CHAUCER STUDIES XXIII

CHAUCER'S APPROACH TO GENDER IN THE *CANTERBURY TALES*

This volume presents a feminist approach to the *Canterbury Tales*, investigating the ways in which the tensions and contradictions found within the broad contours of medieval gender discourse write themselves into Chaucer's text. Four discourses of medieval masculinity are examined, which simultaneously reinforce and resist one another: heroic or chivalric, Christian, courtly love, and emerging humanist models. Femininity is considered from within these dynamics. The book concludes that on the question of gender issues, the *Tales* are best studied as male-authored texts containing representations and negotiations revealing much about late medieval masculinities.

Dr ANNE LASKAYA is an Assistant Professor and Director of the Freshman Writing Program at the University of Oregon.

CHAUCER STUDIES

ISSN 0261-9822

CHAUCER'S APPROACH TO GENDER IN THE *CANTERBURY TALES*

ANNE LASKAYA

D. S. BREWER

First published 1995 by D. S. Brewer
Reprinted in paperback 1992

Transferred to digital printing

ISBN 978-0-85991-481-9

D. S. Brewer is an imprint of Boydell & Brewer Ltd
PO Box 9, Woodbridge, Suffolk IP12 3DF, UK
and of Boydell & Brewer Inc.
668 Mt Hope Avenue, Rochester, NY 14620, USA
website: www.boydellandbrewer.com

A CiP catalogue record for this book is available
from the British Library

This publication is printed on acid-free paper

CONTENTS

DEDICATED TO

Suzanne Lesley Gerhardt
and
Bonnie Jeanne Tull

ACKNOWLEDGMENTS

Like all books, this one arises out of a network of benevolent forces. I am deeply grateful to Russell A. Peck who has given careful, precise, and rigorous response to several versions of this text; his generosity and encouragement, both during my graduate school years and since, have been essential. Whatever is meritorious here is indebted to him; the faults are my own. I would also like to thank colleagues whose work and whose conversations have influenced my thinking about gender and medieval literature, especially Barbara Altmann, Thomas Hahn, Regina Psaki, Eve Salisbury, Marjorie C. Woods, and the innumerable contributors to medieval and feminist electronic discussion networks and conferences.

Although this book grows out of my dissertation (University of Rochester, 1989), both dissertation and book were written while I carried demanding teaching and administrative loads at the University of Oregon, and it has been crucial to have encouragement, intellectual conversation, and advice. With gratitude, I note the support of Marilyn Farwell, John Gage, John Stuhr, and Louise M. Westling; they have, by example and counsel, sustained me in moments of insecurity and doubt. I must also thank Suzanne Clark and James Crosswhite for their collegiality. While many contributed to this project, I especially note those who materially aided in its completion: Jacqueline Longton for financial support which allowed a summer of intense study without teaching; my great-aunt, Helena M. Williams (now deceased), for monetary assistance during my graduate school years and for her nurturing during my own severe illness; Christy Bradford Racy for hours of careful bibliographical research assistance; and Mike Stamm for his consistent generosity of spirit and for his aid with administrative responsiblities while my mind kept wandering back to the Middle Ages. Deep gratitude belongs also to my family and friends: to Suzanne L. Gerhardt for her patience, understanding, and enthusiasm, whose help was fundamental for the completion of this project; to Bonnie J. Tull for her hours of wisdom, conviction, and confidence; and to my mother, C. Janet Houser, who taught me from my earliest years to love the world of books.

And finally, I thank all those colleagues whose work has helped to create an exciting international intellectual community. Many of their names are cited throughout my text, offering up a dialogue of both agreement and dissent so crucial to the life of the mind.

ABBREVIATIONS

AnM	*Annuale Mediaevale*
ChauR	*Chaucer Review*
ELH	*Journal of English Literary History*
JEGP	*Journal of English and Germanic Philology*
MAE	*Medium Aevum*
MLQ	*Modern Language Quarterly*
MP	*Modern Philology*
MS	*Mediaeval Studies*
NM	*Neuphilologische Mitteilungen*
PL	*Patrologia Latina*
PMLA	*Publications of the Modern Language Association*
PQ	*Philological Quarterly*
RES	*Review of English Studies*
SAC	*Studies in the Age of Chaucer*
SAQ	*South Atlantic Quarterly*
SP	*Studies in Philology*
TSE	*Tulane Studies in English*
TSLL	*Texas Studies in Literature and Language*
UTQ	*University of Toronto Quarterly*

CHAPTER ONE

Introduction

Literature is no one's private ground: literature is common ground. . . .
Let us trespass freely and fearlessly and find our own way for ourselves.

Virginia Woolf

. . . there can be neither a first nor a last meaning; [meaning] always
exists among other meanings as a link in the chain of meaning, which in
its totality is the only thing that can be real. In historical life, this chain
continues infinitely, and therefore each individual link in it is renewed
again and again, as though it were being reborn.

M. M. Bakhtin

Academic discussions of gender issues within Chaucer's texts have tended to
align themselves with the postmodern distrust of the sign, for if we ground an
inquiry on more or less stable categories of gender, the 'masculinist' and
misogynist aspects of Chaucer's writings are undeniable. Finding these elements
of the text disconcerting or distasteful after having spent years of one's life
preparing to 'profess' literature, many of us take comfort in the reading
strategies of postmodernism or gender studies. When we *do* discuss gender, we
deconstruct the categories male/female, masculine/feminine, and/or we consider
the feminized nature of writing and the feminization of any writer, male or
female (but particularly the male). Although much can be said for these projects,
and although I will, at times, echo them and participate in them, as a feminist, I
find it noteworthy that we are often trying our best to slide past gender
differences.

Frequently the point of discussing concepts like 'masculinity' and 'femininity'
seems to be to dismiss or avoid them and to aim for 'gender' as a preferable
term. Indeed, collapsing sex role differences into one word, 'gender,' may
indicate the discomfort we seem to be experiencing with difference. But any
dream of escaping differences or of combining differences into 'androgyny,'
'polysexuality,' or 'performance' often suggests an erasure of women and can be
a way for a patriarchal society to disguise its on-going powerful preference for
the masculine.[1] If we adopt a critical strategy from deconstruction and strive to

---

[1] See Kari Weil, *Androgyny and the Denial of Difference* (Charlottesville: University of Virginia

put differences into 'play,' revealing the interdependence and hierarchy of various conceptual binaries like male/female, heterosexual/homosexual, we still have to re-enter the socialized and embodied world which does not live in 'play.' So while deconstruction can indeed add much to our understanding of gender, the deconstructive move can also be a way to ignore gender's power as an on-going discourse and institution, one which persists in categorizing human beings as 'men' or as 'women,' as 'boys' or as 'girls.' Although we may resist notions of a fixed and permanent male/female binary opposition, we must also acknowledge the power of these conceptual binaries. In other words, we need to continue the project of understanding what those arbitrary and conventional terms of sexual and gender difference mean now and what they meant in the past. Of course, postmodernism is helpful to the extent that it is congruent with feminist aims and enhances efforts to construct new, feminist readings. But, as Carmen Luke and Jennifer Gore have commented, a 'hidden agenda of erasure . . . drives much of current postmodernist theory and analysis.'[2] Whereas the liberal-humanist tradition encourages the female reader to locate herself in the perceptual space of the generic male reader, postmodernism and deconstruction encourage her to locate herself within the perspective of a polygendered reader; in other words, she is to locate herself anywhere but within an embodied female reader.

Obviously gender, regardless of any biological considerations, exists as a complex cultural construct. In their text, *Sexual Meanings: The Cultural Construction of Gender and Sexuality* (Cambridge, 1981), Sherry B. Ortner and Harriet Whitehead assert: 'natural features of gender and natural processes of sex and reproduction, furnish only a suggestive and ambiguous backdrop to the cultural organization of gender and sexuality.'[3] This assumption, now well-documented in anthropology and sociology, leads to the conclusion that gender and sexuality are cultural (symbolic) constructs and that, like all symbols, they are invested with meaning. In his essay, 'Men loving Men,' Gary Kinsman elaborates this: 'Our biological, erotic, and sexual capabilities are only the precondition for the organization of the social and cultural forms of meaning and activity that compose human sexuality. Our biological capabilities are transformed and mediated culturally, producing sexuality (gender) as a social need and relation.'[4] Michael Foucault has addressed this feature of gender in his *History of Sexuality, Volume I*, arguing that the meaning of sexuality is almost

Press, 1992); Leslie Wahl Rabine, 'A Feminist Politics of Non-identity,' *Feminist Studies* 14 (1988):16; and Teresa de Lauretis, 'Upping the Anti(sic) in Feminist Theory,' in *Conflicts in Feminism*, ed. Marianne Hirsch and Evelyn Fox Keller (New York and London: Routledge, 1990), 255-270.

[2] Carmen Luke and Jennifer Gore, eds., *Feminisms and Critical Pedagogy* (New York and London: Routledge, 1992), 5.

[3] Sherry B. Ortner and Harriet Whitehead, eds., *Sexual Meanings: The Cultural Construction of Gender and Sexuality* (Cambridge: Cambridge University Press, 1981), 1.

[4] Gary Kinsman, 'Men Loving Men,' in *Beyond Patriarchy: Essays by Men on Pleasure, Power, and Change*, ed. Michael Kaufman (Toronto and New York: Oxford University Press, 1987), 107. See also Kinsman's work, *The Regulation of Desire* (Montreal: Black Rose, 1986); John D'Emilio, *Sexual Politics, Sexual Communities* (Chicago: University of Chicago Press, 1983); Jeffrey Weeks, *Sex, Politics, and Society* (London: Hutchinson, 1981); Jonathan Dollimore, *Sexual Dissidence* (Oxford: Clarendon, 1991).

entirely constructed in culture and that, furthermore, it is constructed so as to assist the political interests of the dominant social class.[5] Language, religion, politics, law, as well as medical and economic institutions all participate in that construction. Although Foucault's thesis arises out of an examination of nineteenth- and twentieth-century European contexts, it holds broad implications for any culture. Particular constructions of gender may vary, but gender *is* constructed. Foucault's work follows a long line of feminist theorists and writers going back to Simone de Beauvoir, who have been ascribing just such an artifice to gender for quite some time.[6] An easy way to see the artificiality of gender is to examine the difference between the words 'woman' and 'man' (which are artificial constructions and carry connotations from various dominant discourses in our culture like science, religion, literature) and the lives of actual historical human beings whom we classify as women and men.[7] Still, despite their artificiality, gender construction and linguistic categories also impact greatly on men's and women's real lives. In her book, *Technologies of Gender*, Teresa de Lauretis maintains that 'we need a notion of gender that is not so bound up with sexual difference as to be virtually coterminous with it'; we need to understand that gender does not 'derive unproblematically from sexual difference.' Equally important, she argues, is our need to be alert to ways 'gender can be subsumed in sexual differences as an effect of language, or as pure imaginary – nothing to do with the real.' Addressing both of these concerns, de Lauretis defines gender as 'the representation of a relation, that of belonging to a class, a group, a category.' It is also

(a) representation – which is not to say that it does not have concrete or real implications, both social and subjective, for the material life of individuals. On the contrary, the representation of gender *is* its construction – and in the simplest sense it can be said that all of Western Art and high culture is the engraving of the history of that construction . . ..[8]

---

[5] Michael Foucault, *The History of Sexuality, Volume I* (New York: Vintage, 1980). Foucault's theories are not without their problematic for feminism. Teresa de Lauretis writes that his 'critical understanding of the technology of sex did not take into account its differential solicitation of male and female subjects,' and that it 'ignor[es] the conflicting investments of men and women in the discourses and practices of sexuality . . .,' *Technologies of Gender: Essays on Theory, Film, and Fiction* (Bloomington: Indiana University Press, 1987), 3.

[6] Cf. Simone de Beauvoir, *The Second Sex*, trans. H. M. Parshley (1952; rpt New York: Vintage, 1974).

[7] See Teresa de Lauretis's discussion of this in her introduction to *Alice Doesn't: Feminism, Semiotic, Cinema* (Bloomington: Indiana University Press, 1984), 5–7. The ability of a sign, like 'woman,' to carry us into the ideological realm (the value-laden, connotative realm) was commonly acknowledged by medieval rhetoricians. St Augustine defined a sign as 'a thing that causes us to think of something beyond the impression the thing itself makes upon the senses,' *On Christian Doctrine*, trans. D. W. Robertson, Jr (New York: Bobbs-Merrill, 1958), 34.

[8] Teresa de Lauretis, *Technologies of Gender*, 2–4. She has also pursued this issue in her most recent study, *The Practice of Love: Lesbian Sexuality and Perverse Desire* (Bloomington: Indiana University Press, 1994), where she examines gender construction and sexuality 'as semiosis, as the mutual overdetermination in experience of habits, representations, fantasy, and the practice of love' (312).

As teachers, we are, I hope, aware of the pain, anger, frustration, and disgust our students (particularly our female or gay students) experience when they read the *Reeve's Tale*, the *Clerk's Tale*, the *Wife of Bath's Tale*, the *Pardoner's Tale*, and the *Second Nun's Tale*. Whatever our sophisticated scholarship on the text might advocate, our students usually read and interpret much of Chaucer's work as misogynist and homophobic. Like many of my colleagues, I have found myself an apologist for the *Tales*, and, like them, I cannot ignore my students' repeated observations that narrators in the *Canterbury Tales* seem obsessed with feminine sexuality and/or male domination. I cannot ignore the high esteem the text accords to women's self-abnegation nor the harsh condemnation it frequently levels at women's autonomy. And I cannot ignore the power the text accords to men nor the judgments it makes about men who do not conform to culturally-accepted forms of masculinity. From 'a' feminist perspective, the *Canterbury Tales* is, at times, undeniably misogynist, masculinist, and judgmental toward anything even approaching male or female polymorphous sexuality. Without a vested interest in defending the text, my students have challenged me to consider my own vested interest. Thus, I began to ask myself, how might a Cassandra, a Philomela, or a Hyacinth read the *Canterbury Tales*? And I wondered to what extent Chaucer's depictions of human perception, his imagery, narrative structures, assumptions, and judgments are bound up with medieval patriarchal traditions and perspectives on the world. I have also wondered why it is that feminists continue to read, reread, and write about the *Tales*.

Clearly, Chaucer's text is homosocial – written by a man, primarily about men, and primarily for men. Although we could explore ways Chaucer 'writes like a woman' (to borrow from Jonathan Culler), I aim to examine the text assuming that Chaucer (like Culler) lived, thought, and wrote from within a male body socialized in, even if resisting, particular masculinities.[9] Although scholars often ignore or mute this rhetorical/sexual context, it needs to be acknowledged and explored since criticism and canon-formation are so political in nature.[10] If, for example, we uncritically develop reading strategies which prefer to read misogyny as 'play,' what *are* we advocating? How might such reading strategies (if used unreflectively) reinforce those elements of our own culture which persist in ignoring or purposefully misreading women's 'no' as

---

[9] Cf. Susan Crane, *Gender and Romance in Chaucer's Canterbury Tales* (Princeton: Princeton University Press, 1994). Following the constructionists, especially Judith Butler, Crane writes: 'Taking seriously the idea that sex and gender are both constructed and continually renegotiated through an array of social forces entails untying the bond between, in the case of Chaucer, a historical man and masculine discourses. The sex of an author fixes discourse no more securely than sex fixes gender' (5).

[10] That literary judgments are political in nature has become commonplace. Besides feminist critics, from Simone de Beauvoir to Audre Lorde, who all assume this, see Leslie Fiedler, 'Literature as an Institution: The View from 1980,' in *English Literature: Opening Up the Canon, Selected Papers from the English Institute, 1979*, ed. Leslie A. Fiedler and Houston A. Baker, Jr (Baltimore: Johns Hopkins University Press, 1981), 73–91; Fredric Jameson, *The Political Unconscious: Narrative as a Socially Symbolic Act* (Ithaca: Cornell University Press, 1981); and Louis Kampf and Paul Lauter, eds., *The Politics of Literature: Dissenting Essays on the Teaching of English* (New York: Pantheon, 1972). For a discussion of the feminist perspective, see Judith Fetterley, *The Resisting Reader: A Feminist Approach to American Fiction* (Bloomington: Indiana University Press, 1981).

'yes' or 'maybe'? The complex relationship between interpretive methods and ideologies warrants inquiry and reflection. In his work, *Negotiating the Past: The Historical Understanding of Medieval Literature*, Lee Patterson argues a similar point, when he says, 'The refusal of criticism to acknowledge [its political valence], and its counterclaim that it is called into being by an object that exists wholly apart from itself, is simply an effect of its reluctance to reflect upon the political nature of its authority.'[11] Now, if we understand the *Canterbury Tales* and other texts in the traditional 'canon' of English literature to have political valence, to be tools of enculturation as well as agents of aesthetic and intellectual delight (also interwoven with the political), we would do well to confront and discuss the misogyny, anti-semitism, racism, heterosexism, and elitism frequently encountered there. To do otherwise is a denial of, or worse yet, a complicity with, those forces in our culture and in ourselves that would oppress others or would deny the oppression of others. This forms a crucial assumption of my inquiry: namely, that literature classified and taught as canonical is, like any other empowered and privileged communication, an agent of enculturation. For us to ignore or to remain uncritical of such authority is not only contrary to the purpose of education and scholarship, it is also potentially dangerous. Hence, the importance of feminist, marxist, postmodernist, and as yet unborn critical stances to reread the 'canon.'

Additionally, I want to acknowledge the appeal the *Canterbury Tales* has for feminist scholars working on medieval literature, an appeal which stems, at least in part, from the complex narrative structure of the text. The *Tales* are constructed as a celebration of many voices, and the celebration of multiplicity and difference is at the heart of much feminist theory and practice. Audre Lorde, for example, maintained that 'difference [multiplicity] must be not merely tolerated, but seen as a fund of necessary polarities between which our creativity can spark like a dialectic. . . . Only within that interdependency of different strengths, acknowledged and equal, can the power to seek new ways of being in the world generate.'[12] In a culture which has, for quite some time, privileged that which pretends to transcend difference and multiplicity, feminist thought has sought to expose the illusion and the price of such transcendence. Men's experiences are not the same as women's; documenting this difference and valuing women's experiences and perceptions forms the basis for feminist scholarship. The nature of women's difference and 'otherness' has been privileged and eulogized by some feminists and condemned and renounced as a source of women's oppression by other feminists; nevertheless, the issue of difference remains at the center of feminist theory.[13]

[11] Lee Patterson, *Negotiating the Past: The Historical Understanding of Medieval Literature* (Madison: University of Wisconsin Press, 1987), 42.

[12] Audre Lorde, 'The Master's Tools will Never Dismantle the Master's House,' in *Sister Outsider: Essays and Speeches by Audre Lorde* (Trumansburg, New York: Crossing Press, 1984), 111. This frequently anthologized speech was originally given in September, 1979.

[13] A good introduction to the concept of difference in feminist theory (and it is defined variously by various feminists) can be found in Hester Eisenstein and Alice Jardine eds., *The Future of Difference* (Boston: Barnard College Women's Center, 1980) and in Alice Jardine's book, *Gynesis: Configurations of Women and Modernity* (Ithaca: Cornell University Press, 1985), 118-44. See also Diana Fuss's important discussion of the tensions between (and interdependence of)

The *Canterbury Tales*, with its dramatization and careful depiction of many different narrators, is fertile ground for feminist analysis. Differences of status, profession, personality, and gender are deemed significant within the frame tale, beginning with the *General Prologue*. That the text is a collection of voices which are in tension with one another and which are incapable of being simplified or reduced to an easy generalization or one unified perspective is obvious from the plethora of Chaucerian scholarship and commentary. Furthermore, the misogyny in the text is somewhat qualified by Chaucer's careful creation of fictional narrators who are never assumed (by the text, at any rate) to be without bias. No human narrator in the *Canterbury Tales* has a view of life or of truth that really includes all the experiences and truths of the others. In its diversity of voices, the text disallows unqualified authority to any one human voice. Some voices are more misogynist than others, some far more narrow in their definitions and attitudes toward men and women than others, and some may appear to us to have more authority than others, but the ambiguity of the text defies hasty or sweeping generalizations. In fact, the voices we accord authority may well indicate more about our own world views and biases as readers than anything about judgments made in the text. Lee Patterson notes, '. . . by privileging one context at the expense of others we decide how the text's ironies should be read, whence they derive their authority, and against whom they are directed.'[14] If we privilege the *Parson's Tale* as the perspective from which we should judge the other tales because it is placed last or because it is a sermon, we get one reading; if we privilege the *Knight's Tale*, because it is the most artful and is placed first, we get a different reading; and if we disregard placement and thereby privilege a tale or a teller on some other grounds, we will get yet another reading.

This dilemma is not only of our time; it isn't a particularly modern situation. Medieval readers and listeners must have held differing interpretations of the *Tales* also. Patterson argues that 'unless we accept the notion of a culturally monolithic Middle Ages, we cannot assume that the habits of one group of [medieval] readers can simply be extended across the cultural field as a whole.'[15] The narrative voice given highest authority by a clergical reader could well be different from the one accorded the greatest authority by a merchant or by a man of law, a court lady, a lover, a young reader, or an old reader, and so on. Similar variables, as well as the distance of history and culture, influence modern literary interpretations of the *Canterbury Tales*.

My inquiry into the issue of gender and its relationship to perception, genre, and representation in the *Tales* is obviously shaped by questions deemed crucial in the late twentieth century, and I tentatively explore and question Chaucer's text using modern feminist analysis, close textual readings, and techniques and assumptions from theories of analysis as diverse as deconstruction, formalism, hermeneutics, and historicism. I begin, then, at the intersection of several different critical orientations, so that following one road may seem to be leading away from another road at times. To borrow from Paul Zumthor's comment on

---

essentialism and constructionism in feminist thought, *Essentially Speaking* (New York and London: Routledge, 1989).

14 Patterson, *Negotiating*, 151.

15 *Ibid.*, 116.

his own critical methodology, 'the ground on this work site is shifting under my feet.'[16] My discussion can be said to be making forays out and back, around and around, first one way and then another; and this is because (as daughter to Athena-Cassandra-Philomela and heir to the many voices of twentieth-century scholarship) I am never completely comfortable with any one viewpoint.[17] In this way, I share Gayatri C. Spivak's appreciation for deconstruction. She comments:

> The aspect that interests me most is . . . the recognition, within deconstructive practice, of provisional and intractable starting points in any investigative effort; its disclosure of complicities where a will to knowledge would create oppositions; its insistence that in disclosing complicities the critic-as-subject is herself complicit with the object of her critique; its emphasis upon 'history' and upon the ethico-political as the 'trace' of that complicity – the proof that we do not inhabit a clearly defined critical space free of such traces; and, finally, the acknowledgement that its own discourse can never be adequate to its example.[18]

And so, like deconstructionists, we can explore ways Chaucer's text constructs and deconstructs masculinity, ever mindful that what we may see 'in' the text is, in many ways, an expression of our own 'complicity' with the text and an expression of our own culturally-constructed vision.

Like any interpretation, or, to use a medieval term, like any 'gloss,' my readings will surely manipulate and distort Chaucer's text. All efforts at literary criticism do this. As Robert Hanning has noted, 'the idea that a gloss manipulates rather than explains its text may seem a peculiarly modern one, but medieval scholars and satirists were by no means unaware of the possibilities of such textual harassment.'[19] The idea that a text is a revision of an earlier text, which is, in turn, a revision of an earlier text, and so on, can be seen in the account of St Anselm's composition of the *Proslogium*. According to the story, St Anselm received his text in a vision, awoke, and wrote it down on wax tablets. He then gave it to a monk for safe-keeping. A few days later, Anselm asked to see the tablets, but they had mysteriously disappeared, whereupon he recorded his vision again only to find the tablets broken in fragments all over the floor the following day. For a third time, he recalled, revised, and pieced together the account (the interpretation) of the experience: '*Adunat ipse ceram, et licet vix scripturam recuperat*' (He pieced together the wax and recovered the

---

16 Paul Zumthor, *Speaking of the Middle Ages*, trans. Sarah White, ed. Eugene Vance, Regents Studies in Medieval Culture (Lincoln: University of Nebraska Press, 1986), 86.

17 That this eclecticism is a common feature of feminist scholarship can be seen in Susan Sherwin's article, 'Philosophical Methodology and Feminist Methodology: Are They Compatible?' in *Feminist Perspectives: Philosophical Essays on Method and Morals*, ed. Lorraine Code, Sheila Mullett, and Christine Overall (Toronto: University of Toronto Press, 1988), 13–28. It is also a feature of some scholars working in the field of gender studies; see Jonathan Dollimore's articulation of his own diverse methodology in *Sexual Dissidence*, 21.

18 Gayatri Chakravorty Spivak, 'Translator's Forward to "Draupadi" by Mahasweta Devi,' *Critical Inquiry* 8 (1981): 382–83.

19 Robert Hanning, ' "I Shal Finde It in a Maner Glose": Versions of Textual Harassment in Medieval Literature,' in *Medieval Texts and Contemporary Readers*, ed. Laurie A. Finke and Martin B. Schichtman (Ithaca: Cornell University Press, 1987), 29.

writing though with some difficulty). Finally, Anselm transferred the text to parchment and added an answer to objections which were raised by his readers.[20] Between the 'text' and the interpretation falls the shadow; and so it is with twentieth-century criticism of a medieval text, regardless of one's methodology or critical stance: our distance from that original context and author is immense.[21]

We should not, however, simply discard the effort to piece the fragments together nor discard the effort to place the text in its own historical context. Inquiring into literary interpretations of medieval texts, Paul Zumthor has noted: 'We steer a course between Scylla and Charybdis. The ultimate turn we aim for is really to bring the ancient text into the present, that is, to integrate it into that historicity which is ours. The pitfall is that in doing so we may deny or obscure its own historicity; we may foreshorten the historical perspective and, by giving an achronic shape to the past, hide the specific traits of the present.'[22] Consequently, I identify some of the prevalent discourses constituting masculine and feminine gender in the late Middle Ages and situate Chaucer's text in relationship to them.[23] But I also, inevitably, approach the text through the perspective of my own historicity. Indeed, the critic cannot do otherwise. As Fredric Jameson comments, 'we never really confront a text immediately, in all its freshness as a thing-in-itself. Rather, texts come before us as the always-already-read; we apprehend them through sedimented layers of previous interpretations. . . .'[24] Like all critics, I speak from a particular place within time and culture, having been shaped by numerous institutions and discourses: academic, political, economic, racial, sexual, religious, psychological, legal, and so on. Julia Kristeva, in her essay, 'How Does One Speak to Literature?' reminds us that criticism involves both *desire* (where the critic as subject is implicated via body and history) and *symbolic order* (where language, culture, and 'intelligibility' are implicated). Interspersing material from Roland Barthes, she writes:

As for the 'critic,' he [*sic*] takes on the task of pointing out heteronomy. How? Through the presence of enunciation in the utterance, by

---

[20] This account of the composition of the *Proslogium* can be found in *The Life of St Anselm Archbishop of Canterbury by Eadmer*, ed. and trans. R. W. Southern (London: Thomas Nelson, 1962), 31-32. See also Louis H. Mackey, '*Inter Nocturnas Vigilias*: A Proof Postponed,' in *Medieval Texts and Contemporary Readers*, ed. Finke and Schichtman, 90-99.

[21] Of course, our distance from the text would still be pronounced, even if we sat right next to Chaucer as he read from his manuscript some summer evening in 1393. See Michael Riffaterre's comments on reading in his article 'The Mind's Eye: Memory and Textuality,' in *The New Medievalism* ed. Marina S. Brownlee, Kevin Brownlee, Stephen G. Nichols (Baltimore: Johns Hopkins University Press, 1991), 29-45; esp. 32-34.

[22] Zumthor, *Speaking*, 33.

[23] In this way, I follow a method of inquiry similar to 'the new medievalism.' Eugene Vance defines 'the new medievalism' as that which 'tends to respect the inherent poetics of a literary text, yet to stress the interaction between the constitutive discourse(s) of literature and those other discourses (the scientific, the theological, the judicial, the political, the historiographical, etc.) coinhabiting a given cultural context. . . . The new medievalism is a science not of things and deeds, but of discourses; it is an art, not of facts, but of *encoding* of facts,' Eugene Vance, 'Semiotics and Power: Relics, Icons, and the *Voyage de Charlemagne à Jérusalem et à Constantinople*,' in *The New Medievalism*, 226-27.

[24] Jameson, *The Political Unconscious*, 9.

introducing the agency of the subject, by assuming a representative, localized, contingent speech, determined by its 'I' and thus by the 'I' of its reader. Speaking in his *name* to an *other*, he introduces *desire*: 'Clarity [. . .] is all this desire that lies within writing' (*Critique et vérité*, p. 33); one should ask the critic to 'make me believe in your decision to speak' (*Ibid.*, p. 75); 'To move from reading to criticism is to change desires; it is no longer to desire the work but to desire one's own language' (*Ibid.*, p. 79).'[25]

By desiring to find our 'own language,' we are looking to discover new and potential meanings within medieval texts. One assumption lying behind such a methodology is summed up quite clearly by M. M. Bakhtin, in his essay, 'Response to a Question from the *Novy Mir* Editorial Staff:'

> Semantic phenomena can exist in concealed form, potentially, and be revealed only in semantic cultural contexts of subsequent epochs that are favorable for such disclosure. . . . Shakespeare took advantage of and included in his works immense treasures of potential meaning that could not be fully revealed or recognized in his epoch. The author himself and his contemporaries see, recognize, and evaluate primarily that which is close to their own day. The author is a captive of his epoch, of his own present. Subsequent times liberate him from this captivity, and literary scholarship is called upon to assist in this liberation.[26]

Obviously, the same can be said of twentieth-century interpretations of Chaucer. This is exactly what Chaucer himself does with the ancient tale of Troilus and Criseyde; he situates the classical tale in a medieval philosophical context and thereby reveals 'immense treasures of potential meaning that [otherwise] could not be fully revealed or recognized' in the source material. Bakhtin argues for the value of such re-vision, saying:

> Of course, a certain entry as a living being into a foreign culture, the possibility of seeing the world through its eyes, is a necessary part of the process of understanding it; but if this were the only aspect of this

---

[25] Julia Kristeva, 'How Does One Speak to Literature?' in *Desire in Language: A Semiotic Approach to Literature and Art*, trans. Thomas Gora, Alice Jardine, and Leon S. Roudiez, ed. Leon S. Roudiez (New York: Columbia University Press, 1980), 116, 115. Kristeva continues, citing Barthes: Critical works are, she explains, ' "works crisscrossed by the great mythic writing in which humanity tries out its significations, that is, its desires" [critique et vérité, p. 61]; "there is no other primary *significatum* in literary works than a certain desire: to write is a mode of Eros" (*Critical Essays*, p. xvi); "the same writing: the same sensual pleasure in classification, the same mania for cutting up [. . . the same enumerative obsession [. . . the same image practice [. . . the same erotic and phantasmatic fashioning of the social system" (*Sade, Fourier, Loyola*, p. 3) . . .' (115).

[26] M. M. Bakhtin, 'Response to a Question from *Novy Mir* Editorial Staff,' in *Speech Genres and Other Late Essays*, trans. Vern W. McGee, ed. Caryl Emerson and Michael Holquist, University of Texas Press Slavic Series, No. 8 (Austin: University of Texas Press, 1986), 5. This essay, according to the *Novy Mir* editors, first appeared in November 1970. Bakhtin's bias implying that the text is a 'captive' in its own time and that it can be 'liberated' by the present is, obviously, problematic, but his understanding of the critical process that revels in the discovery of potential meaning is very useful.

understanding, it would merely be duplication and would not entail anything new or enriching. *Creative Understanding* does not renounce itself, its own place in time, its own culture; and it forgets nothing. In order to understand, it is immensely important for the person who understands to be *located outside* the object of his or her creative understanding – in time, in space, in culture. For one cannot even really see one's own exterior and comprehend it as a whole, and no mirrors or photographs can help; our real exterior can be seen and understood only by other people, because they are located outside us in space and because they are *others*.

In the realm of culture, outsideness is a most powerful factor in understanding. It is only in the eyes of *another* culture that foreign culture reveals itself fully and profoundly (but not maximally fully, because there will be cultures that see and understand even more). . . . We raise new questions for a foreign culture, ones that it did not raise itself; we seek answers to our own questions within it; and the foreign culture responds to us by revealing to us its new aspects and new semantic depths.[27]

Using feminist analysis (and other twentieth-century approaches to literature) to uncover potential and concealed semantic phenomena in the *Canterbury Tales* is in some ways 'to raise new questions for a foreign culture.' The questions I address to the *Canterbury Tales* revolve around the text's construction and analysis of gender – primarily masculinity – and its relationship to perception and representation. But even though our understanding of these issues may well differ from Chaucer's, he also raised similar issues directly or indirectly in his text as he participated in the on-going cultural construction of gender in the late Middle Ages.

The 'gender narrative,' inscribed within most narratives, and, indeed, inscribed within the *Canterbury Tales*, is a story that locates itself at the very origins of humanity, for one of the most powerful narratives told in any culture is the story of creation. Such a myth, in a very real sense, 'names' the world and, as such, provides a framework for our perceptions. It creates assumptions and categories by which we judge and interpret our world. In our culture, the creation myth has often shaped, either directly or indirectly, what we have perceived of relationships in the world: birth and death, nature and society, human and divine, and men and women, among other things. It has been a framework for perceptions, creating categories of existence which have profoundly influenced *what* we perceive and *how* we judge what we perceive; it has thus had tangible consequences.[28] One of the tangible consequences of this creation myth is that male and female become distinct conceptual categories which identify differences, even opposites. And the difference is emphasized.

---

[27] Bakhtin, 'Response,' 7.

[28] See Claude Lévi-Strauss, *The Raw and the Cooked*, trans. John and Doreen Weightman (New York: Harper and Row, 1969). See also Ernst Cassirer, *Language and Myth*, trans. Susanne Langer (New York: Harper, 1946). Mircea Eliade, too, in his work, *Myth and Reality*, trans. Willard R. Trask (New York: Harper and Row, 1963; rpt Harper Colophon, 1975), 6, writes that the Creation myth is an essential myth which shapes our sense of ourselves as 'mortal, sexed, and cultural beings.'

To categorize and separate life into opposites is characteristic of the European and American dominant cultural heritage; it is a propensity for order which disregards life's variety, particularity, and multiplicity. Joseph Campbell has remarked that our culture can, in fact, be characterized 'by its setting apart of all pairs-of-opposites – male and female, life and death, true and false, good and evil – as though they were absolutes in themselves.'[29] Among the basic distinctions in our mythologies, continuing powerfully to influence our social organization, is the distinction of gender. More than any other trait, gender has consistently prescribed a person's role and function in society (though these roles and functions vary). From the moment of birth, children are assigned a sex category; parents announce to the world (and we say to ourselves) that here is, not simply a new life, but a new male or female life. Subsequently, the child's relationships with parents and others, his or her education, clothes, toys, and hobbies all become agents and artifacts to shape his or her identity.[30] The sex role difference is so pervasive a force in our lives, that even what is clearly imposed by the culture can easily seem natural. We assimilate our category so thoroughly that we can hardly define ourselves without reference to it. Mary Ellmann believes our culture encourages us to think 'by sexual analogy,' that we 'comprehend all phenomena, however shifting, in terms of our original and sexual differences,' and that we 'classify almost all experience by means of sexual analogy.'[31] Gender has determined our divisions of labor, the structure of our languages and the structures of our lives. Consequently, it has influenced the way we think and the way we perceive reality. Hélène Cixous asserts: 'every theory of culture, every theory of society, the whole conglomeration of symbolic systems – everything, that is, that's spoken, everything that's organized as discourse, art, religion, the family, everything that seizes us, everything that acts upon us – it is all ordered around hierarchical oppositions that come back to the man/woman opposition. . . .'[32]

It is little wonder, then, that Chaucer, a poet so concerned with epistemological issues and with how we define our worlds and ourselves, should also be a poet who explores gender issues, since gender and perception are intimately intertwined. That he is a poet concerned with gender issues is obvious: almost every narrative in the *Canterbury Tales* deals with how the sexes relate to one another or envision one another. The prodigious critical material on the marriage

[29] Joseph Campbell, *The Masks of God: Occidental Mythology* (New York: Viking Press, 1964), 26–27. See also Hélène Cixous and Catherine Clément, *The Newly Born Woman*, trans. Betsy Wing, Theory and History of Literature, Volume 24 (Minneapolis: University of Minnesota Press, 1986), 63–64: 'Always the same metaphor: we follow it, it carries us, beneath all its figures wherever discourse is organized. If we read or speak, the same thread or double braid is leading us throughout literature, philosophy, criticism, centuries of representation and reflection. [Western] thought has always worked through opposition. . . . Through dual, hierarchical oppositions. Superior/Inferior. Myths, legends, books. Philosophical systems. Everywhere (where) ordering intervenes, where a law organizes what is thinkable by oppositions (dual, irreconcilable; or sublatable, dialectical). And all these pairs of oppositions are *couples*. Does that mean something? Is the fact that Logocentrism subjects thought – all concepts, codes, and values – to a binary system, related the "the" couple, man/woman?'

[30] See Carol Gilligan, *In A Different Voice: Psychological Theory and Women's Development* (Cambridge, Mass.: Harvard University Press, 1982).

[31] Mary Ellmann, *Thinking About Women* (New York: Harcourt, 1968), 6.

[32] Hélène Cixous, 'Castration or Decapitation,' trans. Annette Kuhn, *Signs* 7 (1981): 44.

group and on courtly love leads fruitfully in such a direction. But there is more to discover here. Whereas a path has begun to be cleared in the direction of examining Chaucer's gender discourse, it is by no means a road.[33] We can find studies of Chaucer's knights, his clerks, his lovers, but not many studies which fully explore these roles in terms of masculinity or gender; particularly absent are studies of masculinity. This is not surprising. Even though much social science research concentrates on men and often assumes the male subject can generate information about the universally human, research placing masculinity in the foreground of investigation is rare.[34] For most of the twentieth century, scholars considered Chaucer's male and female characters as types of humans rather than as distinctively males or females, even though Chaucer's characters are quite obviously drawn to illustrate traits (good or bad) and ways of thinking that late medieval culture saw as distinctively masculine or feminine. Chaucer's characters may, of course, function as emblems of vices or virtues, of inner states of being common to both men and women, but they also function as emblems of gender, identifiably male or female. Indeed, the literary context of the fourteenth century encourages us to see male characters as specifically 'men' and female characters as 'women.' The many hundreds of romances, lyrics, sermons, treatises, and plays that discuss gender in one way or another give ample testimony to a culture concerned with sex roles, as Francis Lee Utley's 1944 work, entitled *The Crooked Rib*, indicated.[35] Furthermore, the debate

[33] H. A. Kelly began to work in this direction, though not from a feminist perspective, in his now classic study, *Love and Marriage in the Age of Chaucer* (Ithaca: Cornell University Press, 1975). Traugott Lawler has addressed the issue somewhat cursorily in his text, *The One and the Many in the Canterbury Tales* (Hamden, Conn.: Archon, 1980). Gender has formed a significant issue in the following books on Chaucer: David Aers, *Chaucer* (Brighton, Sussex: The Harvester Press, 1986), 62–102; H. Marshall Leicester, Jr's post-structuralist reading, *The Disenchanted Self: Representing the Subject in the Canterbury Tales* (Berkeley: University of California Press, 1990); Elaine Tuttle Hansen's collection of essays, *Chaucer and the Fictions of Gender* (Berkeley: University California Press, 1992); Jill Mann's *Geoffrey Chaucer* (Atlantic Highlands, NJ: Humanities Press International, 1991); Carolyn Dinshaw's post-structuralist/ feminist reading of *Chaucer's Sexual Poetics* (Madison: University of Wisconsin Press, 1989); and Susan Crane's recent *Gender and Romance in Chaucer's Canterbury Tales* (Princeton: Princeton University Press, 1994).

[34] Only recently have scholars begun writing critically about our culture's concepts of masculinity and male identity. In his book, *The Inward Gaze: Masculinity and Subjectivity in Modern Culture* (New York and London: Routledge, 1992), Peter Middleton cites a comment by Michael Kimmel, 'I believe that most men do not know they have a gender' (11). Middleton explores this issue as well as others in his discussion of the construction and representation of masculinity. Although feminists have written about masculinity as it relates to women's positionings in the culture, few men have taken up the project. In the seventies and eighties, however, men began to examine their gender roles – among them, J. H. Pleck, Warren Farell, Marc Fasteau, Clyde Franklin, Jack Nichols, Michael Kaufman, and Jack Sawyer. Their work first appeared in marginalized presses and gradually found its way into mainstream and more prestigious presses like the Oxford University Press. See, for example, *The Making of Masculinities*, ed. Harry Brod (Winchester, Mass.: Allen & Unwin, 1987); *Changing Men: New Directions in Research on Men and Masculinity*, ed. Michael S. Kimmel (Newbury Park, Calif.: Sage, 1987); Arthur Brittan, *Masculinity and Power* (Oxford: Basil Blackwell, 1989); and Kaja Silverman, *Male Subjectivity at the Margins* (New York: Routledge, 1992). Within medieval studies, see the recent *Medieval Masculinities: Regarding Men in the Middle Ages*, ed. Clare A. Lees (Minneapolis: University of Minnesota Press, 1994). See also the citations in footnote 4, above.

[35] Francis Lee Utley, *The Crooked Rib* (Columbus: Ohio State University Press, 1944). For information on sermons, see G. R. Owst, *Literature and Pulpit in Medieval England*, 2nd ed.

about the nature of women – the 'Querrelle des femmes,' which began in the tenth century – was widespread throughout Europe in the thirteenth, fourteenth, and fifteenth centuries. This period in Western history, like our own twentieth century, 'was a period when "woman" was at [a] height of discursive circulation,' as Alice Jardine observes. In her book, *Gynesis: Configurations of Woman and Modernity*, Jardine asks us to consider a question which can open the door on potential intersections between late medieval culture and modern culture:

> . . . might it not be that a series of if not causal at least etiological links could be established between those periods in the West when women were most vocally polemical and those so called 'epistemological breaks'? . . . Could it be that the 'two major transitions in Western thought' [the Renaissance and Modernity] might be directly linked to the subject (of) woman? . . . Such major conceptual changes as the breakdown of the sign, the questioning of the Subject and his quest for the Object, could only come about in a culture once again radically changing its conception of conceptualization: the loss of *the* Quest, the disappearance of *the* Object.'[36]

In other words, 'woman' perhaps becomes a central intellectual, political, and emotional topic *for men* at exactly the same time men experience a crisis in their own systems of knowledge. But if 'woman' becomes central for men, so do the concepts 'man' and 'masculinity,' as the growing criminalization of homosexuality in the late Middle Ages demonstrates. Imbedded in their historical moment, the *Canterbury Tales* reflect these gender issues.

Obviously Chaucer's work is not, by any stretch of the imagination, 'feminist' in the way we commonly use that term. But the *Tales* do discard unexamined notions of gender as misrepresentation, to some degree. Just as his work can be said to call other ideals into question, so it can be said to call gender ideals into question. It offers up a sophisticated discussion of masculinity and strongly indicts some of the prevalent medieval notions of ideal masculinity while still remaining firmly homosocial and homophobic. Its representations of femininity are also created at a conjunction of inquiry and reinscribed misogyny. With regard to gender issues, the *Canterbury Tales* is best studied as a male-authored text containing representations which tell us much about late medieval constructions of masculinity/masculinities. Such a position risks (or at times seems to embrace) essentialism, as does any feminist project. The binary of essentialism/anti-essentialism has, however, been deconstructed in Diana Fuss's work, *Essentially Speaking*, with each side of the divide shown to be implicated in the other.[37] Indeed, we cannot confer meaning to language at all without

(New York: Barnes and Noble, 1966), esp. 108–20; 376–406. Sermons obviously had far-reaching influence on standards of masculinity and femininity (regardless of practice) because they were heard by all classes, unlike Courtly love literature which circulated primarily among the upper classes. Sermons also had the authority of the Church, of damnation or blessedness, to give them power in shaping people's perceptions.

[36] Jardine, *Gynesis*, 93, 96–97.

[37] Diana Fuss, *Essentially Speaking: Feminism, Nature & Difference* (New York: Routledge, 1989).

risking essentialism. In terms of gender, I will join Patricia Waugh in assuming that 'one's experience of being a 'woman' or a 'man' [is not] simply the consequence of a 'false consciousness' which can be rationally deconstructed and thrown off.' And, simultaneously, I will concur with her that 'the basis of one's subjectivity as 'masculine' or 'feminine' is formed out of real needs and desires which are constructed outside of one's consciousness.'[38] Gender and sexuality exist, then, as a 'nexus of reciprocally constitutive effects between psychic and social realities,' to borrow a phrase from de Lauretis.[39]

The goals for my inquiry are three-fold: first, to examine the essentialist gender discourses surrounding Chaucer and his text in the late Middle Ages to see how these write themselves into the *Tales*; second, to suggest ways the text registers resistance to that discourse; and third, to offer close readings of the *Tales* which explore ways gender and perception are co-constituted by Chaucer's text. I will assume that a 'politics of location' which situates contemporary scholars also (and differently) situates Chaucer.[40] Chapter two briefly outlines dominant cultural discourses surrounding masculinity and femininity in the late Middle Ages for the purposes of exposing tensions and confluences of gender prescriptions. This chapter is followed by sections which offer close readings of the *Canterbury Tales*: chapter three examines the frame narrative and gender; chapter four explores Chaucer's representations of the heroic; chapter five discusses men in love; chapter six investigates Chaucer's representations of intellectual men and the competitive nature of literacy; connections between spirituality and competitive masculinity are examined in chapter seven; and chapters eight and nine explore Chaucer's representations of women as characters and narrators, concluding with the *Wife of Bath*. Final observations reside in the tenth chapter.

---

[38] Patricia Waugh, *Feminine Fictions: Revisiting the Postmodern* (New York: Routledge, 1989), 36–37.

[39] de Lauretis, *The Practice of Love*, 312.

[40] The phrase 'politics of location' becomes a theoretical grounding for Adrienne Rich in her essay 'Notes toward a Politics of Location (1984).' The essay, first written as a talk, is available in Rich's *Blood, Bread, and Poetry: Selected Prose 1979–1985* (New York and London: W. W. Norton, 1986), 167–187.

CHAPTER TWO

Dominant Medieval Discourses on Gender

I. MASCULINITY

Just what fourteenth-century Europeans believed about gender differences is hard to determine, especially since definitions of masculinity and femininity vary according to class and, to some degree, according to country or region, but the cultural assumptions about gender and gender *ideals* can be found codified in law, education, religion, the arts, the economy, the court, and in texts generated by, or about, fourteenth-century political and social institutions. Undoubtedly these ideals and assumptions reflect only a portion of historical reality. Recent scholarship has uncovered exceptions, but the codified beliefs about gender which existed within powerful institutions were tremendously influential, just as our own culture's beliefs about, say, democracy or equality (whatever the actuality) are highly influential.

The late Middle Ages promoted at least four different literary discourses of ideal heterosexual male behavior which were often in tension with one another.[1] One was the heroic, or epic, discourse inherited from the non-Christian past which praised men who were successful warriors and rulers. Men were to be strong physically and mentally, assert themselves over their adversaries both abroad and at home, and conquer and maintain rule over a wild, threatening world. This 'heroic male' was to be a fighter and a leader who could exhibit prowess and skill in any form of earthly competition. He was required to demonstrate courage and loyalty first to his leader, his king, or his father's legacy; second to other male comrades; and third to his family. Heroic masculinity surfaces with various faces in the depiction of many men in the *Canterbury Tales*, but Theseus is the most obvious example. The culture of the Middle Ages promoted and perpetuated this discourse particularly within the aristocratic class and its political and military institutions. But such an ideal, once established for a powerful group of men, spills over into other classes and

---

[1] On the force of discourse and its role in social formation and re-formation, see Bruce Lincoln, *Discourse and the Construction of Society: Comparative Studies of Myth, Ritual, and Classification* (Oxford: Oxford University Press, 1989); and Michael Herzfeld, *The Social Production of Indifference: Exploring the Roots of Western Bureaucracy* (Chicago: Chicago University Press, 1992).

social arenas and promotes competition between men of any class or group. It urges men to succeed or win regardless of whether the arena is a battleground or a struggle for land, political power, recognition, wealth, women, labor, or knowledge. Understood in this way, all of Chaucer's male characters can be said to express some aspect of competitive heroic masculinity.

Contrasting with this secular discourse of heroic masculinity was the discourse of Christian masculinity based on the life of Christ. It encouraged a non-competitive attitude toward the world and praised non-violence, self-renunciation, and devotion to an inner world. Its quest was not for earthly fame and achievement, but for heavenly reward. The masculinity of Christ stressed service to others (John 13: 12–16). Following the teachings of the Church Fathers, Christ-like men were to renounce their flesh and sexuality and value the spiritual over the physical. That Chaucer depicts this type of masculinity has been well-established by D. W. Robertson, Jr and his followers. One can easily see ways these two discourses – the heroic and the spiritual – created tensions in the culture (as perhaps they still do). One prescribed seeking power and fame through an outward-directed struggle in the world. The other praised men who sought glory through an inward-directed struggle; it honored men who renounced the world and who directed their energies toward a reward in the afterlife. Despite their differences, some common threads run through both discourses. Both encouraged men to sacrifice their bodies, either in war or in asceticism; both valued rational qualities and intelligence over emotion (or approved of overwhelming emotion only in certain, restricted moments and spaces); both demanded allegiance to a superior male (either human or divine); both ascribed value to the struggle against obstacles, adversaries, and weaknesses; and both discourses praised men for the ability to control others as well as oneself.

Some of these same prescriptions are found in yet a third ideal, the masculine discourse of courtly love. This heterosexual discourse was, like the heroic discourse, aimed primarily at the upper classes. In fact, as Richard F. Green explains in his book, *Poets and Princepleasers: Literature and the English Court in the Late Middle Ages*, 'the capacity to experience [romantic] love had long been regarded as an exclusively aristocratic prerogative.'[2] The lover-knight suffered psychologically and physically in pursuit of his goal; the courtly male body was to endure hardship and sacrifice itself for glory. In literature, the courtly lover struggled against physical obstacles just as the epic hero did, battling nature, other men, dragons, witches, disease, and even death to prove himself worthy. And, like the ideal Christian man, he was to remain forever obedient to his god (the secular god of love, now) and forever faithful to his lady. Both discourses applauded men for resisting sexual temptation, but the lover-knight did so usually to prove how great his love was for *one* woman, whereas the Christian did so to prove how great his love was for God.

Loyalty, honor, bravery, and, at times, mercy, were part of the requirements for men pursuing the courtly love model, and the lover-knight sought these goals

---

[2] Richard F. Green, *Poets and Princepleasers: Literature and the English Court in the Late Middle Ages* (Toronto: University of Toronto Press, 1980), 112. One must keep in mind, however, who regarded and inscribed love in this exclusively aristocratic way.

either in severe isolation or within elaborate rituals of an aristocratic court world. But always, whether in isolation or in the midst of a public spectacle, the lover-knight was to exhibit exquisite, meticulous manners which placed him securely in the aristocracy and marked him as a 'civilized' man. Unlike the epic warrior, however, the courtly lover was often at odds with superior male authority as Lancelot was with Arthur and Tristan was with King Mark. Some key elements of courtly love discourse obviously conflicted sharply with the tenets of traditional heroism and Christianity. Unlike the heroic or the Christ-like man, the lover-knight was to hold women as the source of inspiration, the worthy cause of hardship, and as a superior reason for action in the world. This placed courtly love discourse in tension with the other two discourses on masculinity which located women on the periphery as nurturers of male endeavors, seductive temptresses, temporary obstructions, or lesser objects of conquest. Courtly love discourse appeared to rebel against the debasement of women, although it continued to objectify them. Still, its fictions placed women above men and assumed women appropriately made decisions which governed men's lives. Within the topos of courtly romance narrative, women frequently established herculean feats for men to achieve, even though, as Susan Crane notes, 'the dubious merit ascribed to women's specific demands sharpens the image of courtship as a process of masculine self-improvement rather than mutuality or intimacy.'[3] But even if women's roles as governors over men's lives are compromised within courtly love narrative or absorbed into its larger project of constructing masculinity, the discourse does accord women a central role. It places women and heterosexuality at the center of the male protagonist's world, thereby resisting ecclesiastical preferences for virginity and the Church's harsher view of active human sexuality. In her work, *Love and War in the Middle English Romances*, Margaret Gist comments:

> The essential spirit of courtly love is, then, revolt against the bargain marriage that bought and sold women like commodities; against a concept of sex that debased the physical relationship; and against the theory that the divine punitive system penalized most stringently the expression of the God-given emotion of love.[4]

Whether ideals of courtly love were ever actually practiced or whether they formed simply a literary convention is another question. Richard F. Green, in his article 'The *Familia Regis* and the *Familia Cupidinis*,' argues that 'men in the late Middle Ages put less store by living up to the code of the chamber [involving relations with women] than they did that of the battlefield.' He maintains that the fear of women's judgment in the courtly love tradition 'can be seen as merely the metaphorical embellishment of a literary feud; there is no compulsion to regard it as reflecting a formalised social ritual.' Some men, he says, had a 'chivalric attitude' toward women which 'owed as much to publicity

---

[3] Susan Crane, *Gender and Romance in Chaucer's Canterbury Tales* (Princeton: Princeton University Press, 1994), 65.
[4] Margaret Gist, *Love and War in the Middle English Romances* (Philadelphia: University of Pennsylvania Press, 1947), 105.

value as to genuine sentiment.'[5] Regardless of what history may establish as actual practice, the code of courtly love helped shape the culture's encoded images of masculinity. It parades through Chaucer's *Canterbury Tales* with quite a flourish, often parodied, but pervasively present.

Much evidence, however, indicates that the fourteenth century had begun to turn away from the model of courtly masculinity and toward yet another model – the intellectual male lauded by late medieval and early renaissance humanism. This fourth prescription for masculinity promoted the virtue of knowledge above all else. The increased influence of 'intellectual masculinity' can be seen quite easily if we note simply the growth of universities during the late Middle Ages. In 1200, there were 6 universities in Europe (including Oxford). By 1300, the number had more than doubled to 14 (including Cambridge). By 1400, there were 36; by 1500, there were 80. The late medieval and early renaissance humanist discourse encouraged men to develop their rational and intellectual abilities rigorously. Boccaccio, for example, writes that poets must know grammar and rhetoric, as well as 'the other Liberal Arts, both moral and natural'; they must 'possess a strong and abundant vocabulary, . . . behold the monuments and relics of the Ancients,' and 'have in [their] memor[ies] the histories of the nations' as well as their geographies.[6] Educated men were still expected to be active and in control, but the goals of activity had been altered. Whereas the warrior, the heroic man, strained and disciplined his muscles and his fears for the purposes of gaining land and fame, and whereas the Christian man struggled and disciplined himself to achieve a heavenly afterlife, the educated man struggled to achieve intellectual goals and the perfection of the intellect, achievements we associate with early modern humanism.[7]

Like the discourse surrounding ideal Christian masculinity, the humanist discourse privileged mind over body, but the goal was control of the world by knowledge and rational thought. John Boswell, in his *Christianity, Social Tolerance, and Homosexuality*, claims: 'The single most prominent aspect of the period from the later twelfth to the fourteenth century was a sedulous quest for intellectual and institutional uniformity and corporatism throughout Europe.'[8] It

[5] Richard F. Green, 'The *Familia Regis* and the *Familia Cupidinis*,' in *English Court Culture and the Late Middle Ages*, ed. V. J. Scattergood and J. W. Sherborne (London: Duckworth, 1983), 101, 103, 105. On the truth and fiction of the courtly love tradition see also R. Howard Bloch, *Medieval Misogyny and the Invention of Western Romantic Love* (Chicago: University of Chicago Press, 1990); John F. Benton, 'Clio and Venus: An Historical View of Medieval Love,' in *The Meaning of Courtly Love*, ed. Francis. X. Newman (Albany: State University of New York Press, 1968), 19–42; and Benton's article: 'The Court of Champagne as a Literary Center,' *Speculum* 36 (1961): 551–91. See also Jo Ann McNamara and Suzanne Wemple, 'The Power of Women through the Family in Medieval Europe 500–1100,' *Feminist Studies* 1 (1973): 126–41; and Herbert Moller, 'The Social Causation of Courtly Love Complex,' *Comparative Studies in Society and History* 1 (1958/59): 137–63.

[6] Giovanni Boccaccio, *Genealogy of the Gentile Gods* XIV, vii, in *Boccaccio on Poetry*, trans. and ed. Charles G. Osgood (Princeton: Princeton University Press, 1930), 40.

[7] For an appraisal of historical context see Janet Coleman, *Medieval Readers and Writers, 1350–1400* (New York: Columbia University Press, 1981), esp. Chapter 2 entitled 'Vernacular Literary and Lay Education,' (18–57).

[8] John Boswell, *Christianity, Social Tolerance, and Homosexuality* (Chicago: University of Chicago Press, 1980), 270.

was a quest that depended upon a uniformity of ideas perpetuated and assisted by early renaissance/late medieval education. The *trivium* and the *quadrivium*, gradually extending across a larger literate population, shaped what men thought valuable or important in knowledge; and what was important was the abstract concept. Whether grammar, rhetoric, logic, arithmetic, geometry, astronomy, or music, the elements of formal education were abstract subjects, involving what Marilyn French calls 'an approach to experience that [was] distant.' She notes, 'There is no history, no study of human relations, no study of the arts for the sake of pleasure: the study of music was a mathematical exercise. By so defining what mattered, this kind of education also taught men what they were expected to be, how they were to approach life. It separated men from all women (for no women were permitted to enter the universities) and from uneducated men, and made them a new elite dedicated to knowledge as a form of power. All other kinds of and approaches to knowledge became illegitimate, insignificant.'[9] The early renaissance, despite its dedication to knowledge, emphasized certain kinds of knowledge and texts, and it muted, erased, or lost other kinds. Theology became much more rigorously unified, and secular knowledge was gathered and systematized into encyclopedias. The creation of the Inquisition gives testimony to this institutional drive to eradicate 'erroneous' opinions and forms of knowledge, though, of course, efforts to eradicate heresies existed in the Middle Ages as well. The difference is one of degree; for the late medieval/ early renaissance world, the strengthening and centralizing of civil and ecclesiastical bureaucratic powers made the enforcement of conformity easier and more likely than it had been in the past.

With the possible, but not inevitable exception of the courtly love ideal, the masculinity of warrior-king, lover-knight, saint, or humanist, involved recognition, reward, and acceptance into an ordered hierarchy of men. For the most part, the culture actively promoted these ideals among the more privileged classes of society. The need for some form of patriarchal hierarchy was by and large assumed. Vincent de Beauvais writes, 'If man had not ruled man, the human race by the absence of justice would have slaughtered itself to extinction.'[10] This view is corroborated by many writers, among them Giraldus Cambrensis who argued in his *De Instructione Principum* that 'princely power is necessary for men, since where there is no government, the people will come to ruin.'[11] (Obviously one assumption here is that lower class men, particularly, tend toward violent disorder if uncontrolled by superiors.) Medieval theorists, who had no elaborate aggression or repression theories to explain men's violence, believed this tendency toward chaos and brutality stemmed from original sin, a sentiment echoed throughout patristic and philosophic texts. Alexander of Hales writes, 'Natural law ordains the equal freedom of all in the state of original nature; but according to the state of fallen nature it ordains that

[9] Marilyn French, *Beyond Power, On Women, Men, and Morals* (New York: Simon & Schuster, Summit, 1985), 160.

[10] Vincent de Beauvais, *Tractatus de morali principis institutione* (cap. 3), cited in Bede Jarret, *Social Theories of the Middle Ages 1200–1500* (Boston: Little Brown, 1926), 9.

[11] Cited in Jarrett, *Social Theories*, 9. See also *Chronicles and Memorials of Great Britain and Ireland During the Middle Ages*, in *Cambrensis Opera* vol. 8, ed. George F. Warner (London: Eyre and Spottiswoode, 1891), 8.

subjection and lordship are necessary for the constraint of evil.'[12] If the need for hierarchy and control stems from 'man's' 'fallen nature,' 'man's' right to control or govern others stems from his 'original nature.' That men should govern is a deeply engraved cultural assumption supported by the creation myth. Aquinas argued that 'in the state of innocence, before man had disobeyed, nothing disobeyed him that was naturally subject to him.'[13] Aquinas justified men's superiority and right to govern by likening the will and reason of men to the will and reason of God, and he cites Genesis 1:26 as his evidence: God says 'Let us make man after our own image and likeness and let him have dominion' over the world. Because men (not women) are made the most like God, Aquinas argued that they should have habitual domination over all other creatures, including women.[14]

The appropriateness or 'order' of male rule extended from the power of Popes and kings who ruled over large masses of people to the landlords who ruled over peasants, from priests who ruled over parishes to husbands who governed wives and children. That men were told, by the culture, to rule over their respective subordinates is clear. The crucial question facing men, then, was never *whether* to rule, but *how* to rule. Men were concerned with questions like 'What are the limits of governance?' 'When does rule become tyranny?' 'What should be the relationship between punishment and mercy?' 'What constitutes just governance for a king, a bishop, a confessor, a husband?' So it is not surprising to find Chaucer examining the nature of male power and the implications of men's rule in the *Canterbury Tales*. Indeed, these are quite clearly the questions he raises with his male characters. The depiction of men in the *Tales* demonstrates that Chaucer knew quite well how men exerted their power and control over the world using physical strength, military might, money, rhetoric, law and religion, not to say the arts to effect their own aims. In so far as Chaucer raises the question of male rule, his text reinscribes the cultural discourse surrounding men, but often Chaucer's representation of men's rule is critical or comical.

The premium medieval culture placed on male governance meant that physical force could be used, and often was used, to attain power. Medieval society was an intensely masculine world organized around war, land, and combat. Wars, skirmishes, and military campaigns were common occurrences. They overshadowed government, politics, and finances in England from the late thirteenth to the mid-fifteenth centuries.[15] The image of the brave warrior was central to a culture engaged in such frequent conflicts. Shulamith Shahar observes that of all the appellations given to a nobleman, 'the name of *miles* predominated . . . since it stressed his military function and image.'[16] The culture had to promote the

---

12 Alexander of Hales, *Summa Theologica*, ques. 47, m. I, a. I. cited in Jarrett, *Social Theories*, 9.

13 Thomas Aquinas, *Summa Theologica* 96, art. 1 in *The Basic Writings of St Thomas Aquinas*, 2 vols., trans. and ed. Anton C. Pegis (New York: Random House, 1945) I: 918.

14 Aquinas, *Quest.* 93, 'The Image of God in Man,' in *Basic Writings* I: 885 and *Summa Contra Gentiles*, chapter LXXXI in *Basic Writings* II: 152–53.

15 On wars as a common phenomenon see John Barnie, *War in Medieval English Society: Social Values and The Hundred Year's War 1337–99* (Ithaca: Cornell University Press, 1974); Philippe Contamine, *War in the Middle Ages*, trans. Michael Jones (Oxford: Basil Blackwell, 1984); May McKisack, *The Fourteenth Century 1307–99* (Oxford: Oxford University Press, 1959; rpt 1971).

16 Shulamith Shahar, *The Fourth Estate: A History of Women in the Middle Ages*, trans. Chaya Galai (London and New York: Methuen, 1983), 127.

image of the strong warrior as an heroic ideal since so many men were needed to fight in the wars. Shahar, citing demographic research conducted by T. H. Hollingworth, found the following:

A study of ducal families in England in 1330–1475 shows that the average life-expectancy of men at birth was 24 years, and of women 32.9 years. The average life-expectancy of men who survived the age of 20 was 21.7 and of women at 20 was 31.1 years. The source of this discrepancy was the fact that 46 percent of all men died violently after their fifteenth year: in wars, tournaments, or by execution during civil wars. . . . if violent death was taken into account, then in the 20–54 age-group, only 18 percent of the men survived throughout (i.e. reached the age of 54), while among women of 20–49, 50 percent lived out the period (i.e. reached the age of 49).[17]

Secular struggles for power unequivocally exacted a heavy toll on men's lives. But secular conflicts were not the only culprits; the Church, too, involved men in brutal crusades. Pope Urban II, with the proclamation of the First Crusade in 1095, declared that war undertaken to defend and maintain the faith was holy. He even went so far as to assure crusaders that if they died *en route* to holy battle or in the melee itself, their sins would be remitted and that they would guarantee themselves a place in heaven. Urban also promised temporal rewards of plunder and prosperity: 'The possessions of the enemy, too, will be yours, since you will make spoil of their treasures and return victorious to your own; or empurpled with your own blood, you will have gained everlasting glory.'[18] Besides the Church, civil law granted special favors and immunities to warriors, and the praise of war inevitably left its imprint on art and literature. Writers – from chroniclers to theorists to poets – admired, analyzed, recorded, and encoded the chivalric/heroic discourse into the culture. John Clanvowe, a friend of Chaucer's and one of the King's chamber knights, noted sadly in his text, *The Two Ways*, that the world honors men 'þat been greete werreyours and fiȝteres and þat distroyen and wynnen manye loondis . . . þat woln been venged proudly and dispitously of every wrong þat is seid or doon to hem.' These are the men, he says, whose lives and deeds are preserved in 'bookes and soonges . . . for to hoolde þe mynde of here deedis þe lengere heere vpon eerth.' However, Clanvowe wrote, God finds all this 'riȝt shameful.'[19] True, there were voices of dissent, but heroic action – violence – was overwhelmingly admired, if it was undertaken for the 'right' reasons. John Gower, in his *Vox Clamantis*, complained that late medieval knighthood had lost its commitment to justice. He

---

[17] Shahar, *Fourth Estate*, 129. She gets her statistics from T. H. Hollingworth, 'A demographic study of the British ducal families,' *Population Studies* XI (1957): 36.

[18] There are several versions of Urban's speech; this one is taken from Baldric of Dol's account in *The First Crusade: The Chronicle of Fulcher of Chartres and Other Source Materials*, ed. Edward Peters (Philadelphia: University of Pennsylvania Press, 1971). Peters includes the translation of Baldric found in A. C. Krey, *The First Crusade: The Accounts of Eye-Witnesses and Participants* (Princeton: Princeton University Press, 1921). See also F. H. Russell, *The Just War in the Middle Ages* (Cambridge: Cambridge University Press, 1975), 36.

[19] *The Two Ways*, lines 485–501 in *The Works of Sir John Clanvowe*, ed. V. J. Scattergood (Cambridge: D. S. Brewer, 1975).

lamented that knights had become greedy, sluggish, and lecherous. The solution to their sloth was, notably, participation in a just war:

> O knight, you who prefer pleasures and abandon your arms and seek to have rest at home and plunder spoils from the poor like a lion: you seek the fat of the land for yourself, thereby causing others to waste away. Sluggishness motivates you and voluptuous lust urges you on, together with money and the driving force of avarice. Undertake the awesome duties of bloody warfare and I believe that your vices will flee you at once.[20]

As a military society, the Middle Ages honored bravery in battle as an essential masculine characteristic, but the applause was not unanimous. The New Testament taught that forgiveness and mercy were far more virtuous than brawn. Vincent de Beauvais argued against force, claiming that 'Christ's triumph was won by sweetness and not by swords.' He upheld patience as 'the best protection' against evils of the world and argued that violent, 'impatient' men were the ones truly 'alone' and the ones 'truly unarmed.' War, he said, 'produces little good and it wastes much more than it produces . . . Wise men, then, avoid war.' Peace, he believed, is achieved far more rapidly 'by giving than by taking.'[21] This sentiment is also reflected in the writings of Chaucer's contemporary, John Wyclif, who wrote that 'wise men . . . vencuschen [vanquish] hor enmyes withouten any strok, and men of tho gospel vencuschen by pacience, and comen to reste and to pees by suffryng of deth.'[22] The *Twelve Conclusions of the Lollards*, which were posted on the doors of Westminster Hall during the Parliamentary session of 1395, contain the following:

> Þe tende conclusiun is þat manslaute be batayle pretense lawe of rythwysnesse for temperal cause or spirituel withouten special reuelaciun is expres contrarious to þe newe testament, þe qwiche is a lawe of grace and ful of mercy. Þis conclusiun is opinly prouid be exsample of Cristis preching here in erthe, þe quiche most taute for to loue and to haue mercy on his enemys, and nout for to slen hem . . . aftir þe firste strok, charite is ibroke; and qwoso deyth out of charite goth þe heye weye to helle . . . þe lawe of mercy þat is þe newe testament, forbad al mannisslaute: *in euangelio dictum est antiquis, Non occides* . . . And knythtis þat rennen to hethnesse to geten hem a name in sleinge of men geten miche maugre of þe King of Pes; for be mekenesse and suffraunce oure beleue was multiplied, and fythteres and mansleeris Ieus Cryst hatith and manasit. *Qui gladio percutit, gladio peribit.*[23]

---

[20] John Gower, *Vox Clamantis, The Major Latin Works of John Gower*, trans. and ed. Eric W. Stockton (Seattle: University of Washington Press, 1962), 208.

[21] Vincent de Beauvais, *De Eruditione Principum*, Books 7–8, cited in Jarrett, 185–86.

[22] John Wyclif, 'On the Seven Deadly Sins,' cited by C. T. Allmand, *Society at War: the Experience of England and France during the Hundred Year's War* (Edinburgh, 1973; New York: Barnes and Noble, 1973), 37. Allmand's book is a valuable collection of medieval documents which comment on war. See also Contamine's *War in the Middle Ages*, 292–95.

[23] *Selections from English Wycliffite Writings*, ed. Anne Hudson (Cambridge: Cambridge

Secular literature sometimes expressed the same sentiment. In a poem from Digby 102, *Mede and Muche Thank*, a poor but honorable man debates with a foppish knight about war:

> Thou woldest evere more were werre,
> (ffor profyt and pilage thou myght glene,)
> Cristen bold destroyed clene,
> And townes brent on a glede.
> Thy conscience is ful lene;
> Thou noldest not come there but for mede.[24]   (ll. 67–72)

The 'travaylyng man' in this poem condemns war undertaken for booty, and his outrage can be found echoed in numerous other secular texts.[25] But even though some writers lamented war, most of them granted war a place. Baldus de Ubaldis (ca. 1320–1400), for example, grudgingly admits that 'in this age it is necessary for there to be wars, and the slaughters and infinite sufferings of war.'[26] In the Middle Ages, as in our own time, the exaltation of peace and the frequency of war were simultaneous phenomena.

A permanent readiness to do battle was not, however, simply a necessity for the warrior in times of war; violence between the classes was, apparently, a common occurrence. Despite the myth of an ordered hierarchy of blissful interdependence among the Estates, history speaks a different story. Peasants were frequently controlled by the physical force of their lord and his armed representatives. A poem written 'On the Deposition of Richard II,' for example, records the lower classes' dissatisfaction with the King's retainers:

> [they] reden with realté
> ȝoure rewme thoruoute
> and as tyrauntis of tiliers
> token what hem liste,
> and paide hem on her pannes,
> whan her penyes lacked.
> Ffor non of ȝoure peple
> durste pleyne of here wrongis,
> ffor dred of ȝoure dukys,
> and of here double harmes.[27]

University Press, 1978), 28. See a similar position in the fifteenth point of *Sixteen Points on which the Bishops accuse Lollards* in Hudson, 23–24.

[24] This poem can be found in *Twenty-Six Political and Other Poems (Digby 102)*, ed. J. Kail, EETS OS 124 (London, 1904), 6–9.

[25] See Coleman, *Medieval Readers*, 84–92.

[26] Baldus de Ubaldis, *Consilia* V, com 439 cited in *The Cambridge History of Later Medieval Philosophy*, ed. Norman Kretzmann, et al (Cambridge: Cambridge University Press, 1982), 771. See also the chapter on 'The Just War,' in the same volume (771–84).

[27] 'On the Deposition of Richard II,' in *Political Poems and Songs relating to English History, Composed during the Period from the Accession of Edw.III. to that of Ric. III.*, 2 vols., ed. Thomas Wright (London: Longman, 1959) I: 376. See also the poem, 'On King Richard's Ministers,' (1399) which attacks Bushey, Greene, and Bagot also in Wright I: 363–66.)

The sentiment recurs in sermons delivered during the last years of Richard II's reign: 'officers of gret men that wercth her lyverethes . . . by colour of lawe and azens lawe, robbeth and dispoyleth the poure people, now betynge, now sleyinge, now puttynge hem from hous and landes.'[28] Lords and their officials did not hesitate to use violence to coerce the peasants.[29] James B. Given cites the following account as a typical example of such coercion:

> In east Sussex the prior of Hastings brought a suit of villeinage against his tenants at Burwash. His efforts to deprive his men of their legal freedom failed in the courts. He therefore decided to take direct action. With some 30 men, including Ralph Harengod – who had also brought a suit of villeinage against his tenants in the nearby village of Iklesham – and some other members of the local gentry . . . , he attacked Burwash, destroyed the villagers' houses, and carried off their goods.[30]

Barbara A. Hanawalt found similar cases recorded in the *Bedfordshire Coroner's Rolls*, among them accounts of lords who murdered peasants.[31] Lamenting this kind of abuse, William Langland writes:

> And mysbede nouzte þi bonde-men þe better may þow spede; þowgh he be þyn vnderlynge here, wel may happe in heuene, þat he worth worthier sette and with more blisse, þan þow, bot þou do bette, and lyue as þow shulde;
>
> *Amices, ascende superius.*
>
> *Piers Plowman* B-text VI, 46–49

The peasants had little recourse, for the courts seldom prosecuted men of the upper class. If a villager deigned to challenge a knight in court, there was little chance he would get a sympathetic hearing. Richard Kaeuper describes the case of Henry of Lincoln, a 'notorious Lincolnshire Knight,' who 'caught one of the jurors who had indicted him in a criminal inquest, stole his horse, beat the man

---

[28] Cited by G. R. Owst, *Literature and Pulpit in Medieval England*, 2nd ed. (New York: Barnes and Noble, 1966), 324. See also *Mum and the Sothsegger*, ed. Mabel Day and R. Steele, EETS OS 199 (London: Oxford University Press, 1936); Thomas Hoccleve's *Regement of Princes*, ed. F. J. Furnivall, EETS ES 72 (London: Oxford University Press, 1897); and V. J. Scattergood, *Politics and Poetry in the Fifteenth Century* Blandford History Series (London: Blandford Press, 1971).

[29] Barbara A. Hanawalt, 'Peasant Resistance to Royal and Seigniorial Impositions,' in *Social Unrest in the Late Middle Ages* Papers of the Fifteenth Annual Conference of the Center for Medieval and Early Renaissance Studies, ed. Francis X. Newman (Binghamton, New York: Center for Medieval and Early Renaissance Studies, 1986), 26: 'Seignorial violence toward the peasantry often exhibited an arrogance of class superiority.'

[30] James B. Given, *Society and Homicide in Thirteenth-Century England* (Stanford: Stanford University Press, 1977), 88. Richard Kaeuper, 'An Historian's Reading of the *Tale of Gamelyn*,' *Medium Aevum* 52 (1983): 53, cites the case of one Sir Thomas Ingaldersthor, a knight, who misused his powers as Keeper of the Peace to ambush, beat, and imprison a villager simply because he wanted the man's land. The villager was freed only after giving Sir Thomas a bond for £20.

[31] Hanawalt, 'Peasant Resistance,' 26–27.

soundly, and warned him that any of the other jurors caught outside the safety of Lincoln town walls would be killed' or beaten savagely.[32] Although individual peasants rarely retaliated by murdering their lords, they frequently stole from them.[33] Similar dynamics of strife were common between lords and townsmen, between students and townsmen. Frequent conflicts, such as these, mark yet another tension in masculine discourse: the tension between control and obedience. The command given to men to control others is countermanded by another command: obey your male superiors. Consequently, writes Marilyn French, 'the myth shaped for men taught them to shine with reflected glory in their village streets, to walk with bravado in their neighborhoods, but to approach other men, men of more power, with humility, obedience, and subservience.'[34] It would not do to have lower class men assume a sense of power, except over their wives and children. They might, otherwise, demand too much or rebel. But this is, obviously, what frequently happened, as any history of the late Middle Ages will document.

Conflicts between individuals of the same class were also common. Members of the upper class apparently had considerable distrust for one another and feared one another. As James Given has found, individual nobles were, however, somewhat reluctant 'to engage in direct violent conflict with their fellow nobles.' Of course conflicting economic and political interests within the upper class caused considerable civil strife, but individual differences were often resolved so as to avoid direct hand-to-hand struggles. Noblemen appealed to the courts, held tournaments (which ritualized the violent conflict), or sent other men out to do their dirty work for them.[35] This elite class also went about accompanied by retainers, deterring outbreaks of individual acts of violence against themselves, although the retainers were notoriously abusive toward the lower classes.[36] As a class, nobles discouraged personal and uncontrolled outbreaks between themselves and encouraged compromise or controlled violence in the form of the tournament. Obviously, this effort to control violence among the upper class failed miserably at times, as the deposition of Richard II illustrates.

The Clergy, contrary to modern misconceptions, lived in considerable apprehension of one another, as violence among them was not uncommon, and peasants – marginalized members of the culture, deprived of prestige, authority, and land – often turned to intra-class violence as the only available means of influence. Given finds that the lower classes and wandering bandits account for the highest percentages of individual-to-individual violence.[37] Where men had little, they had little to lose by engaging in violent behavior. Where they had wealth and power, they could lose a great deal; consequently, acts of individual violence were much more common, Given claims, among the lower classes:

---

[32] Kaeuper, 'An Historian's Reading,' 53. See also Kaeuper's recent book, *War, Justice and Public Order: England and France in the Later Middle Ages* (Oxford: Clarendon, 1988).

[33] Hanawalt, 'Peasant Resistance,' 35.

[34] French, *Beyond Power*, 265.

[35] See Given's chapter on 'Social Status and Violent Conflict,' in *Society and Homicide in Thirteenth-Century England*, 66–90.

[36] See Coleman, *Medieval Readers*, 58–156 and Scattergood, *Politics and Poetry*, 107–116 and 298–322.

[37] Given, *Society and Homicide*, 70.

The willingness of a person to resort to violence is heavily influenced by his social status. Some groups within a society have better access to means of settling their conflicts than others. Some can draw upon a wide array of institutionalized means of settling differences whereas others cannot. Different groups within a society also have different attitudes about the use of violence. Among some status groups violence may be shunned as uncouth and unmannerly, the man or woman engaging in it rendering himself a pariah. Yet for others within the same society, violence may be highly esteemed and combativeness regarded as a sign of manliness.[38]

In their private lives, too, men received contradictory messages about physical force. On the one hand, men were generally entitled to beat their wives and children. Just as physical might could be used to vanquish an enemy on the battlefield, it could be (and frequently was) used to subdue individuals in personal relationships. The legal code in fourteenth-century Flanders, for example, guaranteed men the right to beat their wives (a law common in much of Europe). Shahar notes, it 'stipulated that the husband may beat his wife, injure her, slash her body from head to foot and "warm his feet in her blood." If he succeeds in nursing her back to health afterwards he will not have transgressed against the law.' The right, indeed, the obligation men had to maintain control over their wives was so valued by the culture that Shahar found evidence of 'certain places [in Europe where] men were punished for being beaten by their wives.'[39] If the legal code promoted physical force as an appropriate measure men could take to rule their homes, so did the Church. Sermons addressing domestic life frequently counseled men to beat their wives, and the Church upheld men's right and obligation to rule their families.[40] Even though Christ's teachings counseled non-violence, the culture promoted violence as a means to control; so that, even though we can locate countless debates about the ethics of imprisoning people, torturing, beating, and killing people, common practice sanctioned much cruelty and violence in the age of Chaucer.[41]

If men were both praised and blamed for aggressive physical behavior, they were also in a conflicted situation in terms of their sexuality; men received conflicting messages from the culture when it came to their relationships with women. The secular world valued sexuality, even celebrated it, but the Church was forever teaching men that women were potentially the gateway to hell. Heroic discourse promoted virility and praised men's sexual prowess with women.[42] It cast women as prey to be hunted and conquered or as objects to be

---

[38] *Ibid.*, 66.
[39] Shahar, *Fourth Estate*, 89–90.
[40] See Owst, *Literature and Pulpit in Medieval England*, 108–20 and 376–406.
[41] For a look at some of the more base realities of fourteenth-century violence, see Herbert J. Hewitt's works which detail the brutalities common during the Hundred Years' War: *The Organization of War Under Edward III, 1333–62* (Manchester: 1966; New York: Barnes and Noble, 1966) and *The Black Prince's Expedition of 1355–57* (Manchester: University of Manchester Press, 1958).
[42] Vern L. Bullough discusses virility and anatomical maleness in his article, 'On Being a Male in the Middle Ages,' in *Medieval Masculinities: Regarding Men in the Middle Ages*, ed. Clare A. Lees (Minneapolis: University of Minnesota Press, 1994), 31–45.

possessed.[43] Courtly love discourse elevated women into distant objects for adoration by men and depicted men as thralls to feminine beauty. And if that weren't enough tension, Christian discourse warned men to worship only God and that the desire for intense intimacy with women was a sign of moral weakness. The educators promoting renaissance humanism were generally in accord with the Church. Women, they argued, had negative influences on men. Mothers were to be replaced with male tutors and mentors. Wealthier male children were taken, at age seven, away from the domestic world of women and placed under a tutor, a master. Mafeo Vegio, for example, argued in his *De Liberorum Eruditione* that male children who were to be educated should be 'spared' from intimate acquaintance with the domestic world, what he called 'the more sordid and domestic business of the home,' a sentiment common in ancient, medieval and modern treatises on education.[44]

Besides the tensions obvious in these traditions, the legacy of tribal, Roman, and feudal codes taught men that their relationships to each other were to be the source of their most meaningful exchanges. Homosocial male bonding was primary; women were objects to be exchanged; men's relationships with men took precedence over any allegiance to women. But the chivalric code and its literary narratives often depicted men as adversaries rather than as colleagues, celebrating the individual quest more than the quest of a community of men and frequently representing men as adversaries with women as the prize. Despite their differences, however, both ancient epic and medieval chivalric traditions cast women as objects to be possessed or controlled. Christianity, even though it often defined women as base creatures in need of male rule, also valued women as souls, not simply as objects. Whereas courtly, chivalric, and epic traditions celebrated feminine beauty and sexuality, Christianity did not; it consistently represented women's bodies as sources of temptation. As if this weren't enough to confuse the matter, early modern humanists began wondering about women's intellectual capabilities and often found value in educating women and teaching them to read, though for the purposes of raising better children, sons in particular. The culture was clear, however, in its message to men: they were to rule and to do. Women were to submit, bear children, and be passive recipients of men's decisions, actions, and knowledge.

[43] Susan Crane, *Gender and Romance*, 81–82, discusses the conflation of violence and sexuality in the heroic discourse of the OF *Eneas*. She cites and translates lines 7076–78, 7084–88, Tarcon's words to the dying virgin-warrior, Camille:

> Feme ne se doit pas combatre,
> se par nuit non tot an gisant;
> la puet fere home recreant . . .
> . . . ne mostrez vostre proësce.
> Ce ne est pas vostre mestier
> mes filer, coldre et taillier;
> en bele chanbre soz cortine
> fet bon esbatre o tel meschine.

[A woman should not enter into combat, except at night lying down; there she can defeat a man. . . . Do not show your prowess. That is not your business, but rather spinning, sewing, and clipping. In a pretty room behind the bedcurtains it's good to fight with a maiden like you.]

[44] Mafeo Vegio, *De Liberorum Eruditione*, Book XXVI cited in Jarrett, *Social Theories*, 56. See also Nicholas Orme, *From Childhood to Chivalry: The Education of the English Kings and Aristocracy, 1066–1530* (London: Methuen, 1984).

Wealth had the same sorts of tensions for men as sexuality: it was both sinful temptation and glorious evidence of a man's success. Men were faced with conflicting cultural messages if they accumulated wealth. Christianity blessed the meek and the poor, and Church Fathers argued that property ownership was something which originated with the fall (consequently evil) – that ownership and wealth could easily damn one's soul in the afterlife. Avarice even came to share with Pride the appellation of the 'most deadly of sins,' especially in the fourteenth century.[45] Besides traditional Christian doctrine which praised asceticism and poverty, the Lollards, Wycliffites, and Waldensians also denounced wealth as sinful. Thomas Hoccleve, in his 1412 treatise, *The Regement of Princes* writes:

> But þis me þinkiþ an abusioun,
> To se on walke in gownes of scarlet,
> xij ȝerdes wyd, wit pendant sleues downe
> On þe grounde, & þe furrour þer-in set
> Amountyng vnto twenty pound or bet.
> . . .
> ffor al þe good þat men may repe or glene,
> Wasted is in outrageous array.   (421–25, 495–96)[46]

But prosperity had long been one aim of heroic male action, and medieval society usually rewarded, honored, and granted special privileges to men with wealth; material success brought men very real and tangible comforts and power. Despite the moral arguments of the Church, society taught men that wealth was desirable and was part of establishing one's masculine power. Alec Myers, writing on *The Household of Edward IV*, notes:

> If a lord did not ceaselessly strive to maintain and to enlarge his affinity, he might find himself in the position of a modern bank if the rumour should begin to spread that its finances were no longer sound. No more than a bank could a magnate afford to look shabby and poverty-stricken; on the contrary, in this lethally competitive society he must impress men by his ostentation and attract them by his hospitality.[47]

Chaucer, as a member of the emerging middle class, was keenly aware of the emphasis the culture placed on wealth. Wealth assumed increasing power and importance as the culture made the transition from a feudal economy to a capitalistic one. Money began to accrue power once reserved for land, and so it is not surprising to find Chaucer depicting men in terms of monetary wealth and evaluating men in terms of how prudently they use their wealth.[48] However we

---

[45] For a thorough discussion of Avarice, see Lester K. Little, 'Pride Goes before Avarice: Social Change in Latin Christendom,' *American Historical Review* 76 (1971): 16–49.

[46] Thomas Hoccleve, *Regement of Princes*, ed. F. J. Furnivall, EETS ES 72 (London: Oxford University Press, 1897).

[47] Alec R. Myers, *The Household of Edward IV* (Manchester: University of Manchester Press, 1959), 2.

[48] Money and coins are prominent images in the *Tales* with implications R. A. Shoaf has explored in his book, *Dante, Chaucer and the Currency of Word: Money, Image, and Reference in Late Medieval Poetry* (Norman, Oklahoma: Pilgrim, 1983).

understand the causes and contours of the economic transition which was building a capitalistic economy on the foundations of a feudal one, the fourteenth century was obviously witnessing a gradual shift from a rather stable system of inheritance by caste to a somewhat more dynamic market system aligned with tensions between price and profit, wages and resources, and competition.[49] And the rising emphasis on wealth created tensions in male ideals which surfaced in the social and political realms.

Traditionally (or at least theoretically), each man was assumed to have his own place in the political and social hierarchy of the Three Estates. And theoretically, each man was to accept his place and be the best peasant, the best priest, or the best knight he could be. If men accepted the positions they were born into, society would be ordered. But in the late Middle Ages, the plague created a shortage of labor and enabled workers to demand higher wages for their work. This set the stage for workers to begin questioning the privileged status of the higher classes, a phenomenon evident in the Jacquerie in France (1358), the Ciompi in Italy (1378), and the Peasants' Revolt in England (1381). Additionally, men were moving out of the villein role into roles with greater economic status more frequently than ever before, and the incessant wars occurring during the century allowed men to enter a new world of economic advancement through plundering (a commonplace of medieval warfare). Many fortunes were made from the fruits of war. Janet Coleman notes that the 'middle class' grew considerably 'particularly from the increasing upward social mobility of the third estate, largely as a result of . . . war.'[50] Challenges posed to the Estate system by labor's demands and by the very presence of an emerging middle class, offer firm evidence that the ideology of the Three Estates was fast becoming a thing of the past.[51] As C. G. Crump noted many years ago in a statement which has received corroboration from more recent historical research, 'society in the Middle Ages was not a rigid form in which every man had a place and a life fixed for him. There were . . . ways of escape.'[52] Even though upward (and usually downward) mobility wasn't as rapid or as frequent as it was to become in later centuries, it was happening, and it was noticeable; this phenomenon seems to have sparked a backlash in the fourteenth century.

---

[49] For discussions of this transition, see M. M. Postan, *The Medieval Economy and Society* (1972; Harmondsworth: Penguin, 1975) and his *Essays on Medieval Agriculture and General Problems of the Medieval Economy* (Cambridge: Cambridge University Press, 1973); Harry A. Miskimin, *The Economy of Early Renaissance Europe, 1300–1460* (Cambridge: Cambridge University Press, 1975); Rodney H. Hilton and T. H. Aston, eds., *The English Rising of 1381* (Cambridge: Cambridge University Press, 1984); R. H. Hilton, *The English Peasantry in the Later Middle Ages* (Oxford: Clarendon, 1975); Hilton, ed., *The Transition from Feudalism to Capitalism* (London: Verso, 1978); and his *Class Conflict and the Crisis of Feudalism* (London: Hambledon, 1985).

[50] Coleman, *Medieval Readers*, 62.

[51] John Gower's *Vox Clamantis* expresses outrage at the Peasants' Rebellion of 1381 and offers complaints against the Estates from a more conservative perspective. As such, it offers testimony that the system was eroding. See Stockton's translation, *The Major Latin Works of John Gower*, 208–209. See also Christopher Dyer, 'The Social and Economic Background to the Rural Revolt of 1381,' in *The English Rising of 1381*, ed. R. H. Hilton and T. H. Aston (Cambridge: Cambridge University Press, 1984), 9–42.

[52] C. G. Crump and E. F. Jacob eds. *The Legacy of the Middle Ages* (Oxford: Clarendon, 1926), 20. Crump wrote the introduction from which this citation is taken.

Chris Given-Wilson claims that in both the fourteenth and fifteenth centuries, 'social distinctions . . . became more rigidly defined, more blatantly advertised, and more jealously guarded' than in earlier centuries.[53] If the peerage guarded its membership more carefully, monied wealth, and consequently power, still continued to accumulate in the hands of an emerging urban middle class and in the hands of small land owners in rural areas.

So, although a perfect hierarchical order between men was held as an ideal by the culture, reality obviously demonstrated otherwise. Even the king's power in England (which had never been absolute), was more and more frequently checked by laws and by the power of the citizens. Richard II, stepping over the boundaries of appropriate governance, found himself faced with dissent which intensified until he was deposed. Chaucer, friend to John of Gaunt and various other powerful men of the English Court, was in a position to observe the complex relationship of men and power, and he explored this relationship in his writings.[54] We may not find a direct assessment of contemporary kingship in his works as we do in the works of his contemporary, John Gower, but the issue of male power and its consequences finds reflection and commentary in the *Canterbury Tales*.

Masculinity in the fourteenth century, involved, then, exerting power and control over women, over other men, the world, and oneself. These are key characteristics of men and/or masculinity which are written into the *Canterbury Tales*. Of course, power and control reveal themselves in different forms of behavior: the spiritual male may seek to control others by converting them or by asserting power over their souls; the heroic male and the chivalric male may struggle in combat, controlling others physically or with the authority of wealth and status; and the intellectual/humanist male may seek to exert power through the agency of knowledge and art. But each prescription for masculinity, and its accompanying discourse, lauds male power and values the rewards men get for exerting that power properly. Although conflicts arise among these codes of masculinity (revolving around the means men choose to exert power), all four codes assume that power in some form and masculinity or maleness are synonymous.

If Chaucer, retained by the Countess of Ulster, Edward III, John of Gaunt, and Richard II, was in a position to observe the tensions interwoven in the lives of courtly and chivalric nobility, he was also always on the edges of such a world. His own socio-political and economic life located him in a nebulous space between more clearly designated class and career roles; consequently, the tensions between the various discourses of masculinity were most likely quite keenly present in his own life. As a squire, he belonged to the 'gentil' estate and could bear arms, but his actual military experience was brief. Attending Parliament in 1386, he went not because he was a member of the wealthy, landed gentry but because he was an agent of the king.[55] And his government

53 Chris Given-Wilson, *The English Nobility in the Late Middle Ages* (London: Routledge and Kegan Paul, 1987), 57.
54 See Lee Patterson, *Chaucer and the Subject of History* (Madison: University of Wisconsin Press, 1991).
55 Anthony Tuck, *Richard II and the English Nobility* (New York: St Martins, 1974), 112; see *Chaucer Life-Records*, ed. Martin Crow and Clair C. Olson (Oxford: Oxford University Press, 1966).

positions as controller of the customs (1374–87) and as clerk for the king until 1391 placed him in the newly emergent role of civil servant. Son of a wine merchant, an urban resident lacking landed wealth, employed in the king's service, Chaucer's adult social position as an 'esquire' situated him, as Paul Strohm describes it, 'at a particularly volatile and ambiguous point in the social structure of his day.'[56] Friendship with some of the king's chamber knights (John Clanvowe, Lewis Clifford, Philip de la Vache) as well as other members of the chivalric class allowed him to observe the world of the nobility. His civil service for the king placed him in jobs rarely filled by men of his background; in fact, Patterson notes 'Chaucer was . . . the first layman in positions that had previously been filled by clerks.'[57] And his urban, bourgeois beginnings connect him with the emerging middle class. Patterson concludes, 'what the evidence reveals is a Chaucer on the boundary between distinctive social formations. Not bourgeois, not noble, not clerical, he nonetheless participates in all three of these communities.'[58] These overlapping venues of identity most likely created tensions as well as opportunities and would, therefore, contribute to Chaucer's complex vision of gender, particularly masculinity.

If these overlapping gender discourses form a cultural context for the *Canterbury Tales*, does Chaucer's depiction of men as warriors, lovers, scholars, and clergymen uphold the codes of masculinity or challenge them? Exactly how does his text represent masculinity, and which types of masculine behavior seem to be valued? Is Chaucer's stance critical, ironic, neutral, or laudatory? We will need to search for the patterns of male behavior and identity which emerge within individual tales and within the frame narrative to ascertain whether Chaucer's text generally chastises or approves of the masculine traits propounded by medieval culture.

II. FEMININITY

The medieval ideals prescribed for women and preserved in the discourses of law, religion, and literature grew out of two sources – the Church and the aristocracy, both bastions of male power. And most of the recorded voices speaking of what women ought to be or ought not to be are male. Eileen Powers comments: 'The ideas about women were formed on the one hand by the clerkly order, usually celibate, and on the other hand by a narrow caste, who could afford to regard its women as an ornamental asset, while strictly subordinating them to the interests of its primary asset, the land.'[59] The culture's ideology about women's nature and behavior was formed, then, by two groups of powerful men who had little knowledge of the everyday lives of the majority of women. What women thought of themselves is less often preserved in the

---

[56] Paul Strohm, *Social Chaucer* (Cambridge, Mass.: Harvard University Press, 1989), 10.
[57] Patterson, *Chaucer and the Subject of History*, 37.
[58] Patterson, *Chaucer and the Subject of History*, 39.
[59] Eileen Powers, *Medieval Woman*, ed. M. M. Postan (Cambridge: Cambridge University Press, 1975), 9.

documents we have from the Middle Ages. Regardless of the exceptions we can discover from records of real women's lives, the ideas about women held by powerful men and perpetuated in the discourses of the culture had strong influence, undoubtedly shaping the mental constructs and thought processes of both men and women.[60]

Surveying medieval chronicles from Gregory of Tours's *History of the Franks* and Bede's *History of the English Church and People* to the historiography of the late Middle Ages, Jane T. Schulenburg finds that women were gradually written out of history.[61] Whereas early medieval chroniclers praised women who were active in shaping history, who were intelligent and capable leaders, chroniclers of the twelfth through the fourteenth centuries discouraged women's active participation in history by neglecting to record women's deeds and/or by praising women who were passive ornaments or objects of male exchange. Schulenburg writes, 'Highly constricted by the codes of proper deportment, the aristocratic "lady" was nearly "refined out of existence".'[62] Indeed, historians have ascertained that the late fourteenth century marks 'a period in which women's experiential realm had become substantially circumscribed; in general, their previous options in political, religious, and economic spheres had sharply contracted.'[63] Chaucer's world was, then, a world in which the lived experiences of men and women had become more profoundly divergent.

Christine de Pisan, educated, sophisticated, and a woman of privilege, was overwhelmed by the antifeminist ideology which pervaded written culture, and she was aware of her vulnerability to it. In the *Book of the City of Ladies*, she recalls: 'I . . . argued vehemently against women, saying that it would be impossible that so many famous men – such solemn scholars, possessed of such deep and great understanding, so clear-sighted in all things, as it seemed – could have spoken falsely. . . . And so I relied more on the judgments of others than on what I myself felt and knew.'[64] She even decided male authorities must be right – that women were abominations of nature, and she succumbed to self-doubt and self-hatred: 'As I was thinking this, a great unhappiness and sadness

---

[60] Powers comments, 'the medieval theory about women, bequeathed as a legacy to future generations and enshrined alike in law and in literature, was destined to have profound social effects for centuries to follow . . .' *Medieval Woman*, 9. Alcuin Blamires has edited an anthology of medieval writings on women in his *Woman Defamed and Woman Defended* (Oxford: Oxford University Press, 1992). To ascertain the effects of the discourse, see Shulamith Shahar, *The Fourth Estate: A History of Women in the Middle Ages*, trans. Chaya Galai (New York and London: Methuen, 1983). See also David Nicholas, *The Domestic Life of a Medieval City: Women, Children, and the Family in Fourteenth-Century Ghent* (Lincoln, Nebraska: University of Nebraska Press, 1985).

[61] Jane Tibbets Schulenburg, 'Clio's European Daughters: Myopic Modes of Perception,' in *The Prism of Sex*, ed. Julia A. Sherman and Evelyn Torton Beck (Madison: University of Wisconsin Press, 1977), 33–53.

[62] *Ibid.*, 43.

[63] *Ibid.*, 37. See also David Herlihy, *Medieval Households* (Cambridge, Mass.: Harvard University Press, 1985). Contrasting the early Middle Ages when women frequently took on administrative duties, with the late Middle Ages, Herlihy writes (100–101): 'In the late Middle Ages women lost these [important administrative and economic] functions. . . . women were not so indispensable in high administration as they once were.'

[64] Christine de Pisan, *The Book of the City of Ladies*, trans. Earl Jeffrey Richards (New York: Persea Books, 1982), 4–5.

welled up in my heart, for I detested myself and the entire feminine sex, as though we were monstrosities in nature. . . . I considered myself most unfortunate because God had made me inhabit a female body in this world.'[65]

As Christine de Pisan was so keenly aware, what determined a woman's position was, above all else, her sex. First and foremost, the dominant cultural discourse surrounding femininity encouraged the perception of women as physical objects, as bodies. They were identified with the flesh, with nature, and with the 'concupiscential part' of humanity.[66] The written discourse surrounding 'the feminine' in the Middle Ages stressed woman as body and frequently found her sexuality powerfully frightening and often repulsive. On the one hand, woman was placed on a pedestal and praised for her physical beauty or her virginity; on the other hand, she was reviled as a grotesque and lascivious temptress who could lead men to hell. This way of seeing women generally prevailed in both secular and religious realms.

Since many arenas of medieval culture were establishing that men's most precious achievement was control, sexual attraction to women – that biological drive beyond rational control – was a potential source of humiliation and frustration, particularly in a culture that placed a very high value on men who entered the clergy and took a vow of chastity. Church fathers, writing to protect and encourage chastity among monks and priests, portrayed women's bodies as outwardly attractive and inwardly filthy or grotesque. The female body was considered duplicitous and sinisterly seductive. Of course, if clergy believed this, they would be more liable to remain in their ecclesiastical roles and devote their lives to the male institutions of ecclesiastical power. The Church needed men as much as the armies did. We can find Thomas Aquinas arguing that a woman's body is so powerful that simply touching it can cast a man down from spiritual and intellectual heights: 'venereal pleasures above all debauch a man's mind . . . nothing so casts down the manly mind from its height as the fondling of a woman.'[67] Even though statements like these were directed at a monastic audience, the ideas spread to the secular world and had tremendous influence there. Robert of Brunne wrote in his treatise, *Handlyng Synne* (1303), that even eye contact and conversation with women could lure a man to mortal sin.[68] Walter Map (whose work was known to Chaucer) wrote:

> Being ensnared by the beauty of a lovely person thou knowest not, poor wretch, that what thou seekest is a chimera. But thou art doomed to know that this triform monster, although it is beautified with the face of a noble

---

[65] *Ibid.*, 5.
[66] Augustine, 'Of the Work of Monks,' trans. H. Browne *Select Library of the Nicene Fathers* (Buffalo, 1887) III: 524.
[67] Thomas Aquinas, *Summa Theologica*, II, part 2, ques 152, ed. and trans., the Fathers of the English Dominican Province (New York: Benzinger, 1947). See St Paul, I Corinthians 7:1, 'It is good for a man not to touch a woman.'
[68] Robert of Brunne, *Handlyng Synne*, ed. F.J. Furnivall, EETS 119 (London: 1901), 240, 258. See also Idelle Sullens' more recent edition, *Robert of Brunne's Handlyng Synne*, Medieval and Renaissance Texts and Studies, volume 14 (Binghamton: State University of New York Binghamton, 1983).

lion, yet is blemished with the belly of a reeking kid and is beweaponed with the virulent tail of a viper.[69]

Although such an attitude toward women had its most outspoken advocates among the clergy, it pervades secular writings as well. John Gower, addressing the knightly class in his *Vox Clamantis*, bemoans the knight who would 'subjugate' himself to a woman and thinks him 'more idiotic than an idiot':

> It is not right that lead be mixed with shining gold, nor that Venus prescribe the deeds of a doughty knight. A woman does not often release a man whom she has ensnared so that he may escape. Instead, she envelopes him with her silly love . . . It is practical for a knight to avoid battles in which he might be made captive, when he cannot win. It is not for the wise man to enter a ford in which he could be drowned . . .[70]

Because love of women was seen as 'dangerous' to men, women were commonly commanded by men's discourse to be chaste and deny their bodily passions.[71] After surveying law, homilies, didactic literature, and Church writings, Shulamith Shahar concludes, 'Chastity appears as the most important trait of all women, irrespective of their social class, vocation, or marital status.'[72] In a handbook of manners, Philippe de Navarre writes:

> Women have one great advantage: it is enough for them to cultivate a single virtue if they wish to be well thought of. Men, however, must have several if they wish to be esteemed. A man must be courteous, generous, brave, and wise. But if a woman keeps her body intact, all her other defects are hidden and she can hold her head high.[73]

The most esteemed women, in the discourses surrounding femininity, were virgins. Although marriage and sex within marriage received the Church's blessing, virginity was always considered more admirable (at least theoretically).[74] Since women were thought to be far more controlled by their bodies than men, a woman's triumph over her body was seen as heroic. It was the one

---

[69] Walter Mapp, *De Nuqis Curialium*, trans. Frederick Tupper and Marbury. B. Ogle (London: Chatto and Windus, 1924). See also *De Nugis Curialium, Courtiers' Trifles*, ed. and trans. M. R. James; rev. C. N. L. Brooke and R. A. B. Mynors (Oxford: Clarendon, 1983). This edition includes the Latin text as well as an English translation. The passage I have cited is readily available in *Chaucer: Sources and Backgrounds*, ed. Robert P. Miller (New York: Oxford University Press, 1977), 439.

[70] Gower, *Vox Clamantis*, trans. Stockton, *The Major Latin Works of John Gower*, 196-97.

[71] See Diane Bornstein, *The Lady in the Tower: Medieval Courtesy Literature for Women* (Hamden, Conn.: Archon, 1983).

[72] Shahar, *The Fourth Estate*, 109.

[73] Philippe de Navarre, *Les Quatre Ages de L'Homme*, ed. Marcel de Freville (Paris: Librairie de firmin didot, 1888), 20. The French reads: 'Fames ont grant avantage d'une chose: legierement pueent garder lor honors, se eles vuelent estre tenues a bones, por une seule chose; mès a l'ome en convient plusors, se il vuet estre por bons tenuz: besoigs est que il soit cortois et larges et hardiz et sages. Et la fame, se ele est prode fame de son cors, toutes ses autres taches sont covertes, et puet aler partot teste levée.'

[74] For an excellent discussion of women as mothers, see Clarissa W. Atkinson, *The Oldest Vocation: Christian Motherhood in the Middle Ages* (Ithaca: Cornell University Press, 1991).

way women could atone for, and transcend, the legacy of Eve with all of its abhorrent faults.[75] As sexless beings, women could gain admiration. Schulenburg writes, 'For their espousal of virginity, they often won the highest patristic compliment: they were praised for becoming "male" or "*virile*". For heroic defenses of their virginal purity, they were often designated as saints and martyrs.'[76] Their stories fill volumes. St Jerome, whose writings on women were well-known in Chaucer's time, even argued that suicide was an appropriate action for a virgin to take if she were threatened with rape. In *Against Joviniam*, he lists examples of pagan virgins from ancient history whom he praises for killing themselves to preserve their chastity. His views were also corroborated by numerous others, including St Ambrose (St Augustine disagreed). History reports that many nuns indeed did mutilate themselves or sacrifice their lives when threatened with rape. Of course, monks and priests were to be virginal also, but the male spiritual's sexual state was never emphasized to the extent that female virginity was. Schulenburg argues, 'It never dominated the total mode of perception of the male religious, nor defined the parameters for the state of masculine perfection as it did for women. For women, it was the single most essential prerequisite for a life of Christian perfection.'[77]

The culture's fear and fascination with women's bodies can be seen in secular literature as well. Almost all female characters are identified as chaste or unchaste, and the literature was fond of making lists of good women and bad women. Chaucer, himself, creates such lists in the *Legend of Good Women* and in *The Canterbury Tales*. Popular chivalric romances also emphasized the desirability of virginal women and usually judged women's sexual experience harshly. Within patriarchal social structures, 'good women' were women who guarded their wombs so that men could be assured of their children's legitimacy. The inheritance rights of men's legitimate offspring were to be guaranteed, and the only way to guarantee the fusion of property and blood relation was to regulate women's wombs carefully. The genre of the fabliau, which presented peasant and middle class women as sex objects and sexual predators, also reflects the prominence the body played in the portrait of any female character. Furthermore, the cultural ideals of feminine beauty, frequently found in literature, attest to the culture's prevalent discourse on the woman as 'body.' The ideal woman was delicate, small-waisted and small-boned, grey-eyed, and blond. Upperclass status was also assumed as a requirement for beauty.[78]

---

[75] In *Saints and Society :The Two Worlds of Western Christendom, 1000–1700* (Chicago: Chicago University Press, 1982), 220–38, Donald Weinstein and Rudolph Bell found a significant difference in the locus of evil for male and female saints. For male saints, they argued, evil was most often located outside the body as an external temptation; sin occurred as an impure response to demonic stimuli. For women saints, evil was located inside the body, the devil being represented as an internal parasite.

[76] Jane T. Schulenburg, 'The Heroics of Virginity: Brides of Christ and Sacrificial Mutilation,' in *Women in the Middle Ages and the Renaissance: Literary and Historical Perspectives*, ed. M. B. Rose (Syracuse: Syracuse University Press, 1986), 32.

[77] Schulenburg, 'Heroics,' 31. See also Donald Weinstein and Rudolph M. Bell, *Saints and Society: The Two Worlds of Western Christendom, 1000–1700* (Chicago: University of Chicago Press, 1982), 220–38; and *Medieval English Prose for Women: Selections from the Katherine Group and Ancrene Wisse*, ed. Bella Millett and Jocelyn Wogan-Browne (Oxford: Clarendon, 1990).

[78] On medieval standards of beauty see *The Poetria Nova of Geoffrey of Vinsauf*, trans. Margaret F.

Medical literature of the late Middle Ages paralleled the literary discourse, assuming that women were far more controlled by their bodies than men and far more sexual than men.[79] Shahar notes that 'theologians and canonists did not differ from the authors of medical works . . . [or] from secular writers in their attitude to woman's sexuality.'[80] Obviously, this preoccupation with women's bodies and women's sexuality expresses a great anxiety and concern about 'bodily boundaries.' Carroll Smith-Rosenberg notes that when a culture exhibits such concern it may well 'reflect actual change[s] in the functions and structure of the family, alterations in the lines that divide the family from other social institutions, redefinitions of public and private space, and, most especially, changes in relations between the world of men and the world of women.'[81] These kinds of changes were precisely the ones occurring in the urban world of the emerging middle class, a world Chaucer knew well.

Because the representations and evaluations about women are articulated by male voices and perspectives, they may reflect more about men's views of women than women's views of themselves. Men are the ones who perceive woman as 'body' and thereby may project the body (their own body) onto the 'other' sex. The cultural discourse surrounding female corporeality emphasizes it as matter which will gratify men's (bodily) needs: sucking at the breast, feeding, being clothed, being nurtured and comforted, realizing sexual desire, and procreating. Identifying 'woman' as the body permitted and/or encouraged men to project their own physicality elsewhere. Men were not to be subject to the frailty and the needs of the body; they were, according to written discourse, to be warriors, ascetic clergymen, intellectuals. And if they were lovers following in the courtly love tradition, they were depicted as suffering dearly for their attraction to women.

The primary virtue women were to cultivate, besides chastity, was obedience; in no way were women to assert themselves as equals to men. They were to recognize, accept, and uphold male sovereignty. Although Christian discourse generally considered the female soul equal to the male, it also considered women to be 'the weaker vessel[s] who were to remain in subjugation to their menfolk' (see I Peter 3:1–7). And although there were supposedly neither male nor female in heaven, the twelfth-century chronicler, Hugh of Flavigny described the

Nims (Toronto: Pontifical Institute, 1967), 36–38; E. T. Donaldson, 'Idiom of Popular Poetry in the *Miller's Tale*,' in his *Speaking of Chaucer* (1970; rpt Durham: Labyrinth, 1983), 20–22.

[79] About women's biological inferiority, see, for example, Galen, *Oeuvres*, ed. and trans., C. Daremberg (Paris, 1854–56) II: 99–101. See also the short passages from Galen included in Blamires, *Woman Defamed and Woman Defended*, 41–42, and Elizabeth Robertson, 'Medieval Medical Views of Women and Female Spirituality in the *Ancrene Wisse* and Julian of Norwich's *Showings*,' in *Feminist Approaches to the Body in Medieval Literature*, ed. Linda Lomperis and Sarah Stanbury (Philadelphia: University of Pennsylvania Press, 1993), 142–67.

[80] Shahar, *Fourth Estate*, 71.

[81] Carroll Smith-Rosenberg, 'Writing History,' in *Feminist Studies/Critical Studies*, ed. Teresa de Lauretis (Bloomington: Indiana University Press, 1986), 49. Although Smith-Rosenberg's article concerns changes in nineteenth-century Euro-American culture, this particular point applies appropriately to late medieval culture since it, too, faced tremendous social change. See the now dated, but still provocative studies by Norbert Elias: *The History of Manners: The Civilizing Process, Volume I*, trans. Edmund Jephcott (New York: Pantheon, 1978), 160–90 and *Power and Civility: The Civilizing Process, Volume II*, trans. Edmund Jephcott (Oxford: Blackwell, 1982), 76–90.

following hierarchy of souls to be admitted into heaven at the Last Judgment: 'Peter, Paul, John the Baptist, the rest of the Apostles, holy hermits, perfect monks, good bishops, good priests, good laymen, [and lastly] women.'[82] The creation myth established the inferiority of women and the superiority of men on earth. Men, it said, were made in God's image and for 'the glory of God'; women were made in man's image and for 'the glory of man' (see I Corinthians 11:7-9). Just as the creation narrative was cited as God-given evidence of man's 'innate' superiority over others, so, too, the creation myth formed the most powerful 'reason' for women's inferiority. It was believed to represent divine will and thereby a divine expression of social truth. Firstly, Eve was made *for* Adam, to be his helpmate; and, secondly, her weakness was the primary cause of humanity's fall from paradise. Consequently, women were not only created to serve men, they were also inexplicably intertwined with moral weakness and associated with the evils of sin and disobedience. Eve's legacy was imprinted on women's lives by the culture. Peter Damian wrote: 'It is not surprising that there still quivers in the descendants of Eve that same spear which the ancient enemy (Satan) flung at Eve.'[83] Perhaps the most severe correspondence made between contemporary women and Eve is found in Tertullian, an early Church Father well-known and often quoted in the late Middle Ages:

> [Women] should wear rags and mourning clothes, weep and show an Eve plunged in repentance, trying to expiate by her contrite appearance the disgrace of that first crime and the shame of having brought destruction to humanity. . . . And do you not know that you are Eve? God's sentence hangs still over all your sex and His punishment weighs down upon you. You are the one who opened the gate for the devil; you are the one who first violated the forbidden tree and broke the law of God. You were the one who persuaded him whom the devil had not the power to attack. So easily did you shatter that image of God: Adam. Because of the death you merited, the Son of God had to die.[84]

Although there were dissenting voices among patristic writers, most ecclesiastical teachings represented women as Tertullian did, though seldom with as much venom.

The law, too, upheld women's inferiority. Women could not hold public office or participate in any level of government. They were barred from religious and secular positions of authority. Estates literature reinforced the exclusion, 'Women must be kept out of all public office. They must devote themselves to their feminine and domestic occupations.'[85] The English jurist Glanville corroborates this view, writing that women 'are not able, have no need to, and are not accustomed to serving their lord the King, either in the army or in

[82] From the *Monumenta Germaniae Historica*, Scriptores VIII, 384, cited in Gerd Tellenbach, *Church, State and Christian Society*, trans. R. F. Bennett (1940, Oxford: Basil Blackwell, 1948), 52.

[83] Peter Damian, *De Sancta Simplicitate*, *PL* 145, col. 695. Here as with other citations from Latin or Italian, I thank David Nolens for help with translation.

[84] Tertullian, *De Cultu Feminarum*, *PL* 1, col. 1417–19.

[85] Ruth Mohl, *The Three Estates in Medieval and Renaissance Literature* (New York: Columbia University Press, 1933; rpt New York: F. Ungar, 1962), 341.

any other royal service.'[86] Women's legal and civil rights were, in fact, severely restricted, and this was justified on the grounds that women were less intelligent than men, more sly and duplicitous than men, and particularly avaricious. Laws very often fell back on the Church's explanation of Eve's heritage to deprive women of equality or legal recognition. Even though recent scholarship has produced examples of women who did wield authority of some kind, the exception proves the rule; Shulamith Shahar maintains, 'Reality generally matched the law.'[87]

Judith Bennett, in her recent study, *Women in the Medieval English Countryside*, found that women's subordinate position in fourteenth-century culture was the same kind of subordination, regardless of class. It was a subordination maintained by excluding women from the public sphere, the only sphere that granted social power. Unlike women, men had 'public options [which] enabled them to be better neighbors – through pledging, official largesse, loans, and the like . . . [they consequently] accrued both power and prestige.'[88] Bennett believes women were usually offered only 'second rank legal status, disadvantaged access to land and work, . . . relatively limited social horizons . . .' and little public or political power.[89] Women's worlds 'were particularly narrow and oriented toward family members'; in fact, she says, 'the everyday social experiences of women and men in Brigstock [the community she studies carefully] suggest a society that not only often segregated the sexes, but also offered many more associations to men than to women.' The worlds of men and women were thus 'dissimilar as well as separate.'[90] Numerous studies by sociologists and anthropologists have established that 'women most approach equality in their private relations with men when their public actions are more nearly symmetrical'; consequently, public activities and records reveal a great deal about the dynamics of medieval women's private lives. As Judith Bennett comments, 'public actions usually illuminate private matters.'[91]

If women were instructed to accept their inferior status in the Church and in the public world, they were also instructed to accept an obsequious role at home. 'Ideally,' and by in large actually, fathers, husbands, brothers, and other male relatives shaped and controlled women's domestic lives. Corporal punishment – condoned (even encouraged) by social, legal, and ecclesiastical institutions – kept women in line at home. Paolo da Certaldo, a husband himself, writes: 'The female is an empty thing and easily swayed: she runs great risks when she is away from her husband. Therefore, keep females in the house, keep them as close to yourself as you can, and come home often to keep an eye on your affairs and to keep them in fear and trembling.'[92] Cherubino da Siena expresses the

---

[86] Glanville's remarks are cited in Frederick Pollack and F. W. Maitland, *A History of English Law* 2 vols., 2nd ed. (Cambridge, 1898; rpt Cambridge: Cambridge University Press, 1968) I: 485. See the chapter on women, I: 482–85.

[87] Shahar, *The Fourth Estate*, 12.

[88] Judith Bennett, *Women in the Medieval English Countryside* (Oxford: Oxford University Press, 1987), 44.

[89] *Ibid.*, 47. See also Barbara Hanawalt, *The Ties That Bound: Peasant Families in Medieval England* (Oxford: Oxford University Press, 1986), 124–55.

[90] Bennett, *Women*, 37, 36–37.

[91] *Ibid.*, 44.

[92] Paolo da Certaldo, *Libro di buoni costumi*, ed. Alfredo Schiaffini (Firenze: F. Le Monnier,

same attitude in his book, the *Rules of Marriage*: 'if your wife is of a servile disposition and has a crude and shifty spirit, so that [your] pleasant words have no effect, scold her sharply, bully, and terrify her. And if this doesn't work . . . take up a stick and beat her soundly.' He justifies the beating by claiming it will 'redound to your merit and her good.' Women's souls, he argues, could be saved if men beat them into appropriate womanly behavior.[93] As I mentioned above, severe beatings were common and were considered acceptable forms of regulating women's behavior. It was widely accepted throughout Europe that if a husband caught his wife in adultery and killed her in a rage, he would be pardoned and would go free. If a woman killed her husband, for any reason, her action was usually considered treason, and she was most often executed.[94] But women did not commit murder as often as men, partly because they were not socialized into violence to the same degree. Aristocratic women were not sworn to the assize of weapons and were not commonly trained to use weapons from childhood like men were.[95]

If women were subjected to violence in the domestic realm, they were subjected to it in the public realm as well. That the upperclass man often considered women of his feudal realm fair game is common knowledge. The lower a woman's class, the more vulnerable she was to physical outrage – beatings, rape, even murder. Widows were often targets also, their lack of male protection making them vulnerable to rape and assault. Court documents from northern France provide evidence of widows who were raped by gangs of young men and who were then charged (themselves) with immorality.[96] War also frequently became an excuse for brutalizing women, even one's own compatriots. According to the chronicler Thomas Walsingham, Sir John Arundell and his men, *en route* to war with France, raided a Southampton convent in 1379 and kidnapped sixty nuns to use as sexual 'recreation' during the campaign. Taking the women on board their ships, the men raped the women and threw them overboard into the sea when a storm came up.[97] The Church, too, held potential danger for women since priests and clergymen could use their power to gain access to women sexually and could use their privileged position to cover up violence. Petrus Cantor, writing in the twelfth century, bemoaned the fact that 'certain honest matrons, refusing to consent to the lasciviousness of priests, have been written by such priests into the Book of Death, and accused as

1945), 105–06. See also *The Book of the Knight of the Tower*, trans. William Caxton, ed. M. Y. Offord, EETS, SS, no. 2 (London: Oxford University Press, 1971), 35; section one, chapter xvii, 'How a good woman ought not to stryue with her husbond.'

93 Cherubino da Siena, *Regole della vita matrimoniale* (Bologna, 1888), 12–14. See also Alcuin Blamires, *Woman Defamed and Woman Defended*; Robert P. Miller, *Chaucer: Sources and Backgrounds*, 397–474.

94 Given, *Society and Homicide*, 56.

95 *Ibid.*, 136.

96 Jean-Luc Dufresne, 'Les comportements amoureux d'après les registres de l'officialité de Cérisy (XIV–XVe siècle),' *Bulletin philologique et historique du comité des travaux historiques et scientifiques, 1973* (1976): 131–56; cited in Claudia Opitz, 'Life in the Late Middle Ages,' in *A History of Women in the West*, vol. 2, ed. Christiane Klapisch-Zuber (Cambridge, Mass.: Belknap Press of Harvard University Press, 1992), 308.

97 Thomas Walsingham, *Historia Anglicana*, 2 vols., ed. Henry T. Riley, Rolls Series (London: Longman, 1863–64), I: 418–25. Walsingham also condemns the action throughout his account, concluding with God's judgment on the men who were drowned at sea.

heretics and condemned to the fire.'[98] The violence threatening women, whatever its source or its intention, enforced women's obedience to men and dependence on men.

Women who stepped beyond proper roles prescribed by the culture were called 'mannish' or labelled 'viragos' and were severely chastised. In his *Chronicon* (1348), Henry Knighton records an incident at a tournament when forty or fifty women 'came in divers and marvellous men's garments.' Dressed like men, 'they rode forth,' he says, 'to the place of the tourney on choice chargers or richly decked palfreys, thus wasting their own goods, and debasing their bodies with folly and . . . wantonness.' Knighton reads the women's cross-gendered behavior as a betrayal of their own bodies and as a sin against the community and God: 'they neither feared God nor blushed for the modest outcries of the people but made nought of their marriage vows.' As if to imply divine judgment, the chronicler concludes his account of the episode with the comment that rain and lightning poured down on their 'vain sports.'[99] More violent responses to women's role-refusal can be found in judicial and ecclesiastical trials, the trial of Joan of Arc (d. 1431), and the accounts in the *Malleus Maleficarum* perhaps the most famous.[100]

Women's dependency and self-abnegation were structured not only by a code of womanly obedience, but also by a code which encouraged them to cultivate silence. This, too, originates in Biblical discourse: 'Let your women keep silence in the churches, for it is not permitted unto them to speak. . . . I suffer not a woman to teach, nor to usurp authority over the man, but to be in silence' (see I Corinthians 14:34; I Timothy 2:12). Church Fathers, citing Genesis, maintained that women's words were dangerous. St Bernard is said to have remarked that Eve 'spoke but once and threw the world into disorder,' and John of Garland, in his *Parisiana Poetria*, wrote, 'in death's eternal kingdom Woman is enthroned forever; from her mouth flows gall that is taken for nectar, and kills body and soul.'[101] The feminine virtue of silence was encoded in secular fictional literature and handbooks of manners; and it was reinforced by a negative caricature of women as chattering, gossiping animals. Despite the obvious silencing undertaken by most all the institutions within the culture, women were taught to fear speaking too much. In a lengthy disquisition on women's speech and silence, the *Ancrene Riwle* urges women to imitate the Virgin Mary: 'Oure lefdy seint Marie we rede in holy wrytt þat sche ne spake bot foure syþes and þo were woordes of gret myrȝth.'[102] Shulamith Shahar recounts the now well-

[98] Petrus Cantor, *Verbum Abbreviatum*, PL 205: 230 cited and translated by G. G. Coulton, *Life in the Middle Ages*, 4 vols. (Cambridge: University Press, 1928), I: 32.

[99] *Chronicon Henrici Knighton*, ed. J. R. Lumby, Rolls Series, no. 92, vol. 2 (London, 1895), 57–58; translated in Richard Kay, *Medieval Anecdotes* (Lewiston, NY: Broadview, 1988), 282–83.

[100] See Charles T. Wood, *Joan of Arc and Richard III: sex, saints, and government in the Middle Ages* (New York: Oxford University Press, 1988) and *The Malleus Maleficarum of Heinrich Kramer and James Sprenger*, trans. and ed. Montague Summers (1928; New York: Dover, 1971).

[101] St Bernard's comments are recorded by Humbert of Romans, *De Eruditione predicatorum, Treatise of Preaching*, ed. W. M. Conlon, O.P. (Westminster, Md.: Newman Press, 1951), 48. John of Garland, *Parisiana Poetria*, ed. and trans. Traugott Lawler (New Haven: Yale University Press, 1974), VII, 1909–10.

[102] *The English Text of the Ancrene Riwle* (MS. Pepys 2498), ed. A. Zettersten (London: Oxford University Press, 1976), 31.

known story of Esclarmonde, a widow of a great lord of Glascony, who tried to participate in disputations between Cathars and Catholics. Frustrated with her abilities, one Catholic cleric said, 'Madame, go home and spin threads. It is not meet for a woman to take part in a religious discussion.'[103] One reason silence was essential to the feminine ideal was, apparently, to guarantee or assist men's sovereignty. Nothing must challenge that authority, and so, Christine Brooke-Rose argues, 'the male imagination constructs a mute ideal' for women.[104] Jean-Paul Debax has pursued this issue in his article, 'Et voilà pourquoi votre femme est muètte.' He believes that there are a number of reasons why women's silence is part of the feminine ideal. First, he says, it represents virginity – a kind of sexual/vocal innocence that knows nothing of sexual commerce. Secondly, 'to reduce woman to silence is to reduce her to powerlessness,' and control over women is a key element in the cultural discourse surrounding masculinity. Thirdly, Debax writes, 'Language, the tongue, is woman's weapon'; her 'will to fight back against intolerance necessarily involves the use of language.' So it is a weapon that must be neutralized.[105] When, within a community, power derives more and more from knowledge than from physical prowess, regulating who speaks becomes crucial for those who want to possess power. Notably, formal education in early modern Europe existed nearly exclusively for men, and access to public and printed forums was, for the most part, reserved for men. There were, it must be noted, men who disagreed. Heretical sects commonly encouraged women's active participation, and women flocked to them.[106] And some men – such as William of Ockham, the influential fourteenth-century philosopher whose ideas were familiar to Chaucer – advocated greater rights for women in the Church, including their right to speak and contribute to church councils.[107]

The feminine prescription of subordination, virginity, obedience, and silent acceptance achieved its zenith in the Virgin Mary. She was the self-sacrificing, long suffering and nurturing mother (yet ever-virginal), the vessel in whom the male god was translated into flesh. She did not choose her role; she was chosen. Her acquiescence and passive, pious response to men's rule over her were enshrined as virtues for women. And the sorrows of Mary were incorporated into many rituals and prayers to demonstrate the ideal feminine response to adversity: acceptance, silence, patience, and piety. The Virgin adored her husband (God) and her son (Jesus). She was the most prominent model, though not the only cultural model of femininity. As such, she enacted an adoration of the male.[108] But even this kind of motherly-virginal affiliation with men was still

---

[103] Shahar, *Fourth Estate*, 259.
[104] Christine Brooke-Rose, 'Woman as a Semiotic Object,' in *The Female Body in Western Culture*, ed. Susan R. Suleiman (Cambridge, Mass.: Harvard University Press, 1986), 310.
[105] Jean-Paul Debax, 'Et voilà pourquoi votre femme est muètte,' *Caliban* XVII Tome XVI (L'Universite de Toulouse Le Mirail, 1980), 32-35; cited in Brooke-Rose, 'Woman as a Semiotic Object,' 310.
[106] See Shahar's chapter on 'Witches and the Heretical Movements,' *Fourth Estate*, 251-280.
[107] Shahar, *Fourth Estate*, 258.
[108] Simone de Beauvoir comments: 'For the first time in human history the mother kneels before her son; she freely accepts her inferiority. This is the supreme masculine victory, consummated in the cult of the Virgin – it is the rehabilitation of woman through the accomplishment of her defeat,' *The Second Sex*, trans. H. M. Parshley (New York: Vintage, 1974), 193. If the culture

too much for some theologians. In the Gnostic *Gospel of St Thomas*, Simon Peter says, 'Let Mary go out from our midst, for women are not worthy of Life!' Christ answers him, saying, 'See, I will draw her so as to make her male so that she also may become a living spirit like you males. For every woman who has become male will enter the Kingdom of heaven.'[109] In other words, when 'she' becomes 'he,' she will be purified and thereby deserve salvation. This was not just an idea found in Gnosticism; St Jerome writes: 'As long as woman is for birth and children, she is different from man as body is from soul. But when she wishes to serve Christ more than the world, then she will cease to be a woman and will be called man.'[110] And St Ambrose asserted, 'She who does not believe is a woman and should be designated by the name of her sex, whereas she who believes progresses to perfect manhood, to the measure of the adulthood of Christ.'[111] It is a notion which found support from Aristotle, who maintained that 'the female is, as it were, a mutilated male.'[112]

The Virgin Mother (chaste and yet a mother) spells out the primary tension in the cultural discourses of the Middle Ages surrounding femininity, and that tension revolved around the body. She also established an ideal no woman could attain – for if a women were a virginal nun, she would have no son; and if she had a son, she could not be virginal. Within the discourses of the heroic male, the spiritual male, and the intellectual male, women were quite consistently instructed to be passive and dependent upon men. Within courtly love narratives, women were imagined to exert control over their lovers for a time, remaining distant, and often moral and pure; but, as in the *Roman de la Rose* and most romances, women were also being instructed finally to give the lover what he wanted, what he had 'earned.' As Susan Crane notes, courtly love discourses 'do not admit [women] a language of refusal.'[113]

Since men were assumed to govern, these discourses represented the most crucial question facing women as a question of how to submit. And so, women in literature can be found wondering, 'Are there any limitations on my obedience to my husband or father?' 'How can I influence the governor?' 'When does influence become rebellion?' 'When does submission become slavery?' 'How do I submit and still maintain self-respect?' As these are questions posed by a predominately male-created discourse, we cannot mindlessly assume that they are necessarily women's questions. We can, however, quite easily see them as the questions *about* women that most concern men; and, because of the powerful

---

believed as Augustine did that 'through the woman, death; through the woman, life,' (*Sermo* 232, 2 in *PL* 38, 1108), it is no wonder that motherhood becomes translated into a controlled and subservient ideal. De Beauvoir comments, 'It was as Mother that woman was fearsome; it is in maternity that she must be transfigured and enslaved,' so that only 'through being his docile servant . . . she will also be a blessed saint' (193).

[109] *The Secret Books of the Egyptian Gnostics*, intro., ed., and trans., Jean Doresse (Paris, 1958; rpt New York: Viking, 1960), 370. The full text is translated in appendix ii (355-77).

[110] St Jerome *Commentariorum in Epistolam ad Ephesios* III, 5 in *PL* 26, col. 567.

[111] St Ambrose, *Expositio Evangelii secundum Lucam*, Book X, n. 161, in *PL* 15, col. 1938. Augustine, taking a slightly different view, still assumes that woman is only restored to the image of God in spirit, not body because only man in body and spirit is made in the likeness of God. *De Trinitate* XII, 7, *PL* 42, col. 1003-05.

[112] *De Generatione Animalium* II, chap. 3 (737a, 26-31), trans. Arthur Platt, *The Works of Aristotle*, vol. 5, ed. J. A. Smith and W. D. Ross (Oxford: Clarendon, 1912).

[113] Crane, *Gender and Romance*, 65.

cultural resonances these questions had, they must have been often significant for women, as well. And that is the tack I will take in examining codes of femininity in the *Canterbury Tales*. So, besides identifying how female characters and narrators answer the questions posed by the discourse surrounding femininity, we will want to see what the depiction of women here indicates about the male-narrators and/or Chaucer. The fictional women in the *Canterbury Tales* are all creations of men, and they will bear, in one way or another, traces of their creators.

CHAPTER THREE

Pervasive Competition and Fragile Control: Chaucer's Appraisal of Masculine Stereotypes in the Frame Narrative

As a supreme ironist, Chaucer was fond of looking at any human value, belief, behavior, or emotion commonly exhibited in his culture from several different perspectives. Consequently, it is no wonder that we find him exploring the nature of masculine power and control, particularly calling attention to its achievements, its limitations, and its price. If, as I have established in the previous chapter, the desire for control is one pervasive feature of late medieval masculinity, inevitably Chaucer (the poet who studied human nature so closely) will include it in his portraits of male characters. And, indeed, tale after tale explores the extent of men's control over themselves, over others, and over the world around them. The *Tales* demonstrate that men who seek power over others inevitably run into conflict with one another; that is, that competition between men is an obvious consequence of men trying to realize, in their lives, a masculine identity based upon control. In his essay, 'The Construction of Masculinity,' Michael Kaufman observes that competition between men takes a variety of forms in Western culture, and one key purpose of this competition – whether physical or mental, intellectual or emotional, whether individual, social, or national – is, he argues, to 'reinforce the reality that relations between men . . . are relations of power.'[1]

[1] Michael Kaufman, 'The Construction of Masculinity,' in *Beyond Patriarchy: Essays by Men on Pleasure, Power, and Change*, ed. Michael Kaufman (Toronto and New York: Oxford University Press, 1987), 17. See also Julian Henriques, Wendy Hollway, et al, who assert, 'power is not a property but a relationship. One can only examine its reality in its exercise. . . .' Furthermore, Henriques says, 'Power is always exercised in relation to a resistance,' *Changing the Subject: Psychology, Social Regulation and Subjectivity*, ed. Julian Henriques, Wendy Hollway, et al. (London and New York: Methuen, 1984), 117, 115. See also Peter Middleton, *The Inward Gaze: Masculinity and Subjectivity in Modern Culture* (New York: Routledge, 1992), for discussion of contemporary theories of masculinity, particularly for its work on relations between men. Also Eve Kosofsky Sedgwick, *Between Men: English Literature and Male Homosocial Desire* (New York: Columbia University Press, 1985) and Jonathan Goldberg, *Sodometries: Renaissance Texts, Modern Sexualities* (Stanford: Stanford University Press, 1992).

Clearly the conflicts between, say, the Miller and the Reeve or the Pardoner and the Summoner (even between the Parson and the Host) highlight the competition for power among the narrators themselves. Within the individual tales, too, competition among men often forms the basic dramatic tension for the plot. It is central to the contest between Palamon and Arcite in the *Knight's Tale*, to Nicholas, Absalon, and old John, the carpenter, in the *Miller's Tale*, to the tragedy of the *Physician's Tale*, to the greed played out in the *Pardoner's Tale*, to the conflict between the Fox and Chaunticleer in the *Nun's Priest's Tale*, and so on. Competition, in fact, forms the very occasion for the telling of the *Tales* when Harry Bailly, the pilgrims' host, initiates a storytelling contest. He is described in the *General Prologue* as 'a semely man' who is large, merry, bright-eyed, and successful; he is 'boold of his speche, and wys, and wel ytaught, / And of manhod hym lakkede right naught' (755-56). This host proposes that the pilgrims pit their narrative talents against one another on their journey. For incentive, he promises a reward to the winner (the losers will pay for the winner's meal). He also promises punishment for anyone who refuses to cooperate or participate. The pilgrims approve the plan, making Harry the 'governour' who will judge the storytelling contest. They decide to be 'reuled . . . at his devys / In heigh and lough; and thus by oon assent,' they agree to be 'acorded to his juggement' (813-18). From the first moment of action on the journey, one man has established his authority over others and has shaped the others' experience; he has shaped it in the form of competition. Of course, the purpose here is entertainment, but the structure of the entertainment is competition. The comedy of the gaming situation establishes hierarchies of power and struggles for success and control which frame the *Tales*. In so far as the *Canterbury Tales* are grounded on the dynamic of competition, they are aligned with what the culture considers an aspect of the ideal masculine, at least in the heroic, courtly love, and intellectual traditions.

Perhaps it is not surprising that Chaucer would build his serial narrative on the dynamics of competition. Because the *Canterbury Tales* depict the process of telling a tale (each narrator taking us through this process again and again), one story the text itself tells is the story of storytelling; and there is a close affinity between competition, or the struggle to dominate, and the way Chaucer's narrators speak about creating narrative. We are frequently reminded that the storyteller must exert control over his or her tale. Each narrator must choose the tale he or she will tell, fashion its beginning, middle and end, select details, create syntax, rhythms, meters, and rhymes, and exert control over language, experience, characters, plot, and audience. Creating a tale involves the storyteller in a competitive relationship with disorder. Each narrator, like Harry Bailly, will set himself or herself up as governor and judge over all the elements in the story. What we see in the dynamics between Harry and the pilgrims is reenacted in the dynamics between author and text material.[2] Sometimes Harry has control; sometimes he does not. Sometimes narrators successfully shape and control their tales; sometimes tales get the best of their narrators.

---

[2] Cf. Alan T. Gaylord, 'Sentence and Solaas in Fragment VII of the *Canterbury Tales*: Harry as Horseback Editor,' *PMLA* 82 (1967): 226-35.

The discourse Chaucer and his contemporaries used to discuss literary creation intersects with the cultural discourse surrounding masculinity. To create or shape a narrative is defined most often in terms of a male activity. Medieval rhetoricians who spoke of the writer, spoke of the writer as male; Boccaccio, for example, asserts: 'true poets have always been the rarest of men.'[3] Geoffrey of Vinsauf, in his *Poetria Nova*, equates the artist with a man who builds a house: 'if a man has a house to build, his impetuous hand does not rush into action. The measuring line of his mind first lays out the work, and he mentally outlines the successive steps in a definite order.'[4] In *Troilus and Criseyde*, Chaucer translates this very passage:

> For everi wight that hath an hous to founde
> Ne renneth naught the werk for to bygynne
> With rakel hond, but he wol bide a stounde,
> And sende his hertes line out fro withinne
> Aldirfirst his purpos for to wynne.   (I, 1065-69)

Like Geoffrey of Vinsauf's description of the creative project, Chaucer's assumes a masculine subject, a male 'builder' who erects a monument by achieving control over his materials. Additionally, Chaucer claims that creating poetry is like 'sending out a line to win a purpose'; in other words, it involves some sort of competition. Chaucer's imagery of the poet casting out a 'line' to 'win' something carries connotations in Middle English of fishing or snaring birds.[5] To create narrative, then, is not merely to erect something, it is also to hunt, overpower, and capture something.[6] Chaucer's assumptions about the nature of writing and storytelling suggest that he conceived of it most often as a masculine activity but one women could engage in as well. If we can trust the descriptions within his texts, writing was, for him, an activity involving control over his 'matere.' It was also, at least sometimes, an activity he depicted as competitive. This is true of Dante and Boccaccio, who, at least on occasion, assumed a competitive potential in creative endeavor. In Book II of Dante's *De Vulgari Eloquentia*, language is described connotatively as an agent of status, power, and combat: '. . . language is the necessary vehicle of our thought no less than the horse is of the soldier, and since the best horses are suited to the best soldiers, . . . the best language will be suited to the best thought.'[7] Boccaccio, in his defense of poetry found in Book XIV of the *Genealogy of the Gentile Gods*, imagines that the pursuit of poetry is always a fight with those forces in late medieval culture that would quell imaginative literature: 'I am about to enter the arena, a manikin against these giant hulks – who have armed

---

[3] Giovanni Boccaccio, *Genealogy of the Gentile Gods*, Book XIV in *Boccaccio on Poetry*, 39.

[4] *The Poetria Nova of Geoffrey of Vinsauf*, trans. Margaret F. Nims (Toronto: Pontifical Institute of Mediaeval Studies, 1967), 16-17.

[5] Donald R. Howard, *The Idea of the Canterbury Tales* (Berkeley: University of California Press, 1976), 136.

[6] Cf. Teresa de Lauretis, *Alice Doesn't: Feminism, Semiotics, Cinema* (Bloomington: Indiana University Press, 1984), especially chapter five, pp. 103-157. Her chapter, entitled 'Desire in Narrative,' explores connections between sadism, narrative, and narrativity.

[7] Dante, *De Vulgari Eloquentia*, Book II in *Dante in Hell: The De Vulgari Eloquentia: Introduction, Text, Translation, Commentary*, ed. Warman Welliver (Ravenna: Longo Editore, 1981), 91.

themselves with authority to say that poetry is either no art at all or a useless one.
. . . But . . . the fight must be fought.' A bit later, in the same text, addressing
those who would condemn literature, he continues in these bellicose and
gladiatorial terms:

> And now, O men of sense, . . . calm your indignation. . . . Our contest
> has grown perhaps too bitter. You began by taking up the cudgel against an
> innocent class of men, with the intention of exterminating them. I came to
> their defense, and . . . did what I could to save deserving men from their
> deadly enemies. Yet, if the poets in person had fairly taken the field
> against you, you would see how far their powers surpass both yours and
> mine, and repent. . . . But the fight is over; with some glory of war, and a
> good deal more sweat, we have reached the point where the lust for victory
> may be a bit qualified, and we may part company with a fair settlement,
> . . . for the prizes of the contest have been awarded.[8]

Besides the rhetoric of contest which dramatizes poetic creation, the medieval
poet, in fact, like any modern poet, struggles 'to carve' a text out of tradition,
language, experience, and imagination. 'He' is always faced with the choice of
duplicating an established narrative, elaborating or embellishing it, or diverging
from it. In this way, the poet resides in a state of tension with tradition. This was
particularly true for the late medieval English poet who would write in the
vernacular, since the aristocracy had what Elizabeth Salter has termed
'stubbornly foreign reading habits.' English vernacular literature, she says, 'had
to battle [against other literatures] in order to survive and develop.'[9]

   Then, too, each of Chaucer's narrators is in constant tension with all that is not
said, not selected, and not allowed within his or her narrative, as the interpretive
strategies of deconstruction and semiotics have so persuasively demonstrated.
On at least a literal level, Chaucer appears aware of this aspect of storytelling.
Pandarus, in *Troilus and Criseyde* remarks that definitions always involve
tensions: "A wheston is no kervyng instrument, / But yet it maketh sharppe
kervyng tolis":

> 'By his contrarie is every thyng declared.
> For how myghte evere swetnesse han ben knowe
> To him that nevere tasted bitternesse?
> Ne no man may ben inly glad, I trowe,
> That nevere was in sorwe or som destresse.
> Eke whit by blak, by shame ek worthinesse,
> Ech set by other, more for other semeth . . .'
>
> (I, 631-32; 637-43)

In the *Knight's Tale*, the narrator tells us what he says he will not tell us about
Arcite's funeral (I, 2919-2966), and in the *Retractions*, we may also detect a

---

[8] Boccaccio, *Genealogy of the Gentile Gods* Book XIV in *Boccaccio on Poetry*, 36, 97.
[9] Elizabeth Salter, *English and International: Studies in the Literature, Art and Patronage of Medieval England*, ed. Derek Pearsall and Nicolette Zeeman (Cambridge: Cambridge University Press, 1988), 75

spoof on 'un-naming' where Chaucer's deliberate yet ineffective censorship
calls our attention to the very tales he would reject. He may deny them (at least
in a stylized retraction), but renunciation always calls to mind that which is
renounced, and obviously Chaucer did not destroy his text nor did others who
might insist upon reading the retractions seriously. Similarly, the Man of Law,
in his introduction, gives us a rehearsal of the tales he will not tell – tales
Chaucer has already told: Ceys and Alcione, Lucresse, Dido, Ariadne, Medea,
Alceste, and so forth. Then the Man of Law adds:

> But certeinly no word ne writeth he
> Of thilke wikke ensample of Canacee,
> That loved hir owene brother synfully;
> (Of swiche cursed stories I sey fy!)
> Or ellis of Tyro Appollonius,
> How that the cursed kyng Antiochus
> Birafte his doghter of hir maydenhede,
> That is so horrible a tale for to rede,
> Whan he hir threw upon the pavement.
> . . .
> Of swiche unkynde abhomynacions,
> Ne I wol noon reherce, if that I may.   (II, 77–89)

In this passage, the narrator alludes to John Gower who, in his *Confessio
Amantis*, rehearsed such 'abhomynaciouns.' Notably, the Man of Law not only
reminds us of the tales, he also condemns Gower for telling them, thus entering
into a competitive relationship with another poet.[10] Laura Kendrick has
commented that denial and affirmation are essential components of any artistic
(or critical) endeavor: 'The basic device of artistic fictions – and of their
criticism – seems to be a combination of denial and substitution or
transformation whose purpose is to allow the interpreter to have it both ways, to
express and savor the forbidden desire while controlling it through a kind of
sublimation.'[11] Fiction, whether a child's game of make-believe or an adult's
narrative, is a deliberate refusal of reality. Fiction-making allows us to deny
reality and to exert our own control over an artificial world. It involves both
mimesis and distortion, qualities which dance in competitive tension within any
fiction. Competition and control are, in various senses, at the heart of the
creative process, and so it is hardly surprising that Chaucer should situate his
tale about storytelling within a competitive dynamic.

There may also be a historical reason why Chaucer associates storytelling with
competition. Richard Firth Green, studying relationships between literature and
the English Court in the late Middle Ages, has documented quite clearly that for

---

[10] For a discussion of Chaucer's relationship with Gower, see John Fisher, *John Gower: Moral
Philosopher and Friend of Chaucer* (New York, 1964), 204–302. Richard Hazelton has also
argued that the *Manciple's Tale* may be a satire on the serious moralizing of poets like Gower in
'The *Manciple's Tale*: Parody and Critique,' *Journal of English and Germanic Philology* 62
(1963): 1–31. Cf. Derek Pearsall, 'The Gower Tradition,' in *Gower's Confessio Amantis:
Responses and Reassessments*, ed. A. J. Minnis (Cambridge: D. S. Brewer, 1983), 180.

[11] Laura Kendrick, *Chaucerian Play: Comedy and Control in the Canterbury Tales* (Berkeley:
University of California Press, 1988), 30.

Chaucer, or any other Court Poet, creating a poem or a narrative meant entering into a competition. To write for a courtly audience meant that one might receive a reward of some kind – greater prestige or an invitation into closer association with the political power base of the nation or region.[12] Presumably, it might also mean one was silenced, ignored, or deemed inadequate, if the work was not well-received. As Elizabeth Salter points out, 'rigid distinctions between political and cultural activities cannot ever have really existed.'[13] Chaucer probably knew that poets, like Phebus's crow, needed to be careful about what they said and how they said what they said. He surely knew that writing well could enhance the career of a diplomat, a custom's clerk, or a King's servant. Thus, for Chaucer to conceive of narrative arising out of a competitive contest, as it does in the *Canterbury Tales*, may well reflect his own experience within a Courtly environment as well as common cultural assumptions about the 'masculine nature' of creative endeavor.

Situating the *Tales* at the site of competition carries with it several interesting critiques of the dominant medieval gender discourse. Of course, by placing his narrators within a competitive game, under the direction of a man, Chaucer reproduces the hierarchies of power which the dominant cultural discourse surrounding gender assumes: men will control. But, the subtleties lying potential in the choice of competition as the setting for the narratives do not always simply reinscribe the cultural discourse about men's rule. First of all, Chaucer's inclusion of women's voices in his storytelling competition suggests that, contrary to the ideals prescribed for women, competition is not just the purview of men. Whereas gender discourse in the Middle Ages encouraged men to compete, it did not encourage women to compete with men. Men were to control; women were to submit. Men were to speak; women were to be silent. Although they number far fewer than the men, the women in Chaucer's frame tale are not silent; they speak, much to our delight. They participate in the competitive game, openly competing with, and challenging, men – and they are not chastised for their participation. All the narrators, whether male or female, have equal opportunity to win the game. If the frame narrative suggests competition is not just a feature of relationships between men, but is also a feature of the relationships between men and women, it does not, however, depict overt competition between the women narrators. In so far as the Wife of Bath, the Prioress, and the Second Nun participate in the game, they compete with each other, but they never speak directly to one another as the male pilgrims do. Their tales are commented upon by men, surrounded by men's narratives, and told at the invitation of men. Whereas the frame narrative records overt conflict between male pilgrims, it nowhere dramatizes open conflict between women. The women compete primarily with men. At every immediate site of competition in the frame tale, men are always involved; women are not. Nevertheless, the inclusion of women's voices in the competition suggests that

---

[12] Richard Firth Green, *Poets and Princepleasers: Literature and the English Court in the Late Middle Ages* (Toronto and Buffalo: University of Toronto Press, 1980), 135–67. Green notes that successful 'court writers came to see themselves as the mentors of royalty' (135).

[13] Salter, *English and International*, 243. See also chapter 12, 'Chaucer and Internationalism' (239–44), and her discussion of the close relationships between literature and politics in chapter 3 (75–100).

women need not be, nor are not, silent – that they can, and do, participate in the creation of narrative – and that they can be, and are, an active part of shaping the life of the community.

A critique of the power relations *between* men themselves is also made potential in the competitive setting of the frame narrative. The man who governs the company is an innkeeper, not a knight, a monk, or a man of law. The man who becomes 'governour,' albeit within the fiction of the game, is not the man of highest degree or status in the company of pilgrims. To the extent that we find his rule haphazard, ineffective, and humorous, we may interpret Harry's governance as an example of the unruly and inadequate leadership capabilities of the lower-status male, but Harry *is* the one who originates the plan or design for the entertainment, and, in rough form, his plan is realized. If the *Canterbury Tales* gives us a representation of the world, as is often argued, it represents a world arrangement initially conceived of, and ruled over, by an innkeeper. Potentially, the reader may see in this move a criticism aimed at the arbitrary nature of privilege. If merits and capabilities (rather than lineage or status) determined who ruled, perhaps the Harry Baillys would emerge as rulers. It is an idea suggested, too, by the lines on 'gentillesse' in the *Wife of Bath's Tale*:

> For, God it woot, men may wel often fynde
> A lordes sone do shame and vileynye;
> And he that . . .
> Ne folwen his gentil auncestre that deed is,
> He nys nat gentil, be he duc or erl;
> For vileyns synful dedes make a cherl.
> For gentillesse nys but renomee
> Of thyne auncestres, for hire heigh bountee,
> Which is a strange thyng to thy persone.
> Thy gentillesse cometh fro God allone.
> Thanne comth oure verray gentillesse of grace;
> It was no thyng biquethe us with oure place.
>
> (III, 1150–51; 1156–64)

This sentiment reverberates in the *Clerk's Tale*, where Griselde, born in poverty and of humble birth, becomes an able and saintly queen, much loved by her people and quite capable of ruling (IV, 394–441). The competitive frame, then, with its innkeeper-host, helps Chaucer contribute to what Nigel Saul calls 'one of the most vigorous and long-running of medieval debates, that on the essence of gentility.'[14]

These more subtle critical potentialities lie submerged and latent within the competitive world of play and game, and they suggest yet another kind of challenge to the hierarchical relationships between men promoted by Estates ideology. Initially, Harry attempts to sequence the telling of the tales so that the Knight and the Monk will commence the game. Harry orders his world (his game) to mirror those cultural institutions which grant greatest privilege to men

[14] Nigel Saul, 'Chaucer and Gentility,' in *Chaucer's England: Literature in Historical Context*, ed. Barbara A. Hanawalt, Medieval Studies at Minnesota, volume 4 (Minneapolis: University of Minnesota Press, 1992), 41. The full article is found on pages 41–55.

of highest status in the company of pilgrims. Harry's position as governor and his ordering design reinscribe familiar hierarchies, even though the innkeeper is now king. This design is, however, disrupted by the aggressive and boorish Miller and Reeve. The competitive setting allows for, and even encourages, this disruption of order so that competition becomes a way for the text to demonstrate the limitations of hierarchical systems and male rule, regardless of which male rules. Within the drama of the frame narrative, the tension between competition and control is the only successful 'governour.' In the world of the frame tale, the male pilgrims, especially, are in perpetual tension. They re-enact the script of heroic masculinity in that they struggle to establish order, hierarchy, and control; and yet, because order can only be established in contest with other forces and potentialities, the possibility always exists that the order will fail. Even though Harry asserts a modicum of control over others, and even though he creates rules for a game, his rules and his authority are not, in fact, always honored. Chaucer frequently creates challenges to his authority in the frame narrative. Harry Bailly has commanded the pilgrims: 'stonden at my juggement, / . . . for to werken as I shal yow seye' (778–79), but this edict does not hold. After the Knight concludes his tale, for example, Harry asks the Monk to 'quyte' the Knight with another tale. It is, obviously, Harry's plan to control who speaks and when, but the Miller intrudes, drunken and loud, unwilling to abide by the rules, and insisting on speaking next:

> Oure Hooste saugh that he was dronke of ale,
> And seyde, 'Abyd, Robyn, my leeve brother;
> Som bettre man shal telle us first another.' (3128–30)

The Miller angrily retorts:

> 'By Goddes soule . . . that wol nat I;
> For I wol speke, or elles go my wey.' (3132–33)

The Miller's aggression wins him second place in the temporal succession of narratives so that he is the one who gets to 'quyte' the Knight. Harry Bailly's control, his designated authority, bends before the aggressiveness of the Miller. A similar challenge to the host resides in the epilogue to the *Man of Law's Tale* and erupts when Harry asks the Parson to tell the next tale. The Shipman, this time, insists, 'Nay . . . that schal he nat . . . My joly body schal a tale telle' (1178–85). And when Harry later requests that the Pardoner tell a funny tale to cheer everyone up after the dreary *Physician's Tale*, not one, but several pilgrims object to his plan:

> But right anon thise gentils gonne to crye,
> 'Nay, lat hym telle us of no ribaudye!
> Telle us som moral thyng, that we may leere
> Som wit. . . .' (323–26)

It is not just the order of the *Tales* or the nature of the *Tales* that the pilgrims occasionally try to take control of, however; they also intrude on the entertainment by arguing with one another. Again, Harry is not always successful at controlling the situation. When discord breaks out between the Friar and the Summoner, for example, his efforts to prevent animosity fail. The 'governour' himself even winds up in a combative confrontation with the Pardoner, yelling: 'I wolde I hadde thy coillons in myn hond / . . . Lat kutte hem of . . . / They shul be shryned in a hogges toord!' (952–55). So Harry's authority is always tenuous, thereby calling into question men's ability to control events and people.[15]

The frame narrative establishes the tenuousness of each individual's authority, as each tale is 'repayed' or 'quyted' in some way by one of the other tales; thus, the *Tales* themselves compete with one another. And despite the orderly progression of tales Harry tries to orchestrate, each narrator is subject to the possibility of interruption, with the consequence that the authority of narrative voice is frequently disrupted in the *Tales*. Which tales and voices will be heard and for how long becomes a question imbedded in the contest of the frame. The Cook never completes his tale; the Squire is cut off by the Franklin, the Monk by the Knight, Chaucer by the host, and the Wife of Bath by the Friar and Summoner (who also argue with one another and interrupt each others' tales).

The competitive setting for the *Tales* also implicates any efforts readers may make to establish a hierarchy or a 'winner' among the tales. Unquestionably, the frame encourages us to make such judgments, to think of the 'play' between the tales, and to assume that the tales are, in some way, competing. However, since the text gives no assurances about who 'wins,' at least in the literary game, we cannot form any unassailable decision. The text prevents us from gaining control over it in the same way competition always threatens Harry Bailly's control and his decisions. We may be invited to make an aesthetic judgment about which tale 'wins,' but it is a decision nearly impossible to make. If we are pulled into making a decision, our decision will always be subject to disagreement. At the least, the ambiguity in the unresolved competitive setting forces us to acknowledge the assumptions that come to play when we make aesthetic judgments, when we choose a 'winner.'

Clearly, the struggle to order, restrain, challenge, and win is essential to the drama of the frame narrative; it therefore provides evidence that competition functions as a central dynamic within the *Canterbury Tales*. To the extent that it creates competitive relationships between men, it adopts one key, structural dynamic found in those medieval masculinities prescribed by the heroic, courtly love, and intellectual traditions. But it disrupts those discourses by suggesting that women also should and do participate in the competition as capable players. In so far as the competitive gaming situation creates a hierarchy of power between Harry and the pilgrims, the *Tales* re-enact the medieval assumption that men must rule. But the game also demonstrates that the ideal of male control is an illusion, that hierarchies are arbitrary at best and are always subject to challenge by those placed in lower status positions. The dynamics of competition place limitations on men's ability to govern. Competition between men may serve the purpose of establishing men's power, but it also limits men's power.

---

[15] Judith Ferster, *Chaucer on Interpretation* (Cambridge: Cambridge University Press, 1985) discusses the reciprocal relationship that exists between Harry and the pilgrims in her last chapter entitled, 'The Politics of Narrative in the Frame of the *Canterbury Tales*' (139–156).

Likewise, the competitive setting draws the reader into arguing for or against the qualities of any given tale, but it inevitably limits our power as interpreters of the text, since the text itself refuses to resolve the competition.

There is yet more to consider if we examine the implications of the framing competition: namely, that there may be a critical comment on competition implicit in the narrative frame. Though competition forms the motive for the rehearsal of stories, it occurs within a spiritual and, ideally, non-competitive event: the pilgrimage. Of course, Chaucer could have written his collection of tales within a frame that more overtly reinforced competitive values and behaviors. He could have sent his narrators on a journey to market where they would enter a competitive economic world. He could have placed them on board a ship travelling to crusade against the French or against the 'Infidel,' where they would be entering the world of physical combat and military competition. He could have situated his collection of tales in a great hall during a feasting game, where social and political competition would constitute a congruent stage. Instead, he chose to situate his narrators within the context of pilgrimage. They play their competitive game against a backdrop that does not advocate a quest for land or temporal power of any kind. Instead, pilgrimage promotes a personal and internal quest for greater spiritual understanding. Although competition arises among the pilgrims, competitiveness is not, ideally, a feature of pilgrimage, as the *Parson's Tale* makes clear. Christian ideology (though not always practiced) judges spiritual competition negatively. As the Parson asserts, pilgrimage and penitence are about renunciation, not acquisition, the love of God instead of the human and worldly, faith instead of reason. To be sure, pilgrimage is a quest, but it is a non-combative, non-competitive quest for forgiveness, for healing, for penance rather than a quest for power or ascendancy over others. It is a quest that urges one to achieve control over one's own soul, not one's neighbor, and it thereby contrasts with the competitive nature of the storytelling game and with the competitive worlds often found within the individual tales themselves. From a Christian perspective, the pilgrimage setting demonstrates the follies of competitive values.[16]

The frame tale, with its tension between game and pilgrimage, dramatizes the conflict between competitive acquisition and obedient renunciation; in doing so, it reflects tensions that can be found in the culture's assumptions about masculinity. Whereas the hierarchical gaming situation is part of the heroic, courtly love, and intellectual discourse, it is not congruent with spiritual pilgrimage or with Christian apotheosis. Thus, the conflict between Christianity

---

[16] Several scholars have established and discussed the festive and gaming quality of pilgrimages during the Middle Ages. Historical evidence affirms that gamesmanship often did, in actuality, accompany pilgrimages. But, in the fourteenth century, the Church as well as the emerging, rather austere religious leaders often condemned such activities. See Johan Huizinga, *Homo Ludens: A Study of the Play-Element in Culture* (London: Routledge, 1949); J. J. Jusserand, *English Wayfaring Life in the Middle Ages*, trans. Lucy Toulmin Smith (London: Benn, 1884); Christian Zacher, *Curiosity and Pilgrimage: The Literature of Discovery in Fourteenth-Century England* (Baltimore: Johns Hopkins University Press, 1976); Victor Turner and Edith Turner, *Image and Pilgrimage in Christian Culture: Anthropological Perspectives* (New York: Columbia University Press, 1978); Carl Lindahl, *Earnest Games: Folkloric Patterns in the Canterbury Tales* (Bloomington: Indiana University Press, 1987).

and competitive male ideals found in medieval culture is reinscribed in the frame narrative of the *Canterbury Tales*. Just as Chaucer's frame does not ignore these tensions or deny them, neither do the individual tales. Whether the tales address heroic, courtly love, religious, or intellectual assumptions about men, they, too, represent the complexity of late medieval 'masculinity.'

CHAPTER FOUR

The Heroic Discourse: the *Knight's Tale*

If the *Canterbury Tales* can be said to comment upon the cultural discourse advocating heroic masculinity, it can also be said to call that ideal into question. Heroism even becomes, at times, the butt of humor, as it does in the mock-heroic material scattered throughout the *Tale of Sir Thopas*. In the *Knight's Tale*, where heroism in the character of Theseus is praised, Boethian and Christian philosophic contexts modify and temper the heroic. Even *Troilus and Criseyde*, a work heavily indebted to the ancient heroic world, presents Troilus primarily as a lover, a private man of feeling and thought. Very few lines in the text are concerned with military action or public event. Chaucer's early poems also focus on the internal world of male characters, not on their public actions.[1] From the early dream visions to the pilgrimage in the *Canterbury Tales*, Chaucer's poetry downplays or ignores the world of serious epic action and heroism. For traditional heroic narratives, one must look elsewhere. Wars and national events are in the background and are subordinate to a close look at individual worlds. The rulers and warriors depicted in the *Tales* usually function first as fathers and husbands, rulers of domestic worlds, and only secondarily as rulers of nations and their destinies. Instead of warriors, the text is filled with men who are fathers, husbands, lovers, tradesmen, clerks, and low-status clergymen.

The tales which concern the lives of kings and queens and warriors foreground the domestic world. Walter's importance in the *Clerk's Tale* resides primarily in his marriage to Griselda, not in his relationship to some other head of state. Even though his position as a ruler has a crucial bearing on the story, the quality of his rule is evidenced in his private relationship to his wife. The Wife of Bath's knight goes out on a quest, but he does not fight dragons or awesome opponents; instead, he seeks an answer to a question. His is not a physical quest like those

---

[1] Elaine Tuttle Hansen has explored what she calls the 'feminized' poet in her article, 'The Feminization of Men in Chaucer's *Legend of Good Women*' found in *Seeking the Woman in Late Medieval and Renaissance Writings*, ed. Janet Halley and Sheila Fisher (Knoxville: University of Tennessee Press, 1989) and included as part of her introduction to her own book, *Chaucer and the Fictions of Gender* (Berkeley: University of California Press, 1992), 1–25. See Lee Patterson's reading of the early poems, especially the Theban materials: *Anelida and Arcite*, *Troilus and Criseyde*, and the *Knight's Tale* in his exquisite study, *Chaucer and the Subject of History* (Madison: University of Wisconsin Press, 1991), 47–243.

found so often in chivalric romances but an intellectual and psychological quest. In the *Franklin's Tale*, Arveragus goes to campaign in glorious tournaments in Great Britain, but not much is said of his activity. His knightly exploits exist simply to account for his absence. He must be off the set, so to speak, to make room for the private relationship between Dorigen and Aurelius. In the *Man of Law's Tale*, the Sultan and King Alla are portrayed mainly in relation to Custance, not in relation to international struggles for land and power. Although power struggles and battles occur in the tale, they have the status of background material; they are not the focus of the plot. This is not to say that such details are unimportant, but that they are less critical to the plot. When King Alla goes north to fight a war, he does so because his absence from Court allows Donegild to use the counterfeit letter as a maneuver which drives Custance into exile. Although the narrative tells us the king is at war, we get no description of the battles; the event exists to make room for a twist of the plot essential to the tale's focus: Custance's life and sufferings. The public outlines of King Alla's identity are mentioned, but they are downplayed, and the only public events recorded in the narrative which involve King Alla's court occur because Custance is their central focus.

The *Monk's Tale*, with its repetitious assessment of heroic achievement and tragic loss, underscores a more Boethian or Christian perspective on heroic achievement. Here, the tales of Hercules, Alexander the Great and Julius Caesar are not told for the purposes of singing praises to heroism in epic manner, nor to laud heroic achievements, but to teach us, by example, to avoid the sins of pride. As the Monk says, 'For hym that folweth al this world of prees, / Er he be war, is ofte yleyd ful lowe' (VII, 2137–38):

> Lordynges, ensample heerby may ye take
> How that in lordshipe is no sikernesse;
> For whan Fortune wole a man forsake,
> She bereth awey his regne and his richesse,
> And eek his freendes, bothe moore and lesse. (VII, 2239–43)

Instead of fame and fortune, the *Monk's Tale* urges the audience to seek an introspective and spiritual wealth: 'Ful wys is he that kan hymselven knowe!' (2139). What the *Monk's Tale* records is that high chivalry and great achievement spark jealousy, and either may easily place one in jeopardy. His tragedies are a rereading or a revision of the epic material from a medieval Christian and Boethian perspective. The Monk's ominous interpretation of heroism may well be one of the reasons (though not, of course, the only reason) why the Knight-narrator interrupts him:

> 'Hoo!' quod the Knyght, 'good sire, namoore of this!
> That ye han seyd is right ynough, ywis,
> And muchel moore; for litel hevynesse
> Is right ynough to muche folk, I gesse.
> I seye for me, it is a greet disese,
> Whereas men han been in greet welthe and ese,
> To heeren of hire sodeyn fal, allas!

And the contrarie is joye and greet solas,
As whan a man hath been in povre estaat,
And clymbeth up and wexeth fortunat,
And there abideth in prosperitee.
Swich thyng is gladsom, as it thynketh me,
And of swich thyng were goodly for to telle.'   (VII, 2767-79)

Even though the Knight may find the Monk's repetitious tragedies boring, that is not what the Knight articulates in his objection. Instead, he objects to dwelling on sadness, tragedy and loss. (It is Harry Bailly who says he's bored.) The Knight, the man whose profession aligns him most intimately with heroic virtues, doesn't want to hear the Monk's rendition of chivalry and heroism. It may well be for him a great 'dis-ease' to be reminded that fragile fame and fortune accompany feats of war. The Knight can appreciate Boethian philosophy as long as he speaks it and controls it, as long as he places it within the ordered and highly artful rendition of his own tale. Even though the *Knight's Tale* and the *Monk's Tale* carry some of the same messages about men's ability to control events in the world, the Knight is uncomfortable with the *Monk's Tale*. He can tell a tale about the necessity of accommodating oneself to change, but he finds it uncomfortable to hear one that is so blunt, heavy-handed, and tirelessly unadorned. Perhaps it is also worthy to note that the Knight, despite his seeming awareness of mutability, shapes his tale around Theseus, a warrior and ruler who retains his wealth, power, and nation throughout the narrative. Theseus may learn that he cannot completely control fate, but he acquires this lesson by watching the events crucial in other people's lives, not his own. Arcite is the one who dies in a contest, not Theseus; Palamon is imprisoned for years, not Theseus; Emelye's marriage is arranged for her, not Theseus's; and Ypolita and Creon lose wars and nations, not Theseus. Perhaps the Knight's interruption of the Monk's tragedies reveals just how well he really knows or has experienced loss or the wheel's turn.

Not surprisingly, the Knight-narrator, the company's experienced warrior, tells a tale incorporating heroic values associated with masculinity. Theseus is, however, reconstructed in a late medieval context and hence reveals qualities consistent with Boethian Christian masculinity not just with the heroic.[2] Still, as in epic narrative, the political world of the *Knight's Tale* is represented as a place where men establish victory over adversaries by warring against them, imprisoning them, banishing them, or by building alliances and establishing political influence over them through marriage. Relations between men in this tale are overwhelmingly competitive. Male relationships in the foreground of the story all involve competition: Palamon with Arcite, Theseus with Creon as well as the two young cousins, and the two hundred men who accompany Palamon and Arcite into the arena for the tournament. In this tale, competition between men always culminates in physical struggle, except at the very end of the tale where Theseus's struggle with Palamon (Athens vs. Thebes) is concluded with a

---

[2] Cf. Jill Mann who, following a powerful tradition of reading Theseus as ideal, claims that he 'represents the fullest development of an ideal of feminised masculinity' *Geoffrey Chaucer* (Atlantic Highlands, N.J.: Humanities Press, 1991), 171.

marriage alliance rather than with a battle. But what does the text reveal about this struggle for power? Theseus is often read by twentieth-century scholars as an admirable warrior-prince, as a force of order and, therefore, as a positive image of masculinity.[3] Opposing interpretive camps argue that the tale presents an indictment of aristocratic, chivalric values. Like a number of scholars, I see ways in which Chaucer writes his character so as to emphasize Theseus's tenuous ability to maintain order.[4] Furthermore, Chaucer seems to find the young Theseus, the warrior-king who is modelled on the heroic male topos, somewhat limited and to prefer the older Theseus, the merciful diplomat.

In the *General Prologue* immediately preceding the *Knight's Tale*, and throughout the tales which follow, we are made keenly aware of the ironic stance Chaucer often takes with his narrators and their stories. The *General Prologue*'s description of the Monk, for example, demonstrates that the Monk obviously aspires to greater freedom and greater status than is appropriate for a Benedictine. But this evaluation is not to be found in blatant judgments made by a naive Geoffrey, the pilgrim-narrator; it is, instead, made by Chaucer's careful manipulation and selection of details. It is made ironically. Chaucer does not want us to view the Monk with the same apparently naive view Geoffrey has, nor with the same elitist view the Monk has of himself. We hear that the Monk is an 'outridere,' a man for whom rules exist to be broken, challenged, or circumvented. He scorns the labor, study, asceticism, poverty, and cloistered life of prayer established for his order by St Benedict. He likes hunting, fine horses, excellent hounds, rich garments, sumptuous banquets, and sex. But our narrator, Geoffrey, does not draw these conclusions; we do. Geoffrey merely describes what can be seen or learned by observation. It is up to us to make a judgment. Beryl Rowland maintains that irony is Chaucer's 'most consistent position' and that 'he has no sense of commitment to any class or cause . . . [Consequently,] his detachment frequently creates ambiguities so pronounced

---

[3] Scholars who identify Theseus as a force of order and as an idealized image of aristocratic masculinity include Charles Muscatine, *Chaucer and the French Tradition* (Berkeley: University of California Press, 1957); E. Talbot Donaldson, *Chaucer's Poetry: An Anthology for the Modern Reader*, 2nd ed. (New York: Ronald, 1975); D. W. Robertson, Jr *A Preface to Chaucer: Studies in Medieval Perspectives* (Princeton: Princeton University Press, 1962); John Halverson, 'Aspects of Order in the *Knight's Tale*,' SP 57 (1960):606–21; P. Boitani, *Chaucer and Boccaccio* (Oxford: Society for the Study of Mediaeval Languages and Literature, 1977); Douglas Brooks and Alastair Fowler, 'The Meaning of Chaucer's *Knight's Tale*,' MAE 39 (1970): 123–46; John P. McCall, *Chaucer Among the Gods* (University Park: University of Pennsylvania Press, 1979); A. J. Minnis, *Chaucer and Pagan Antiquity* (Cambridge: D. S. Brewer, 1982); Paul A. Olson, *The Canterbury Tales and the Good Society* (Princeton: Princeton University Press, 1986).

[4] Cf. David Aers, *Chaucer, Langland and the Creative Imagination* (London: Routledge and Kegan Paul, 1980); Stephen Knight, *Geoffrey Chaucer* (Oxford: Blackwell, 1985). Lee Patterson, *Chaucer and the Subject of History*, 167–68, writes 'I do not believe that Chaucer's engagement with chivalry took the form of either moral or social polemic. [He was] analytic rather than rhetorical. . . . his analysis focused, finally, neither on moral standards nor on social conditions but on attitudes . . . on socially determined and therefore historically contingent values and beliefs. Ultimately, this is the more radical critique.' Patterson's discussion argues that the *Knight's Tale* presents a 'demystification' of the Order of Chivalry and that it allows Chaucer 'to explore chivalry's contradictions both in its contemporary practices and, more profoundly, in the idea of chivalry itself.'

that critics still argue over his intentions.'[5] Edmund Reiss has even argued that the Knight's portrait in the *General Prologue* contains the potential for an ironic reading: 'The "chivalrie, / Trouthe and honour, fredom and curteisie" professed by the Knight (I,45–46) are controverted by such deeds as his fighting as a mercenary for a heathen lord.'[6] Because irony is Chaucer's prevalent stance, we must beware of assuming the Knight and/or Theseus are simply mouthpieces for Chaucer. The Knight's perspective on Theseus and Chaucer's need not always coalesce.

The Knight-narrator fully admires Theseus and describes him as a 'lord and governour' who 'in his tyme [was] swich a conquerour, / That gretter was ther noon under the sonne' (I, 861–63). Theseus is (from this perspective) rich, wise, strong, powerful, of noble blood, and well-wedded. These are the preliminary generalizations about his character; then we get the particulars which illuminate the generalization. Given Chaucer's propensity for irony, we need to see whether the Knight-narrator's interpretation of Theseus is undercut at all by the plot, the tone, or the details within the narrative. Does the tale itself support the Knight-narrator's appraisal? The first bit of supporting evidence the Knight provides us to convince us that Theseus is, indeed, wise and chivalric is that Theseus defeated the Amazons:

> What with his wysdom and his chivalrie,
> He conquered al the regne of Femenye,
> That whilom was ycleped Scithia,
> And weddede the queene Ypolita,
> And broghte hire hoom with hym in his contree
> With muchel glorie and greet solempnytee,
> And eek hir yonge suster Emelye.   (I, 865–71)

We learn that Theseus warred against Ypolita and won. Violent encounter is left unsaid, even though it presses against the silence between the lines. How Theseus managed to marry Ypolita is also left unsaid; what Ypolita thought is of no concern; what matters is that Theseus won a battle, a kingdom, and a wife.[7] The description cuts against the grain of traditional heroic discourse in so far as it downplays the violence and the physical prowess involved in the battle. All we know is that Theseus won the war 'by wysdom and chivalrie.' The opportunity

---

[5] See Beryl Rowland's introduction to Earle Birney's *Essays in Chaucerian Irony*, (Toronto: University of Toronto Press, 1985), xxvii.

[6] Edmund Reiss, 'Chaucer's Parodies of Love,' in *Chaucer the Love Poet*, ed. Jerome Mitchell and William Provost (Athens: University of Georgia Press, 1973), 40, n. 13.

[7] For a general discussion of the Amazon figure in literature, see Abby W. Kleinbaum, *The War Against the Amazons*, (New York: McGraw-Hill, 1983). Kleinbaum calls attention to Chaucer's reduction of Amazons (who in ancient mythology are, indeed, ferocious) to passive women. She also writes that 'The Amazon is a dream that men created, an image of a superlative female that men constructed to flatter themselves. . . . The conquest of an Amazon is an act of transcendence, a rejection of the ordinary, of death, of mediocrity – and a reach for immortality'; it is a way 'to be certified as a hero' (1). See also W. Blake Tyrell, *Amazons: A Study in Athenian Mythmaking* (Baltimore: Johns Hopkins University Press, 1984); Page duBois, *Centaurs and Amazons: Women and the Pre-History of the Great Chain of Being* (Ann Arbor: University of Michigan Press, 1982).

to praise the warrior in the heat of battle is bypassed.[8] The Knight-narrator glosses over the war between Amazons and Athenians, saying, 'I wol nat letten eek noon of this route'(889). Instead, he chooses to focus on Theseus's heroic adventures in battle against Thebes, a war against male adversaries. On the way home 'in his mooste pride,' Theseus is interrupted by women mourners who are crying beside the road:

> . . . swich a cry and swich a wo they make
> That in this world nys creature lyvynge
> That herde swich another waymentynge;
> And of this cry they nolde nevere stenten
> Til they the reynes of his brydel henten.
> 'What folk been ye, that at myn homcomynge
> Perturben so my feste with criynge?'
> Quod Theseus. 'Have ye so greet envye
> Of myn honour, that thus compleyne and crye?   (900–908)

His first thought is that they are disrupting *his* homecoming. His second thought is that they are envious of *his* honor. The self-centered thought process is noteworthy. Theseus does not ask simply, 'Why are you mourning?' Instead, he assumes that his own actions have something to do with their condition. Thirdly, he perceives them as potential victims, asking, 'Who hath yow mysboden or offended?' (909). Lastly, he asks them if they need his help.[9] The oldest woman in the group corrects his first mistaken assumption:

> She seyde: 'Lord, to whom Fortune hath yiven
> Victorie, and as a conqueror to lyven,
> Nat greveth us youre glorie and youre honour,
> But we biseken mercy and socour.
> Have mercy on oure wo and oure distresse!'   (915–19)

She tells him she and the other mourners are Theban noblewomen who have been bereft of everything by the new King of Thebes who has murdered their husbands and made them 'caytyves.' Hoping Theseus will redress Creon's wrongs, they beg for his help. Once informed, Theseus opens his heart to them. Although the Knight-narrator thinks it unimportant to mention Theseus's emotional reaction to marrying Ypolita, his emotional response is a crucial part of his reaction to the Theban women. Here, early in the text, the narrative

---

[8] It may well be neglected because the courtly code of conduct regulating knights' behavior toward ladies forbids and finds reprehensible any violence directed against women. Susan Crane, *Gender and Romance in Chaucer's Canterbury Tales* (Princeton: Princeton University Press, 1994), reads this episode assuming that the defeat of the Amazons and the pity shown to the Theban women are an appropriation of the feminine into the masculine (18–23): 'Traits marked feminine can indeed be integrated into masculine behavior, but the current does not run in reverse from masculine behavior into feminine identity;' and she notes that femininity and feminine figures 'complicat[e]' masculinity, 'enlarging and universalizing rather than feminizing the masculine experience' (21).

[9] Cf. Jill Mann, *Geoffrey Chaucer* (Atlantic Highlands, NJ: Humanities Press, 1991), 174: 'The "compassioun" Theseus feels for women is itself a womanly quality implanted in him. It feminises him without making him effeminate.' See her full discussion (165–85).

reveals its alliance with the heroic, or chivalric, codes and its rejection of the courtly love scenario. Theseus is most moved by the plight of widows and orphans, a reaction consistent with late medieval codes of chivalry. His emotional response to his own marriage can scarcely be discerned. Aside from considering the influence of Chaucer's sources, historical context provides a reason why the emotional side of a king's marriage might be neglected in favor of his reaction to the community since it was common practice for aristocrats to marry for economic or political reasons. Theseus, a king, will marry in order to gain greater political power, much like Chaucer's friend, John of Gaunt, married Costanza of Spain, laying claim to lands and power in another country.

In the first few lines describing Theseus, the heroic discourse is evident in the silence surrounding Theseus's marriage to Ypolita; the *Knight's Tale* downplays the warrior's private emotional life; what is important is his public life. The chivalric or heroic discourse is also evident in Theseus's oath to protect widows and orphans, but it is noticeably absent in the actual description of violent confrontation between the Amazons and the Athenians. It is also tempered by the knight-narrator's emphasis on Theseus's empathy toward the Theban women:

> This gentil duc doun from his courser sterte
> With herte pitous, whan he herde hem speke.
> Hym thoughte that his herte wolde breke,
> Whan he saugh hem so pitous and so maat,
> That whilom weren of so greet estaat;
> And in his armes he hem alle up hente,
> And hem conforteth in ful good entente . . .   (952–58)

Singing a duet with courtly masculine sentiment, Theseus's heroic masculinity is voiced through this same passage. He swears he will defend the women and fight Creon 'That al the peple of Grece sholde speke / How Creon was of Theseus yserved' (962–63). At least part of his motivation to assist the women stems from his desire for fame, a motivation consistent with the heroic.

If the heroic discourse is tempered by the Knight-narrator's desire to make a medieval courtly gentleman out of his Greek hero, the appraisal of Theseus as a wise and gentle man is also ever so slightly ambiguous and tempered by empathy the text creates for the Thebans (at least for a modern reader).[10] On the one hand, Creon's defeat is unambiguously presented as Theseus's triumph over evil because Creon is so despicable: Theseus 'faught and slough hym manly as a knyght' (987). But, on the other hand, what of Theseus's relationship to the other Thebans? He 'putte the folk to flyght' (988) and proceeded to ravage and pillage the city:

---

[10] In their article, 'The Meaning of Chaucer's *Knight's Tale*,' *Medium Aevum* 39 (1970): 123–46, Douglas Brooks and Alaistair Fowler maintain that Theseus seems an ideal figure to the Knight-narrator 'because the Knight shares in his faults and to some extent his virtues' (141). Arguing on different grounds, Brooks and Fowler maintain that Theseus' character is 'presented ambivalently . . . and though a formidable character of many strengths, [he] is never completely satisfactory from a moral standpoint. . . . He falls short of the ideal' (140–41).

> And by assaut he wan the citee after,
> And rente adoun bothe wall and sparre and rafter.   (989–90)

He becomes an agent of destruction in his quest for victory, 'And dide with al the contree as hym leste' (1004).[11] Chaucer's source, Boccaccio's *Teseida*, provides telling contrast. Teseo is not challenged by the Thebans after he enters the city, and the conquering warrior wanders around the city amazed by its beauty. Teseo gives Creon an elaborate funeral and 'had the plain searched and every wounded man who was found was given medical aid, and every corpse was buried.'[12] But Chaucer changes the emphasis. Theseus permits his forces to 'ransacke in the taas of bodyes dede, / Hem for to strepe of harneys and of wede' (1005–06). In Chaucer's version, the Thebans – the defeated city – are described as victims of war. As the Athenian scavengers pillage and search through the bodies of Thebans who have been wounded or who have died, they find 'Thurgh-girt with many a grevous blody wounde, / Two yonge knyghtes liggynge by and by, / Bothe in oon armes . . .' (1010–1012). The description of victims who are assaulted, ransacked, stripped of their possessions and whose city is 'rente adoun' hardly creates sympathy for Theseus, regardless of the Knight-narrator's enthusiasm for him. In the midst of this melee, two young knights are pulled out of a pile of bloody bodies and taken to Theseus, and when Theseus learns the two young men are of royal Theban blood, he takes them prisoner and sends them 'to dwellen in prisoun perpetually – he nolde no raunsoun' (1023–24).[13] Such severe retribution is unchivalric according to manners of war codified in late medieval handbooks of chivalry. Christine de Pisan, for example, in her *Book of Fayttes of Armes and of Chyualrye* (1410; translated in 1489), argues that ransom should 'be not so cruell that the man be not vndoo thereby, and his wiffe and children distroied and brought to poverte. Other wise it is tirannye ayenst conscience and aienst al ryght of armes . . . But for to putte a man in an euyll pryson and constrayne by tormentynges to paye more then hys power may bere, it is an homynable horreur and the dede of a cruel . . . tyraunt.'[14]

Once the city is plundered and the two young knights taken captive, Theseus rides home triumphant. Juxtaposing Theseus's victory with the young cousins' woe, Chaucer writes:

> And whan this worthy duc hath thus ydon,
> He took his hoost, and hoom he rit anon
> With laurer crowned as a conquerour;
> And ther he lyveth in joye and in honour

[11] For a discussion of the deviations Theseus makes from medieval codes of war, see John Reidy, 'The Education of Chaucer's Duke Theseus,' in *The Epic in Medieval Society: Aesthetic and Moral Values*, ed. Harald Scholler (Tubingen: Max Niemeyer Verlag, 1977), 391–408.

[12] Boccaccio, *The Book of Theseus*, trans. Bernadette M. McCoy (New York: Medieval Text Association, 1974) II: 84. See *Sources and Analogues of Chaucer's Canterbury Tales*, ed. W. F. Bryan and G. Dempster (Chicago, 1941; rpt New York: Humanities, 1958).

[13] Chaucer's Theseus refuses to grant ransom for Palamon and Arcite, a harsh move unknown to Boccaccio's Teseo. It is also an unchivalric action, according to the codes of war. See C. T. Allmand, ed. *Society at War* (New York: Barnes and Noble, 1973), 83–84.

[14] Christine de Pisan, *The Book of Fayttes of Armes and of Chyualrye*, trans. William Caxton, ed. A. T. P. Byles, EETS OS 189. (London: Oxford University Press, 1932), 223–24.

Terme of his lyf; what nedeth wordes mo?
And in a tour, in angwissh and wo
This Palamon and his felawe Arcite
For everemoore; ther may no gold hem quite.   (1025–32)

The contrast between the conqueror and the conquered is abrupt and dramatic.
Of course, this juxtaposition shows Fortune's Wheel at work, but the word
choices and the abrupt contrasts are also certainly shaping our responses to the
characters.[15] Palamon and Arcite are clearly the victims and are described as
'woful prisoner[s],' 'sorweful prisoner[s],' 'piteously' held by a jailer behind 'a
wyndow, thikke of many a barre / Of iren greet' (1063, 1075–76). By contrast,
the celebratory warrior seems harsh, indifferent, and somewhat cold. Such
evidence seems to call the Knight-narrator's initial appraisal of Theseus into
question. Whereas the Knight-narrator – our warrior – is unabashed by the
violence between men, considering it 'manly' to slay adversaries in battle, the
reader may recall Chaucer's *Ballade to a Former Age* and wonder:

What sholde it han avayled to werreye?
Ther lay no profit, ther was no rychesse.
. . . [In a former age]
Unforged was the hauberk and the plate;
The lambish peple, voyd of alle vyce,
Hadden no fantasye to debate,
But ech of hem wolde other wel cheryce;
. . .
Allas, allas! now may men wepe and crye!
For in oure dayes nis but covetyse,
Doublenesse, and tresoun, and envye,
Poyson, manslauhtre, and mordre in sondry wyse.
                              (25–26; 49–52; 60–63)

What Theseus has accomplished early in the tale, consistent with the heroic
masculine code, is a triumph of physical force. Competition has erupted into war
against Scithia and against Thebes. As a consequence, Theseus is rewarded with
greater political power and wealth, but his competitive actions have also resulted
in the destruction and possession of human bodies. Ypolita and Emelye are taken
in battle and wind up under the protective surveillance of Theseus; many
Thebans lie wounded or slain, dispossessed of their wealth in the plundering that
occurs after the battle; Palamon and Arcite are imprisoned without ransom.

Notably, in terms of a discourse on masculinity, this tale registers a tension
between the heroic nature of the actions in the plot and the Knight-narrator's
characterization of a genteel hero. Notice, too, that the Knight-narrator, the one
who has, according to the *General Prologue*, fought in so many wars abroad, the

---

[15] Joerg O. Fichte notes 'the juxtaposition of joy and misery is so immediate that Chaucer connects
the two states by the same end rhyme, in order to achieve the greatest possible tension.' Because
of all the sudden reversals of fortune in this world, Fichte sees the world of Theseus in great
confusion. 'Man's Freer Will and the Poet's Choice,' *Anglia* 93 (1975): 340.

one who returns 'Al bismotered in his habergeroun,' never judges Theseus negatively, but the tone of his narrative and the shape of his narrative create a fantastic account of violent competition. His account is pollyannaish. He tells a Romance tale which, by definition, takes place in an ideal nether world; and it may be intended to show us his allegiance to courtly sophistication or perhaps to 'obsolescence,' as Donald Howard has argued, but it may well be ironic that the pilgrim who knows the most about the realities of war refuses to reveal or turns away from what he knows perhaps all too well.[16] His descriptions of war and imprisonment are tightly shaped and controlled, and they seem pat, so that fantasy hides much of the violence in the tale.[17] The tension between epic warrior and courtly gentleman also emerges in a pattern of reactions which Theseus exhibits throughout the tale. Theseus first wars against Ypolita and then marries her; violence is replaced with a contract. Then he wars against the Thebans, but spares Palamon and Arcite; violent death is replaced with imprisonment. Theseus is, at first, somewhat abrupt with the Theban women on the roadside, and then he gets down off his horse to embrace them all and comfort them in his arms. This pattern of heroic action tempered by a genteel heart repeats itself over and over again in numerous events within the tale, and it underscores a shift in Theseus's function within the tale from warrior to diplomatic governor.

So it is not surprising to find the imprisoned young cousins eventually freed, but first a harsher Theseus rules. Early within the tale, Palamon cries out to Venus, calling Theseus a tyrant :

> Out of this prisoun help [us] that we may scapen
> And if so be my destynee be shapen
> By eterne word to dyen in prisoun
> Of oure lynage have som compassioun
> That is so lowe ybrought by tiryannye.   (1107–11)

A bit later in the narrative, Arcite accuses Theseus of 'martyring' 'wrecched' Palamon (1561–62). Despite the exaggerated language the captives use, our empathy may well be aroused for two young men held prisoner for life. Additionally, Theseus does not decide, on his own, to spare them a bleak destiny; instead, an agent of mercy intervenes on their behalf. Perotheus – Theseus's long-time friend – finally secures Arcite's release, but the release is provisional. Theseus must still exert control over his enemy, and so Arcite is banished on pain of death. Theseus attempts to control him by banishing him, just as he had previously controlled him by imprisonment. The motivation here is to protect his city and his own wealth and power, for this descendent of the royal house of Cadmus could threaten Athens. The dramatization of his softening toward (male) adversaries has begun, and it continues when Theseus

---

[16] Donald R. Howard, *The Idea of the Canterbury Tales* (Berkeley: University of California Press, 1976), 89–93; 108–110; 115.

[17] H. Marshall Leicester, Jr notices similar dissonances in the tale, arguing that 'the track of the Knight's historical disenchantment with chivalry as an institution is most clearly registered, at least at first, in his dissatisfaction with its most cherished fantasies, which are also his own,' *The Disenchanted Self*, 223. See also his pp. 221–382.

discovers Palamon (who escapes) and Arcite (who has returned to Athens disguised) fighting over Emelye in a grove. This time, Queen Ypolita and her ladies intercede on behalf of the young knights; kneeling and weeping, they beg Theseus to have mercy. Whereas his initial impulse is to execute the young men ('Ye shal be deed, by myghty Mars the rede!' [1747]), his final decision is to grant mercy ('at the laste aslaked was his mood, / For pitee renneth soone in gentil herte' [1760–61]). Theseus stands before the two cousins, many years after having captured them, and finally forgives them. He says, 'Fy / Upon a lord that wol have no mercy' (1773–74). And so Theseus avoids committing the kind of murderous and tyrannical absolutism Creon had exhibited in Thebes; although, as Susan Crane notes, 'the scene locates pity in women as a way of describing the subordinate place it holds in the all-encompassing masculine deliberation.'[18] Still, the man of action is commanded by the man of thought. From a Boethian or Christian perspective, this development is positive.

Throughout the remainder of the *Knight's Tale*, Theseus relinquishes direct physical control of his adversaries and pursues new ways of maintaining his control. Since the two cousins are now pitted against one another, rather than against him, he finds it strategic to orchestrate their conflict by establishing a tournament where they will return in a year and settle their differences. When one cousin successfully slays 'his countrarie, or out of lystes dryve,' Theseus says, 'Thanne shal I yeve Emelya to wyve' (1859–60). Still careful to protect his own power, Theseus forces the two younger men to swear 'That nevere mo ye shal my contree dere, / Ne make werre upon me nyght ne day, / But been my freendes in all that ye may' (1822–24). Henry J. Webb sees Theseus as having many characteristics of the Renaissance Machiavel; and, indeed, if the story stopped here, we might agree; Theseus could take advantage of his enemies' quarrel and have them kill each other off, but he doesn't.[19]

Boccaccio's Teseo follows just such a Machiavellian strategy. In Chaucer's source, the two men fight to the death and many men die. But Chaucer deviates from Boccaccio's version of the story; he creates a Theseus who modifies the rules of his tournament to prevent massive injury and slaughter. When Palamon and Arcite return to Athens to fight for Emelye's hand, 'to shapen that they shal nat dye' (2541), Theseus announces that many weapons will be disqualified from the arena, and he establishes rules to make the tournament less bloody.[20] The people's response reinforces a favorable view of this decision:

> The voys of peple touchede the hevene,
> So loude cride they with murie stevene
> 'God save swich a lord, that is so good.
> He wilneth no destruccion of blood!'[21]   (2561–64)

---

[18] Crane, *Gender and Romance*, 22.

[19] Henry J. Webb, 'A Reinterpretation of Chaucer's Theseus,' *RES* 23 (1947), 298, 294. See also L. K. Born, 'The Perfect Prince: A Study in 13th and 14th Century ideals,' *Speculum* 3 (1928): 470–504.

[20] See G. A. Lester, 'Chaucer's Knight and the Medieval Tournament,' *Neophilologus* 66 (1982): 460–68, and Juliet R. V. Barker, *The Tournament in England, 1100–1400* (Woodbridge: Boydell Press, 1986).

[21] Cf. The Conciliar Condemnations of Chivalry (1130–1215) translated and edited by David Carlson in his article, 'Religious Writers and Church Councils on Chivalry,' in *The Study of*

Obviously, by deviating from Boccaccio early in the tale and creating a Theseus who was harsher than Teseo and then, by deviating from his source toward the end of the tale and creating a Theseus far more merciful than Teseo, Chaucer purposefully shapes a maturation process for this character.[22] The young Theseus who controlled the world around him through violence and physical force gives way to a mature Theseus who is more merciful and humane, who attempts, like the intellectual or humanist male ideal, to control by knowledge, art, and diplomacy.

Theseus's initial callousness toward his male adversaries has been replaced once again with compassion. When, in the tournament, Arcite is thrown from his horse and dies, Theseus grieves. His sorrow is so pronounced that 'No man myghte gladen Theseus / Savynge his olde fader Egeus' (2837-38). This reaction is a far cry from the younger war-like Theseus who 'rente adoun' Thebes 'bothe wall and sparre and rafter' (990), and who 'dide with al the contree as hym liste' (1004). Instead of destroying, this more mature Theseus would nurture and preserve; the Theseus who, at the beginning of the tale destroys the 'Land of Femenye' and razes Thebes, becomes, at the end of the story, a builder of elaborate lists and temples and a maker of peaceful treaties and marriages. He finally secures peace between Thebes and Athens with the marriage of Palamon and Emelye.[23]

The Knight-narrator appears to admire Theseus from beginning to end without ever judging him negatively, but the shape of the narrative encourages us to make a subtle judgment against violence and in favor of a merciful and gentle masculinity. A narrative ending, at least in medieval literature, usually carries with it a moral reflection on earlier plot events, so for the story to begin with war and end with efforts to avoid massive violence suggests a moral preference for nonviolence. Although powerful forces in medieval culture valued aristocratic men who effectively control others by physical force if necessary, the *Knight's Tale* subtly calls men's control by violence into question. It does this by showing us an heroic warrior who again and again softens toward his adversaries and who matures out of the warrior code into a peaceful and merciful code of diplomacy. Elaine Penninger's comments on knighthood in the *Canterbury Tales* support

---

Chivalry, ed. Howell Chickering and Thomas H. Seiler (Kalamazoo: Western Michigan University Press, 1988), 141-171. The article also includes text and translation of objections to tournaments raised by Bernard of Clairvaux and Jacques de Vitry. In the same volume, see Helmut Nickel, 'The Tournament: An Historical Sketch' (213-62).

22 John Reidy believes, 'the events of the Tale are designed' to bring the self-confident man of action to more acceptable views and attitudes,' 'The Education of Duke Theseus,' in *The Epic in Medieval Society*, ed. Scholler (1977), 403. Charles Muscatine has noted that 'The pace of the story is deliberately slow and majestic. Random references to generous periods of time makes it chronologically slow,' *Chaucer and the French Tradition*, 177. And Fichte, 'Man's Freer Will' (340), has noted that Chaucer's story involves a far greater time period than Boccaccio's. Perhaps one reason the time is lengthened is to allow for this change in Theseus, this maturation process.

23 This movement in Theseus's character may possibly carry with it an historical analogue. Richard II, in the later years of his reign, was influenced by Michael De la Pole, among others, who urged him toward a policy of peace with France rather than war. The *Knight's Tale*, in this light, may reinforce the arguments against war and violence found in the *Tale of Melibeus*. See Gardiner Stillwell, 'The Political Meaning of Chaucer's *Tale of Melibee*,' *Speculum* 19 (1944): 433-44. Chaucer's own career followed this movement, from his early military campaign and captivity to his later diplomatic and governmental roles.

this interpretation. She maintains that knightly combat in the *Tale of Sir Thopas* (which Chaucer assigns to himself) 'is made absurd,' and finds knighthood in the *Tale of Melibee* (also told by Chaucer, the pilgrim) 'eschewed as unchristian.' Melibee, she says, 'acts as a man should: he forgives.'[24] V. John Scattergood has also argued that the parody of romance and chivalry found in *Sir Thopas* may well express an opposition to 'the values of the warrior ethos' and to 'those sorts of literature which served to sustain them.'[25] In the *Tale of Melibee*, an 'olde wise' man rejects the same values in a different way:

> 'ther is ful many a man that crieth "Werre! werre!"
> that woot ful litel what werre amounteth./
> . . .
> soothly, whan that werre is ones bigonne, ther is
> ful many a child unborn of his mooder that shal
> terve yong by cause of thilke werre, or elles
> lyve in sorwe and dye in wrecchednesse. . . .'
> (VII, 1038, 1041)

Scattergood writes: 'the burlesque in *Sir Thopas* and the rational argument in *Melibee* add up to the same thing in "sentence" – that a concern for military glory is vain and futile, at times, indeed, rather foolish.' He interprets Geoffrey's two tales as a jibe against competitive values found in the discourses surrounding masculinity in the late fourteenth century: 'Chaucer's performance as a whole evinces the view that men are not particularly heroic creatures and that their best interests are served by caution, circumspection, compromise, and even forgiveness.'[26] These are exactly the behaviors developed in the main character of the *Knight's Tale*, the traits lauded in a tale told by an old and experienced warrior. Although the Knight-narrator may praise much in Theseus that is consistent with heroic masculinity, to the extent that his tale promotes thoughtful compromise and mercy, he challenges the heroic discourse. In this way, the tale is subtly ironic, since such a revision or challenge to heroic masculinity comes to us in the garb of a story drawn from the heroic past.

In his essay 'The Arming of the Warrior in European Literature and Chaucer,' Derek Brewer finds details in Chaucer's text supporting such a contention. Chaucer models his arming scene in the *Tale of Sir Thopas*, after the heroic topos, but he modifies and exaggerates the topos to make the portrait 'splendidly absurd,' and, according to Brewer, 'even more so when read against the long

---

[24] Elaine Penninger, 'Chaucer's *Knight's Tale* and the Theme of Appearance and Reality in the *Canterbury Tales*,' *South Atlantic Quarterly* 63 (1964): 403. D. W. Robertson, Jr suggests that Theseus' mercy 'is a reflection of the wisdom of the New Law . . . of mercy as opposed to the Old Law' of strict justice,' of an eye- for-an-eye found in the Old Testament: *A Preface to Chaucer*, 261. However, Robertson believes Theseus is 'an exemplar of wisdom and chivalry' and does not trace any maturation process in the narrative. He does admit that Theseus is not wholly consistent as a figure of wisdom: Theseus 'exhibit[s] mercy . . . in all but the first episodes' (261).

[25] V. John Scattergood, 'Chaucer and the French War in *Sir Thopas* and *Melibee*,' in *Court and Poet: Selected Proceedings of the Third Congress of the International Courtly Literature Society*, ed. Glyn Burgess (Liverpool: Francis Cairns, 1981), 291.

[26] *Ibid.*, 292.

tradition of solemn splendor.'[27] Brewer points to several epic arming scenes for comparison. In the *Aeneid*, for example, Virgil describes Turnus's arming:

> Then round his shoulders Turnus donned his cuirass
> Glinting with golden and pale copper scales,
> Made ready sword and shield, and helm with horns
> To bear his crimson plume. The sword was one
> The Fire God himself had forged for Daunus,
> Dipping it white-hot in the wave of Styx.
> And finally, from where it leaned against
> A pillar of the hall, he picked a spear,
> His powerful hand gripping that hardy shaft
> He took in battle from Auruncan Actor.
> Shaking it, making it vibrate, he cried out:
> 'Spear that never failed me once when called on,
> Now the time has come. . . .'[28]

From within the native British heroic tradition comes the arming scene in Laȝamon's *Brut*, also full of 'solemn splendor':

> Þa dude he on his burne ibroide of stele,
> þe makede on aluisc smið mid aðelen his crafte;
> he wes ihaten Wygar, þe Witeȝe wurhte.
> His sconken he helede mid hosen of stele.
> Calibeorne his sweord he sweinde bi his side;
> hit wes iworht in Aualun mid wiȝelefulle craften.
> Halm he set on hafde, hæh of stele;
> þeron wes moni ȝim-ston, al mid golde bigon;
> he was vðeres þas aðelen kinges;
> he wes ihaten Goswhit, ælchen oðere vnilic.
> He heng an his sweore ænne sceld deore;
> his nome wes on Bruttisc Pridwen ihaten;
> þer wes innen igrauen mid rede golde stauen
> an onlicnes deore of Drihtenes moder.
> His spere he nom an honde, þa Ron wes ihaten.
> Þa he hafden al his iweden, þa leop he on his steden.[29]

---

[27] Derek S. Brewer, 'The Arming of the Warrior in European Literature and Chaucer,' in *Chaucerian Problems and Perspectives: Essays Presented to Paul E. Beichner, C.S.C*, ed. Edward Vasta and Zacharias Thundy (Notre Dame: University of Notre Dame Press, 1979), 238.

[28] Virgil, *Aeneid* Book XII: 124–34, trans. Robert Fitzgerald (New York: Vintage, 1990), 370. This passage is cited by Brewer who supplies his own translation, 'The Arming of the Warrior,' 224. Brewer cites a number of arming scenes in his discussion, including Biblical material, the *Iliad*, the *Táin Bó Cúalnge*, *Beowulf*, *Le Chanson de Roland*, *Erec et Enide*, passages from Arthurian literature, and several late Middle English romances.

[29] Laȝamon, *Brut*, lines 2828–44; Brewer ('Arming,' 232–33) cites these lines from *Selections from Laȝamon's Brut*, ed. G. L. Brook (London: Oxford University Press, 1963) and translates them: 'then he put on his corslet of woven steel, which a smith with magical powers made by his noble skill; it was called Wygar, which Widia made. He covered his legs with steel stockings. Calibeorn his sword he hung by his side; it was made in Avalon with magic skills. His tall helmet of steel he set on his head: there were many jewels on it, and it was encircled with gold. It was the noble king

And then, there is Chaucer's rendition of an arming scene in the *Tale of Sir Thopas*:

> He dide next his white leere,
> Of cloth of lake fyn and cleere,
>   A breech and eek a sherte;
> And next his sherte an aketoun,
> And over that an haubergeoun
>   For percynge of his herte;

> And over that a fyn hawberk,
> Was al ywroght of Jewes werk,
>   Ful strong it was of plate;
> And over that his cote-armour
> As whit as is a lilye flour,
>   In which he wol debate.

> His sheeld was al of gold so reed,
> And therinne was a bores heed,
>   a charbocle bisyde;
> And there he swoor on ale and breed
> How that the geaunt shal be deed . . .   (VII, 857–73)

The greaves, as Brewer notes, are situated in a ridiculous location and are made from leather rather than steel; Sir Thopas's shield is made from soft gold; his horse is meek; his helmet is of lattern, not a strong metal. To top off the absurdity, Sir Thopas swears on bread and ale. Brewer believes Chaucer created this portrait to mock the Flemish bourgeoisie and to please an elitist English Court, but he also believes Chaucer 'was . . . mocking . . . the whole ancient formal aggrandizement of fighting, Arthurian bravery and bravado, "and al that longeth to that art." '[30] Looking at the *Knight's Tale*, Brewer notes that Chaucer had plenty of opportunity to inscribe the arming of the warrior topos into his text, but he chose not to do so. It does not occur when Theseus fights Ypolita or Creon; nor does it surface when Palamon and Arcite fight in the grove, nor even before the grand tournament. If traditional heroic tales and chivalric romances used the arming scenes to build the warrior's prestige and to set him apart from all the other men in the tale (or from the audience, for that matter), Chaucer turns away from that topos. Even in *Troilus and Criseyde*, Troilus's armor is only described when the lover-knight is returning from war with his armor hanging in shreds around him. Nowhere are we given the arming of Troilus. Brewer notes that this image of the ragged, exhausted warrior returning from battle is similar to the portrait Chaucer gives us of the Knight-narrator in the General Prologue: he is 'bismotered' and ragged and wears his habergoun, not his armor. Making a pilgrimage to atone for his sins, the Knight is far from the

---

Uther's; it was called Goosewhite, and was unlike any other helmet. He hung a precious shield around his neck: in British it was called Pridwen. On the inside was engraved with red-gold markings a precious likeness of God's Mother. He took his spear, which was called Ron, in hand.'

[30] Brewer, 'Arming,' 238. See also Patterson's chapter on 'The *Knight's Tale* and the Crisis of Chivalric Identity,' in *Chaucer and the Subject of History*, 165–230.

triumphant, returning warrior. He is a pilgrim, tired and in search of forgiveness. As Brewer notes, 'Both [Chaucer's] treatment of [the arming topos] and his refusal to use it . . . are significant. What Chaucer finds moving is suffering, not aggression.'[31]

The subplot of the *Knight's Tale* documents a 'war' between Mars and Venus. In this contest between the god of war and the goddess of love, the goddess of love wins. The same contest has occurred within Theseus himself: competition based upon physical prowess is gradually replaced by a more mature masculinity that acknowledges and reintegrates the 'feminine' aspects of the self. But whatever reading we come up with to explain Theseus's transformation, Chaucer's text encourages us to admire most that masculinity which is informed by wisdom and mercy. When men try forcibly to control other men, the result is chaos and bloodshed. Creon shows no mercy for his foes and, consequently, devastates his entire nation and destroys his own life. Theseus shows little mercy for Thebes and, consequently is always trying to protect himself from the potential retaliation of Palamon and Arcite (even to the end). Palamon and Arcite struggle in a ridiculous physical contest that leaves Arcite dead. However, in the *Knight's Tale*, Chaucer is even subtly questioning men's ability to assume control of their worlds by any means, and in this questioning resides the Boethian and Christian influences on Chaucer's text. Because of all the sudden reversals of fortune, Theseus's world is in great confusion. Despite his attempts to control the outcome of human events, Theseus is often unsuccessful. Robert Lumiansky records fourteen events in the narrative which are determined by Fate.[32] And, indeed, Fate and other humans unravel Theseus's plans as fast as he makes them. He is intercepted on his triumphant orderly return from Scithia by women whom Fortune has placed before him and whose pleas pull him into the chaos of war with Creon. He establishes control over Palamon and Arcite by putting them in a tower, but under Perotheus's influence, he releases and banishes Arcite, only to have the young man return to Athens disguised. He keeps Palamon in the tower, only to have him escape. He declares Arcite the winner of the tournament, except fate intrudes and kills the young knight. Consequently, the tidy conclusion Theseus makes by marrying Palamon and Emelye seems fragile, even though the Knight-narrator does not appear to have any doubts. What we see is a hero who often takes action or makes decisions which need emendation. His reign over events and men is tenuous. As Thomas Van asserts, Theseus's attempts to exert control have minimal significance 'before the flux which controls all.'[33]

Theseus's reaction to this 'flux' is worthwhile to note. When Arcite is killed amidst his triumph over Palamon, Theseus falls into a depression and is consoled only by his aging father, one who knows 'this worldes transmutacion, / As he hadde seyn it chaunge bothe up and doun.' His father defines the world as 'a thurghfare ful of wo' where death is the only sure thing (2839–40; 2847–49). After Arcite's death, it is Theseus who declares the world a 'wrecched,' 'corrumpable,' 'foule prisoun,' where all 'moot deye' (2995, 3010, 3061,

[31] Brewer, 'Arming,' 238.

[32] Robert Lumiansky, 'Chaucer's Philosophical Knight,' *TSE* 3 (1952): 54.

[33] Thomas A. Van, 'Imprisoning and Ensnarement in *Troilus* and the *Knight's Tale*,' *Papers on Language and Literature* 7 (1971): 3–12.

3034). Theseus's perception of the changeable world as a 'foule prisoun' is a perception formed in the context of an heroic masculine identity. Even though it would seem reasonable for him to have these foreboding thoughts when he gazes out over a battlefield – when he participated in the brutality and carnage of war – instead, he perceives the world as a 'wrecched' place where all 'most dye' only when his own plan is defeated, not when others are defeated. He finds the world despicable when it doesn't give him what he wants. Because Theseus's control of events has been disrupted, he becomes depressed and sees the world as a depraved place. He resists change, blaming the world for its natural changeableness. He has tried to preserve order; he desires permanence and transcendence, values associated with heroic masculinity. Theseus finds solace only in affirming his separation from the world of time, change, mutation. Flux is feminine (allegorically represented as Lady Fortune); flux is, for Theseus, frustrating, to say the least.

Charles Muscatine, in his study, *Chaucer and the French Tradition*, sees the disruption differently. He writes that what gives the world of the *Knight's Tale* 'its perspective, its depth and seriousness, is its constant awareness of a formidably antagonistic element – chaos, disorder – which in life is an ever-threatening possibility.' A bit further he writes:

> This subsurface insistence on disorder is the poem's crowning complexity, its most compelling claim to maturity. We have here no glittering, romantic fairy-castle world. The impressive, patterned edifice of the noble life, its dignity and richness, its regard for law and decorum, are all bulwarks against the ever-threatening forces of chaos, and in constant collision with them.[34]

Fortune, fate, flux, and change are all features our own culture, as well as medieval culture, associates typically with the feminine. The masculine, seen as opposite, is solid and stable, what Muscatine calls 'a bulwark against the ever-threatening force of chaos.' The masculine is the 'law,' the 'edifice,' the 'pattern' Theseus tries to impose on the world. And when Fortune, the feminine, forces her ascendancy, when the human will is unable to control, Theseus is overcome with depression and grieves his loss. So the feminine disrupts the masculine in the tale, just as Venus does Mars.

On one side, male power comes up against itself – other agents of male power. On the other side, male power confronts a feminine force – mutability – a force that limits achievement and the dream of permanence. But Chaucer does not depict disruption as ultimately tragic; rather, flux and chaos offer up the possibility for wisdom, for growth. Recall for a moment Muscatine's comment that disorder 'is the poem's crowning complexity, its most compelling claim to maturity.' The narrative sets up a development here: from Flux (feminine) to Disorder to Complexity to Maturity. In other words, because we live in a complex world, our designs are often frustrated by chance and circumstance (Flux and Disorder). We can become rigid and read the world wrong, desiring simplicity and sameness and ease, or we can learn flexibility and read the world

---

[34] Muscatine, *Chaucer and the French Tradition*, 181, 189–90.

right, appreciating its complexity as well as our own. It is an idea discussed at length in the *Consolation of Philosophy*, a text Chaucer translated and often mined for wisdom. Speaking to a despairing Boece, Lady Philosophy says:

> Yif thou committest and betakest thi seyles to the wynd, thow schalt ben shoven, nat thider that thow woldest, but whider that the wynd schouveth the. Yif thow casteth thi seedes in the feeldes, thou sholdest han in mynde that the yeres ben amonges outherwhile plentevous and outherwhile bareyne. (II. Prosa 1, 101–107)

To live, to participate in life, one must be flexible. To resist the changeableness of reality, she argues, is to become a 'fool of alle mortel foolis' (113–14). The desire for sameness is a kind of greed or covetousness which needs correction. To become wise is to acknowledge that in the world of lived experience, 'nothyng that is engendred nys stedfast ne stable' (II. Metrum 3, 22–23). From this perspective, flux, change or disorder, is good, because it results in maturation. Here, then, is a crucial contradiction. To be a man is to meet a challenge and overcome it, to participate in a change. Yet, the heroic discourse on masculinity urges men to transcend change, or death, to attain a stability that is impervious to change, to value 'sameness.' It is a conflict inherent in heroic discourse itself but emphasized here by Chaucer's Boethian reading of an heroic text. Even Lady Philosophy seeks the *summum bonum*.

If the movement of Fortune's wheel disrupts men's plans for control over the external world in the *Knight's Tale*, the 'feminine,' embodied in individual women, also has the potential to reveal men's very limited ability to control themselves. Women, simply by being, can be powerful agents who spawn chaotic competition among men. Emelye, unaware, becomes an object for which Palamon and Arcite compete solely on the basis of her physical beauty. And the power of her beauty is considerable. Dividing men and threatening them, it does violence to their souls. Emelye's beauty 'hurte' and 'wounded' the young cousins; it stings Palamon 'unto the herte,' leaving him pale and deathly. It 'sleeth' Arcite so that when he is banished from Athens he contemplates suicide:

> And over al this, to sleen me outrely,
> Love hath his firy dart so brennyngly
> Ystiked thurgh my trewe, careful herte,
> That shapen was my deeth erst than my sherte.
> Ye sleen me with youre eyen, Emelye!   (1563–67)

Ultimately, it leads men to an encounter with death.[35] Arcite returns to Athens disguised as a squire and risks discovery and death; Palamon escapes from prison and risks capture and death. Both cousins wind up fighting fiercely in the grove, ankle deep in blood when Theseus discovers them. Later, at the

---

[35] Although this may seem excessive, Chaucer, apparently, wants us to see the rivalry this way. Angela Lucas, in her work on *Women in the Middle Ages* (New York: St Martins, 1983), 83–104, establishes that treating women as property and battling over them did actually occur. On the relationship between love and death, see Denis de Rougemont, *Love in the Western World*, rev. ed., trans. Montgomery Belgion (Princeton: Princeton University Press, 1940; 1983).

tournament, each risks his own life and the lives of two hundred other men to achieve the reward of possessing Emelye. The text does not ennoble this violent eruption of competition between the two cousins. Their conflict is depicted as comical, excessive, petty, irrational, and bestial. At one point, Arcite equates it to two dogs fighting over a bone. The conflict also has the effect of keeping the two cousins subordinate to Theseus. It thereby establishes that men who let passion overtake them – passion, that is, for a woman – are less manly than the man who remains aloof from such feelings. Theseus can be passionate about war and winning, 'honour' and 'chivalrie'; he can be passionate about building temples and arenas; he can be passionately committed to honor his friendship with Perotheus, but he is not passionate about women. He is, he says, *beyond* that.

Theseus is a man who remains dutiful to men. The bond between men is primary and the bond with women secondary for him. Even as he brings his new wife home to Athens for the first time, he can be called away to war for other men's souls. In fact, the most powerful relationship in Theseus's life that is discussed in the tale is not with Ypolita (his wife), but with Perotheus. Nowhere in the Tale is the word 'love' used to describe Theseus's relationship with Ypolita; instead, it is used to describe his feelings for his comrade:

> For in this world he loved no man so,
> And he loved hym als tendrely agayn.
> So wel they lovede, as olde bookes sayn,
> That whan that oon was deed, soothly to telle,
> His felawe wente and soughte hym doun in helle.   (1196–1200)

Theseus has compassion for women and exhibits gentleness toward them, but, according to the text, he *loves* only Perotheus. Modelled after the epic hero, Theseus finds his identity and intense connection first with men.[36] The love of women, the irrational, he claims to have experienced as a young man, but as a mature man, he is in possession of himself and exerts considerable control *over* women. His attitude toward men's love of women is clear when he discovers Palamon and Arcite fighting over Emelye:

> A man moot ben a fool, or yong, or oold –
> I woot it by myself ful yore agon,
> For in my tyme a servant was I oon.
> And therefore, syn I knowe of loves peyne,
> And woot hou soore it kan a man distreyne,
> As he that hath ben caught ofte in his laas,
> I yow foryeve. . . .   (1812–18)

Men who are 'caught' in love's 'laas' suffer 'peyne' and are 'fools' but are to be tolerantly forgiven.[37] Palamon and Arcite, controlled by the love of a woman,

---

[36] For a discussion of the classical hero and the primacy of his male bonding, see Eva Keuls, *The Reign of Phallus: Sexual Politics in Ancient Athens* (New York: Harper, 1985).

[37] David Aers, (*Chaucer*, 77), notes, 'The ironic dimensions of these comments . . . are highlighted by recalling how [Chaucer] fills out the allusions in his *House of Fame* and *Legend of Good Women*. In both these poems, Theseus symbolises the classic example of male egotism inhabiting

become excessive, melodramatic, and even humorous. Along with Theseus, we laugh at their irrationality. Theseus, on the other hand, the man who 'conquered al the regne of Femenye,' takes possession of Ypolita and Emelye, marries Ypolita himself, and arranges Emelye's marriage with Palamon at the end of the tale. So whereas he gradually relinquishes control over the world and over other men, he is always in control of women. The Knight-narrator holds him up as the preferable model of masculinity, and Chaucer does not undercut his narrator's judgment. The tale offers us no serious treatment of the man who desires women. He is absent from the male images depicted here; for the Knight-narrator, man the lover is not as esteemed as man the rational governor. To have control over one's emotions is valued; to let one's emotions rage passionately is sinful, humorous, or pathetic in the sacred and secular texts of the late Middle Ages, particularly for men. So, although we see Chaucer subtly criticizing the masculinity of the warrior code with its attendant violence between men, and although we see him prefer the masculinity of a mature, philosophic Theseus over the young man of action, his depiction of men's relationships with women are very stereotyped in the *Knight's Tale*. Men are emasculated by love. Woman's beauty, woman's body, is her only power, and it is depicted as a very threatening, even if passive, power. This power is not acquired actively by deciding to *do* something or to *say* something. It is a power that comes from *being* something, the power of being an object which men desire, fight for, and exchange.

Women in the *Knight's Tale* are 'creatures' whose worlds are controlled by men. Ypolita and Emelye, defeated by Theseus, are taken far from their own home to live in Athens as Theseus's property. The Theban women's fortunes are first dashed by Creon and then restored by Theseus. They do not act themselves; men act on their behalf. They remain passive. Emelye, too, never has a say in her marriage or her destiny. Unbeknownst to her, two noblemen fall in love, fight for her, and finally win her. Theseus summons her (after having decided with Parliamentary approval to marry her to Palamon), commands her future, names her life, and 'names' her:

> Suster . . . this is my fulle assent,
> With al th'avys heere of my parlement,
> That gentil Palamon, youre owene knyght,
> That serveth yow with wille herte, and myght,
> And ever hath doon syn ye first hym knewe,
> That ye shul of youre grace upon hym rewe,
> And taken hym for housbonde and for lord.   (3075–81)

He delivers a 'litel sermonyng' to convince Emelye to marry. The text of the speech reveals that Theseus has thought about Palamon's feelings: the 'gentil' man has suffered so much, he deserves reward. Theseus has also considered the

the courtly forms of love and service. The key words "pity," "service," "mercy," "true," recur in these accounts which culminate in the duke's abandonment of the woman he has courted and used, now his wife, on an island inhabited by wild beasts. The courtly language is presented as a male's medium for manipulating and exploiting the female, a language of power (*LGW*, 1886–2227; *House of Fame*, 405–26).'

welfare of his country: it will have 'certein countrees alliaunce' and Theban 'obeisaunce' (2973–74). He considers the advice of his Parliament, but he never asks Emelye what she thinks, how she feels, or what she wants. Theseus may be limited by fortune and by the wills of other men, but he has an absolute control over Emelye's exterior world. From this perspective, women in the *Knight's Tale* serve to illustrate the potency of Theseus's power. His attitude toward women is consistent with the model of masculinity upheld by the Germanic and Classical heroic heritage. Peter Weltner argues that the epic hero considers 'the feminine to be merely whatever is; the masculine is whatever becomes. The feminine must be passive; only the masculine is allowed action. . . . Woman defines herself by being; the man, by doing.'[38] Gender roles in the *Knight's Tale* are consistent with this definition. As A. J. Minnis observes in his book, *Chaucer and Pagan Antiquity*, Emelye has no 'freedom of action, other than freedom to ennoble what must be by accepting it bravely.'[39] We are allowed a brief glimpse into her mind when she prays to Diana. There she says she prefers to be 'A mayde, and love huntynge and venerye, / And for to walken in the woodes wilde, / And noght to ben a wyf and be with childe' (2308–10). She prays Diana will secure a peace between Palamon and Arcite so that they will 'fro me turne awey hir hertes so' (2318). But the world of the gods and goddesses is ultimately a patriarchal one, governed by Saturn, and he has decided that Emelye will marry. Her response is acceptance: 'I putte me in thy proteccioun, / Dyane, and in thy disposicioun' (2363–64). Emelye's virtue, consistent with the medieval discourse surrounding ideal femininity, is submission to the will of men. As Theseus says in his speech to her, 'whoso grucceth ought, he dooth folye, / And rebel is to hym that al may gye' (3045–46). And he argues that humans must submit to the First Mover's design; to do otherwise is 'wilfulnesse' (3057).

If anyone needs to heed the wisdom of this speech, however, it is the men who have demonstrated their willfulness again and again. But the command to be passive is directed toward Emelye, the character who is made to accept change more easily. Now, from a Boethian perspective, acceptance is noble, and Theseus's speech, modelled after Boethius, argues exactly this point. But notice the bias in the Knight-narrator's interpretation of women's acceptance: he argues that Emelye and all women 'folwen alle the favour of Fortune' (2682). The Knight-narrator's ambivalence about control and submission is evident here. On the one hand, he praises Emelye because she obeys authority; on the other hand, he accuses her of being capricious and of being easily moved by Fortune.[40] Theseus, as we noted above, is praised for changing his mind, for softening from absolutism to mercy, for yielding to the appeals of people and circumstances. As Peter Elbow has pointed out, 'the activity which Theseus engages in more than

---

[38] Peter Weltner, *Myth and Masculinity*, Harper Studies in Language and Literature (New York: Harper & Row, 1975), 4.

[39] Minnis, *Chaucer and Pagan Antiquity*, 133.

[40] Wolfgang Rudat believes Emelye is to be regarded admirably for her flexibility and that she represents a positive contrast to the inflexibility of Arcite 'in her *varium et mutabile* attitude she is closer to the Boethian precepts as expressed by Theseus than are the two Knights,' 'Chaucer's Mercury and Arcite: The Aeneid and the World of the *Knight's Tale*,' *Neophilologus* 64 (1980): 307–19.

any other is changing his mind.'[41] But the Knight-narrator never criticizes him. The Knight, aligned as he is with the very male world of military exploits, can find himself in Theseus, but not in Emelye. He assumes Theseus changes his mind because he is 'wys'; Emelye (he assumes) changes her mind because of her nature. To Theseus he ascribes a rational process that makes his changeableness noble. To Emelye he ascribes an irrational process that makes her changeableness fickle. Her mutability does not result from her control over anything; it is simply a part of her nature. When the change is seen as controlled, it is respected and honored; when the change is defined as uncontrolled, it is criticized.

The tale upholds a masculinity forged out of the intellect, reason, and justice tempered by mercy. Theseus is the character most admired because he is the man most in control of himself and others. He is the man who finds non-violent ways of exerting that control. Creon, Arcite, and Palamon are men whose masculinity is criticized. Creon is judged harshly because he is too bloodthirsty and tyrannical, Palamon and Arcite because they lose control of themselves and become like 'houndes [fighting] for the boon' (1177). From both epic and Old Testament traditions come the injunctions to men: create and control. Order and control become, in this discourse, synonymous with survival and preservation. In tension with this discourse (which upholds an assertive and powerful masculinity), is the Boethian and New Testament tradition which also informs the *Knight's Tale*.[42] The injunction to men from Boethius is summed up in Theseus's speech at the very end of the story. Control belongs ultimately, he says, to the 'Firste Moevere' who shapes our lives – not us; it is useless to decry Fortune. The wise man accepts what Fortune commands; he does not try to control events or other people. 'The contrarie of this is wilfulnesse,' says Theseus. In this conflict between the active and the passive, caught between heroic action and Christian acceptance, lies the masculinity described by the *Knight's Tale*.

For the reader, however, the tale may hold yet another message. Although, within the story itself, these tensions play off one another to create a significant part of the drama in the tale, for the reader, who, along with the Knight-narrator, identifies with Theseus, the tale is reassuring. It creates a fictional world which momentarily takes the fear out of being controlled by fortune or flux. If we identify with Theseus, the tale reassures us that despite change and the ravages of time and fortune, we can endure, and we can exert *some* (not absolute) control over our worlds. Theseus, after all, preserves his own well-being throughout the tale. Nowhere do we see him seriously threatened with personal loss. He suffers only a few set-backs, ones that really affect other people's lives far more drastically than his own. Here is the vantage point we are encouraged to fantasize for ourselves as we face the uncertainties of life. Consciously or not, what we most likely see at the end of the *Knight's Tale* is a man who triumphs. Even though Theseus concludes the tale with a speech acknowledging the power of chaos and fortune, he, himself, has escaped any deleterious change. He still governs a large kingdom, one that has grown in power, wealth, and size. He still

---

[41] Peter Elbow, 'How Chaucer Transcends Oppositions in the *Knight's Tale*,' *Chaucer Review* 7 (1972): 103.

[42] See Frederick P. Pickering, 'Historical Thought and Moral Codes in Medieval Epic,' in *The Epic in Medieval Society*, ed. Scholler (1977), 1–7.

governs Ypolita, Emelye, the Amazons, the Theban princes, and the Theban cities. With the blessings of Fortune, he has effectively contained or suppressed any potential threat these conquered peoples could pose to his own kingdom. He has disarmed his enemies, and he is safe. If the tale had been constructed around the subjectivity of Emelye, Palamon, Arcite, the Amazons, or the Thebans, it may well have had a much different effect on us. But as it stands, the *Knight's Tale* creates a surface narrative that literally encourages us to submit to Fortune and, at the same time, it creates a subsurface narrative that assures us we can endure and transcend adversity, but only if we pretend we are Theseus.

The tale also negates the 'feminine' power of change by positing two divine 'fathers,' who ultimately determine the design for the universe. Saturn arbitrates in the conflict between Venus and Mars, deciding Arcite's death (consequently, his death is not meaningless – it is part of a transcendent plan). The other transcendent father, the First Mover, 'stable' and 'eterne,' has a design Theseus discusses at length at the conclusion of the tale. It is a design which subsumes the Wheel of Fortune into its own purpose:

> 'The Firste Moevere of the cause above,
> Whan he first made the faire cheyne of love,
> Greet was th'effect, and heigh was his entente.
> For with that faire cheyne of love he bond
> The fyr, the eyr, the water, and the lond
> In certeyn boundes, that they may nat flee.
> That same Prince and that Moevere,' quod he,
> 'Hath stablissed in this wrecched world adoun
> Certeyne dayes and duracioun
> To al that is engendred in this place,
> Over the whiche day they may nat pace . . .' (2987–98)

In the *Knight's Tale*, the feminine – mutable Dame Fortune – is contained within the 'father's' plan so that her awesome power is harnessed and decreased by her subjugation to him. She becomes his handmaiden. It is a relationship mirrored within the human world of the tale as Theseus instructs Emelye to accept the rule of the First Mover and his own decision to marry her to Palamon.

The presence of the First Mover is apparently meant to reassure us that 'a father' ultimately has control, a reinscription of patriarchy. From this perspective, everything that happens, happens for a reason. Events become expressions of a benevolent and creative First Mover's will; we, as his children, should obey his will and trust his wisdom. If we do this, Theseus and the Knight-narrator argue, we (like Palamon and Emelye) may ride off into the sunset without any 'jalousie.' But we also know, despite the Knight-narrator's wish otherwise, that such an ending is an illusion. The tight control the Knight exerts over the ending and the elaborate formal design of his tale testify to conflicting appraisals of control: control is possible, but it is equally an artifice. This is precisely the tale's analysis of heroic masculinity: the heroic is possible, but it is also tenuous.

CHAPTER FIVE

Men in Love and Competition: the *Miller's Tale* and the *Merchant's Tale*

Chaucer's depictions of love, particularly courtly love, have sparked considerable debate throughout the twentieth century. Some readers have ascribed allegorical reading to the material, finding in the love relationships between men and women a suggestion of the soul's movement toward or away from God. Some have focused on Chaucer's parody of courtly love ideals, and still others have assumed that Chaucer was, himself, a Love Poet. Once again, the ambiguity of his texts – their open-endedness and irony – make room for readers to find their own agendas reflected there. Whatever the potential readings, the male narrators on the pilgrimage to Canterbury most often represent men in love as irrational victims of their own desires, as men who have lost control of themselves. Both narrative commentary and plot design encourage us to see them this way. Whether they provoke our laughter or our outrage, male lovers are situated at a distance from us. Narrative strategies sometimes encourage us to identify with, or feel empathy toward, the narrators of the tales or the characters who are victims of circumstance, such as Custance or St Cecile, but we are always placed in an overtly critical relationship to the man in love. Chaucer accomplishes this by undercutting any consistently sympathetic response we might have toward these characters. Through the techniques of hyperbole, satire, and burlesque, as well as by revealing the baser motives lying within a character's desire for women, Chaucer pokes fun at men in love.

Women, the focus of men's amorous desire, are presented as goals to be attained or as sexual territories to be conquered or resisted. It is common for them to be jealously possessed and/or protected by men, not adored. Women usually become the site of a struggle between men so that at the heart of Chaucer's depiction of men in love (within the *Canterbury Tales*) is homosocial competition, rather than a courtly code praising the devotion of men to women.[1]

---

[1] See Eve K. Sedgwick, *Between Men: English Literature and Male Homosocial Desire* (New York: Columbia University Press, 1985). The *Man of Law's Tale* offers a variation on the male-to-male competition. In that tale, evil mothers-in-law jealously guard their own power so that competition erupts between the mothers and their sons and between the mothers and Custance; yet, at the heart of the tale rages a competitive relationship between God and Satan, the divine forces which

No radiant Beatrice emerges in these tales, and no Gawain practices the high arts of courtesy. The text refuses an uncritical reinscription of the maiden on the pedestal and the ever-yearning lover-knight. It is a pattern which begins early. In the *Knight's Tale*, as we have already seen, Palamon and Arcite are made into clowns. Their excessive and ridiculous passion for Emelye makes them the butt of anti-courtly love humor, and it leads them into violent conflict with each other. The intersection of competition and sexual desire is reinforced in many tales throughout the text: in the *Merchant's Tale*, for example, we have Damian and January; in the *Franklin's Tale*, Aurelius and Arveragus; in the *Miller's Tale*, old John, Nicholas, and Absolon; and in the *Reeve's Tale*, the miller and the two young clerks. More ominous is the *Manciple's Tale*, where Phebus kills his wife because she has another lover; and, in a variation on this narrative pattern, the *Physician's Tale* gives us Virginius who slays his own daughter to 'protect' her from Apius.

Regardless of the genre, many narratives in the *Canterbury Tales* depict men in love in a way more consistent with heroic or theological discourse than with courtly love. Frequently, men in love are men in danger. Addressing knights in his *Vox Clamantis*, John Gower writes:

> A knight does not rightly have to fear a bodily wound, since he should receive the world's praises for it. But he should fear the wounds of the spirit, which blind, incurable lust inflicts with fiery darts. Bodily wounds are to be healed, but not even Galen will make a man well who is sick with love. If the knight holds with womanish behavior, his honor dies, bereft of his noble lineage. When a wise knight falls, his fame forsakes him, as though he were fatuous and foolish. When carnal love holds the mind ensnared, an intelligent man's reason becomes irrational. When the brightness of human intelligence is clouded over by the shadow of the flesh, and the spirit of reason withdraws into the flesh, man's reason stands utterly scorned. It is a slave to the flesh, and scarcely retains the post of handmaiden.[2]

The sentiment is interwoven throughout many narratives of the *Canterbury Tales*. Whether the tone of a tale is comedic or serious, its plot usually suggests that a price is paid when men fall in love with women. Men may lose exclusive claim to their wife's sexual body and be cuckolded; they may be discovered and humiliated or chastised in some way for loving women; and/or they may be in danger of losing control over themselves. Rather than ennobling men, as love does in courtly love discourse, it is usually represented, or perceived by male narrators, as demeaning. The very language they use describes 'falling' in love in negative terms. 'Falling' in love is a descent: it is illness, drunkenness, pain, blindness, foolishness, madness, loss, and sometimes even a death.[3] Such a

---

struggle for mastery over human events and souls. Male-to-male competition is still inscribed in the tale as God and Satan struggle to win the allegiance and 'love' of the human characters.

[2] John Gower, *Vox Clamantis*, V, 4, in Stockton, 201.

[3] Again, John Gower's *Vox Clamantis* provides a catalogue of dangers which love holds for men (here, particularly, knights): 'Love is not of one hue, but is conflicting within itself; it tempers its vicissitudes intemperately. Love conceals and reveals, disunites and reunites, and often drives

representation of love encourages us to distance ourselves from it. As listeners or as readers, we are not liable to embrace this kind of love, since it leads to such pain and exposure. In the *Merchant's Tale*, Damyan 'was so ravysshed on his lady May / That for the verray peyne he was ny wood' (IV, 1774–75), and in the *Franklin's Tale*, the 'sike' Aurelius 'langwissheth as a furye dooth in helle' (V, 950).

Within the long tradition of heroic discourse, love frequently begets chaos: it begins the Trojan war, and it spells the doom for Camelot. Love, in heroic or chivalric narrative material, frequently pulls men away from their public and social responsibilities, away from their loyalties to other men. Commenting on this frequent feature of twelfth-century French romances, Joan Ferrante notes that even though these texts arise in the culture at the same time as courtly love literature, 'they present love almost exclusively as an obstacle to social responsibility and knightly glory.'[4] She cites many medieval romances which do just this, including *Le Roman de Troie*, where men's love for women is condemned because it makes them lose 'belief and faith, father and lord, lands and territories' (ll. 18455–59).[5] Such views of human love are surely consistent with Chaucer's presentation in *Troilus and Criseyde*; and, tempered by humor, it is evident in the story of Palamon and Arcite.[6] Love, interpreted this way, poses a threat to the bond between men, to the loyalty of son to father, vassal to lord, and individual to community; it promotes conflict and divisiveness. Outraged at such competitiveness, the Merchant-narrator, for example, cries:

> O perilous fyr, that in the bedstraw bredeth!
> O famulier foo, that his servyce bedeth!
> O servant traytour, false hoomly hewe,
> Lyk to the naddre in bosom sly untrewe,

happy hearts mad with grief. Love is an unjust judge; marrying opposites, it makes the very natures of things deteriorate. In love, discord is harmonious, learning is ignorant, anger makes jest, honor is base, a poor man has plenty, joys grieve, praise reproves, despair hopes, hope is afraid, harms are helpful, assets are harmful. In love, anguish is tasteful, bitterness becomes sweet, winter is springlike, chills perspire, sickness is strengthening. So take greater heed, knight, of the dangers you see. Read what forms love's sickness takes.

Love is sickly health, troubled rest, pious sin, warlike peace, a pleasant wound, a delightful calamity, anxious happiness, a devious path, dark light, gentle harshness, a light lump of lead, both a flowery winter and a withered, flowerless spring, a thorny rose, a capricious law without justice, weeping laughter, laughing lamentation, intemperate temperance, a hostile ally and a gracious enemy, fickle constancy, . . . bitter honey, delicious gall, a prison offering pleasures, irrational reason, foolish discretion, an untrustworthy judge, an ignorant person reflecting on everything, food never digestible and drink ever thirsty, an insatiable mental hunger, a living death, a dying life, harmonious discord, a garrulous mind, mute speech, a secret fever, poor prosperity, prosperous poverty, a slavish prince, a subject queen and a destitute king, drunken sobriety, demented clemency, the port of Scylla, a pestilential cure, a way of health; love is a delightful serpent.' V, 2, in Stockton, 197–98.

4   Joan M. Ferrante, 'The Conflict of Lyric Convention and Romance Form,' in *In Pursuit of Perfection: Courtly Love in Medieval Literature*, ed. Joan Ferrante and George Economou, et al (Port Washington, New York: Kennikat, 1975), 137.

5   Cited in Ferrante, 'Conflict,' 137.

6   See Arlyn Diamond, '*Troilus and Criseyde*: The Politics of Love,' in *Chaucer in the Eighties*, ed. Julian N. Wasserman and Robert J. Blanch (Syracuse: Syracuse University Press, 1986), 93–103.

God shilde us alle from youre aqueyntaunce!
O Januarie, dronken in plesaunce
In mariage, se how thy Damyan,
Thyn owene squier and thy borne man,
Entendeth for to do thee vileynye.
God graunte thee thyn hoomly fo t'espye!
For in this world nys worse pestilence
Than hoomly foo al day in thy presence.   (IV, 1783–94)

Such a reading of love and desire, which places women between competing men, can be found throughout the *Tales*, particularly in the context of most fabliaux. It assumes (by implication) that men's relationships to men are paramount.[7] The women who are desired by men are usually seen, therefore, as a disruption of the male-to-male relationship, a disruption of an assumed order. As such, these tales record a 'masculine' plot – one which reinscribes a psychological scenario familiar to any modern reader acquainted with Freud's account of the son's relationship to the father. An interesting parallel to the Freudian Oedipal narrative emerges in many of Chaucer's tales of love: women are often married to, or controlled by, older more powerful men; and they are sought by younger, less powerful and unmarried men. This is true for Emelye, Alisoun, Maleyne, Dame Simkin, May, and Phebus's wife. The young men who desire the wife are thus challenging or breaking *into* the marriage relationship, into the territory of the older men. They are also frequently seen disrupting the law of marriage and violating the culture's institutionally-prescribed boundaries around sexuality.

Granted, there are men whose love for their wives is represented with more detachment and less passion; notably, however, none of these men's marriages are threatened by younger men's sexual desires. Walter's pursuit of Griselda in the *Clerk's Tale* is more contractual than passionate. Theseus's marriage to Ypolita, in the *Knight's Tale*, originates in military victory and territorial appropriation, not love. And in the *Tale of Melibeus*, Chaucer foregrounds Melibee's intellectual relationship with Prudence. But in tales where men's relationships to women are ones of desire and passion, infidelity and betrayal become what Douglas Kelly has termed a 'nightmare theme.'[8] The difference between passionate love and a more detached love is underscored in the word choices and plot structures of the *Man of Law's Tale*. The Sultan, who falls in love with Custance's bodily image early in the tale, comes down with a bad case of amorous fever: 'Al his lust and al his bisy cure / Was for to love hire' (II, 188–89). His part in the plot concludes when his own mother murders him at his wedding banquet ('he for love sholde han his deeth'). Custance's second husband, King Alla, is not, however, moved by sexual desire to marry but rather by his 'gentil herte . . . fulfild of pitee' (660); notably, the narrative treats him much differently. Instead of being motivated by passion, King Alla is 'made' to

[7] Cf. Eve Sedgwick, *Between Men*, 1–15; 21–66. See also Kaja Silverman's discussion of the placement of women between men's eroticism in Fassbinder's films, *Male Subjectivity at the Margins* (New York: Routledge, 1992).

[8] Douglas R. Kelly, *Medieval Imagination: Rhetoric and the Poetry of Courtly Love* (Madison: University of Wisconsin Press, 1978), 197.

wed Custance 'ful solemprely' according to divine plan. God's design, rather than human desire, unites Custance with her second husband: 'And thus hath Crist ymaad Custance a queene' (693). Of course, King Alla's marriage is threatened by betrayal when his own mother, Donegild, plots to exile Custance and her child, but the plot allows him a final reward. Whereas the Sultan was killed by his mother, King Alla kills his mother, eventually making a pilgrimage to Rome for forgiveness where he is reunited with his wife and his son. (His son even eventually becomes Pope.) The narrative treatment of King Alla differs drastically from the treatment of the Sultan, and the difference is emphasized by parallel plot structures. In addition to the anti-Islamic bias of the tale which partially explains the Sultan's demise, King Alla triumphs in love because his love for Custance is inspired by God; it is not defined as sexual.

The Canterbury narratives most often represent courtly love discourse as an absurdity, and what Chaucer and his narrators appear to find most humorous and ridiculous in the courtly love tradition is men's loss of self control. More than anything women *do* or *are*, men's own desires are emasculating. To the extent that this is true, the *Tales* echo those medieval texts on masculinity advocating control, particularly over one's own heart. Although Chaucer's work challenges and refuses courtly love discourse, it conforms to the value the culture places on control in the construction of late medieval and early modern masculinity. Furthermore, the tales of 'courtly love' are told primarily, but not exclusively, from a male point of view and hence represent men's experience of love in more detail than women's. The Wife of Bath, discussed in chapter nine, will, of course, address this very issue in her Prologue and Tale. In the tales told by the male pilgrim-narrators, men in love are frequently perceived as foolish victims. Nowhere in the *Canterbury Tales* do we get a story depicting sexual passion as unambiguously ennobling. Ascetic and ecstatic religious love that denies the body (such as St Cecilia's in the *Second Nun's Tale*) is said to ennoble others, but sexual love is not represented as a stepping stone to a platonic experience. Sexuality, is, in fact, frequently described in economic terms. The most blatant equation can be found in the *Shipman's Tale* where, as Thomas Hahn has remarked, 'success on the Wall Street of the fourteenth century produces renewed sexual vigor.'[9] The Wife of Bath's Prologue also characterizes sexuality as a commodity of economic exchange, when Dame Alysoun claims that this world is one where 'al is for to selle,' particularly the female body (III, 414, 202, 212).[10]

This view of human sexuality interfaces with late medieval theological interpretations of human love. In doctrinal discourse, human love is cast in a role similar to the one it has within heroic discourse: men's desire for women threatens to separate them from the divine Father, as Adam was tempted away from God. The Parson, representing the standard theological view of human love, says, 'God woot, a man may sleen hymself with his owene knyf, and make hymselve dronken of his owene tonne. / Certes, be it wyf, be it child, or any

9 Thomas Hahn, 'Money, Sexuality, Wordplay, and Context in the *Shipman's Tale*,' in *Chaucer in the Eighties*, ed. Wasserman and Blanch, 235.
10 Alfred David thinks the Wife of Bath 'regards "love" like any other commodity to be bought and sold in the World's market place,' *The Strumpet Muse: Art and Morals in Chaucer's Poetry* (Bloomington: Indiana University Press, 1976), 146.

worldly thyng that he loveth biforn God, it is his mawmet, and he is an ydolastre' (X, 858–59). Speaking against adultery he argues:

> Now lat us speke thanne of thilke stynkynge synne of Lecherie that men clepe avowtrie of wedded folk, that is to seyn, if that oon of hem be wedded, or elles bothe. / Seint John seith that avowtiers shullen been in helle, in a stank brennynge of fyr and of brymston; in fyr, for hire lecherye; in brymston, for the stynk of hire ordure. / . . . 'whoso seeth a womman to coveitise of his lust, he hath doon lecherie with hire in his herte.' (839–40, 844)

Sex in marriage is 'chaste' if husband and wife 'assemble' to pay the debt owed to their spouses, but if they 'assemble' 'oonly' to satisfy desire, they are sinful: 'if they assemble oonly for amorous love . . . to accomplice thilke brennynge delit . . . it is deedly synne' (942). The Parson, in his sermon, follows theological precepts which emphasized procreation as the only truly legitimate purpose of sexual union and downplayed mutual affection and pleasure between spouses; pleasure and mutual desire become, in this discourse, 'fornication' (938–42). The only sexual behavior the Parson endorses is a reluctant submission to sexuality for both men and women, but especially for a wife: 'she hath merite of chastitee that yeldeth to her housbounde the dette of hir body, ye, though it be agayn hir likynge and the lust of hire herte' (940). He advises husbands: 'Man sholde loven hys wyf by discrecioun, paciently and atemprely; and thanne is she as though it were his suster' (860). This idea is reiterated by Justinus in the *Merchant's Tale*:

> I hope to God, herafter shul ye knowe
> That ther nys no so greet felicitee
> In mariage, ne nevere mo shal bee,
> That yow shal lette of youre savacion,
> So that ye use, as skile is and reson,
> The lustes of youre wyf attemprely,
> And that ye plese hire nat to amorously,
> And that ye kepe yow eek from oother synne.   (IV, 1674–81)

As David Aers comments, the theological 'teaching and its language manifest the complete degradation of the erotic, the total separation of love from sexuality, of sexuality from one's full and true humanity.'[11]

Whether Chaucer himself accepted such a perspective or not is an unanswerable question. Still, his depictions of men in love with women are rarely admirable. They are usually comic, at moments tragic, and occasionally some wonderfully ambiguous combination of both. Whether or not his representations of men in love reveal an antipathy toward the love of women, whether they represent only a parody of a literary tradition, or whether they merely reflect the fashionable fourteenth-century stance of an old narrator looking back at the foolishness of youthful love (as in Gower's *Confessio Amantis*), are questions we cannot really ever answer. However, much evidence

---

[11] David Aers, *Chaucer* (Brighton: Harvester Press, 1986), 67.

suggests that Chaucer's stance is consistent with late fourteenth-century literary tastes. Courtly love literature had, even at the end of the twelfth century, undergone a crisis. Douglas Kelly notes that in the *Queste del saint graal* and in Jean de Meun's continuation of the *Roman de la Rose*, as well as in numerous Launcelot-Grail cycles, courtly love was seen as a corruption: 'The knights of the Round Table are blind to their own error in the *Queste*; like Amant in Jean's *Rose*, they sink into clumsy foolishness and sensuality, murder and rape.'[12] The Wife of Bath's rapist knight accords with just such a portrait, although her tale argues for the power of women, the ancient feminine, to effect a transformation of this kind of male violence and immorality. Despite the presence of ideal romance and courtly worlds in late medieval literature, by and large, Kelly argues, the fourteenth-century audience turned away from these lofty and fantastic romance worlds 'to poems about the end of love, and especially the death of a loved one.' Chaucer's time was, according to Kelly, beginning to prefer literary art which recreated a world closer to actual lived experience, with all its ambiguity, variation, and mortality: '[Fourteenth-century] poems [of love] are 'realistic' in the sense that they are set in a given time and place and show forth limitation and finality. The prevailing mood is one of resignation, even despair.'[13] He notes the tendency of fourteenth-century poets to emphasize old age, death, and the passing of time: 'Chaucer's tendency to emphasize the decline of *fyn lovyng* into a worse state is symptomatic of his generation's questioning of the reality or possibility of courtly love as an ideal.'[14]

If Kelly is correct about the fourteenth century's challenge to idyllic love, Chaucer's *Canterbury Tales* reflect their historical context and its growing rejection of courtly love ideals. However, much of Chaucer's challenge to the mythology of love occurs in fabliaux tales which do not emphasize 'sorrow' or 'death' but which, rather, humorously expose the raw physicality lying beneath courteous euphemisms. One purpose of the fabliau as a genre is to overthrow repressive authority, and so Chaucer's text makes exquisite use of bawdy tales to demonstrate the disparity between the culture's myths about love and baser realities (though the fabliaux themselves are not 'realistic' depictions either).[15] The 'decline of *fyn lovyng*' can be seen quite clearly in the *Miller's Tale*, where a competition between men seems much more the point than love. Judson Allen and Theresa Moritz have noted that in the *Miller's Tale*, as in the other tales of the first Fragment, 'Chaucer was interested in . . . rules and intrusions against them. His focus is therefore on the intrusive male and his supposedly sovereign adversary.'[16] Although the Miller-narrator frequently borrows language from courtly love discourse, the desire of Absolon and Nicholas to possess Alisoun nearly in front of her husband underscores the competitive nature of male

---

[12] D. R. Kelly, *Medieval Imagination*, 177.

[13] *Ibid.*, 178.

[14] *Ibid.*, 196.

[15] Laura Kendrick notes, 'To a far greater extent than most writers of French fabliaux, Chaucer builds the authority to be dethroned into the text of his *Canterbury Tales*,' *Chaucerian Play: Comedy and Control in the Canterbury Tales* (Berkeley: University of California Press, 1988), 100.

[16] Judson Allen and Theresa Moritz, *A Distinction of Stories: The Medieval Unity of Chaucer's Fair Chain of Narratives for Canterbury* (Columbus: University of Ohio Press, 1981), 77, n. 4.

relationships in this tale.[17] Rivalry between the two clerks also erupts when Nicholas insists on sticking his arse out the window to get the best of Absolon. It is not enough that Alisoun has made a fool of Absolon; Nicholas must do it too. In this tale, love becomes, in fact, a battle ground for a contest fought by body parts through a window frame. Mouths, eyes, rear ends, and the phallic coulter come together in quite a row. For the Miller-narrator, the clothing of eloquence and courtly love ritual simply obscure the naked truth of human desire and physicality. Although the tone is comic (consistent with its fabliau genre), the plot of the *Miller's Tale* implies a judgment on this kind of behavior, for the lovers who 'quite' one another pay a price for their competitiveness just as they do in the *Knight's Tale*. John winds up cuckolded. He has a broken arm and a whole town that thinks he's crazy. Nicholas, although he gets the girl momentarily, winds up with a burned bum. And Absolon unwittingly kisses Alisoun's 'nether eye' and is 'almoost yblent' by Nicholas's fart. Competition hurts, but, of course, it is also funny.[18]

The *Miller's Tale* goes beyond poking fun at and judging the love-contest, however; men's blindnesses, their fantasies about themselves and their fantasies about women, are also exposed by the tale. Each of the three male characters assumes he's superior to the others for some reason. Old John is the working man, the laborer; Nicholas plays the intellectual; and Absolon fashions himself into the courtly lover. Each assumes his own form of masculinity is somehow better than the others. Old John believes money, younger women, and hard manual labor are ennobling. Thinking and pursuing knowledge are activities he considers even potentially dangerous, and he ridicules the studious and intellectual clerk:

> Men sholde nat knowe of Goddes pryvetee.
> Ye, blessed be alwey a lewd man
> That noght but oonly his bileve kan!
> So ferde another clerk with astromye;
> He walked in the feeldes, for to prye
> Upon the sterres, what ther sholde bifalle,
> Til he was in a marle-pit yfalle;
> He saugh nat that.   (I, 3454–61)

Apparently, he assumes clerks are so preoccupied with their minds that they are unaware of their bodies, and even though he is afraid he will be cuckolded, John expresses no concern about leaving Alisoun home alone with the clerk who rents their spare room. This blind assumption as well as John's prideful ignorance provide Nicholas with just the tools he needs to take advantage of his host. John may mock learning, but we see his own blind ignorance push him into a 'marle-pit' as he is so easily set up by the educated Nicholas. The superstitious

---

[17] The *Miller's Tale* is also, quite clearly, in competition with the *Knight's Tale*, so that the fabliau genre competes with and defeats the chivalric romance genre, at least from the churls' perspective. See Kendrick's *Chaucerian Play*, 5–10.

[18] Cf. Lee Patterson, ' "No man his reson herde": Peasant Consciousness, Chaucer's Miller, and the Structure of the *Canterbury Tales*,' *SAQ* 86 (1987); Elaine Tuttle Hansen, *Chaucer and the Fictions of Gender*, (Berkeley: University of California Press, 1992), 223–36.

carpenter unquestioningly accepts Nicholas's prophecy that the Flood will reoccur imminently, so he sets about constructing his ridiculous life boats and hangs them from the ceiling of his house. Commenting on John's gullibility and his delusion, the Miller says:

> Lo, which a greet thyng is affeccioun!
> Men may dyen of ymaginacioun,
> So depe may impressioun be take.   (3611-13)

But John is not the only man deceived by his own assumptions; so is Absolon.[19] This young clerk plays at idealized or courtly love in a highly self-conscious manner, imagining himself a gallant:

> This parissh clerk, this joly Absolon,
> Hath in his herte swich a love-longynge
> That of no wyf took he noon offrynge;
> For curteisie, he seyde, he wolde noon.   (3348-51)

'For paramours' he dresses himself just so, and wanders around in the middle of the night singing underneath Alisoun's window. He falls madly in love with Alisoun, worshiping her as he imagines courtly lovers do. He sends her sweet wine, spiced ale, hot cakes, and money, and 'Sometyme, to shewe his lightnesse and maistrye, / He pleyeth Herodes upon a scaffold hye' (3383-84). But all of this high drama is for naught; Alisoun repeatedly refuses his advances. Stubbornly, the foppish Absolon interprets her repeated rebukes as insincere, assuming she is also playing his game of courtly love, and so he persists despite them. His subjectivity blinds him to the possibility that Alisoun could have her own desires and wishes beyond, or in contradiction to, his own. He absolutely refuses to grant her any autonomy; she is merely an extension of his own fantasy. The text ridicules this kind of narcissism as Absolon's persistence leads him to kiss Alisoun's 'nether eye.' At first, he cannot even comprehend the truth. Edward Schweitzer has commented that 'Absolon is so comically deluded, so much a victim of his expectations, his judgment so overpowered by his imagination, that he cannot fully comprehend the trick played on him.'[20] If the narrative makes a statement about the courtly love tradition, it may be implying that the courtly man's fantasies ignore women's autonomy. As such, the Absolon material may be remarking on the refusal of men to acknowledge women's desires. But the tale may also illustrate ways that men's adherence to the courtly love ideal and their 'excessive love' for women can weaken them and make them vulnerable to abuse not only from women but from men as well, for both Alisoun and Nicholas play the bum-baring trick on the adoring Absolon. Here the 'servant of love' topos from the courtly love tradition receives a thorough-going fart in the face. As Laura Kendrick remarks, 'a kiss bestowed on

---

[19] For an article that examines the self-delusion in Absolon's character, see especially Edward Schweitzer's 'The Misdirected Kiss and the Lover's Malady in Chaucer's *Miller's Tale*,' in *Chaucer in the Eighties*, 223-33.

[20] Schweitzer, 'Misdirected Kiss,' 226.

the lower orifice, instead of on the mouth, puts woman "on top" in a grotesque parody of the ceremony of vassalage.'[21]

Nicholas and Alisoun are not the only ones who ridicule Absolon, however. There is yet another character who plays rather roughly with him: namely, the Miller-narrator. He apparently sees men who worship women, who posture themselves after the courtly love tradition, as effeminate. In fact, the Miller-narrator first describes Absolon using a rhetorical *effectio* modelled after those commonly reserved to describe feminine beauty.[22] The beautiful woman was traditionally described in a descending catalogue from head to toe. She had blond hair and grey eyes, rosy lips and cheeks, small round breasts and a tiny waist.[23] The Miller describes Absolon from head to toe, as having golden hair like a 'fanne,' grey eyes and blushed complexion; 'Yclad he was ful smal and proprely' (see ll. 3320f). As has been noted by numerous scholars, Absolon's namesake, King David's son, had a beautiful and generous head of hair that cost him his life.[24] In biblical exegesis, Absolom's hair was often seen as an emblem of the effeminacy of sin. As further signs of Absolon's effeminacy, he is 'somdeel squaymous of fartyng' (3337–38), and he sings in quivering voice that is 'gentil and smal' like a nightingale's (3360). He coughs 'softe . . . with a semy soun' (3697) before he begins his performance beneath Alisoun's window, and he 'moorne[s] as dooth a lamb after the tete' (3704). Although the presence of 'feminine' features in a male body challenges gender stereotypes to some degree, the message the Miller intends to communicate here is fully masculinist: things womanly or child-like are weak and unbecoming when they exist in a man. Absolon is the only man in this tale who is described as feminine, and he is the man most maligned by the crude events in the tale. Apparently the Miller-narrator believes that the working man who creates with his hands and the intellectual who designs with his mind are more masculine than the courtly lover whose goal is to love women and revel in desire.

Absolon does not remain lost in his love-sickness for very long, however. He is rudely awakened to a 'naked' truth about Alisoun, for no lady would bare her bottom to her lover in such a manner. And so, as Robert Miller observes, 'In Absolon's misplaced kiss, the Miller subjects the code of courteous love (as he sees it) to the indecent exposure he feels it deserves.'[25] Absolon's response to 'truth' is revenge. He bites his lip in anger and 'to hymself he seyde, "I shal thee quyte" ' (3745–46). He gets a hot iron and intends to regain his dignity by luring Alisoun to the window and burning her bottom. He regains his sense of manhood and control by retaliating physically. The hot coulter may well be more than a

[21] Kendrick, *Chaucerian Play*, 188, n. 10.

[22] See E. Talbot Donaldson, 'Idiom of Popular Poetry in the Miller's Tale,' in *Speaking of Chaucer* (Durham, 1970; Labyrinth Press, 1983), 20–22; Robert P. Miller, 'The *Miller's Tale* as Complaint,' *ChauR* 5 (1970): 147–60. See also *The Poetria Nova of Geoffrey of Vinsauf*, trans. Margaret F. Nims (Toronto: Pontifical Institute, 1967), 36–38.

[23] For a discussion of the catalogue device as it is applied to women see Kevin Kiernan, 'The Art of the Descending Catalogue, and a Fresh Look at Alisoun,' *ChauR* 10 (1975): 1–16.

[24] See Paul Beichner 'Absolon's Hair' *Mediaeval Studies* 12 (1950): 222–33 and his 'Characterization in the Miller's Tale,' in *Chaucer Criticism: The Canterbury Tales*, ed. Richard J. Schoeck and Jerome Taylor (Notre Dame: University of Notre Dame Press, 1960), 117–29. See also D. W. Robertson, Jr, *A Preface to Chaucer*, 385.

[25] R. P. Miller, 'The *Miller's Tale* as Complaint,' 153.

weapon, as Charles Owen noted some time ago; it may suggest an ironic symbol of Absolon's sexual inadequacy: a phallus.[26] To be healed of his effeminacy, Absolon must become aggressive. If he was love-sick before, he is cured 'at the end':

> His hoote love was coold and al yqueynt;
> For fro that tyme that he hadde kist hir ers,
> Of paramours he sette nat a kers;
> For he was heeled of his maladie.   (3754–57)

The Miller-narrator represents Absolon's love of women as an illusion which is 'sick' and unmanly.[27] Losing that illusion, 'cooling' the heart, and regaining control over one's emotions, are seen as 'healing' and positive. To be healed of his effeminacy, Absolon becomes aggressive. Instead of yearning for the 'tete' as a babe, he asserts himself with the coulter-phallus as a weapon. The development of Absolon's character traces a movement from oral desire to phallic retribution, a development the Miller-narrator apparently sees as a remedy for Absolon's unmanliness. Notably, the agent for Absolon's 'cure' is Alisoun's nakedness. In this way, the tale establishes sexuality as a field of knowledge and power, albeit humorously. Here, the woman's body is represented much as it appears in a modern pornographic film: her body becomes the knowledge to be 'seen' and possessed by men. As Yann Lardeau has commented, 'the naked woman has always been, in our society, the allegorical representation of Truth.'[28]

If Absolon is a man who has been molded by a cultural discourse to such a degree that he becomes a fool, Nicholas represents yet another kind of distorted perception. V. A. Kolve has suggested that Nicholas is a 'shaper of fictions.'[29] He uses his intelligence to compete with other men, to seduce women, and to exert some control over his world. Not surprisingly, he 'Hadde lerned art, but al his fantasye / Was turned for to lerne astrologye'(3191–2). Although this educated man gets the best of the uneducated Carpenter, and although the

---

[26] Charles Owen, 'Chaucer's *Canterbury Tales*: Aesthetic Design in Stories of the First Day,' *English Studies* 35 (1954): 53.

[27] E. T. Hansen, in her analysis of the tale, stresses the homoerotic and homophobic elements in the Nicholas-Absolon exchange. *Chaucer and the Fictions*, 223–236. On pages 230–31, she writes of Absolon's retaliation against Nicholas: 'this reaction identifies what is most disturbing: the actual and feared lack of distinction between men and women, which in turn suggests the related possibilities of castration and homosexuality. A relation between (the fear of) castration, homosexual behavior, and the rape or mutilation of the female (who is presented in this tale as definitely asking for it) is equally . . . brought out in the revenge Absolon hastens to enact.'

[28] Yann Lardeau, 'Le sexe froid du porno au dela,' *Cahiers du Cinéma*, 289 (June, 1978): 49, translated by and cited in Teresa de Lauretis, *Alice Doesn't: Feminism, Semiotics, Cinema* (Bloomington: Indiana University Press, 1984), 26. De Lauretis, incorporating Lardeau's work on pornographic film, writes, 'The pornographic film is said relentlessly to repropose sexuality as the field of knowledge and power, power in the uncovering of truth . . . the close-up is its operation of truth, the camera constantly closing in on the woman's sex, exhibiting it as object of desire and definitive place of *jouissance* only in order to ward off castration . . . . The porno film is constructed on the disavowal of castration, and its operation of truth is a fetishistic operation.'

[29] V. A. Kolve, *Chaucer and the Imagery of Narrative: The First Five Canterbury Tales* (Stanford: Stanford University Press, 1984), 166.

Miller-narrator obviously enjoys telling his audience about Nicholas's ruse, Nicholas hardly represents an admirable masculine model. He is 'subtile,' 'sleigh and ful privee,' and he knows and practices 'deerne love' well. Edmund Reiss has established that Chaucer and many of his contemporaries used this term 'deerne love' to indicate a 'more artificial than natural' love, and that the word 'deerne' carries with it connotations of sinfulness.[30] Reiss claims, 'The evidence would seem to indicate strikingly that *deerne love* is not noble, not an expression of *fin amour*, but, rather, a low love, one illicit and sinful.'[31]

Nicholas sees Alisoun as an object to be won in a game.[32] He does not carry on an affair with her when John goes on business trips (which happens twice). Instead, his thrill lies in staging a ruse, deceiving John, and having Alisoun as a result of his fiction-making. V. A. Kolve has suggested that 'Nicholas's ultimate intent' may be 'as much the witty exploration of an old man's gullibility as the 'swyvyng' of the wife.'[33] But even though Nicholas succeeds at gulling John and 'swyvyng' Alisoun, he is punished. His desire to compete with men gets the best of him when he decides to bare his bum to Absolon. In his eagerness, he falls for Absolon's ruse and suffers the scarring consequences. Absolon applies the red-hot poker, and

> Of gooth the skyn an hande-brede aboute,
> The hoote kultour brende so his toute,
> And for the smert he wende for to dye.
> As he were wood, for wo he gan to crye,
> 'Help! water! water! help, for Goddes herte!' (3811–15)

So a pattern emerges from the representations of men in the *Miller's Tale*. We have here men who seek to control their worlds by fantasy, cultural code, or cunning design and yet who remain vulnerable to the designs of others. Their vulnerability arises out of their erroneous assumptions about other men and about women. John falls for Nicholas's ruses; Absolon falls for Alisoun's; and Nicholas falls for Absolon's. Edmund Reiss suggests that in this tale all secrets and all things concealed are finally exposed. Nicholas reveals his 'deerne love' to Alisoun who has been kept 'caged,' or concealed, by her jealous husband. Alisoun quite easily escapes from her 'cage,' at least for a night, to play with Nicholas. Nicholas reveals his secret prophecy to John. Alisoun exposes her 'privetee' to Absolon whose pretenses and misperceptions are discovered. Absolon's secret plan burns Nicholas's private parts which are exposed awaiting a kiss, and John falls from the ceiling into a realization that he's been duped. 'At

---

[30] Edmund Reiss, 'Chaucer's *deerne love* and the Medieval View of Secrecy in Love,' in *Chaucerian Problems and Perspectives: Essays Presented to Paul E. Beichner, C.S.C.*, ed. Edward Vasta and Zacharias P. Thundy (Notre Dame: University of Notre Dame Press, 1979), 165. See also E. Talbot Donaldson, 'Idiom of Popular Poetry in the *Miller's Tale*,' in *Speaking of Chaucer*, 19–20. The *MED* II, 1006 defines the word, 'deerne' as 'stealthy, insidious, crafty, dishonest, deceptive, immoral, and evil.'

[31] Reiss, 'Chaucer's deerne love,' 171.

[32] For an article that examines the *Miller's Tale* as a game, see Gerard Joseph, 'Chaucerian "Game" – "Ernest" and the "Argument of Herbergage," in the Canterbury Tales,' *ChauR* 5 (1970): 88–89.

[33] Kolve, *Chaucer and the Imagery of Narrative*, 189.

the end of the tale,' says Reiss, 'all that had been *deerne* is made public with great commotion and outcry.'[34] The tale opens out into the entire community as the town learns of all the private matters in the lives of the main characters. The tale, he says, serves 'to show the inadequacy of that which is illicit and hidden,'[35] and, I might add, that which is fantasy and affectation.

In this tale, only the men, apparently, have fantasies, affectations, and hidden motives which need to be exposed; Alisoun does not. She may have fantasies; she may parody a courtly lady and thoroughly relish her seduction, but her primary purpose in the tale is the same as Emelye's in the *Knight's Tale*: the female-as-body, the object to be possessed. She is in the tale to reveal something about the male characters. Her experience, her thoughts, her desires, though mentioned briefly, are not the focus. Paul Olson, in his article, 'Poetic Justice in the *Miller's Tale*,' writes:

> In the *Miller's Tale*, Alysoun becomes what each of her lovers wants her to be: to the lecher [Nicholas], she is mere animal satisfaction, and she springs as a colt for him; for the proud Absolon, she is elevated to celestial regions as the Bride of the Canticum; for the greedy John, she is what he hopes to save from the flood. Pierre Bersuire remarks that a man may have three 'wives': carnality, avarice, and pomposity. Alysoun serves for all three.[36]

If we explore the implications of Olson's analysis, then, men's misperceptions of women are punished in the *Miller's Tale*. Each of the three men fashion their actions around the delectable prize: Alisoun – her name means 'of delight' – and yet none of them can see her as anything but an object. They may 'know' her (sexually) and yet not know her. Their inability to acknowledge her subjectivity as well as their own fantasies about her lead them into errors of judgment and into trouble. The men are, then, similar to medieval versions of Adam who, because he was so fond of Eve, loses his judgment and suffers punishment. But we cannot assume too close a correspondence between the tale and gender issues in Genesis, for Absolon and Nicholas are the subjects who initiate the action; Alisoun is the object; the only innovative thing she does in the story is to stick her rear end out the window in a rather conventional fabliau move. Like Emelye, she plays a predominantly, though not exclusively, passive role.

That subjectivity revolves around the male characters and objectivity around Alisoun is also apparent in the way the narrative describes the two genders.[37] The description of Alisoun emphasizes her body and her sexuality. She is, as David Aers has described her, 'an assortment of desirable bits.'[38] The descriptions of the men do, of course, emphasize their bodies and their sexual appetites in so far as we are in the genre of the fabliau, but we learn much more about them than that. Nicholas may be lecherous, but much of his

---

[34] Reiss, 'Chaucer's deerne love,' 174.
[35] *Ibid.*, 174.
[36] Paul Olson, 'Poetic Justice in the *Miller's Tale*,' *MLQ* 24 (1963): 233.
[37] Cf. Kolve, *Chaucer and the Imagery of Narrative*, 158–90; and Thomas B. Hanson, 'Physiogamy and Characterization in the *Miller's Tale*,' *Neuphilologische Mitteilungen* 72 (1971): 477–82.
[38] Aers, *Chaucer*, 84.

description establishes him (humorously) as a student with textbooks, an astrolabe, augrym stones, and a harp which he plays well. He also sings beautifully and can act a part superbly.[39] Absolon is also lecherous, and yet we learn that he is a barber of sorts, that he can 'maken a chartre of lond or acquaintance,' and that he knows many fashionable dance steps. He can play a fiddle, 'wel kan' play and sing with the guitar, and can even participate in the town's amateur play productions. And what of John? Although John's gullibility is hilarious and his superstitiousness ridiculous, we do see him engage in business activities, and we witness his skill in carpentry. But Alisoun? She, like Emelye, is first introduced as a body in a description linking her with the natural world. Granted, Nicholas's breath is described as sweeter than the root of licorice, and Absolon is compared to a cat, a nightingale, a goose, and a blossom, but Alisoun's description is overwhelmingly sprinkled with references to Nature:

> Fair was this yonge wyf, and therwithal
> As any wezele hir body gent and smal.   (3233-34)

She has 'a likerous eye' and is compared to a budding peach tree, 'wolle of a wether,' swallows, colts, kids and calves, honey, apples, primroses, and 'a piggesnye.' She is a 'popelete' or doll. She is the prize 'for any lord to leggen in his bedde / Or yet for any good yeman to wedde' (3269-70). But what of her work? Her accomplishments? Very little. The point here is that the woman is described not in terms of her achievements or aspirations, not in terms of her mind, but in terms of her physicality and sexuality, her body alone. She is the object of the male gaze, to borrow terminology from contemporary film criticism, and her body is fragmented by the Miller-narrator's representation and made into pieces of a body apparently desired by men – mouth, eye, eyebrow, waist, breasts, genitals, and a naked rear-end. The subject of Chaucer's tale is the male gaze and its consequences, not Alisoun. 'Alisoun,' Judson Allen and Theresa Moritz argue, 'functions more as occasion than person, as do the other 'awardable' women in the first fragment.'[40] Whereas Emelye is taken prisoner and becomes a war prize after the conflict between the Amazons and Theseus, Alisoun is held 'narwe in a cage' by her husband and is seen as a colt to be tamed by Nicholas. The ending of the tale is telling:

> [The Carpenter] was holde wood in al the toun.
> . . .
> Thus swyved was this carpenteris wyf,
> For al his kepyng and his jalousye;
> And Absolon hath kist hir nether ye;
> And Nicholas is scalded in the towte.   (3846; 3850-53)

---

[39] J. Burke Severs discusses the nature of Nicholas' pursuits and their relationship to the gulling of John in 'Chaucer's Clerks,' in *Chaucer and Middle English Studies in Honour of Rossell Hope Robbins*, ed. Beryl Rowland (London: Allen & Unwin, 1974; Kent, Ohio: Kent State University Press, 1974), 140-52; especially 140-43.

[40] Allen and Moritz, *A Distinction of Stories*, 77, n. 4. Robert P. Miller has also argued that the *Miller's Tale* is an 'offensive thrust at women' where wives are 'simply sexual instruments,' 'The *Miller's Tale* as Complaint,' 158.

It is Alisoun who is copulated *with*, not Nicholas. She is the sexual object, not he. Johan Huizinga argued quite some time ago that 'all the conventions of love are the work of men: even when it dons an idealistic guise, erotic culture is altogether saturated with male egotism.'[41] Such egotism reveals itself in the *Miller's Tale*, but not without ironic exposure.

If blindness, particularly men's blindness about women, is figuratively an epistemological condition of the men in the *Miller's Tale*, it becomes literally represented in the Merchant's story about old January. The male gaze is, once again, the object of Chaucer's satire, but the *Merchant's Tale* offers a more complex satiric comment on courtly love, and that complexity stems, partially, from the more active and ingenious role given to May, January's young wife.[42] At the beginning of the tale, however, May is obscured, and the focus is on January. Despite the counsel of his friends, despite the wisdom one might expect from his age, and despite incontrovertible evidence to the contrary, the old knight persists in his belief that marriage is bliss. He believes in his own fantasies and the fictions of cultural ideals. Marriage, he thinks, will give him an heir, 'a lyf blisful and ordinaat,' an obedient wife who will mother him whenever he is in need, and some measure of economic security. A wife, he fantasizes, will be his helpmate just as the sermons prescribe; she will provide him with emotional stability and will never abandon him. He imagines that women are 'Goddes yifte' to men, a kind of property far better than 'londes, rentes, pasture, . . . commune, / Or moebles' (IV, 1311, 1313-14). Each ideal he holds is ironically answered by the events in the tale. Except that his marriage to May is blessed by a priest and may well produce an heir, the marriage (and May, particularly) exists to reveal the old knight's inadequate knowing. Contrary to any courtly depiction of love, January's devotion to an ideal of conjugal bliss is not laudable within the tale; it literally blinds him to truth.

Juxtaposed in ironic fashion against the 'factual experience' of the Merchant-narrator's own wedded life, January's beliefs become ridiculous right from the beginning of the tale, for the Merchant predicates his tale on the assumption that marriage is pain. In the Prologue to his tale, he reveals his own 'cursed' condition as a henpecked husband:

> I have a wyf, the worste that may be;
> For thogh the feend to hire ycoupled were,
> She wolde hym overmacche, I dar wel swere.
> What sholde I yow reherce in special
> Hir hye malice? She is a shrewe at al.
> . . .
> I wolde nevere eft comen in the snare.
> We wedded men lyven in sorwe and care.
>
> (IV, 1218-22; 1227-28)

---

[41] Huizinga, *The Waning of the Middle Ages*, 138.

[42] Cf. Hansen's reading of the *Merchant's Tale* sees it as a far more sinister tale than I do here. Her argument establishes ways the tale reinscribes sexual-gender anxieties around sexual differentiation, rape, coercion, and the power of the sex-gender system. *Chaucer and the Fictions*, 245-66.

Strategically prefacing the tale with such statements, Chaucer situates competing interpretations of women and marriage at the center of his story. This guarantees that we will question the idyllic and formulaic disquisition on love and marriage which January delivers early in the narrative. Furthermore, within the tale, itself, January's perceptions of marriage are challenged by Justinius's skepticism and by the antifeminist authoritative voices of Seneca, Theophrastus, and others, again guaranteeing that the audience will not accept the old knight's interpretations.

The correlation between epistemology and the knowledge of women is emphasized early in the tale by two images drawn quite obviously from the platonic tradition. January imagines that knowing or possessing a wife will accord him far more comfort than any of the 'yiftes of Fortune, / That passen as a shadwe upon a wal' (1314–15). Even though January believes he will find some kind of 'truth' in marriage, the Merchant-narrator interprets January's desire for a wife as if it were only a desire for artificial appearances, for shadows, for reflected images:

> Heigh fantasye and curious bisynesse
> Fro day to day gan in the soule impresse
> Of Januarie aboute his mariage.
> Many fair shap and many a fair visage
> Ther passeth thurgh his herte nyght by nyght,
> As whoso tooke a mirour, polisshed bryght,
> And sette it in a commune market-place,
> Thanne sholde he se ful many a figure pace
> By his mirour; and in the same wyse
> Gan Januarie inwith his thoght devyse
> Of maydens whiche that dwelten hym bisyde.   (1577–87)

Rather than depict the male lover's devotion to courtly love, the Merchant depicts January as a practitioner of mercantile courtesy.

The narcissism of this fantasy comes to life in the action of the tale as January takes May to bed to (consume)mate *his* marriage, and it is a narcissism tainted with overtones of violent conquest. January, Venus's 'knyght / . . . wolde bothe assayen his corage / In libertee and eek in mariage' (1724–26). He begins to imagine his power and dominance over the young maiden:

> . . . in his herte he gan hire to manace
> That he that nyght in armes wolde hire streyne
> Harder than evere Parys dide Eleyne.
> But natheless yet hadde he greet pitee
> That thilke nyght offenden hire moste he,
> And thoughte, 'Allas! O tendre creature,
> Now wolde God ye myghte wel endure
> Al my corage, it is so sharp and keene!
> I am agast ye shul it nat susteene.
> But God forbede that I dide al my myght!   (1752–61)

The passage recreates January's thoughts, and they are thoughts of physical domination, not adoration, as the word choices so obviously indicate ('assayen,' 'manace,' 'armes,' 'knyght,' 'corage,' 'streyne harder,' 'offenden,' 'sharp,' 'keene,' 'myght'). The reference to Paris and Helen (with its inevitably military connotation) as well as January's fantasy that May, a little creature, might not 'susteene' his powerful sexual advances, help create a subtext of a sexual assault as a dominant feature of his sexual imaginings. Even more explicitly violent is the knight's metaphorical reference to his penis as 'a knyf': 'A man may do no synne with his wyf, / Ne hurte hymselven with his owene knyf' (1839–40). But January's fantasies are ludicrous; outside the fantasy we see an old man who needs aphrodisiacs and fictions to bolster his courage in his own sexual performance. Damyan, his servant and meat-carver, will serve better than he, albeit in bizarre circumstances. For both men, May is the delectable prize, the feast for their sexual appetites.

In this supremely anti-courtly tale where 'love' is simply lust with violent overtones and where the 'lover' is a lecherous old man, Chaucer emphasizes January's egocentrism and the chasm which, consequently, separates him from May. This is accentuated by constructing the narrative so that it initially reveals January's subjectivity and obscures May's. We know Venus enjoys arousing January's sexuality (1723–29), but what she thinks of May is not recorded. We know how January found subtle ways to get his guests to leave the wedding banquet (1765–71); we know what he thought (1750–64), what he drank (1805–12), and what he said (1814–15). Consistent with this male-oriented passage, we know of Damyan's sexual arousal (1772–82) and the Merchant's reaction (1783–94); we know how masculine time (the sun) 'Parfourned hath . . . his ark diurne' so that masculine 'night with his mantel, that is derk and rude, / Gan oversprede the hemysperie aboute' (1795; 1798–99), but the feminine representative – May? 'The bryde was broght abedde as stille as stoon' (1818). However obscured May is during these lines, after January consummates his desire, the Merchant says:

> But God woot what that May thoughte in hir herte,
> Whan she hym saugh sittynge in his sherte,
> In his nyght-cappe, and with his nekke lene,
> She preyseth nat his pleyyng worth a bene.   (1851–54)

Despite her earlier obscurity, or perhaps precisely because of it, this momentary stop at the doorstep of May's subjectivity is powerful, for her perception of January is, presumably, correct. Like us, she can see what he cannot. Even though only five lines of the 156 lines describing the wedding festivities indicate May's experience and perceptions, her five lines of precise and accurate observation point to the excessive fantasies of the male characters.[43]

---

[43] The lengthy discussion on marriage at the beginning of the tale, which takes up almost half the narrative, is a discussion involving only men. The inclusion of the exclusively male discussion of women within a tale which satirizes men's objectification of women may well comment on the exclusion of women from the debate. For a discussion of the aesthetics of the tale, see Robert M. Jordan, *Chaucer and the Shape of Creation: The Aesthetic Possibilities of Inorganic Form* (Cambridge, Mass.: Harvard University Press, 1967).

As the narrative progresses, May's character and her perceptions gradually become clearer and clearer, accompanied by January's greater and greater blindness. While the men in the tale are blinded or consumed by jealousy and lust, May takes control. She acts. Feigning roles and concocting plots, she takes on an active role in the tale similar to Nicholas's role in the *Miller's Tale*: 'For craft is al, whoso that do it kan' (2016). Here is no distant paragon of courtly love virtue, no passive recipient of male action; here is a determined and resourceful artisan of fictions and affairs. Although the men – Damyan and January – first fall in love with May, May herself chooses to pursue an affair with Damyan despite his poverty ('he namoore hadde than his sherte' [1985]). She chooses to defy and her husband's possessiveness and to satisfy her own desires, ingeniously finding ways to skirt his fierce jealousy; and she is the one who cleverly destroys Damyan's billet-doux by throwing it down the privy. She is the one who writes Damyan:

> And sotilly this lettre doun she threste
> Under his pilwe, rede it if hym leste.
> She taketh hym by the hand, and harde hym twiste
> So secrely that no wight of it wiste.   (2003–06)

In Chaucer's spoof on the courtly love tradition, his Merchant says:

> Lo, pitee renneth soone in gentil herte!
>   Heere may ye se how excellent franchise
> In wommen is, whan they hem narwe avyse.
> Som tyrant is, as ther be many oon,
> That hath an herte as hard as any stoon,
> Which wolde han lat hym sterven in the place
> Wel rather than han graunted hym hire grace;
> And hem rejoysen in hire crueel pryde,
> And rekke nat to been an homycide.   (1986–94)

At least twice the Merchant-narrator tells us that Damyan goes along with May's plans because he 'knew al hire entente' (2120, 2212); and her 'entente,' or will, governs once January loses his eyesight. She is the one who devises the plan to duplicate the garden gate key from a wax imprint (2117–18), and she is the stage director in the garden scene: 'For in a lettre she hadde toold [Damyan] al / Of this matere, how he werchen shal' (2215–16). Carefully orchestrating her 'play,' she gestures:

> On Damyan a signe made she,
> That he sholde go biforn with his cliket.
> This Damyan thanne hath opened the wyket,
> And in he stirte, and that in swich manere
> That no wight myghte it se neither yheere,
> And stille he sit under a bussh anon.   (2150–55)

Then leading blind old January 'down the garden path,' May deceitfully sings and gives testimony to her fidelity. She feigns pregnancy and a sudden craving for fruit; stepping on her blind husband's back in a bitter representation of the courtly lover's vassalage to women, May hoists herself into a pear tree to frolic with Damyan. At just this moment, the Merchant-narrator interrupts the action with a digression reminiscent of the courtly past-time of competitive debating.

Imagining Pluto and Proserpina as divine witnesses to the human scene, the Merchant freezes the action to allow for a discussion. Pluto, outraged that May should cuckold her husband, decides to restore old January's eyesight. He condemns May, and all women, citing Solomon's words: 'Thus preiseth he yet the bountee of man: / "Amonges a thousand men yet foond I oon, / But of wommen alle foond I noon," ' (2246–48). But lest we, as listeners or readers, should accept such a categorical evaluation of women, Proserpina launches into a defense of women (2264–2310), and forces a reconsideration. From Proserpina's perspective, young women forced into marriage with older, lecherous men are to be pitied. And Proserpina, unlike Pluto, can see that even if one woman is adulterous, it is not logical to conclude that all women are adulterous. Pluto, like January, is far more illogical and absolute. Women, he thinks, are, without exception, lustful and 'untrouthe.' But that is not, apparently what Chaucer wants us to think, otherwise Proserpina's commentary would not stand in counterpoint to Pluto's. At this moment in the narrative, the complexity of textual interpretation becomes explicit: are we going to side with Pluto or with Proserpina? Their interpretations of the January-May relationship offer us two possibilities.

If we agree with Pluto, we fall into the kind of misperception January exhibits at the beginning of the tale: an insistence on absolute judgments, on either/or thinking. If we side with Proserpina, we are left with what may seem like an uncomfortable decision to sanction adultery: an approval of deceit and duplicity. This dilemma is, apparently, the one Chaucer wants for us, otherwise the narrative would never have been so abruptly interrupted by questions of interpretation. In the dilemma, made even more problematic by the Merchant's Prologue, the only conclusion we can draw for sure is that the way one answers the question depends upon one's experience. Pluto, the old king of the underworld, king of darkness, feels outrage when he sees old, blind January being cuckolded by his wife. Proserpina, the young goddess of Spring, abducted, ravished, and made wife of Pluto, understandably feels for May. The scales may well tip in Proserpina's favor, since most of us would find an alliance with life (rebirth, youth, Proserpina) more amenable than an alliance with death (the underworld, old age, Pluto). It may also be tempting for the feminist reader to revel in May's rebellion, in her clever response to January, for as Joan Ferrante notes: 'With limited opportunities to exercise real power over their own or others' lives, women in medieval literature and sometimes in real life find subtle or hidden ways to exercise such power, to manipulate people and situations, and to spin out fictions which suit them better than their reality, fictions by which they can, or hope to, control reality.'[44] But to revel in May's clever response, to side with Proserpina, is not completely comfortable, for

---

[44] Joan Ferrante, 'Public Postures and Private Maneuvers: Roles Medieval Women Play,' in *Women and Power in the Middle Ages*, ed. Mary Erler and Maryanne Kowaleski (Athens: University of Georgia Press, 1988), 213.

Proserpina's gift of duplicity to May also has the effect of making her consistent with the representations of women which the antifeminist tradition maintains. That is quite clearly the way Harry Bailly reads the tale: he remarks, 'Lo, whiche sleightes and subtilitees / In wommen been!' (2421-22).

Consistent with his absolutist mode of thinking, Pluto, even after listening to Proserpina's defense of women, still vows to restore January's eyesight so that he will know the truth of his wife's adultery. Proserpina, consistent with her compassion toward May, vows that if Pluto does restore January's eyesight, she will provide May with 'suffisant answere, / And alle wommen after, for hir sake' (2266-67). Their plans proceed exactly. January opens his eyes and accuses his wife. She maintains coolly:

> . . . 'Sire, what eyleth yow?
> Have pacience and resoun in youre mynde!
> I have yow holpe on bothe youre eyen blynde.
> Up peril of my soule, I shal nat lyen,
> As me was taught, to heele with youre eyen,
> Was no thyng bet, to make yow to see,
> Than strugle with a man upon a tree.'   (2368-74)

Still, January persists, outraged by what he has witnessed: ' "Strugle!" quod he, "ye algate in it wente! / . . . He swyved thee, I saugh it with myne yen" ' (2376, 2378). Once again, May, using the cleverness of language and argument, simply denies him his seen reality:

> 'But sire, a man that waketh out of his sleep,
> He may nat sodeynly wel taken keep
> Upon a thyng, ne seen it parfitly,
> Til that he be adawed verraily.
> Right so a man that longe hath blynd ybe,
> Ne may nat sodeynly so wel yse,
> First whan his sighte is newe come ageyn,
> As he that hath a day of two yseyn.
> Til that youre sighte ysatled be a while
> Ther may ful many a sighte yow bigile.
> Beth war, I prey yow; for, by hevene kyng,
> Ful many a man weneth to seen a thyng,
> And it is al another than it semeth.
> He that mysconceyveth, he mysdemeth.'[45]   (2397-2410)

Here is, perhaps a serious Chaucerian appraisal of the man in love, and it is a warning: beware of your own misperceptions. The power of January's desire for

---

[45] Cf. Hugh of Folietto, *De nuptiis libri duo* (*PL* 176, col. 1212): 'What a woman does without a witness, she forgets as if it never happened. If, however, there was a witness, she forces him to believe by her artful use of language (*artificio linguae*) that he had not seen what he actually saw.' This passage is translated by and cited in Katharina M. Wilson and Elizabeth M. Makowski, *Wykked Wyves and the Woes of Marriage: Misogamous Literature from Juvenal to Chaucer* (Albany: State University of New York Press, 1990), 90.

the ideal negates his sensory experience, so that he kisses May and leads her home, apparently content to deny reality and believe fiction.

In the *Miller's Tale*, Absolon's kiss forces his recognition of truth, his recognition of his own ridiculous delusions, but here, in the *Merchant's Tale*, January is even more ridiculous because he never does fully recognize the truth of his own illusions (or the truth of real experience, for that matter). As a comment on the culture's discourse surrounding women, characterized by the January-Justinius debate which begins the tale, the *Merchant's Tale* laughs at men's very human tendency to swallow ideology without thinking, to believe in the myths without hesitation, to imagine that signifier and signified are synonymous, that marriage and 'paradys' are necessarily the same because some authority says so, or that women are always manipulative because some other authority says so. Where the *Miller's Tale* parodies the courtly love discourse, the *Merchant's Tale* takes the challenge even further by daring the audience to formulate a judgment; and since, according to the tale, we can only 'glympse' at truth, it comments as much on us as on January. It suggests that we often give credence to particular definitions of 'men' and 'women' (and to particular interpretations of reality) because those interpretations happen to complement our own fantasies.[46]

---

[46] Hansen writes, 'Characters and narrator alike are at once constituted and deconstructed by the misogynistic discourses that they use, and so again the *Merchant's Tale* reminds us that the fused problems of identity and writing cannot be divorced from the fundamental problems of gender difference and gender relations. No one escapes into the position of asexuality and nonrepresentability, here – except, more visibly than ever, perhaps, the Chaucer that modern criticism has nervously attempted to discern,' *Chaucer and the Fictions*, 266.

CHAPTER SIX

Competing Ideas: Chaucer's Clerks and Academic Disputes

> For alle oure sleightes
> we kan nat conclude

To venture into Chaucer's representation of the intellectual male is to run the risk of falling into a 'marle-pit,' because the topic raises so many questions. To speak of an intellectual or educated male model could take us in many directions. We could examine Chaucer's depiction and use of rhetorical and grammatical paradigms and theories, his borrowings from Classical, French, and Italian literatures, the *disputatio* form, mathematics, science, medicine, history, physiogamy, theology, philosophy, and so forth. Furthermore, it is difficult to know exactly how much education Chaucer himself had, and it is impossible to know exactly what versions of various intellectual debates were readily available to him.[1] Then, too, because of his penchant for irony, it is really quite impossible to establish what he seriously thought or concluded about the philosophical and theological debates of his own time. However, it is easy to see that he addresses some of the major intellectual questions of his day within the *Canterbury Tales*. Chaucer's contemporaries certainly thought he did. Thomas Usk considered Chaucer 'the noble philosophical poete in Englissh'; Eustace Deschamps compared him to Socrates; William Caxton called him a 'noble & grete philsopher'; and Thomas Hoccleve claimed he was a 'vniversel fadir in

---

[1] Edith Rickert, 'Chaucer at School,' *Modern Philology* 29 (1931-32): 257-74. See E. Rickert, 'Was Chaucer a Student at the Inner Temple,' in *The Manly Anniversary Studies in Language and Literature* (Chicago: University of Chicago Press, 1923), 20-31; R. W. V. Elliot, 'Chaucer's Reading,' in *Chaucer's Mind and Art*, ed. A. C. Cawley (Edinburgh and London: Oliver and Boyd, 1969), 46-68; J. A. W. Bennett, *Chaucer at Oxford and Cambridge* (Toronto: Oxford University Press, 1974); and George A. Plimpton, *The Education of Chaucer: Illustrated from the School Books in Use in his Time* (London: Oxford University Press, 1935). Source studies and influences of other writers and thinkers like Ovid, Boccaccio, Boethius, Dante, and others, suggest yet more to consider in appraising Chaucer's representations of learning. Cf. Marcia L. Colish, *The Mirror of Language: A Study in the Medieval Theory of Knowledge*, rev. ed. (Lincoln: University of Nebraska Press, 1983).

science' and was, of all the poets 'in oure tonge,' closest 'in philosophie to Aristotle.'[2]

Indeed, research into Chaucer's historical context demonstrates that men's scholastic and theological disputes were of considerable interest outside the University in the late fourteenth century. Scholars often drew up propositions, or theses, posted them publically, and invited all comers to an intellectual form of jousting. As a result of a greater exchange between the academic and non-academic worlds, which was occurring for a variety of reasons, philosophical disputes can be found surfacing quite frequently within secular literature.[3] As Hastings Rashdall observes, 'philosophy literally descended from the schools into the street.' This was, he maintains, to have quite an impact on the late medieval academic world because in the popularization of philosophy, the academic disputes began 'to come into contact with practical life.'[4] The intellectual world of the late fourteenth century formed an intricate mosaic of competing ideologies, including scholasticism, nominalism, realism, mysticism, lay piety, and emerging humanism. The power, the potential, and the limitations of human knowledge (defined as primarily men's knowledge) were hotly debated topics.[5] The *Canterbury Tales* also presents just such a mosaic, and competing philosophic perspectives dance within the text.

Traditional philosophy and theology were particularly challenged by the Oxford school, where Robert Grosseteste, Roger Bacon, and William Ockham raised new questions about the nature of authority, experience, experimentation, reason, individual responsibility (will), language, faith, and contingency which sparked considerable debate.[6] According to Gordon Leff, three challenges to traditional thought dominated philosophy in the fourteenth century. The first was an insistence on separating issues of faith and reason. The second challenge, growing out of the first, was that faith could not inform reason and reason could not illuminate faith. Knowledge of this world was to rest upon human reason and empirical evidence; knowledge of God was beyond human reason. Leff explains, '. . . fact became the touchstone; and to move beyond its boundaries was to enter the realm of speculation and leave certainty. Matters of belief, and God Himself, could not be a subject for reason, but for faith alone. To discuss them was to conjure up possibilities, not to assert the truth.'[7] Influenced by Grosseteste, Bacon maintained that induction, experimentation, and logic could reveal truths about the world when united with and tested against human

---

[2] See Caroline F. E. Spurgeon, *Five Hundred Years of Chaucer Criticism and Allusion*, 3 vols. (Cambridge: 1925), I: 8, 21, 22, 62; III: Appendix B, 16. Russell Peck, 'Chaucer and the Nominalist Questions,' *Speculum* 53 (1978): 745, n. 2. also notes that John Leland lauded him: '*hinc artus dialectus, hinc dulcin retor, hinc lepidus poeta, hinc gravis philosophus, hinc ingeniosus mathematicus . . . hinc clerique sanctus theologus,*' (Spurgeon III: Appendix A, 13).

[3] See Janet Coleman, *Medieval Readers and Writers, 1350–1400* (New York: Columbia University Press, 1981), 232.

[4] Hastings Rashdall, *The Universities of Europe in the Middle Ages*, 3 vols., ed. F. M. Powicke and A. B. Emden (1895; Oxford: Oxford University Press, 1936), III: 254.

[5] See Gordon Leff, *The Dissolution of the Medieval Outlook* (New York: New York University Press, 1976).

[6] See Gordon Leff, *Paris and Oxford Universities in the Thirteenth and Fourteenth Centuries: An Institutional and Intellectual History* (New York & London: John Wiley & Sons, 1968), 271–309.

[7] Leff, *Medieval Thought: St Augustine to Ockham* (Baltimore: Penguin, 1958; rpt 1965), 258–9.

experience: 'Reasoning draws a conclusion and makes us grant the conclusion, but it does not make the conclusion certain, nor does it remove doubt so that the mind may rest on the intuition of truth, unless the mind discovers it by way of experience. . . . For if a man who has never seen a fire should prove by adequate reasoning that fire burns and injures things and destroys them, his mind would not be satisfied thereby, nor would he avoid fire until he placed his hand or some combustible substance in the fire so that he might prove by experience that which reasoning taught. But when he has actual experience of combustion his mind is made certain and rests in the full light of truth.'[8] The third challenge to traditional thought came in a revival of the philosophical struggle between realism and nominalism, so that the relationship between subject and object, between universal and individual, between signifier and signified were scrutinized. For William Ockham, the proper object for intellectual study was no longer to be the platonic 'Idea,' that elusive and transcendent object beyond the senses; instead, it was to be an examination of the discrete individual. In his *Ordinatio* I, d.3, q.2, he writes: '. . . no one can naturally have an abstractive cognition of anything in itself unless he previously had an intuitive cognition of the same thing, since otherwise a man blind from birth could thus have an abstractive cognition of colors, just as anyone else can – which is obviously false.'[9] For him, the philosophical tradition which privileged the universal/ideal and devalued the individual/actual was upside-down and backwards; he regarded the notion that universals were real things as 'the worst error of philosophy.'[10] Instead, universals were less perfect than individuals because individuals could claim ontological validity, whereas universals could only claim logical validity within the limited knowing of the human mind. For Ockham, philosophy was the study of verbal and mental language constructs – names, semantic conveniences, and useful assumptions – that help us interact with a multifarious world full of discrete individuals. In other words, he and his followers recognized that philosophy and logic study the world through a veil of language. Because of that inevitable distortion, fundamental differences between all individuals prevent us from accurately knowing any individual in terms of another, so our knowledge of things remains analogical, metaphorical, or allegorical and hence, to some degree, inaccurate.[11]

The presence of these 'modern' challenges to traditional scholastic thought are felt within the *Canterbury Tales*, and this has been well-established by eminent Chaucerians. Russell Peck has examined connections between Ockham's thought and Chaucer's texts in his article, 'Chaucer and the Nominalist Questions'; Eugene Vance has investigated medieval sign theory in secular literature of the Middle Ages, including Chaucer's *Troilus and Criseyde*; J. D. Burnley and others have examined Chaucer's use of philosophical terminology; and Rodney Delasanta has discussed the dual influences of Nominalism and

---

[8] Roger Bacon, *Opus maius* V, II: 167–8, cited in Leff, *Paris and Oxford*, 287.

[9] Cited in Marilyn McCord Adams, *William Ockham*, 2 vols. (Notre Dame: Notre Dame University Press, 1987) I: 543.

[10] *Expositio in librum Perihermenias Aristotelis* I, Prooemium, cited in Adams, I: 13.

[11] For an introduction to Ockham's thought see Adams, *William Ockham* and Gorden Leff, *William Ockham: The Metamorphosis of Scholastic Discourse* (Manchester: Manchester University Press, 1965).

Boethian realism on Chaucer in his article, 'Chaucer and the Problem of the Universal.'[12] That the *Tales* reiterate the major challenges to realism raised by Ockham and his followers can be seen, for example, in Chaucer's frequent refusal of the ideal. As Donald Howard notes, even those characters traditionally assumed to be ideal such as the knight, the parson, and the clerk are 'obsolescent.' He claims that the *Canterbury Tales'* 'narrative "now" focuses upon actualities and puts ideals back into the blur of history. The ideals which stand immediately before us are false and unappealing – the burghers' ambitions, the Pardoner's avarice, the class-conscious and money-grubbing motives which energize most of the pilgrims.'[13] The *via moderna*, with its keen appreciation for empiricism, can also be seen in Chaucer's representation of Geoffrey, a man who records an experience of life 'in this world' which is overwhelmingly concerned with details and individuals. And consistent with the 'modern' skepticism of the Oxford school, Chaucer demonstrates that Geoffrey's interpretations are inadequate approximations of reality. Regardless of his reassurance to us that he speaks 'accordant to resoun,' that he controls his 'matere,' the *Tales* reveal otherwise. Rodney Delasanta argues that 'Chaucer's radical dependence on singulars experientially and intuitively apprehended necessarily transforms the omniscience of the traditional narrator into unreliability and produces a fiction that tilts narrator against narrator and tale against tale in a dialectical joust that seems to unhorse almost all the players and force the audience into a confrontation with the contingencies and relativities of truth-telling.'[14] This competitive form prevents any one perspective from controlling the game for long. The form of the *Tales* thus suggests a skepticism which questions the efficacy of human knowledge, particularly the power of one man to control others' perspectives or to possess truth.

As I have demonstrated in the previous chapter, January's epistemological blindness in the *Merchant's Tale*, his adherence to a false ideal in the face of reality, testifies to a common propensity of the human mind for illusion. In the same tale, May's speech on men's misperceptions is a good example of discourse which is double-edged with ironic content. Her words, warning of

[12] Russell Peck, 'Chaucer and the Nominalist Questions,' *Speculum* 53 (1978): 745–60; Eugene Vance, *Mervelous Signals* (Lincoln: University of Nebraska Press, 1986); J. D. Burnley, *Chaucer's Language and the Philosopher's Tradition* (Cambridge: D. S. Brewer, 1979) and his article, 'Chaucer's Termes,' *Yearbook of English Studies* 7 (1977): 53–67; Rodney Delasanta, 'Chaucer and the Problem of the Universal,' *Mediaevalia* 9 (1983): 145–63; See also Joerg O. Fichte, *Chaucer's Frame Tales: The Physical and Metaphysical* (Tubingen: Gunter Narr Verlag, 1987; Cambridge: D.S. Brewer, 1987); Robert B. Burlin, *Chaucerian Fiction* (Princeton: Princeton University Press, 1977); *Medieval English Religious and Ethical Literature: Essays in Honour of G. H. Russell*, eds. Gregory Kratzmann and James Simpson (Cambridge: D. S. Brewer, 1986); Joseph E. Grennen, 'Science and Poetry in Chaucer's *Hous of Fame*,' *Annuale Mediaevale* 8 (1967): 38–45; Walter Clyde Curry, *Chaucer and the Medieval Sciences*, rev. ed. (New York: Barnes and Noble, 1960); Geoffrey Shepherd, 'Religion and Philosophy in Chaucer,' in *Geoffrey Chaucer: Writers and Their Background*, ed. Derek Brewer (1974; Athens, Ohio: University of Ohio Press, 1975); and Winthrop Wetherbee, 'Some Intellectual Themes in Chaucer's Poetry,' in *Geoffrey Chaucer: A Collection of Original Articles*, ed. George Economou (New York: McGraw Hill, 1976), 75–91.
[13] Donald Howard, *The Idea of the Canterbury Tales* (Berkeley: University of California Press, 1976), 113.
[14] Delasanta, 'Chaucer and the Problem of the Universal,' 149.

deception, are meant simultaneously to deceive January, to convince him to disregard the reality of his visual experience. The prevalence of ambiguities in the *Tales*, the frequent road signs pointing us in several directions at once, attest to the influence of 'modern' thought (nominalism) on Chaucer.

Competing for ascendancy, traditional philosophic assumptions certainly have a voice in his text as well, for Chaucer also argues that 'the wordes moote be cosyn to the dede.'[15] In the *Canterbury Tales*, he directs our outrage toward characters and narrators who use words for personal profit and who are 'subtil clerks' of linguistic deception. The Pardoner is a good example of just such an 'horrific' distance between word and intent.[16] Drawing on the Platonic tradition via Boethius's *Consolation of Philosophy*, Chaucer's text also seems, at times, to long for a 'Former Age,' when word and meaning were one. In his poem, 'Lak of Stedfasteness,' he laments:

> Somtyme the world was so stedfast and stable
> That mannes word was obligacioun;
> And now it is so fals and deceivable
> That word and deed, as in conclusioun,
> Ben nothing lyk, for turned up-so-doun
> Is al this world for mede and wilfulnesse,
> That al is lost for lak of stedfastnesse . . .
> Trouthe is put doun, resoun is holden fable . . .   (1–7, 15)

Since Chaucer translated the *Consolation of Philosophy* we can reasonably assume, though not prove, that he was drawn toward the Platonic epistemology of universal 'Ideas' contained in that text, especially since he used it so frequently to illuminate the psychology of his characters and borrowed its philosophical vocabulary so extensively. Thus, reflecting historical context, the *Tales* not only incorporate nominalist perspectives, they also reiterate the thinking of contemporary realists like Thomas Bradwardine or John Wyclif, as well as the realism found in the 'Auctorities,' Boethius and Augustine.[17]

---

[15] Cf. P. B. Taylor, 'Chaucer's *Cosyn to the Dede*,' *Speculum* 57 (1982): 315–27.

[16] Cf. Carolyn Dinshaw's discussion of the Pardoner in her chapter, 'Eunuch Hermeneutics,' in *Chaucer's Sexual Poetics* (Madison: University of Wisconsin Press, 1989), 156–84. Dinshaw reads the fragmentation of body and language which pervades the Pardoner's prologue and tale as a confounding of realism, and she argues that this material forms a critique of 'patriarchal, androcentric discourse; he [the Pardoner] in fact shows the inadequacy of the very categories – masculine/feminine, letter/spirit, literal/figural – by which it proceeds' (160). Grounding her discussion in poetics, hermeneutics, and Lacanian psychology, Dinshaw can conclude that 'the Pardoner, not-man, not-woman, is the unlikely best pilgrim' to open and expose the limitations of binary thinking, and that his body and his speech suggest new possibilities, 'for in the ideal Christian society too, according to Saint Paul, "non est masculus neque femina" [Galatians 3:28]' (184).

[17] Since Wyclif was considered a saint and martyr by the Lollards, and since Chaucer associated with men known to be sympathetic to him (such as John of Gaunt, who was Wyclif's patron for a time), it is not surprising to find realism surfacing in Chaucer's text as well as nominalism. In his text, *De Universalibus*, Wyclif writes: 'That more universal goods are better than private goods is clear from this, that what is more universal is prior by nature to its inferior. The inferior is ordained for the maintenance of the universal, for it is something naturally prior, and a greater object of concern to God, that there should be human beings at all, than that there should be this particular man. . . .,' Wyclif, *De Universalibus*, trans. Anthony Kenny (Oxford: Clarendon,

The *Canterbury Tales* surely indicates a preference for realism in so far as it asks us to see beyond the literal to a transcendent meaning. At the end of the *Nun's Priest's Tale*, the narrator charges us to 'Taketh the moralite' of his fable – to 'Taketh the fruyt and lat the chaf be stille' (VII, 3440, 3443).[18] Notably, the Nun's Priest's Pertelote, with her 'modern' skepticism, her belief in the physical origins of dreams, and her corresponding disbelief in the revealed truth of Chaunticleer's vision, is proven wrong, for Chaunticleer's dream comes true. And yet, if we look at the same tale wanting to see its nominalist bias we can find it, for the tale simultaneously expresses the nominalist emphasis on empiricism. Chaunticleer's dream doesn't do him much good in the face of actual experience. He is still easily duped by the fox, and he must learn from experience, not revelation. In this way, the tale echoes Roger Bacon's assertion that a man cannot really know fire 'until he place[s] his hand . . . in the fire.'[19]

To the extent that Chaucer's text partakes of these serious philosophical issues and to the extent that it cites hundreds of male writers and thinkers, it promotes learning as a desirable endeavor. But besides the powerful scholastic influences in Chaucer's world, there were also forces afoot in the culture which resisted high-flying theory and the excesses of scholastic disputation. (Both realists and nominalists obviously carried on their debates using logical disputation and relying on human reason to promote their arguments.) Not surprisingly, objections to the presumptuousness of men's intellectual inquiry and quest for control surface in the *Tales*. Of course, the scholastic tradition had always met some resistance. Abelard had aroused the ire of St Bernard of Clairvaux back in the twelfth century. Bernard, ecstatic and ravished by divine Mystery, was perturbed with Abelard's theological philosophy because it addressed such problems as the sacraments, the trinity, and human ethics as intellectual riddles to be solved by human reason. In his letters he writes:

> Virtues and vices are discussed with no trace of moral feelings, the sacraments of the Church with no evidence of faith, the mystery of the Holy Trinity with no spirit of humility or sobriety: all is presented in a distorted form, introduced in a way different from the one we learned and are used to. The faith of simple people is ridiculed, divine mysteries simplified, and the deepest matters become the subject of undignified wrangling. Human acumen presumes to everything and leaves nothing for

1985), 175. Consequently, for him, truth exists in being, and being descends from God, the First Cause, down through a hierarchy of universals to every particular object. In Wyclif's words, 'God has within him the intellectual object which he looks to when he makes creatures.' See J. A. Robson, *Wyclif and the Oxford Schools* (Cambridge: Cambridge University Press, 1961), 152. See also, the more recent discussion of Wyclif and Chaucer in Peggy Knapp, *Chaucer and the Social Contest* (New York: Routledge, 1990), 63–94.

18 Following the lead of D. W. Robertson, Jr, Chaucerians have explored Augustinian and patristic readings of the *Canterbury Tales* extensively. See Robertson, *A Preface to Chaucer* (Princeton: Princeton University Press, 1962). Bernard S. Levy and George R. Adams demonstrate a Robertsonian reading of the *Nun's Priest's Tale* in their article, 'Chaunticleer's Paradise Lost and Regained,' *MS* 29 (1967): 178–92. Cf. E. Talbot Donaldson, 'Patristic Exegesis and the Criticism of Medieval Literature: The Opposition,' in *Speaking of Chaucer*, 134–53.

19 Roger Bacon, *Opus maius* V, II: 168, cited in Leff, *Paris and Oxford*, 287.

faith. All that cannot be illuminated with the help of reason is regarded as trivial, something which it is beneath one's dignity to believe in.[20]

St Bernard's objection to a dispassionate preference for human reason is reinforced by others, including Hugh of St Victor who registered criticisms of scholastic methodology in his *Eruditio Didascalica*:

> In grammar they talk about the construction of syllogisms, in logic the declensions of cases. And, which is even more ridiculous, when commenting on the title of a work they go right through its contents. The first word has hardly been dealt with after three lectures. This is not teaching, it is a demonstration of ostentatious learning. Notice the fallacy in this approach: the greater the number of irrelevant details that are introduced, the less it is possible to discern what is important and remember it.[21]

Although arguing from a different premise, John of Salisbury, an author known to Chaucer, lamented the way logical dexterity could become an end in itself, rather than a tool which could be useful to more important disciplines. In the *Metalogicon*, he writes:

> I do not assert this in order to attack logic . . . but to show that they who devote themselves entirely to it, not for ten or twenty years but for a whole lifetime, have failed in fact to acquire its principles. . . . logic is the only thing they talk about and occupy themselves with. It distracts attention from all other interests. Even as old men scholars like this are absorbed with youthful follies, they scrutinize every syllable they read or hear, even every letter. They turn everything into a problem, they never stop asking questions. Nevertheless they never achieve clarity, in the end they only talk without saying anything . . . . They compile every opinion, they quote and refer to the words and works of even the most trivial people because they have no opinions of their own. They cite everything as they cannot produce anything better themselves. The accumulations of opinions and contradictions are so large that not even their authors can keep track of them. The usefulness of logic is related to one's understanding in other areas. Nothing is easier for the specialist than talking about his own special field. It is more difficult to show the uses of one's knowledge. Any student of ethics can produce an abundance of moral rules as long as they are expressed in words. It is more difficult to demonstrate them through actions. In the same way, it is exceedingly easy to talk about definitions, arguments, and genera with one's colleagues. It is more difficult to show their usefulness in other fields of study.[22]

---

20 St Bernard, *Epistolae* (*PL* 182: cols. 355, 353).
21 Hugh of St Victor, *Eruditio didascalica* (*PL* 176, col. 769).
22 John of Salisbury, *Metalogicon* 2, 7, ed. C. C. J. Webb (London: 1932), 72–73. Cf. *The Metalogicon of John of Salisbury*, trans. Daniel O. McGarry (Berkeley: University of California Press, 1955), 88–89.

Similar objections were raised by writers, reformers, and philosophers living closer to Chaucer's own lifetime as well. Jean Gerson (1363–1429), chancellor of the University of Paris, criticized his faculty for focusing so much of their curriculum on the scholastics. In his treatise, *On Mystical Theology*, he defined the differences between what he saw as the scholastic tradition and what he saw as the preferable spiritual tradition. Scholastics, he says, study God via 'outward effects': Scripture, ecclesiastical history, and the writings of the Church Fathers. Mystical theologians, on the other hand, examine 'internal effects': namely, the 'evidence of divine presence in the recorded history and tradition of the heart.' Whereas mystics valued the emotional experience of faith and remained skeptical of human reasoning, scholastics trusted the intellect and devalued human emotion. The scholastic trusted reason to help him see the truth of God, and the mystic trusted the heart's knowledge of love to help him experience the love of God. Gerson also preferred the mystical way partly because it was much more accessible to the average Christian: 'even young girls and simple people [*ideotae*]' could attain an expertise in mysticism because love and personal experience, not a university education, were the only requirements.[23] Dionysian mysticism, evident in Nicholas of Cusa, Richard Rolle, Walter Hilton, Julian of Norwich and in the anonymous *The Cloud of Unknowing*, advocated a rejection of rational intellect: 'by a rejection of all knowledge, [one] possesses a knowledge that exceeds . . . understanding.'[24]

Traces of this position emerge within Chaucer's Custance whose 'herte' is a 'verray chambre of hoolynesse' (II, 167). She prays rather than debates with her enemies. When the Sultaness puts her out to sea in the rudderless boat, the text tells us:

> She blesseth hire, and with ful pitous voys
> Unto the croys of Crist thus seyde she:
> 'O cleere, o welful auter, hooly croys,
> Reed of the Lambes blood ful of pitee,
> That wessh the world fro the olde iniquitee,
> Me fro the feend and fro his clawes kepe,
> That day that I shal drenchen in the depe.

> 'Victorious tree, proteccioun of trewe,
> That oonly worthy were for to bere,
> The Kyng of Hevene with his woundes newe,
> The white Lamb, that hurt was with a spere,
> Flemere of feendes out of hym and here
> On which thy lymes feithfully extenden,
> Me kepe, and yif me myght my lyf t'amenden.'   (449–62)

---

23 Jean Gerson, *On Mystical Theology*, cited in Steve Ozment, *The Age of Reform, 1250–1550: An Intellectual and Religious History of Late Medieval and Reformation Europe* (New Haven: Yale University Press, 1980), 74.

24 See *Dionysius the Areopagite: On the Divine Names and The Mystical Theology*, trans. C. E. Rolt (London: 1966; New York: MacMillan, 1970), 194. For the influence on English mystics see Wolfgang Riehl, *The Middle English Mystics*, trans. Bernard Standring (London: Routledge & Kegan Paul, 1981), 7–10, 24–26 and David Knowles, *The English Mystical Tradition* (London: Burns & Oates, 1961).

She places her trust in prayer, not reason. Through faith, like Daniel who 'bar [God] in his herte' (476), she survives her ordeal and converts others. Custance preaches to the Britons, as women mystics in the late Middle Ages did: '. . . she gan oure lay declare / That she the constable, er that it was eve / Converteth, and on Crist made hym bileve' (572–74). And her influence reaches an entire nation: 'by Custances mediacioun, / The kyng – and many another in that place – / Converted was, thanked be Cristes grace!' (684–86). Similarly, the *Prioress's Tale* lauds a 'little clerk' who knows nothing of disputation but who has faith. In contrast to the teachers at his grammar school and the abbot, 'which that was an hooly man, / As monkes been – or elles oghte to be' (VII, 642–43), the child-martyr, through his perfect innocence, teaches others with his absolute faith and his miraculous visitation from the Virgin:

> And whan this abbot hadde this wonder seyn,
> His salte terris trikled doun as reyn,
> And gruf he fil al plat upon the grounde,
> And stille he lay as he had ben ybounde.   (673–76)

The primacy of faith also, of course, informs the *Second Nun's Tale* where Valerian's conversion demonstrates an epistemological process requiring the experience of a mystical vision and only subsequently an intellectual apprehension of truth. After Valerian seeks out St Urban, he has a vision of a divine presence:

> And with that word anon ther gan appeere,
> An oold man, clad in white clothes cleere,
> That hadde a book with lettre of gold in honde,
> And gan bifore Valerian to stonde.
>
> Valerian as deed fil doun for drede
> Whan he hym saugh, and he up hente hym tho,
> And on his book right thus he gan to rede:
> 'O Lord, o feith, o God, withouten mo,
> O Cristendom, and Fader of alle also,
> Aboven alle and over alle everywhere.'
> Thise wordes al with gold ywriten were.   (VIII, 200–10)

Only after the overwhelming power of vision has been experienced is the book read. The old man asks Valerian, 'Leevestow this thyng or no?' and Valerian answers, 'I leeve al this thyng.' 'Tho vanysshed the olde man, he nyste where' (211–16). In passages such as these, Chaucer's text acknowledges the mystical tradition in so far as it emphasizes the power of divine faith in the human heart, and it upholds the mystical tradition in so far as it celebrates the power of the innocent child and the female 'saint' to 'know,' exemplify, and communicate truth as well, or better than, men.[25]

---

[25] Wolfgang Riehl's study of *The Middle English Mystics* suggests that, at least occasionally, Chaucer may have borrowed from mystical writings for his philosophical bent. Riehl argues that such material was so much more immediate, popular, and accessible than patristic writings or university debates (35, 50–55, 180, 185–86).

But the mystics were not the only voices in the culture of the late Middle Ages criticizing the primacy of human logic advocated or practiced by the schoolmen. As one of the leading figures in the development of the *Devotio Moderna*, Geert Groote, too, articulated a challenge to the scholastics, arguing that logic was unable to meet the deepest of human needs. In the *Archief voor de Geschiedenis van het Aartsbisdom Utrecht*, he writes:

> Alas, how misguided are the young people today, that they, depending solely on the personal word of Aristotle or of another philosopher whom they personally esteem very highly, persuade and convince themselves of many opinions which they scarcely understand, or indeed even before they have penetrated to the heart of them – solely on account of the person who expresses them.
>
> . . .
>
> There is, however, another greater and more widespread hindrance – and this lies in philosophy itself – namely that apart from the first mentioned method of philosophizing, all students of philosophy, when concerning themselves with the essentials of things, their natures, quiddities, their matter and form, and their genera and species, do not direct their minds to reality but for the greater part only to the verbal expressions themselves. I must confess that I philosophized in this manner for a very long time.[26]

In England, Lollards and Wycliffites took a critical stance toward scholasticism for yet another reason: they argued against the privileged positions of clerks and clergy to read and interpret Scripture, and they objected to the power such privilege accords. Wyclif, in his *De Veritate*, defended a literal reading of Scripture against those who believed it could and should only be read and interpreted by Church officials. Church Fathers had, for centuries, encouraged clerical readers to penetrate beneath literal meaning to deeper figural truths, but, as G. R. Evans has found, Wyclif decried obscure and esoteric readings. He believed the Bible 'should be read in no combative spirit' and that one 'should look for *humilis et quieta concessio equivocacionis signorum*, rather than search for contradictions with which to prove that not all of Scripture is true.'[27] He was not impressed by the extensive academic debate over words: 'Word fights are more common among the moderns than they were among the ancients, as is clear from the questions and difficulties which nowadays mainly concern words.'[28] Lollards also defended the translation of the Bible into English for lay readers claiming, 'And to hem þat seien þat þe Gospel on Engliche wolde make men to erre, wyte wele þat we fynden in Latyne mo heretikes þan of all oþer langagis.' The Prologue to the Lollard Bible maintains that 'God both can and may, if it liketh him, speed simple men out of the university, as much to know

---

[26] Groote, *Archief voor de Geschiedenis van het Aartsibisdom Utrecht*, cited in Post, *The Modern Devotion: Confrontations with Reformation and Humanism* (Leiden: E. J. Brill, 1968), 163–64.

[27] G. R. Evans, 'Wyclif on Literal and Metaphorical,' in *From Ockham to Wyclif*, Studies in Church History, Subsidia 5, ed. Anne Hudson and Michael Wilks (Oxford: Basil Blackwell, 1987), 261. The entire volume edited by Hudson and Wilks is especially valuable.

[28] *De Universalibus*, trans. Kenny, 177.

holy writ, as masters in the university.'[29] In popular texts like *Jack Upland*, *Friar Daw's Reply*, and *Upland's Rejoiner*, we can read charges against Friars for hoarding books:

Frere, what charite is it to gadere vp þe bokis of Goddis lawe, many mo þanne nediþ ʒou, & putte hem in tresorie, & do prisone hem fro seculer preestis & curatis, wher bi þei ben letid of kunnynge of Goddis lawe to preche þe gospel freli?[30]

For Lollards and Wycliffites, reason and knowledge were not to be dismissed, but education (power through knowledge) was not to be elitist; it was not to be in the service of maintaining clerical domination of the secular world. In a passage reminiscent of Virginia Woolf's statements about Oxford in *A Room of One's Own*, one Wycliffite writes: 'Books filled with truth are manifold, but they have been imprisoned and chained up by the private religious in their communities . . . to such a point that poor clerks, . . . prevented from buying books by lack of money, . . . fear to take on the task of preaching.'[31]

In mysticism, lay piety, the *Devotio Moderna*, and periodically within the universities themselves, distrust of learning and scholasticism was expressed. As Heiko Oberman reminds us, fourteenth-century philosophical thought was not some simple academic dispute between nominalists and realists; instead, it included a plurality of forces.[32] Alongside very academic factions were groups which exhibited a growing skepticism about the efficacy of rigorous 'intellectualizing.' Oberman writes, 'The warning against *vana curiositas* and academic speculation gave weight and new authority to *experientia* – the experience of man and nature, of history and society, of daily life – which would soon put the validity of tradition to the test.' It was a period in which '*simplicitas*

---

[29] *The Holy Bible, in the earliest versions made from Latin Vulgate by John Wycliffe and his followers*, ed. Josiah Forshall and F. Madden (Oxford: University Press, 1850) I: 52. See also Anne Hudson, ed. *Selections from English Wycliffite Writings*, 67–72, 107–109 and K. B. McFarlane, *John Wycliffe and the Beginnings of English Nonconformity* (London: English Universities Press, 1952), 91.

[30] *Jack Upland*, 377–78. *Jack Upland, Friar Daw's Reply, and Upland's Rejoinder*, ed. P. L. Heyworth (London: Oxford University Press, 1968), 70. See also Richard H. and Mary A. Rouse, 'The Franciscans and Books: Lollard Accusations and the Franciscan Response,' in *From Ockham to Wylif*, 370.

[31] From the *Floretum* cited in Rouse and Rouse, 372. In *A Room of One's Own*, Virginia Woolf describes the Oxford University library as 'Venerable and calm, with all its treasures safe locked within its breast.' When she wants to use the library to look at Thackerey's manuscripts, she is turned away: 'I was actually at the door which leads into the library itself. I must have opened it, for instantly there issued, like a guardian angel barring the way with a flutter of black gown instead of white wings, a deprecating, silvery, kindly gentleman, who regretted in a low voice as he waved me back that ladies are only admitted to the library if accompanied by a Fellow of the College or furnished with a letter of introduction. . . . [I wondered] what effect poverty has on the mind; and what effect wealth has on the mind; . . . and I thought . . . of the shut doors of the library; and I thought how unpleasant it is to be locked out; and I thought how it is worse perhaps to be locked in . . .' *A Room of One's Own*, (London & New York: Harcourt Brace Jovanovich, 1929; 1957), 7–8, 24. See also 'Fifty Heresies and Error of the Friars,' a Wycliffite tract in *Select English Works of John Wyclif*, ed. T. Arnold (Oxford: Clarendon, 1869–71) III: 396–97.

[32] Heiko Oberman, 'Fourteenth-Century Religious Thought: A Premature Profile,' *Speculum* 53 (1978): 80–93.

and *experientia'* began to flourish.[33] Here, then, may be another source for Chaucer's emphasis on the power of experience. Nominalists were not the only ones in the late Middle Ages calling for the validation of individual experience, reformers and mystics were too.

Although I do not wish, in any way, to cast doubts upon the serious moral and philosophical content in the *Tales* derived from scholasticism, it seems to me that the serious philosophic voice sings a duet with a voice which finds human pretensions to knowledge, reason, and education entertaining at best. In the *Hous of Fame*, Chaucer discusses various theories about dreams and their origins. He concludes that we cannot conclude a truth from human reasoning:

> To my wyt, what causeth swevenes
> Eyther on morwes or on evenes;
> And why th'effect folweth of somme,
> And of somme hit shal never come;
> Why that is an avisioun
> And this a revelacioun,
> Why this a drem, why that a sweven,
> And noght to every man lyche even;
> Why this a fantome, why these oracles,
> I not; but whoso of these miracles
> The causes knoweth bet then I
> Devyne he; for I certeinly
> Ne kan hem noght, ne never thinke
> To besily my wyt to swinke,
> To knowe of hir signifiaunce
> The gendres, neyther the distaunce
> Of tymes of hem, ne the causes,
> Or why this more then that cause is . . .   (3–20)

But he trusts in the efficacy of his wonderful 'drem,' and it is a dream in which human writing and learning is 'fama,' and ephemeral. Skeptical of human learning, Geoffrey remains at the end of the poem a religiously simple man yearning for the vision of 'A man of gret auctorite' (2158). In the *Canterbury Tales*, too, Chaucer's Geoffrey does not present answers; he makes no overt attempt to resolve contradiction or paradox. As Russell Peck notes, Chaucer 'is not a logician, nor is he a systematic philosopher. . .'; he will raise questions 'and will leave the conclusions to the clerks (or rather the clerks to their conclusions).'[34] Such a refusal to assume control over meaning amounts to a rejection of the late medieval male intellectual ideal, because it refuses to play

---

[33] Oberman, 'Fourteenth-Century Religious Thought,' 93.

[34] Peck, 'Chaucer and the Nominalist Questions,' 745. Willi Erzgaber agrees: 'Although he [Chaucer] was familiar with the form of the "débat," which was popular in French literature at the close of the Middle Ages, he was not as intent on solving the contradictions as he was on awakening in the reader [or listener] an appreciation for the complexity of reality, of tradition in general and more specifically of the literary tradition,' ' "Auctorite" and "Experience" in Chaucer,' in *Intellectuals and Writers in Fourteenth-Century Europe*, The J. A. W. Bennett Memorial Lectures, Perugia, 1984 (Cambridge: D. S. Brewer, 1986), 72.

the competitive academic debate-games (at least by their rules). In this move, Chaucer refuses to align himself with the drive to control, the drive to be 'right,' so often seen in the competitive arenas of philosophical disputation.

If we examine particular representatives of that class of men whose profession involves a devotion to the mind, the clerks, Chaucer's ironic outlook is evident. Within the *Canterbury Tales*, the Clerk-narrator especially, represents one such example of the intellectual model, a man many Chaucer scholars have seen as an ideal image of learned medieval masculinity. But the *Canterbury Tales* is full of unambiguously negative clerkly images, as well. The Pardoner and the Summoner both identify themselves as clerks, hardly positive representatives of educated men (*PT* 391, *ST* 1794), and the Wife of Bath, in the autobiographical Prologue to her tale, gives us a scathing analysis of her husband, Jankyn, the clerk of Oxenford, who uses his education to brow-beat his wife. Jankyn so enjoyed the absolute and negative definitions of women found in his 'book of wikked wyves,' that he read them aloud to Alysoun 'every nyght and day' (see III, 669–87). His love for learned clerks who rail against women creates severe discord within his marriage. Alysoun, provoked by this 'clerkly' book, tears a page out in anger; Jankyn responds by beating her severely: 'he smoot me so that I was deef' (668), and 'with his fest he smoot me on the heed, / That in the floor I lay as I were deed' (795–96). Similarly adverse portraits of clerks occur in the *Miller's Tale* and the *Reeve's Tale*, where the Miller's Nicholas and Absolon and the Reeve's John and Aleyn are motivated by more sexual than intellectual desires (a common convention of fabliaux depictions of clerks). Although Nicholas uses his quick wit to deceive old John and 'swyve' Alysoun, his designing mind falls to impulse when he sticks his rear-end out the window without caution. In the *Miller's Tale*, as in many fabliaux, clerks are shown to be men whose education simply obscures the realities of their 'baser' physical desires. If Absolon's misplaced kiss allows the Miller to ridicule the code of courtly love, Nicholas's burned bum allows him to ridicule the scheming lecherous intellectual. Nicholas exposes himself and is branded for what, in some sense, the Miller thinks he really is: an ass.

The *Reeve's Tale* also offers quite a satiric challenge to clerkly pretensions as it demonstrates how easily the two young Cambridge men fall into the scheming designs of the old uneducated Miller. Wanting to steal part of the students' corn, the Miller makes sure the two young clerks spend the whole afternoon chasing their old horse around the neighborhood. When the Reeve's clerks do make use of their learning, they use it to justify rape. Borrowing from the legal language he knows, Alyen says:

> For, John . . . als evere moot I thryve,
> If that I may, yon wenche wil I swyve.
> Som esement has lawe yshapen us;
> For, John, ther is a lawe that says thus,
> That gif a man in a point be agreved,
> That in another he sal be releved.
> Oure corn is stoln, sothly, it is na nay,
> And we han had an il fit al this day;
> And syn I sal have neen amendement
> Agayn my los, I will have esement.   (I, 4177–86)

This clerkly reputation for sexual scheming surfaces again in the *Physician's Tale*, where Claudius, the 'false clerk,' conspires with Apius to steal Virginia from her father.[35] After listening to the story, the Host exclaims, 'Harrow . . . by nayles and by blood! / This was a fals clerk and a fals justise' (var. VI, 288–89). And yet again, it surfaces in the *Franklin's Tale*, where Aurelius's brother, an Orleans-educated man, enlists the aid of a 'subtil clerk,' a 'philosophre,' to help Aurelius deceive Dorigen:

> 'For with an apparence a clerk may make,
> To mannes sighte, that alle the rokkes blake
> Of Britaigne weren yvoyded everichon,
> And shippes by the brynke comen and gon,
> And in swich forme enduren a wowke or two.
> Thanne were my brother warisshed of his wo;
> Thanne moste she nedes holden hire biheste,
> Or elles he shal shame hire atte leeste.'   (V, 1157–64)

'In his studie, ther as his bookis be,' the two brothers are entertained by visions conjured up by the 'maister of magyk,' and after a sumptuous meal, the 'philosophre,' agrees to create a deception for Aurelius for an outrageous fee of a thousand pounds. His great 'jape' – called 'wrecchednesse' and 'supersticious cursedness' by the Franklin – is the creation of an illusion. And it is a momentary illusion at that: 'But thurgh his magik, for a wyke or tweye, / It semed that alle the rokkes were aweye' (1295–96). In this tale, learning serves lust, constructs fleeting illusions, and, perhaps even more ominously, negates human perception of God's creation. Dorigen, questioning God's goodness in placing the rocks along the sea coast, echoes scholastic debates about why God allows evil in the world. In lines 865–72, she cries:

> 'Eterne God, that thurgh thy purveiaunce
> Ledest the world by certein governaunce,
> In ydel, as men seyn, ye no thyng make.
> But, Lord, thise grisely feendly rokkes blake,
> That semen rather a foul confusion
> Of werk than any fair creacion
> Of swich a parfit wys God and a stable,
> Why han ye wroght this werk unresonable?'

In her desire to deny a part of creation she doesn't like or understand, she narcissistically sets herself up for the deceptions of the 'subtil clerk.' But the presence of this passage in the tale calls our attention to the fact that the philosopher, like the narcissist, is obscuring God's creation, hardly a

---

[35] As Robinson notes, 'The MSS. are divided between *cherl* and *clerk*' as the reading throughout the tale (p. 728). Interestingly, modern scholarly editions choose to identify Claudius as a 'cherl' rather than a 'clerk.'

positive image of human intellectual achievement.[36] Perhaps the most damning appraisal of human learning resides in the *Canon's Yeoman's Tale* where alchemy, that forefather of modern science, comes under fire: its pretenses to knowledge are accentuated in the Canon's false experiments, experiments which are designed to dupe the innocent and ignorant and which give the Canon profit. The allusions to hell, to Satan, and to damnation abound in the tale so that in this fiery laboratory, the Canon and the gullible Priest partake of evil. The Yeoman's narrative commentary woven throughout and around the tale stresses failure and loss. The Yeoman-narrator had, in fact, lost himself in the lure of such learning:

> With this Chanoun I dwelt seven yeer,
> And of his science am I never the neer.
> Al that I hadde I have lost therby,
> And, God woot, so hath many mo than I.
> Ther I was wont to be right fressh and gay
> Of clothyng and of oother good array,
> Now may I were an hose upon my heed;
> And wher my colour was bothe fressh and reed,
> Now is it wan and of a leden hewe –
> Whoso it useth, soore shal he rewe! –
> And of my swynk yet blered is myn ye.
> Lo! which avantage is to multiplie!
> That slidynge science hath me maad so bare
> That I have no good, wher that evere I fare;
> . . .
> Lat every man be war by me for evere!
> What maner man that casteth hym therto
> If he continue, I holde his thrift ydo.
> For so helpe me God, thereby shal he nat wynne,
> But empte his purs, and make his wittes thynne.
> And whan he, thurgh his madnesse and folye
> Hath lost his owene good thurgh jupartye,
> Thanne he exciteth oother folk therto,
> To lesen hir good, as he hymself hath do.   (VIII, 720–45)

Despite the appearance of knowledge (we 'semen wonder wise'), and despite a learned vocabulary ('Oure termes been so clergial and so queynte'), despite all their intricate manipulations and calculations, these clerks always fail: 'in oure werkyng no thyng us availle / For lost is al oure labour and travaille' (780–81).

---

[36] Note also the competitive relationship the clerk enters into with Aurelius and, indirectly, with Arveragus, when he decides to forgive Aurelius's debt. This act of generosity is not, apparently, motivated by genuine largesse, but rather by a desire to keep up with the gentility of the Knight and Squire: Just as Aurelius says to Dorigen, 'Thus kan a squier doon a gentil dede / As wel as kan a knyght,' so too, the magician-clerk addresses Aurelius:

> Thou art a squier, and he is a knyght;
> But God forbede, for his blisful myght,
> But if a clerk koude doon a gentil dede
> As wel as any of yow, it is no drede!   (1609–12)

Although the kind of learning being parodied and bitterly criticized is particularly despicable here, we have simply reached the end of a spectrum of 'academic' deception. Rather than conceal creation, as the Franklin's philosopher does, the Canon and his students would manipulate, distort, and alter creation in the *Canon's Yeoman's Tale*. No wonder the Yeoman warns:

> He that semeth the wiseste, by Jhesus!
> Is moost fool, whan it cometh to the preef;
> And he that semeth trewest is a theef.
> That shul ye knowe, er that I fro yow wende,
> By that I of my tale have maad an ende.   (967–71)

If these images of learned men suggest a satire, or at least a word of caution about the power of human learning to deceive us, the Clerk-narrator and his tale is far more problematic. Chaucerians have done all sorts of intellectual gymnastics around him and his tale; and no wonder: the narrative comments throughout the tale and the epilogue set us up for all kinds of disagreements. The Clerk himself suggests several ways of interpreting the text that take us in various (sometimes contradictory) directions.[37] At the end of his tale, he first invites us to read the tale of Walter and Griselde as evidence of a former age, more ideal and 'stronger' than our own. Read that way, the tale both admits to the ideal and regards it as obsolescent. Even if we follow this interpretation of the tale, it remains open and fraught with ambiguity. Are we to grieve the loss of a past world where word and deed were in accord, as represented in the character of Griselde? Or is the tale promoting her 'trouthe' for the present? Is the ideal attainable or unattainable? Are we to aspire to it, or are we to be disgusted by the degeneration of our present world so that we turn away from it? Then again, if the Clerk-narrator means to call our attention to the fiction of his tale – that such behavior does not exist in this world – he may be calling on us to see the fantasy of ideals, period. Thus, his tale may be as much a fantasy as the Wife of Bath's romance. Where her tale demonstrates the way fantasy can grow out of experience, his may illustrate that fantasy can also grow out of vicarious experience: reading. And the text even acknowledges the discrepancy between its fictional world and the actual world:

> Grisilde is deed, and eek hire pacience,
> And bothe atones buryed in Ytaille;
> For which I crie in open audience,
> No wedded man so hardy be t'assaille
> His wyves pacience in trust to fynde
> Grisildis, for in certein he shal faille.   (IV, 1177–82)

But the Clerk won't leave us there; he suggests another reading by asking us to become like Griselde: 'every wight, in his degree, / Sholde be constant in

---

[37] Cf. Wyclif on equivocation. As noted above, Wyclif argued with sophists who claimed to find contradictions in the Bible. He argued for the importance of evaluating the speaker's intention to determine meaning in *De Veritate Sacrae*, and he encouraged humility rather than combativeness as the appropriate stance for the reader of Scripture.

adversitee / As was Grisilde' (1145–47). Turning on the word 'degree,' this interpretation urges us to accept our lot in life (particularly our class standing) and endure suffering patiently. Of course, this somewhat 'realist' interpretation disregards gender distinction and makes Griselde into a universal representative of the human.

Reading further into the meaning of the text, our Clerk suggests a spiritual meaning for the narrative, as well:

> For, sith a womman was so pacient
> Unto a mortal man, wel moore us oghte
> Receyven al in gree that God us sent;
> For greet skile is, he preeve that he wroghte.
> But he ne tempteth no man that he boghte,
> As seith Seint Jame, if ye his pistel rede;
> He preeveth folk al day, it is no drede. (1149–55)

From this perspective, Griselde, still universal, represents the ideal relationship between the human soul and God. Scholars have so enjoyed glossing this that the tale becomes an allegory: Walter represents God and Griselde represents Christ or Job or the Human Soul. Or, is Walter the adversary, the Satan figure? If we interpret the tale allegorically, our interpretations may well get us into trouble, for the equations are slippery. Walter is hardly the God who 'allowed' Satan to test Job, nor is he the God who 'allowed' his son to be tempted and crucified. God always knew and trusted the faith of Job and Christ, whereas Walter continually tests Griselde precisely because he does not seem to know her 'trouthe.' As a grand experimenter, Walter resembles an empiricist more than an all-knowing divinity. Like a precursor to Alymer in Nathaniel Hawthorne's *The Birthmark*, Walter decides he will experiment on Griselde. On the other hand, Walter is hardly Satan either, for he seems to have an unwavering confidence in Griselde's responses. He knows he need not test her; rather, he knows she will endure. Perhaps he is testing the people of his realm rather than Griselde, since they do not really believe she is worthy even though they obviously stand to profit from her heritage. Even her father, Janicula, doubts the outcome of her marriage. No matter what kind of spiritual allegory we use to dress the tale, we have an uncomfortable fit.

Yet a third perspective on the tale emerges in the lines where the Clerk reassures us that God does not test us beyond our limits. In post-plague Europe, war-torn, and enduring the Great Schism, the tale may have its meaning in consolation; we are reassured that suffering can be endured, transcended, and we may, like Griselde, wind up with considerable reward. But then the particular threatens the universal, as the Clerk interprets Griselde as a rare and particular kind of female, not universal:

> But o word, lordynges, herkneth er I go:
> It were ful hard to fynde now-a-dayes
> In al a toun Grisildis thre or two;
> For if that they were put to swiche assayes,
> The gold of hem hath now so badde alayes

> With bras, that thogh the coyne be fair at ye,
> It wolde rather breste a-two than plye.   (1163–69)

For this reading, Griselde is specifically a female, and she is used to slap women in the face: none of them, he says, are anything like her. Furthermore, in examining Griselde from a gender-specific stance, note that the Clerk considers ways her perfection may endanger men, for he thinks it may perpetuate male fantasies about actual women, and Griselde is dead – she is not real! Directed toward men in the audience, the tale could thus carry a meaning similar to the *Merchant's Tale*: men must guard against their fantasies about women! Here, once more, 'woman' represents an epistemological challenge to men. The anti-feminist content also suggests that this tale has meaning as a response to the Wife of Bath; and in that regard, Griselde is a weapon for the Clerk to use against Dame Alysoun. Claiming to move away from 'ernestful matere' (into game?), the Clerk launches into a bitterly misogynist song that pretends to encourage women to rebel against the tyranny of their husbands, but which, like numerous passages in the *Roman de la Rose*, actually attacks women for their lack of submission to men instead:

> O noble wyves, ful of heigh prudence,
> Lat noon humylitee youre tonge naille,
> Ne lat no clerk have cause or diligence
> To write of yow a storie of swich mervaille
> As of Grisildis pacient and kynde,
> Lest Chichevache yow swelwe in hire entraille!
>
> Folweth Ekko, that holdeth no silence,
> But evere answereth at the countretaille.
> Beth nat bidaffed for youre innocence,
> But sharply taak on yow the governaille.
> Emprenteth wel this lessoun in youre mynde,
> For commune profit sith it may availle.   (1183–94)

Or we can reverse this reading and see the Clerk as a man who might side with the Wife, urging her to challenge male fantasies, for only then can there be hope for the goal they both desire: namely, to be the chosen vessel, the bride made new, the mortal translated beyond temporalities. The Clerk's ambiguous ending leaves us exactly where the Franklin left us at the end of his tale: asking questions rather than thinking we have answers.[38] As a technique, this ambiguity reaffirms Chaucer's refusal of definitive authority even over his own work. His Clerk-narrator has, perhaps in a parodic glance at schoolmen, given us several definitions of his *terme*: Griselde.[39] How she is to be defined is the interpretative question we are left with at the end of the tale. Chaucer's Clerk has performed

---

[38] See also the Franklin who ends his tale asking us which of his characters 'was mooste fre, as thynketh yow?' (V, 1621–22).

[39] Here, in the intellectual arena, woman becomes the ground for dispute, the object of inquiry and interpretation, and that which defies interpretation. For a twentieth-century version of this see Alice Jardine, *Gynesis: Configurations of Woman and Modernity* (Ithaca: Cornell University Press, 1985).

the clerkly activity of interpreting his term, his Griselde. Are we to see his several interpretations as a refusal of certainty and laud it, or are we to see in his various interpretations a humorous look at scholastic 'word fights'? If we grant the influence of the Lollards, of Wyclif, of lay piety on Chaucer, we must entertain the idea that the Clerk's multiple interpretations of his text function both as a refusal of certainty (hence a refusal of the scholarly intellectual model) and as yet another demonstration of the seductive powers of human learning. Or it may serve as an endorsement of plurality which empowers the downtrodden heart to seek fulfillment, despite the loss of generalities.

CHAPTER SEVEN

Spirituality and Competition

It is striking that of the major characters in the Canterbury narratives who can claim to imitate Christ, the majority are women, not men. If the essential features of Christ's life include effecting the spiritual transformation of others through words and works, advocating mercy rather than revenge, enduring severe suffering in the face of hostile temporal power and authority, and maintaining a steadfast faith in God and a purity of self, surely Custance, Griselde, Dame Prudence, and preeminently St Cecile exemplify many of these qualities. Penelope Curtis finds that, indeed, 'to a large extent the impulse toward radical Christianity in the *Tales* is narrowed to that of the alienate and disenfranchised soul, whose emblem is the pious woman.' She adds, 'One might even say that the second sex is used to provide models for a . . . metaphysic' of 'dispossession.'[1] Although the Prioress's little clerk exhibits faith and suffering and although he serves as the vessel for divine miracle, at seven years, he is an infantile representative of innocent Christian faith. Notably, he is surrounded and loved by three women: the Prioress, his mother, and the Virgin Mary. For the most part, male characters who appear within the pilgrim-narrator's tales do not exemplify Christ-like virtues. Theseus, it is true, forgives his enemies, but he embraces and represents the political and military power of secular authority; he cannot really be said to suffer in any way comparable to a Custance, a Griselde, or a St Cecile. In Chaucer's *Tale of Melibee*, the main male character, Melibeus, like Theseus, represents the governor who must be persuaded to forgive his enemies rather than retaliate against them. Dame Prudence is the one who uses words to persuade her husband to forgive others; she is the one who quietly and humbly assists peace; and she and her daughter, Sophia, are the ones who endure physical pain. In the *Second Nun's Tale*, St Urban, Valerian, Tiburce, and the men who are martyred for their faith represent some features of Christ, but they are subordinated to the tale's focus on St Cecile. When the pilgrims tell tales of men who are, by profession, spiritual representatives, they revel in satire rather than panegyric.

---

[1] Penelope Curtis, 'Some Discarnational Impulses in the *Canterbury Tales*,' in *Medieval English Religious and Ethical Literature: Essays in Honour of G. H. Russell*, ed. Gregory Kratzmann and James Simpson (Cambridge: D. S. Brewer, 1986), 136. Cf. Caroline Walker Bynum, *Fragmentation and Redemption* (New York: Zone, 1991).

Following in the well-established tradition of antifraternal satire, the *Canterbury Tales* depict 'men of God' as competitive and corrupt. The pilgrims' satiric portraits range from the Miller's affected Absolon and the Shipman's lecherous daun John to the Friar's fiendish summoner; from the Reeve's pretentious social-climbing priest and the Summoner's gluttonous, avaricious friar to the satanic Canon in the *Canon's Yeoman's Tale*. Within the Frame tale, too, the clergy are hardly represented favorably by Chaucer's Monk, Pardoner, Summoner, or Friar. Except for the Clerk, already discussed above, and the Parson, discussed later in this chapter, Chaucer shapes his clergical pilgrim-narrators into competitive men who use religion and their privileged positions within the culture to manipulate others, particularly the laity.[2] The Monk, for example, wears fur-trimmed sleeves, loves to eat (particularly fat swans), fastens his hood with a golden brooch just under his chin, wears 'souple' boots, and rides a palfrey, a horse Paul Beichner considers equivalent to 'the monastery's Cadillac.'[3] Contrary to his monastic vows, the Monk enjoys the things of this world. He is 'fair for the maistrie' and enjoys breaking beyond limits.[4] He is an 'outridere' who spurns the confining rules of his monastic order:

> He yaf nat of that text a pulled hen,
> That seith that hunters ben nat hooly men,
> . . .
> Therfore he was a prikasour aright:
> Grehoundes he hadde as swift as fowel in flight;
> Of prikyng and of huntyng for the hare
> Was al his lust, for no cost wolde he spare.   (I, 177–78; 189–92)

Instead of obedience, this monk exemplifies a desire for domination. He hunts and kills animals, thereby establishing his power over the natural world. He is master of his priory and is exempt from the rules which confine others, thereby establishing his power over other men. And, given the sexual innuendoes of the words describing his hunting, this Monk is, apparently, an active womanizer, a

---

[2] Since this antifraternal satire has been discussed at length in Chaucerian scholarship, only a brief discussion need be undertaken here. For a general introduction, see Jill Mann, *Chaucer and Medieval Estates Satire: The Literature of Social Classes and the 'General Prologue'* (Cambridge: Cambridge University Press, 1973), esp. 1–54, 137–51; Penn R. Szittya, *The Antifraternal Tradition in Medieval Literature* (Princeton: Princeton University Press, 1986), esp. 152–82, 183–246; and see G. R. Owst, *Literature and Pulpit in Medieval England* (New York: Barnes and Noble, 1966), 210–86 for a discussion of the antifraternalism common in fourteenth-century sermons.

[3] Paul E. Beichner, C.S.C., 'Daun Piers, Monk and Business Administrator,' in *Chaucer Criticism: The Canterbury Tales*, ed. Richard Schoeck and Jerome Taylor (Notre Dame: Notre Dame University Press, 1960), 60.

[4] Edmund Reiss suggests that the term 'maistrie' carries ironic content in Chaucer's description just as it did in Caxton's *Mirror of the World*. Reiss, quoting Caxton, writes, 'clerics want "to be called maistres for to be the more preysed and honoured." When they get this title, "they leue the clergye and take them to the wynnynge, lyke as marchants doo and brokers." Furthermore, many "haue the name of maistre, that knowe right lytil of good and reson," ' 'The Symbolic Surface of the *Canterbury Tales*: The Monk's Portrait,' Pt. I, *ChauR* 2 (1967–68): 256.

'prikasour aright.'[5] Fusing hunting imagery with sexual connotation, the passage establishes his sexual domination over women. The metaphor constructing him as a hunter of women (who are his prey) reveals what Richard F. Green has called the Monk's 'denial of women's essential humanity'; indeed, the metaphor resonates throughout the passage and thereby indicates the Monk's relationship to anyone or anything, regardless of gender.[6] His is a desire to have whatever he wishes, regardless of the rules. He obeys his own desires rather than any sacred vow he has made with God.[7]

The Pardoner is also a hunter of sorts, a man who uses words to ferret out money from the laity.[8] He keeps his weapon, his tongue, 'filed' so that like a stinger or an adder's fang he can strike at his audience:

> Of avarice and of swich cursednesse
> Is al my prechyng, for to make hem free
> To yeven hir pens, and namely unto me.
> For myn entente is nat but for to wynne,
> And nothyng for correccioun of synne.   (VI, 400–404)

He boastfully claims that he spits out his 'venym under hewe / Of hoolynesse,' not to benefit his audience in any way, 'but for coveityse' (421–22; 433). Preaching is a sort of camouflage he dons as he hunts for money. Donald Howard has commented on the Pardoner's remarkable 'capacity for dominating others,' which is driven by an 'avowedly rapacious motive.' His tale and his sermons are, according to Howard, a form of 'monstrous verbal rape.'[9]

Similarly, Friar Huberd uses words as agents to manipulate men and women. Geoffrey tells us in the *General Prologue* that 'In alle the ordres foure is noon that kan / So muchel of daliaunce and fair langage' (I, 210–11). Like the Pardoner, Huberd uses his 'power of confessioun' to extract money and sexual favors from the laity, and instead of ministering to the sick and destitute, he fraternizes with innkeepers, tapsters, and rich folks. He purposefully avoids the 'lazar' and the 'beggestere' (240–42):

> For unto swich a worthy man as he
> Acorded nat, as by his facultee,
> To have with sike lazars aqueyntaunce.
> It is nat honest, it may nat avaunce,

---

[5] For a discussion of the punning on words like 'prikasour' and 'venerie,' see Paul F. Baum, 'Chaucer's Puns,' *PMLA* 71 (1956): 242–46.

[6] Richard F. Green comments on the hunting metaphor in his article, 'Chaucer's victimized women,' *SAC* 10 (1988): 18.

[7] For more detailed discussions of the portrait, see Edmund Reiss, 'The Symbolic Surface of the *Canterbury Tales*: The Monk's Portrait,' Pt. I in *ChauR* 2 (1967–68): 254–72; Pt. II in *ChauR* 3 (1968–69): 12–28; Robert B. White, 'Chaucer's Daun Piers and the Rule of St Benedict: The Failure of an Ideal,' *JEGP* 70 (1971): 13–30; David E. Berndt, 'Monastic *acedia* and Chaucer's Characterization of Daun Piers,' *SP* 68 (1971): 435–50.

[8] Cf. Linda T. Holley, 'The Function of Language in Three Canterbury Churchmen,' *Parergon* 2 (1980): 36–44.

[9] Howard, *The Idea of the Canterbury Tales*, 347. See also Robert P. Miller, 'Chaucer's Pardoner: the Scriptural Eunuch and the *Pardoner's Tale*,' *Speculum* 30 (1955): 180–99.

> For to deelen with no swich poraille,
> But al with riche and selleres of vitaille.
> And over al, ther as profit sholde arise,
> Curteis he was and lowely of servyse.[10]   (243-50)

The Summoner, too, hunts people, but he intimidates them with his grotesque appearance and his ecclesiastical power rather than with rhetorical skills, for he is not especially eloquent:

> A fewe termes hadde he, two or thre,
> That he had lerned out of som decree –
> No wonder is, he herde it al the day;
> And eek ye knowen wel how that a jay
> Kan clepen 'Watte' as wel as kan the pope.
> But whoso koude in oother thyng hym grope,
> Thanne hadde he spent al his philosophie;
> Ay '*Questio quid iuris*' wolde he crie.   (639-46)

The Summoner drinks heavily (635-38; 649), and like his adversary, the Friar, he dallies with women (652; 663-65), but most abominably, like both the Friar and the Pardoner, he grants people absolution for their sins in exchange for money and cares little about the condition of their souls (646-58).

Since each arm of the Church needed the economic support of the laity, it is little wonder that competitive relationships blossomed within the *ecclesia*. This clergical competition emerges in the *Canterbury Tales* where it reaches a dramatic apex in the vicious confrontation between the Summoner and the Friar who, like the Miller and the Reeve in the First Fragment, snarl at and verbally assault one another.[11] The Summoner begins the match by calling the Friar meddlesome and by trying to turn the pilgrims against him: 'Lo, goode men, a flye and eek a frere / Wol falle in every dyssh and eek mateere' (III, 835-36). The Friar responds to this name-calling by threatening to tell a tale on the Summoner. The dynamic between these two 'men of God' is one of vengeance and competition, not Christ-like forgiveness and acceptance, so it is hardly surprising that the Summoner vows to tell a tale on the Friar. True to form, as soon as he can, the Friar commences with his 'vileyns word.' Several times over the course of the two tales and their links, Harry Bailly intervenes, attempting to restore order between the two clergymen, but without success. At first he commands, 'Pees! and that anon!' (850). As the animosity breaks out between the two of them again in the Prologue to the *Friar's Tale*, Harry pleads with the Friar:

> . . . 'A! sire, ye sholde be hende
> And curteys, as a man of youre estaat;

---

[10] For an examination of the historical context which gives rise to this kind of portrait, see Thomas Hahn and Richard W. Kaueper, 'Text and Context: Chaucer's *Friar's Tale*,' *SAC* 5 (1983): 67-101.

[11] See Paul E. Beichner, C.S.C., 'Baiting the Summoner,' *MLQ* 22 (1961): 367-76.

> In compaignye we wol have no debaat.
> Telleth youre tale, and lat the Sumonour be.'   (1286–89)

However, the Summoner, eager for the fight, tells Harry to leave the Friar be: 'lat hym seye to me / What so hym list; whan it comth to my lot, / By God! I shal hym quiten every grot' (1290–92). Eventually, Harry is so fed up with the rankling that he even encourages the Friar's viciousness: 'Now telleth forth, thogh that the Somonour gale; / Ne spareth nat, myn owene maister deere' (1336–37). The hunting metaphor – found in Chaucer's portraits of the Monk and Pardoner – surfaces most prominently here as the Friar-narrator deploys it to describe the despicable summoner's desire for control over others:

> This false theef, this somonour, quod the Frere,
> Hadde alwey bawdes redy to his hond,
> As any hauk to lure in Engelond,
> That tolde hym al the secree that they knewe;
> For hire acqueyntance was nat come of newe.
> They weren his approwours prively.
> He took hymself a greet profit therby;
> His maister knew nat alwey what he wan.   (1338–45)

And a bit later in the narrative, the Friar says:

> For in this world nys dogge for the bowe
> That kan an hurt deer from an hool yknowe
> Bet than this somnour knew a sly lecchour,
> Or an avowtier, or a paramour.   (1369–72)

As Janette Richardson has noted, the hunting image 'is the only one in the narrative: all the formal figures of speech depict various kinds of hunters and their prey.'[12] This man, 'evere waityng on his pray,' seeks to control the laity for profit and deceives, or avoids the law of, his superior by withholding money from the archdeacon. Asserting power over women as he wants, he sets himself up even as a pimp in order to extort money from men who are lured into a prostitute's trap. Like the Pardoner, he is anxious 'to wynne' the most money at his 'pley.' But the hunting metaphor takes on a far more sinister connotation in this tale as it gradually reveals the satanic identity of the yeoman dressed in green whom the summoner meets and invites to share in his schemes. In the narrative, the two false 'bailiffs' swear 'to be trewe brother[s]' to each other,

---

[12] Janette Richardson, *Blameth Nat Me: A Study of Imagery in Chaucer's Fabliaux* (The Hague: Mouton, 1970), 75. The homonyms 'pray' (verb), 'prey' (verb), and 'prey' (noun) highlight the significance of rhetorical location. Without specific location, the words dance with playful and potential meanings; with specific rhetorical location, the words acquire meaning so that we understand the Summoner preys on the laity's need to pray, and the devil, in turn, preys upon the Summoner who himself becomes prey. The potentiality of language simultaneously destabilizes (or multiplies meaning) and highlights the importance of rhetorical context to communicate meaning.

but, of course, this pact with the devil backfires on the summoner.[13] Blind to the trap the devil is setting for him, the summoner simply looks for ways he can use the fellow in green for greater profit. Earle Birney comments: 'his deafness to all warnings, his assumptions of his own invulnerability, his very indifference to the subject of souls, of his own soul above all, predetermines his loss of it.'[14] The successful hunter in the tale is, ultimately, the devil who winds up packing the summoner off to hell, promising him, 'Thou shalt with me to helle yet tonyght, / Where thou shalt knowen of oure privetee / Moore than a maister of dyvynytee' (1636–38). The Friar-narrator concludes his tale with a moral, warning the pilgrims to avoid predatory animals such as devils and summoners, for 'The leoun sit in his awayt alway / To sle the innocent, if that he may' (1657–58).

The Summoner-narrator, in a vengeful gesture, begins his tale by immediately quiting the conclusion of the *Friar's Tale*. If the Friar places summoners in hell, the Summoner-narrator will do one better by placing friars in the most grotesque place in hell – under the devil's tale:

> Right so as bees out swarmen from an hyve,
> Out of the develes ers ther gonne dryve
> Twenty thousand freres on a route,
> And thurghout helle swarmed al aboute,
> And comen agayn as faste as they may gon,
> And in his ers they crepten everychon.
> He clapte his tayl agayn and lay ful stille. (1693–99)

If the Friar claims the summoner and the devil 'wente / Where as that somonours han hir heritage' (1640–41), the Summoner will claim that the friar 'for fere yet he quook, / So was the develes ers ay in his mynde, / That is his heritage of verray kynde' (1704–06). In this spiteful 'game' of an eye for an eye, where the Summoner had interrupted the Friar's story to protest against his attack on summoners (1332–33), the Friar will respond by interrupting the Summoner to protest against his accusations: ''Nay ther thou lixt, thou Somonour!,' quod the Frere' (1761). Once again, Harry Bailly intervenes on behalf of peaceful contest, but winds up encouraging the Summoner this time, saying, 'Tel forth thy tale, and spare it nat at al' (1763). Needless to say, the Summoner obliges him. His tale reveals the gluttonous and avaricious nature of a 'false frere' whose motive for preaching is pecuniary gain rather than spiritual healing.

---

[13] The pact between the clergyman and the devil is a common story in folklore and sermon. G. R. Owst, in his text, *Literature and Pulpit in Medieval England*, reports that sermons frequently made use of 'The Devil's Letter,' as a way to attack the *prelati*. In this letter, 'the Prince of Darkness greeted the Princes of the Church as his friends, in acknowledgement of the many souls which they were continually dispatching to him' (242–43). Chaucer's contemporary, John Bromyard, frequently compared prelates and devils. In one sermon, he writes that the clergy 'appear to have made a compact and indenture between them and the demons, to the effect that they themselves should have the wool and milk of their sheep [the laity], that is, the temporal benefits, and that the devils should have the souls of them,' Owst, 261–62.

[14] Earle Birney, ' "After His Ymage": The Central Ironies of the *Friar's Tale*,' *Mediaeval Studies* 21 (1959); rpt in his *Essays on Chaucerian Irony*, ed. Beryl Rowland (Toronto: University of Toronto Press, 1985), 98.

Instead of advocating a genuine and heart-felt spirituality among the laity, this friar 'served hem with nyfles and with fables' (1760).[15] He even admits that his preaching is false when he tells Thomas that he 'seyd a sermon after my symple wit, / Nat al after the texte of hooly writ,' adding insult to injury by assuming that the Bible would be far too difficult for laymen like Thomas to understand: 'For it is hard to yow, as I suppose, / And therfore wol I teche yow al the glose' (1791–92). This pride in his own manipulative sales pitch makes him blind to Thomas's 'odious meschief.' His greed and his over-confidence are repaid by a fart. The friar, thinking the bed-ridden Thomas has been convinced to give his gold to the friar's convent, easily falls for the sick man's ruse:

> 'Now thanne, put in thyn hand doun by my bak,'
> Seyde this man, 'and grope wel bihynde.
> Bynethe my buttok there shaltow fynde
> A thyng that I have hyd in pryvetee.'
> 'A!' thoughte this frere, 'that shal go with me!'
> And doun his hand he launcheth to the clifte,
> In hope for to fynde there a yifte.
> And whan this sike man felte this frere
> Aboute his tuwel grope there and heere,
> Amydde his hand he leet the frere a fart,
> Ther nys no capul, drawynge in a cart,
> That myghte have lete a fart of swich a soun.   (2140–2151)

If the *Friar's Tale* begins by detailing the duplicitous designs of summoners and then ascribes a damnable consequence to those actions, the *Summoner's Tale* begins by detailing the damnable nature of friars and then illustrates how that nature, consequently, emerges in duplicitous designs. The geography of the two tales places hell at the center: the *Friar's Tale* begins with sinful actions set in this world and moves to hell, and the *Summoner's Tale* begins with a vision of hell and then moves to a depiction of hellish behavior on earth. Repeated structures, patterns, and meanings in the two tales suggest that these two clergymen and their tales provide mirrors for one another, but both pilgrims are far too set on competing with one another to see the truths about themselves in the mirror of their dialogue and in the images of their narratives.[16] Both tales establish an interface between hell and false friendships, between Satan and false ministry, weaving the clergical characters and their clergical narrators into a demonic tapestry.

The disparity between the ideal and the actual practice of the clergy had long been decried in song, sermon, treatise, and story. Chaucer's contrast between the degraded motives of his spiritual professionals and the ideal of Christian ministry is but one voice in a chorus of voices heard quite prominently in late fourteenth-century England. The Dominican, John Bromyard, for example, attacked the economic motivations of the clergy, objecting to their concern for

---

[15] Cf. John V. Fleming, 'The Antifraternalism of the *Summoner's Tale*,' *JEGP* 65 (1966): 688–700.

[16] Janette Richardson discusses the repetitions and parallels in the two tales in 'Friar and Summoner: The Art of Balance,' *ChauR* 9 (1974–75): 227–36.

nurturing their treasuries more than human souls: 'So many pecuniary Bulls and excommunications of those stealing temporalities show them to be lovers of moneys; and so many dissimulations of the sins committed against God's Commandments show them to be neglectors of souls.'[17] And because of the clergy's hypocritical materialism and sensuality, he complains:

Foxy they may be called, because, as it is told of the fox in the fable that he lay down in the road and pretended to be dead, so that he might be put into the cart and eat the poultry which it was carrying, . . . so the hypocrites pretend to be modest, humble, compliant and dead, as it were, to all vices and sins, especially in the eyes of those who can assist them further to the thing they are panting after, in order that they may be set in offices and promoted. . . . [and because of their lust, the people say,] 'Why should I give tithe to a rector who keeps a concubine; and why should I help a church in which all the ministers are polluted?', or 'How should I lead a clean life when I have so many foul examples before me?' . . . It would be better that the Church should have no minister at all, than such an one who defiles his flock and the Church's status, violates Christianity and leaves the community desolate with sin and vengeance. . . . 'Woe, woe upon my sanctuary, because it is profaned!'[18]

If Bromyard complained of the clergy's inadequacy, Lollards and Wycliffites levelled even greater accusations at the Church.[19] Wyclif, and at least some of his followers, believed the institutional Church, itself, was illegitimate. Wyclif went beyond antifraternalism to a radical anticlericalism.[20] He denied the authority of the existing institutional ecclesia, the 'visible Church,' and looked to the Bible to formulate a new conception of the true Church. Arguing in his *De Potestate Pape* that the king should have control over the priesthood (rather than bishops, cardinals, and popes), he denounced Papal authority. He even claimed the Pope was an embodiment of the Antichrist in his *De Antichristo*.[21] His thoughts on predestination were also a challenge to the Church, for he believed that the true Church, the 'invisible Church,' consisted of those individuals who had been chosen by God to be part of the elect. Regardless of words or works, God's design determined individuals' ultimate fate.[22] Because the elect could not

17 Cited in Owst, *Literature and Pulpit*, 249.
18 Cited in Owst, *Literature and Pulpit*, 257, 259.
19 For a discussion of Wyclif's ideas see Gordon Leff, *Heresy in the Later Middle Ages: The Relation of Heterodoxy to Dissent, c. 1250–c.1450*, 2 vols. (Manchester: Manchester University Press, 1967; New York: Barnes and Noble, 1967) II: 516–93; MacFarlane, *Wycliffe*, 91–93; Workman, *John Wyclif* II: 3–118; Sittya, *Antifraternal Tradition*, 152–82.
20 Penn Sittya writes that 'after FitzRalph, [Wyclif] must be reckoned the most prolific antifraternal writer of medieval England,' *Antifraternal Tradition*, 152–53.
21 Gordon Leff, *Heresy* II: 519. See also Michael Wilks, 'Royal Patronage and Anti-Papalism,' in *From Ockham to Wyclif*, ed. Anne Hudson and Michael Wilks (Oxford: Basil Blackwell, 1978), 150–63; and Thomas Renna, 'Wyclif's Attack on the Monks,' also in *From Ockham to Wyclif*, 267–80.
22 Leff documents this with a passage from *De Ecclesia*: '*sicut gratia pres cili secundum presentem iustitiam repugnat dampnationi, licet aggregatum ex illa gratia et prescientia inferat necessario dampnationem*,' cited in *Heresy* II: 518, n. 7. See also J. A. Robson, *Wyclif and the Oxford Schools* (Cambridge: Cambridge University Press, 1961), 179–80, 200–07.

be known or recognized, neither those chosen for heaven nor those chosen for damnation could know their status. This insistence on human ignorance wrecked havoc with the established Church. As Gordon Leff describes it:

> If only those who were chosen by God belonged to the Church, and they could not be known, there was no reason for accepting any visible authority or for recognizing the claims of those who exercised it. Even more, there was no reason for such authority at all: if those who were predestined to glory remained of the elect, regardless of temporal vicissitudes, nothing could further or detract from their final destiny. And likewise for the damned. The Church in its traditional form therefore lost its *raison d'être*.[23]

Furthermore, Wyclif refused to acknowledge the authority of anyone in the Church, from Pope to lowly mendicant, who did not abjure material goods. He argued against the efficacy and the spiritual authority of the contemporary ecclesiastical institution because it had abandoned poverty, and he believed avarice was the worst heresy of all for the clergy to commit.[24] Throughout his career, Wyclif censored the Church for its economic and political privileges – and any history of the Church in the late Middle Ages can attest to the kinds of abuses Wyclif decried. The Great Schism, alone, offers an historical instance of two 'men of God' who acted somewhat like Chaucer's Friar and Summoner, each denouncing the other's legitimacy for economic and political gain.

Whatever Chaucer may have thought of the institutional legitimacy of the Church, he shared a world where voices like Bromyard's and Wyclif's condemned ecclesiastical abuses and raised challenges to the Church's power. But if Chaucer's text rejects the abuses of the clergy, it does not reject the ideal of Christian masculinity nor does it reject responsible ministry. His pointed antifraternal satire only condemns deviation from the 'wey' of Christ. By contrast, when the *Canterbury Tales* satirizes courtly love, it does so to reject the ideal of the knightly lover worshiping women and subjecting himself to passion; but when the text satirizes the clergy, it does so to correct imperfect practices. Chaucer's satire on the lover makes fun of the courtly love paradigm; his satire on 'men of God' only makes fun of the disparity between men's practice and the paradigm of Christian masculinity. The paradigm itself is affirmed in the *Canterbury Tales*, though it is most frequently dramatized by the text's 'saintly' female characters. There are, however, two adult male pilgrims in the *Canterbury Tales* who are quite explicitly drawn on a model of Christian masculinity: the Parson and his brother, the Plowman.

In the *General Prologue*, the Plowman is described as a man who would give of himself. He is not interested in economic gain and does not set aside money for his own wealth. Unlike so many other characters included in the *Canterbury Tales*, the Plowman pays his tithe 'ful faire and wel' (I, 539). His relationship to his community is one of self-sacrifice and service, and unlike the much-lauded Knight-narrator who 'loved chivalrie, trouthe and honour, fredom and curteisie'

[23] Leff, *Heresy*, II: 519.
[24] *Ibid.*, II: 528.

(45–46), the Plowman loved 'God . . . best with al his hoole herte' (533). He is a man who obeys the commandment reiterated in Matthew to love God and to love others:[25]

> A trewe swynkere and a good was he,
> Lyvynge in pees and parfit charitee.
> God loved he best with al his hoole herte
> At alle tymes, thogh him gamed or smerte,
> And thanne his neighebor right as hymselve.
> He wolde thresshe, and therto dyke and delve,
> For Cristes sake, for every povre wight,
> Withouten hire, if it lay in his myght.   (I, 536–38)

The Plowman has an awakened spiritual relationship with God, and his labor benefits the entire community, not just himself; his Christ-like charity brings peace to his community. According to Joe Horrell, he exemplifies the kind of charity Aquinas praised when he wrote, 'charity causes peace precisely because it is a love of God and of our neighbor, . . . there is no other virtue except charity whose proper act is peace.'[26] Chaucer's Plowman is obviously literarily related to Langland's Piers Plowman, a common laborer who, within William's dream, merges into Christ. However, Langland's Plowman suffers, endures oppression, and because of this, speaks out against the abuses of the Age, while Chaucer gives us an ideal portrait of a happy farmer, a plowman whose voice is never heard on the pilgrimage.[27] His silence in the *Tales* is noteworthy, since class struggles of the late fourteenth century were often articulated in texts featuring a plowman. Lee Patterson reads this 'psychologically opaque' and 'socially quiescent' character as a 'comforting representative of the third estate' (comforting, that is, to higher estates) 'especially at a time when many of his peers were far from being so . . . docile.' Patterson argues that the Plowman's portrait 'effaces the very real economic struggles of Chaucer's contemporary world.' Consequently, the Plowman's generosity, obedience, and silence may be Christ-like, but his portrait also registers class anxiety.[28] His lower class status, overshadowing his masculinity, serves to silence him so that he takes on a 'feminized' position within the narrative as a whole, a silent, Griselda-like role.

The Plowman's brother, the Parson, is the only clergical representative dramatized in the *Tales* who can be said to imitate Christ. Unlike the other 'priests' in the text who are 'hunters,' the Parson is a 'shepherde.' He is not ambitious to gain power in the world, nor is he anxious to gain wealth or recognition:

---

[25] See Matthew 22:40.

[26] Aquinas, *Summa Theologica* II–II, 4, c, 3 cited in Joe Horrell, 'Chaucer's Symbolic Plowman,' *Speculum* 14 (1939); rpt in *Chaucer Criticism*, ed. Schoeck and Taylor, 95.

[27] See Mann, *Chaucer and Medieval Estates Satire*, 68–73.

[28] Patterson, *Chaucer and the Subject of History* (Madison: University of Wisconsin Press, 1991), 31. Other texts incorporating the plowman as a voice of class struggle (besides *Piers Plowman*), include *The Plowman's Tale*, *The Praier and Complaynte of the Ploweman*, and *Peirce the Plowman's Crede*. See Anne Hudson, 'The Legacy of *Piers Plowman*,' in *A Companion to Piers Plowman*, ed. John A. Alford (Berkeley: University of California Press, 1988), 251–66.

> He sette nat his benefice to hyre
> And leet his sheep encombred in the myre
> And ran to Londoun unto Seinte Poules
> To seken hym a chaunterie for soules,
> Or with a bretherhed to been withholde;
> But dwelte at hoom, and kepte wel his folde,
> So that the wolf ne made it nat myscarie;
> He was a shepherde and noght a mercenarie.   (507–14)

This Parson 'koude in litel thyng have suffisaunce,' and gives unselfishly to his parishioners when they are in need (486–90).[29] This 'povre' man of God is 'riche' in 'hooly thought and werk,' and, unlike the false preachers in the company, he 'trewely wolde preche' (478–81). Even though he has knowledge of the Gospel, his learning does not make him contemptuous of sinners. His manner, according to Geoffrey, is not aggressive; he does not threaten or verbally assault his parishioners:

> And though he hooly were and vertuous,
> He was to synful men nat despitous,
> Ne of his speche daungerous ne digne,
> But in his techyng discreet and benygne.
> To drawen folk to hevene by fairnesse,
> By good ensample, this was his bisynesse.   (515–20)

Given Chaucer's penchant for irony, it seems reasonable to ask whether or not this portrait of an ideal parson is realized in the drama of the *Tales*. Donald Howard suggests not. Although he sees the Parson in the General Prologue as 'a 'figural' priest who stands for the idea of priesthood' and although he reads the *Parson's Tale* seriously, Howard still suggests some subtle discrepancies between the portrait and the Parson-narrator. In the Prologue, Geoffrey emphasizes the Parson's gentle, self-sacrificing, patient, and charitable self, but, Howard maintains, in the course of the pilgrimage, the Parson seems 'astringent' and 'rigid.' 'We catch only . . . [his] tendency to chide and reprimand':

> We never see him in a kindly or charitable act and do not get an impression of his patient or 'benign' qualities. . . . we never see him do or say anything kindly – he doesn't intervene when harsh words and insults are exchanged; leaves it for the Knight to make peace at the end of the Pardoner's tale; is silent over the abusive treatment which the Friar and the Summoner get at each other's hands; and is not in the picture at all when the Cook falls from his horse and is publicly humiliated.[30]

---

[29] Mann notes (*Chaucer and Medieval Estates Satire*, 235, n. 16) that 'Chaucer's phrasing in line 486 may well come from Wyclif, who twice, in his frequent condemnation of "cursynge for tithes," uses these actual words,' *Medieval Estates*, 59. Mann cites as evidence Wyclif's *De Officio Pastorali*.

[30] Howard, *Idea*, 377–79.

Although this observation raises interesting questions about Chaucer's decision, intentional or not, to keep the Parson apart from the activities of the other pilgrims, is Howard's assessment fair? Since the text does not tell us why the Parson refrains from involvement in the various disputes during the pilgrimage, we could easily see in his silence an indication of wisdom rather than neglect. Although the altercations between the various men are tense, none are life-threatening and none erupt into physical combat. The tiffs between the pilgrims do not demand interference, except to encourage the continuation of the game of fables, a game the Parson may see as flippantly loquacious in the setting of pious pilgrimage. Then, too, if our Parson is silent in the midst of the arguing between Summoner and Friar, perhaps it is because he deems their mutual punishments appropriate, or perhaps Chaucer doesn't want to associate him with this competitive and hostile arena. The same could be said for his silence about the Cook's inebriated fall. Then again, we might also see his silence as restraint, as obedience to Harry Bailly's governance, at least until it is his turn to speak. When Howard suggests that the Parson is 'rigid' and exhibits an 'astringent, chiding quality,' he cites the epilogue to the *Man of Law's Tale* as evidence.[31] The Host invites the Parson to tell a tale, and in typical Harry Bailly fashion, he sprinkles his invitation with swear words:

> . . . 'Goode men, herkeneth everych on!
> This was a thrifty tale for the nones!
> Sir Parisshe Prest,' quod he, 'for Goddes bones,
> Telle us a tale, as was thi forward yore.
> I se wel that ye lerned men in lore
> Can moche good, by Goddes dignitee!' (II, 1164–67)

The Parson responds by reprimanding the host for swearing: '*Benedicite!* / What eyleth the man, so synfully to swere?' (1170–71). Although Howard reads this as a strident response, the tone we give to the Parson determines just how rough he seems to us to be with the Host. Whether he is 'chiding' or 'astringent,' at the least we should note that this reprimand takes the form of a question, not a command and not a threat: it asks Harry to look within himself and discover what 'eyleth' him. The Parson shapes his response in the form of a question which probes for understanding unlike the Pardoner or the Summoner who found their discourses on statements meant to intimidate sinners for profit or power. Harry, of course, never directly answers the Parson's question, for he would have the lightness of the game continue. He does not want to stop and examine his conscience. He does not want to face what 'eyleth' him. Instead, he reacts by calling the Parson a Lollard:

> Oure Host answered, 'O Jankin, be ye there?
> I smelle a Lollere in the wynd,' quod he.
> 'Now! goode men,' quod oure Hoste, 'herkeneth me;
> Abydeth, for Goddes digne passioun,
> For we schal han a predicacioun;
> This Lollere heer wil prechen us somwhat.' (1172–77)

---

[31] Howard, *Idea*, 379, 378.

Faced with the proposition of hearing a Lollard sermon, one of the pilgrims interrupts and pleads for the game to continue:

> 'Nay, by my fader soule, that schal he nat!
> . . . heer schal he nat preche;
> He schal no gospel glosen here ne teche.
> We leven alle in the grete God,' quod he;
> 'He wolde sowen som difficulte,
> Or springen cokkel in our clene corn.
> And therfore, Hoost, I warne thee biforn,
> My joly body schal a tale telle,
> And I schal clynken you so mery a belle,
> That I schal waken al this compaignie.'[32]   (II, 1178-87)

This entire passage begs us to listen for tone. If we align ourselves with contemporary aesthetic values or with the ludic features of the *Tales*, we may well laugh at the seriousness of the Parson.[33] If we align ourselves with a theological perspective (one more commonly taken by scholars), we may smile at the stubborn ignorance, or sinfulness, of the churlish characters who resist the Parson's 'matere.' But whatever way we read the passage, if we are evaluating competitive dynamics, what we notice is the Parson's refusal to escalate the conflict.[34] Even though the Host and the churlish pilgrim rail against his seriousness and make fun of him, the Parson does not retaliate in kind. He simply backs off. Consistent with the description in the Prologue, the Parson's teaching here is by example. Unlike the Friar and Summoner who leap into contestation, the Parson's response to a churlish challenge is silence. He bides his time and waits to speak until the pilgrims want to hear from him. When his turn finally arrives, at the end of the story, Harry Bailly again voices a preference for game, begging him 'ne breke thou nat oure pley' (X, 24); 'Unbokele, and shewe us what is in thy male / . . . Telle us a fable anon, for cokkes bones!' (26, 29).[35] But the Parson refuses, saying:

---

[32] MSS vary as to who this pilgrim is. Some attribute the interruption to the Summoner, some to the Squire, and some to the Shipman. F. N. Robinson gives it to the Shipman, but John H. Fisher has argued that the text, if it were left in the *Tales*, should have been revised so that it would be spoken by the Wife of Bath; see his *The Complete Poetry and Prose of Geoffrey Chaucer*, 101, notes to line 1179.

[33] Some critics have, consequently, argued for an ironic reading of the Parson, seeing in him a pedantry and a seriousness that becomes too accentuated to be ideal. See John Finlayson, 'The Satiric Mode and the *Parson's Tale*,' *ChauR* 6 (1971): 94-116 and Judson Boyce Allen, 'The Old Way and the Parson's Way: An Ironic Reading of the *Parson's Tale*,' *Journal of Medieval and Renaissance Studies* 3 (1973): 255-71. For a rebuttal see Rodney Delasanta, 'Penance and Poetry in the *Canterbury Tales*,' *PMLA* 93 (1978): 240-47.

[34] Note lines 75-80, 315, and 1052-53 where he calls attention to the importance of charity.

[35] Notice the Host's swearing here. Depending on how we read his intonation of 'cokkes bones,' we could hear in it a repeated and purposeful challenge to the Parson's former comment on Harry's swearing. Whether we hear the line that way or not, the Parson obviously has learned that the way to Harry's heart will not be made by a discussion of the matter, and so he does not comment on Harry's swearing this time, although he does mention it in general terms within his sermon.

> 'Thou getest fable noon ytoold for me;
> For Paul, that writeth unto Thymothee,
> Repreveth hem that weyven soothfastnesse,
> And tellen fables and swich wreccednesse.
> Why sholde I sowen draf out of my fest,
> Whan I may sowen whete, if that me lest?
> For which I seye, if that yow list to heere
> Moralitee and vertuous mateere,
> And thanne that ye wol yeve me audience,
> I wol ful fayn, at Cristes reverence,
> Do yow plesaunce leefful, as I kan.'[36]   (X, 31–41)

The pilgrims urge him to tell his sermon even though it is not a 'tale,' and they intervene in the conflict between the Host and the Parson on behalf of the Parson. The ruler of the game is replaced by a priest:

> Upon this word we han assented soone,
> For, as it seemed, it was for to doone,
> To enden in som vertuous sentence,
> And for to yeve hym space and audience;
> And bade oure Hoost he sholde to hym seye
> That alle we to telle his tale hym preye.   (61–66)

Instead of continuing the game, 'he buckles up Harry's proverbial bag of fictions,' claims Laura Kendrick, 'and, with the definitive closure of his sermon, Chaucer's Parson re-establishes order and authority' (at least, from a traditional Christian perspective).[37] The *Parson's Tale* returns us to the place where we began our discussion of the *Canterbury Tales*: noting the conflict between pilgrimage and competitive game. Where the General Prologue endorsed game, this final tale endorses the sacred purpose of pilgrimage – contrition, obedience, humility, and serious self-examination. The Parson considers the entire storytelling game to be a diversion – an avoidance of, or alienation from reality and truth, as he sees it. In his discussion of anger, he claims that angry men tell fictions or lies: 'they wol forge a long tale and peynten it with alle circumstaunces, where al the ground of the tale is fals' (610). Rather than speak fictions among themselves, the Parson would have the pilgrims speak to God. Borrowing from Job, he says:

> Loo, heere may ye seen that Job preyde respit a while, to biwepe and waille his trespas; for soothly oo day of respit is bettre than al the tresor of this world. / And forasmuche as a man may acquiten hymself biforn God

---

[36] Paul Strohm notes that the Parson refuses 'to deal with any kind of plot on any terms,' 'Some Generic Distinctions in the *Canterbury Tales*,' *MP* 68 (1971): 325. He also suggests that whereas the other tales have cloaked ideas within allegory and whereas the other pilgrims have been interpreting interpretations (often erroneously), the Parson rejects allegory altogether and aims to communicate clearly so that no misunderstanding, no false gloss, will occur.

[37] Laura Kendrick, *Chaucerian Play: Comedy and Control in the Canterbury Tales* (Berkeley: University of California Press, 1988), 129.

by penitence in this world, and nat by tresor, therfore sholde he preye to
God to yeve hym respit a while to biwepe and biwaillen his trespas.

(X, 178-79)

Somewhat disgusted by the noisy and competitive relationships which have
typified humanity on the road to Canterbury (both the narrators and many of
their characters), the Parson renounces the babble of the storytelling game as
well as the sin rearing its head along the way. One of the things the Parson
emphasizes in his repudiation of the behaviors he has witnessed is competition,
itself. Discussing the seven deadly sins, he claims that almost all sins promote a
disruptive competition between humans. The prideful man, for example, is
'despitous' and 'hath desdeyn of his neighebor . . . his evene-Cristene' (395); he
will 'neither suffre to have maister ne felawe' (400). The envious man will, with
'bakbityng or detraccion,' tear down or tear at his neighbor's reputation and
character. Envy creates 'discord, that unbyndeth alle manere of freendshipe,' he
says (511). Greed, too, involves one in a competitive relationship with others, in
which one may desire to take something from someone else, or in which one
withholds something from someone who needs it (744). It is a sin which
promotes deceit and theft. Lechery, what the Parson calls 'thilke stynkyng
synne', is a kind of theft: a theft of a woman's chastity or, in typically patristic
and misogynist terms, the theft of another man's property. In his discussion of
illicit or pleasure-seeking sex, the Parson casts lechers as sinners against whom
the devil competes and 'wynnes':

This synne, as seith the prophete, bireveth man and womman hir goode
fame and al hire honour; and it is ful plesaunt to the devel, for therby
wynneth he the mooste partie of this world.   (850)

But of all the sins which disrupt and strain the fabric of social order, wrath is the
worst, and the Parson gives it the fullest treatment. In its various forms, it causes
'almoost al the harm that any man dooth to his neighebor' (557). It creates
'discord, thrugh which a man forsaketh his olde freend that he hath loved ful
longe' (562), and it 'unsowen the semes of freendshipe in mannes herte' (622).
Anger is, he says, most detested by Christ 'and no wonder is; for he deyde for to
make concord. / And moore shame do they to Crist, than dide they that hym
crucifiede; for God loveth bettre that freendshipe be amonges folk, than he dide
his owene body, the which that he yaf for unitee' (642-43).

Where so many of the other tales told by male narrators are concerned with
possessions and the desire for power in the world (in its various manifestations),
the Parson's treatise on penance is intended to take individuals on journey into
the inner world of the heart, the soul. It promotes spiritual transformation rather
than worldly domination. And this transformative process of penance offers the
pilgrims (and the audience) a 'weye' to describe themselves, to evaluate
themselves – a 'weye' to find a voice of humility and of self-reflection. The
'verray perfit Penitence' the Parson advocates is not just an intellectual or verbal
process of introspection; it involves 'Contricioun of herte' and 'Confessioun of
mouth,' but it also involves 'Satisfaccioun' (107-08). It demands that actions
follow the intellectual and interior self-evaluation, and these actions are *not* to

be actions of domination or competition. Men are not to control others; they are, instead, to allow God to control them. They are to embrace the transformational power of penitence, to relinquish the desire for power and strive for humility. The *Parson's Tale*, describing human failures, assumes a spiritual equality among humanity. There is a levelling of humans as they are represented in his tale: all have sinned; all can be transformed; all can judge their own performance in the world; and, if they are truly contrite, all can relinquish power and worldly desires to obtain heavenly reward. What the Parson advocates is a life-long process of self-evaluation, judgment, rectification, and renewal. Penance is a process of death and rebirth, a process which imitates the design of Christ's life and the natural cycles of God's creation.

The Parson's 'meditacioun' on the ills of sin and competition is the longest 'tale' within the Canterbury narrative and is constructed like a scholastic tract. It is replete with topic, divisions, subdivisions, definitions, and examples. Structured like a series of chinese boxes, it lacks the more fluid form found in the other narratives. Even the prose treatise, the *Tale of Melibee*, has plot and character, but the Parson gives us a highly schematized sermon on Penitence. Every step of the way, he provides us with an outline and then fills out the outline. Once he has defined what Penitence is, he says, 'And now, sith I have declared yow what thyng is Penitence, now shul ye understonde that ther been three acciouns of Penitence' (X, 96). He identifies them: One, Two, Three (95–105). That task accomplished, he says, 'Now shaltow understande what is behovely and necessarie to verray perfit Penitence. And this stant on three thynges: / Contricioun of herte, Confessioun of Mouth, and Satisfaccioun' (106–07), which he proceeds to explain in systematic fashion.[38] If Laura Kendrick is right that the *Parson's Tale* demonstrates 'Chaucer's ultimate aim,' which is to 'promote social stability,' it is fitting that he should promote stability within a well-ordered, stable form.[39]

If we trust the Parson's assessment of his own narrative, the purpose of his 'tale' is 'To knytte up al this feeste, and make an ende' (47). What better way to end this tale (or tail) of tales than to renounce fiction altogether and offer up a tightly woven treatise about spiritual truths? But the form of his treatise, with its tight control and its refusal of fiction and game is precisely why the reader might recoil from it. As Rodney Delasanta remarks, 'No part of the *Canterbury Tales* has been more unloved than its ending.'[40] Although the Parson's sermon on penitence apparently suited Chaucer's contemporary audiences and although sermons were commonly delivered at the end of a pilgrimage,[41] modern Chaucerians frequently argue that the text's ending is haunting, that we, as modern readers at least, are always drawn back into all the disruptions of order

---

[38] For a discussion of the form and structure of the Parson's sermon, see Robert M. Jordan, *Chaucer and the Shape of Creation* (Cambridge, Mass.: Harvard University Press, 1967), 227–41.

[39] Kendrick, *Chaucerian Play*, 129.

[40] Delasanta, 'Penance and Poetry,' 240.

[41] See, for example, Stephen Knight, 'Chaucer's Religious *Canterbury Tales*,' in *Medieval Religious and Ethical Literature*, 156–66; John Wall, 'Penance and Poetry in the Late Fourteenth-Century,' in the same volume, pp. 179–91; see also Coleman, *Medieval Readers and Writers*, chapters 4 and 5.

and authority which have preceded the *Parson's Tale* precisely because, for us, it is so stark and because the other tales are aesthetically so rich.[42] E. Talbot Donaldson, for example, resists the tale, claiming that it is 'ill-tempered, bad-mannered, pedantic, and joyless.' He says, 'After all, what Chaucer was good at was not the formulation of doctrine on sin but the revelation of the marvelous variety of life in [the] world.' For him, the *Parson's Tale* is 'a most inappropriate gloss for many of Chaucer's best poetic writings.'[43] Donald Howard, taking a more traditional stance on the tale, also acknowledges that 'from a sober point of view the sound 'doctrine' of the Parson must make all the rest seem like so much babble, must make us take seriously the Nun's Priest's and Manciple's injunctions to hold our tongues. Only, the tales are exciting; the Parson's 'doctrine' is not.'[44] And yet, Howard and most modern Chaucerians have generally and overwhelmingly accepted the *Parson's Tale* as an appropriate ending for the pilgrimage, assuming that it establishes the moral standards by which we are to judge the other pilgrims and their tales.[45]

Let us imagine, for the moment, that this is true, that the *Parson's Tale* expresses a serious standard by which we are to judge everything else in the *Tales*. Taken in this light, the tale, even though it opposes competition, is very much a participant in the competitive design of the poem as a whole, for it stands in a competitive relationship with the other tales. Its reflexivity strikes a competitive stance and wins authority over the entire text.[46] From this perspective, the *Parson's Tale* 'wins' the game. And if it wins, then it establishes what definitions of gender are ultimately endorsed by the text. If we trace the outlines of masculinity and femininity urged by the Parson, we see his endorsement of a conservative Christianity which would renounce the body, transcend the world, and seek God through penance and contrition. For the Parson, perfect order involves a hierarchy of faith over reason, reason over desire, and desire over the body:

> For it is sooth that God, and resoun, and sensualitee, and the body of man been so ordeyned that everich of thise foure thynges sholde have lordshipe over that oother; / as thus: God sholde have lordshipe over resoun, and resoun over sensualitee, and sensualitee over the body of man. / . . . whan man synneth, al this ordre or ordinaunce is turned up-so-doun.   (261–63)

---

[42] This seems particularly true for the scholars who have, more recently, considered the text in relation to issues of gender. In their texts which focus on Chaucer, Lee Patterson, Caroline Dinshaw, Elaine Hansen, and H. Marshal Leicester all by-pass any firm chronological arrangement when they consider the gender meanings in the *Tales*, and they by-pass, for the most part, the *Parson's Tale*.

[43] E. Talbot Donaldson, 'Medieval Poetry and Medieval Sin,' *Speaking of Chaucer*, 173. Christian Zacher concurs, arguing that 'only an insensitive reader would refuse to endorse [Donaldson's] sensible, Pelagian attitude toward the whole work and toward the *Parson's Tale*,' in *Curiosity and Pilgrimage: The Literature of Discovery in Fourteenth-Century England* (Baltimore: Johns Hopkins University Press, 1976), 122.

[44] Howard, *Idea*, 381.

[45] Florence Ridley remarked in her survey of Chaucerian scholarship, that 'all the individual Canterbury Tales must be seen in the context of the last, the *Parson's Tale*,' 'The State of Chaucer Studies: A Brief Survey,' *SAC* 1 (1979): 14.

[46] Cf. Lee Patterson, 'The *Parson's Tale* and the Quitting of the *Canterbury Tales*,' *Traditio* 34 (1978): 331–80.

His prescription for manhood is a call for the absolute primacy of a man's relationship to God: 'Certes, be it wyf, be it child, or any worldly thyng that he loveth biforn God, . . . he is an ydolastre' (860). It is a call for the reunion of men with 'the father.' Steeped in Christian culture, the *Parson's Tale* quite typically emphasizes masculine divinity and masculine exemplars. A glance at a Concordance listing of the word 'seinte' in the *Tale* reveals that 17 male saints are named 96 times, whereas only 2 female saints are mentioned 5 times (namely, the 'blisful mooder' of Christ and Mary Magdalene).[47] In fact, the *Tales*, throughout, are filled with reverent references to masculine divinity; the very occasion for the narrative rests on a spiritual quest for rejuvenation which comes from a male saint as the pilgrims travel to seek reward and blessing from St Thomas à Becket 'that hem hath holpen whan that they were seeke' (18). In the *General Prologue*, too, the names of male saints are sprinkled throughout the text in far greater frequency than female saints. Besides St Thomas à Becket, we hear of St Christopher, St Eligius, St Maurus, St Benedict, St Augustine, St Julian, St Peter, St Thomas, Christ, and, of course, God. There are only two references to female saints: St Veronica and the Virgin Mary.[48]

The point is, however, that whereas Chaucer could articulate challenges to the gender discourse of his culture in other parts of his *Tales*, he does not repeat those challenges here in the final tale; instead, the Parson's sermon attempts to stabilize gender. Chaucer's Parson-narrator discusses divinity in almost exclusively masculine terms, and, for him, gender issues and differences reside in the realm of governance and in the realm of the body. In his highly systematized and hierarchical view of the world, he reinscribes ecclesiastical discourse on gender. He assumes that men are superior to women, that men should govern women, and that women are closer to the 'body' than men (see lines 922–40). Answering the Wife of Bath's challenge to male domination, the Parson says, 'ther as the womman hath the maistrie, she maketh to muche desray' (927). And although he urges men to treat women with respect, 'womman sholde be subget to hire housbonde,' and 'sholde setten hire entente to plesen hir housbondes' because he 'is hire lord; algate, he sholde be so by resoun' (930, 932, 931). With regard to women, his text exhibits the kind of misogyny common to patristic writing. In it, we hear the term 'man' used both as a universal and as a gender-specific term; 'woman,' typically, is only gender-specific. There are, certainly, other places in the *Tales* where the pronoun issue could be raised, but it is in the *Parson's Tale* where the word 'man' almost becomes a character because it is so prominent. For modern readers, this can create yet another alienation from the text, but, to my knowledge, no written document composed in the Middle Ages articulates an objection to this linguistic phenomenon. However, there were women in the Middle Ages whose articulated objections to some of the other kinds of misogynist assumptions found in the *Parson's Tale* do survive.

---

[47] John S. P. Tatlock and Arthur G. Kennedy, *A Concordance to the Complete Works of Geoffrey Chaucer and to the Romaunt of the Rose* (Concord: Carnegie Institute, 1927).

[48] The text follows a tradition of similarly biased selection. See Elaine Pagels, 'What became of God the Mother?: Conflicting images of God in early Christianity,' *Signs* 2 (1976): 293–303. Edward Chiera, *They Wrote on Clay* (Chicago: University of Chicago Press, 1938).

The Parson's account of Creation, for example, is a classic reinscription of patristic assumptions about gender. Adam and Eve, the Parson claims, 'naked weren in Paradys, and nothyng ne hadden shame of hir nakednesse' (325). This assumes that one feature of Paradise is sameness, or, at least, an ignorance of difference. But after the Fall, 'whan that they knewe that they were naked, they sowed of fige leves a maner of breches to hiden hire membres' (320). In other words, awareness of difference is a feature of sinfulness. And since the account is grounded in a masculine perspective, a peculiar syllogism emerges: difference itself becomes sinfulness; Eve is different; ergo, Eve is sinful. Adam sins, of course, but he sins (in the traditional telling of the tale) because Eve seduced him. Recall Tertullian's oft-repeated charge levelled at women: 'You are the one who opened the gate for the devil. . . . So easily did you shatter that image of God, Adam. Because of the death which you brought upon us, even the Son of God had to die.'[49] Closer to Chaucer's own lifetime, the charge is horrifically echoed in *The Malleus Maleficarum*: 'All witchcraft comes from carnal lust, which is in women, insatiable.'[50] According to the Parson, Eve was drawn to eat the fruit because she represents 'the delit of the flessh.' She saw that the fruit could feed the body, that it was 'fair to the eyen, and delitable to the sighte' (329). Adam, on the other hand, represents 'the consentynge of resoun,' and so he is persuaded by Eve's invitation to share in her food. Since the Parson makes quite clear to us that reason should rule over the body, Eve is obviously, in his scheme of things, inferior to Adam:

> For trust wel, though so were that the feend tempted Eve, that is to seyn, the flessh, and the flessh hadde delit in the beautee of the fruyt defended, yet certes, til that resoun, that is to seyn, Adam, consented to the etynge of the fruyt, yet stood he in th'estaat of innocence. (331)

Traditional bias emerges, also, in the text's assumption that we descend, not from both male and female, but from the male: 'Of thilke Adam tooke we thilke synne original; for of hym flesshly descended be we alle,' and 'therfore be we alle born sonnes of wratthe and of dampnacioun' (332, 335). Christine de Pisan, quite familiar with this kind of interpretation of women, offers up a different understanding of *Genesis* in her *Book of the City of Ladies* (1405). Defending women against the oppressive misogyny of her day (and Chaucer's), she wonders 'If the Supreme Craftsman was not ashamed to create and form the feminine body, would Nature then have been ashamed? It is the height of folly to say this!' Eve was formed in Paradise, not out of mud, like Adam, but out of 'the noblest substance which had ever been created: it was from the body of man from which God made woman.' Following this logic, 'woman is a most noble creature.' Furthermore, in answer to those who would insist that women must be

---

[49] Tertullian, *De Cultu Feminarum*, PL 1, cols. 1417–19.
[50] *The Malleus Maleficarum of Heinrich Kramer and James Sprenger*, trans. and ed. Rev. Montague Summers (1928; New York: Dover, 1971), 47. The Parson refers to women with this kind of vehemence when he writes, 'seith Salomon that ''whoso toucheth and handleth a womman, he fareth lyk hym that handleth the scorpioun that styngeth and sodeynly sleeth thurgh his envenymynge''; as whoso touchesth warm pych, it shent his fyngres. . . . and trewely he were a greet fool that wolde kisse the mouth of a brennynge oven or a fourney. / And moore fooles been they that kissen in vileynye, for that mouth is the mouth of helle . . .' (854, 856–57).

ruled by men, Christine writes: 'The man or the woman in whom resides greater virtue is the higher; neither the loftiness nor the lowliness of a person lies in the body according to the sex, but in the perfection of conduct and virtues. And surely he is happy who serves the Virgin, who is above all the angels.'[51]

The *Parson's Tale* also advocates a spiritual relationship with the divine which is far more encouraging for a male psyche than a female one. The language of a male-gendered Godhead locates women as 'other,' and outside. Although a 'feminist' understanding of the gender bias within theological treatises on male divinity (the Godhead) does not surface in the written documents of the medieval world (to my knowledge), there certainly were women who felt alienated, not just from the Church hierarchy, but from God himself. In his study of *Women Writers of the Middle Ages*, Peter Dronke records the case of one late thirteenth-century woman, Aude Fauré. She struggled to accept God but found her reason and experience balked:

> . . . one day as I was going to the church . . . to hear Mass, I heard some women . . . saying that a woman had given birth on the roadside, in the village of Merviel: she could not reach a homestead in time. Hearing this, I thought of the disgusting afterbirth that women expel in childbearing, and whenever I saw the body of the Lord raised on the altar I kept thinking, because of that afterbirth, that the host was something polluted. That's why I could no longer believe it was the body of Christ.[52]

She asked her husband, 'My lord, how can it be that I cannot believe in our Lord?' and feared she would consequently lose her place among 'right-thinking people.' Marguerite Porete, too, in her *Mirror of Simple Souls*, certainly believed in a male Godhead, but placed a feminine figure of Amour highest in her pantheon of allegorized divine essences.[53] In her writing, she enjoys an erotic-spiritual relationship with her allegorical 'Lady Love.' Her alienation from the ecclesiastical conception of divinity surfaces in the opening and the closing of her text where God, Christ, and the Virgin are not mentioned, but rather, Dame Amour:

> Theologians and other clerks,
> you won't understand this book
> – however bright your wits –
> if you do not meet it humbly,
> and in this way Love and Faith
> make you surmount Reason:
> they are the mistresses of Reason's house.

---

[51] Christine de Pisan, *The Book of the City of Ladies*, trans. Earl Jeffrey Richards (New York: Persea, 1982), 23–24.

[52] Aude Fauré's testimony is recorded in J. Duvernoy, ed., *Le Registre d'Inquisition de Jacques Fournier, 1318–1325*, 3 vols. (Paris: Mouton, 1978) cited in Peter Dronke, *Women Writers of the Middle Ages: A Critical Study of Texts from Perpetua (d. 203) to Marguerite Porete (d. 1310)* (Cambridge: Cambridge University Press, 1984), 214.

[53] Porete's text is cited in Dronke, *Women Writers*, 217–28; 275–78.

> Reason herself proclaims to us
> in the thirteenth chapter
> of this book, unashamed,
> that Love and Faith make her live:
> she never frees herself from them –
> they have sovereignty over her,
> and she must do obeisance.
>
> So bring low your sciences
> which are founded by Reason,
> and put all your trust
> in the sciences conferred by Love,
> that are lit up by Faith –
> and then you'll understand this book,
> which by Love makes the soul live.

Near the end of her book, she writes:

> Thinking is no more use to me,
> nor work, nor verbal skill:
> Love draws me up so loftily . . .
> with her godlike glances,
> that I've no other goal.[54]

Her alienation culminated in her refusal to acknowledge the authority of the hierarchical Church. She was, consequently, imprisoned, tried, condemned, and burned at the stake in 1310. We also know that women flocked to the various popular heresies which sprang up in the late Middle Ages, and surely some portion of the attraction expresses alienation from the gendered practices of the Church.[55]

The Parson's desire for humanity's reconciliation with the 'Fader celestial' is echoed in twentieth-century theological discourse. Gregory Baum, in 1970, writes:

> To believe that God is Father is to become aware of oneself not as a stranger, not as an outsider or an alienated person, but as a son who belongs or a person appointed to a marvelous destiny, which he shares with the whole community. To believe that God is Father means to be able to say 'we' in regard to all men.[56]

---

[54] Marguerite Porete, *Mirror of Simple Souls*, cited in Dronke, *Women Writers*, 224, 227; Dronke also provides the French in an appendix (275-78). Cf. M. Doiron, 'Margaret Porete: *The Mirror of Simple Souls*: A Middle English Translation,' *Archivio italiano per la storia della pieta* 5 (1968): 241-355. Dronke notes that although the Church tried to eliminate all copies of her book, threatening people with excommunication if they were discovered to possess it, Porete's text survives in numerous translations.

[55] Cf. Shahar, *The Fourth Estate*, 251-80; C. Gross, 'Great Reasoner in Scripture: the activities of women Lollards, 1380-1530,' in *Medieval Women*, ed. Derek Baker (Oxford: Oxford University Press, 1978), 359-80.

[56] Gregory Baum, *Man Becoming* (New York: Herder and Herder, 1970), 195. See Mary Daly, *Beyond God the Father: Toward a Philosophy of Women's Liberation* (Boston: Beacon Press, 1973; rpt 1974), 20.

Of course, both the Parson and Baum appear to assume that this relationship is applicable to women as well as men, but regardless of sophisticated theological conceptions of 'God as Spirit' present in the Middle Ages or current now, 'God the Father' can be problematic for women. Mary Daly writes:

> Sophisticated thinkers . . . have never intellectually identified God with a Superfather in heaven. Nevertheless it is important to recognize that even when very abstract conceptualizations of God are formulated in the mind, images survive in the imagination in such a way that a person can function on two different and even apparently contradictory levels at the same time. Thus one can speak of God as spirit and at the same time imagine 'him' as belonging to the male sex.[57]

There are Chaucerians who would argue that this is rather immaterial for modern readers who have, after all, grown beyond such 'simplistic' readings of a male Godhead or Genesis, or who have abandoned religious belief all together. But, as Mary Daly notes, the myth exists in residual and disguised forms in our twentieth-century culture. She writes: 'Silence about the destructiveness of the myth's specific content is oppressive because it conveys the message – indeed *becomes* the message – that sexual oppression is a nonproblem.'[58] Additionally, for the reading strategies of the 'new medievalism,' which would situate the text within its time, a consideration of how a literate female contemporary of Chaucer's, like Christine de Pisan, responded to this kind of material surely comprises important features of the text's historical context.

Although the *Parson's Tale* alienates women and reinscribes a traditional and conservative Christian discourse, in terms of defining masculinity, it advocates behaviors for men which would repudiate the competitiveness of the world, which would urge peaceful co-existence rather than secular heroic struggle, and which would value faith and good works above wealth, status, and learning. Consequently, this concluding Christian discourse, which urges self-sacrifice, penance, and a transcendence over materialism and physicality, poses a challenge to the courtly, heroic, and intellectual ideals promoted among men in the cultural constructs of the late Middle Ages. But, because it fully embraces the standard ecclesiastical and patriarchal perception of gender, it also advocates masculine domination – in theology, in society, and in the home. The same kinds of tensions surrounding masculinity in the *Knight's Tale* emerge here, only we

---

[57] Daly, *Beyond God the Father*, 17–18. As evidence, Daly (201, fn. 10) notes that John L. McKenzie, S.J., in his book *The Two Edged Sword* (New York: Bruce, 1956), 93–94 exhibits just such a contradiction when he claims 'God is of course masculine, but not in the sense of sexual distinction.' See Simone de Beauvoir, *The Second Sex*, for additional discussion of the Church's role in enculturating women with gender stereotyping. A parallel phenomenon is evident in contemporary discussions of the 'phallus' as privileged signifier of the Symbolic order in psychoanalytic theories. As Diana Fuss comments, 'To the extent that the phallus risks continually conjuring up images of the penis, that is, to the extent that the bar between these two terms cannot be rigidly sustained, Lacan is never very far from the essentialism he so vigorously disclaims. . . . this metaphor derives its power from the very object it symbolizes; the phallus is pre-eminently a metaphor but it is also metonymically close to the penis and derives much of its signifying importance from this by no means arbitrary relation,' *Essentially Speaking* (New York: Routledge, 1989), 8.

[58] Daly, *Beyond*, 45.

come at things from a different vantage point. Here, men are to submit to God, rather than to the First Mover, and they are to maintain peace amongst themselves; but they are also to rule benevolently over women, children, servants, and anyone placed beneath them on the socio-economic scale. The Parson-narrator, like the Knight-narrator, is no radical challenging the hierarchy; he lays the blame for social disorder on individuals rather than on oppressive social structures. In the *Knight's Tale*, the text questions and probes the limitations of heroism and secular governance within its own plot where the powers of chaos continually undermine or challenge the heroic. In the *Parson's Tale*, too, because we have in our memories the evidence of all the earlier tales and events which comprise the *Canterbury Tales*, we know that the balancing act the Parson would have men perform, between piety and governance, is not likely to be successful, even if the text itself endorses the ideal.

CHAPTER EIGHT

Masculinity, Representations of Ideal Femininity in Men's Narratives, and the Challenge

If control and competition are hallmarks of masculinity within medieval gender discourse and are demonstrably pervasive issues surrounding men in the *Canterbury Tales*, obedience and rebellion mark key characteristics of femininity within that same discourse. And in so far as Chaucer's text situates the issue of obedience and rebellion at the center of its depictions of women, the text can be said to reinscribe the culture's dominant codes of femininity. Unlike men, for whom the issue of good governance is crucial, women are most often perceived as subjects for whom obedience is crucial. Although the powerful and disruptive voice of the Wife of Bath allows none of the male representations of women to stand unquestioned, Chaucer's challenge to the culture's discourse surrounding femininity is elusive and fraught with ambiguity. This ambiguity has led modern readers, feminists among them, to interpret images of women in the *Tales* in revisionary ways, ways congruent with modern perspectives or desires. It is possible to read articles claiming Griselde more powerful than Walter in the *Clerk's Tale* and Custance more powerful than the men residing in the *Man of Law's Tale*.[1] Within an exclusively Christian framework, such arguments can stand, for these women exhibit superhuman, Christ-like obedience and humility in the face of oppression and suffering; however, they only have 'power' in the eyes of readers who fully believe that men should

---

[1] Eugene Clasby argues for Custance's heroism in 'Chaucer's Constance: Womanly Virtue and the Heroic Life,' *ChauR* 18 (1979): 221-33, and V. A. Kolve maintains she represents 'the only true source of power' which is faith and acceptance, *Chaucer and the Imagery of Narrative: The First Five Canterbury Tales* (Stanford: Stanford University Press, 1984), 305. Joseph Grennan thinks the *Man of Law's Tale*, strikes 'a blow . . . against the inequity of woman's position under civil law,' 'Chaucer's Man of Law and the Constancy of Justice,' *JEGP*, 84 (1985): 513. Although her argument is complex, Elaine Tuttle Hansen makes the statement that Griselde, 'by being utterly submissive and fundamentally silent,' can exert 'power' over her world, and she writes that Chaucer 'simultaneously . . . understand[s] and critique[s] the misogyny of his world' in the *Clerk's Tale*, 'The Powers of Silence: The Case of the Clerk's Griselda,' in *Women and Power in the Middle Ages*, ed. Mary Erler and Maryanne Kowaleski (Athens: University of Georgia Press, 1988), 230-47. Unlike some discussions of the tale, Hansen's article fully recognizes the misogyny contained in the idealized image of Custance.

behave likewise and/or who fully believe in a hierarchical Christian afterlife with specific Christ-like prerequisites. The 'power' these 'ideal' women have can also be repugnant for twentieth-century readers. Sheila Delany, for example, writes: 'Constance is among the least attractive of Chaucer's women, sharing with patient Griselda . . . the repulsive masochistic qualities of extreme humility and silent endurance.'[2] Attempts to ascribe 'power' to Chaucer's obedient female characters may well reveal how a modern scholar who has spent years of her/his life studying literature would like to find Chaucer, would like to read the text as if it were advocating greater autonomy and power for women. Although such a reading is viable from an idealistically moral and Christian perspective, it runs the risk of praising women for using all their inner strength to achieve silence and a stillness of soul in the face of oppression; in other words, it runs the risk of appearing to endorse women as victims, as though passive-aggressive power were laudable, and as though martyrdom were a powerful and appropriate goal, particularly for women. Just as the Parson advocates benevolent male domination of women, so do other male narrators. Men are to govern all subordinates; and women, who are defined as subordinate, are to be governed: they are to be obedient to men, for, as the Parson argues, 'ther as the womman hath the maistrie, she maketh to muche desray' (X, 927). This perspective not only informs most of Chaucer's male narrators' views of women, it also shapes ways his female characters view men and ways he has his female characters represent themselves.

For men to focus on women as obedient or disobedient was common in the late Middle Ages. As I noted in chapter two, the favorite antifeminist attack on women was for disobedience, and women's disobedience was seen to extend across a spectrum of behaviors, from speaking (or speaking too much) to physical resistance, from attempting self-assertion to struggling for domination over men. Medieval homilists and Church Fathers frequently emphasized obedience as 'The first womanly virtue.'[3] Thomas Aquinas is typical: 'Man is the beginning and end of woman, as God is the beginning and end of every creature. . . . Woman is subject to man on account of frailty of nature as regards both vigour of soul and strength of body.'[4] The idea is echoed in secular literature. Geoffrey de la Tour de Landry, who composed a detailed discussion of all the sins of Eve, writes in his *Book of the Knight of the Tower* (1371-72), 'a woman ought not in no wyse to refuse to come at the commaundement of her lord yf she wylle haue and kepe his loue and pees. And also by good reason humylyte ought to come fyrste to the woman. For euer she ought to shewe her self meke and humble toward her lord.' And a popular medieval proverb warned, 'Let not the hen crow before the rooster.'[5] The husband-author of a late

---

[2] Sheila Delany, 'Womanliness in the *Man of Law's Tale*,' in her collection of essays, *Writing Woman: Women Writers and Women in Literature Medieval to Modern* (New York: Schocken, 1983), 36.

[3] G. R. Owst, *Literature and Pulpit in Medieval England* (Cambridge, 1933; New York: Barnes and Noble, 1966), 389.

[4] *Summa Theologica* I, 93, 4. *Supp* 81, 3.

[5] Geoffrey de la Tour, *The Book of the Knight of the Tower*, trans. William Caxton, ed. M. Y. Offord, EETS, SS, 2 (London: Oxford University Press, 1971), 103. The proverb is quoted by Shulamith Shahar in her text, *The Fourth Estate: A History of Women in the Middle Ages*, trans. Chaya Galai (New York: Methuen, 1983), 89.

fourteenth-century treatise, *Le Ménagier de Paris*, equates husbands with God and domineering wives with Lucifer: 'some women . . . take upon themselves authority, command and lordship, first in a small thing, then in a larger, and a little more every day. Thus they attempt [to] advance and rise, . . . and climb to domination, . . . then those women are all at once, by their husband's rightful will, cast down even as Lucifer was. . . . Wherefore you should be obedient.'⁶ The English jurist Bracton, typical of many legal writers, believed 'a woman was obliged to obey her husband in everything as long as he did not order her to do something in violation of Divine law.'⁷ The law saw women's obedience to men as so fundamental that it often excused women who were accessories to their husband's crimes, considering them *sub virga sui* (under their husband's rule).⁸ The Church and the legal courts even approved of wife-beating to keep women in subjection. Abused wives were encouraged to think of their abuse as a spiritual challenge, to respond to such treatment with obedience and meekness and to dispel men's anger with increased devotion.

Whereas competition between men in the *Tales* occurs between 'equals' – that is, between members of the same gender category – competition between men and women (when it arises) is represented as if it were occurring between distinctly unequal 'players'; consequently, it is interpreted and articulated in quite different terms. Women who compete with men for power or who challenge men's authority within the *Canterbury Tales* are defined as rebellious.⁹ They may exhibit exactly the same behavior men do, but that behavior is perceived differently because of the gender of the subject. When women are overtly assertive or aggressive, they are most often seen (by male narrators) as underlings refusing to accept their proper roles. But when men compete with each other, male narrators usually characterize this behavior as either 'game' (in which case it is comic) or as 'war' (in which case it is noble and/or tragic). If male competition were defined negatively as rebellion by the pilgrims, many of the fabliaux tales would not be funny; the trespass of one man on another man's domain would carry with it more serious consequences and would be expressed in more sober tones. There is a crucial difference, then, between the perceptions of men in competition with men and the perceptions of men in competition with women. Eve Kosofsky Sedgwick, discussing similar patterns of tension in Shakespeare's sonnets, claims, 'for a man to undergo even a humiliating change in the course of a relationship with a man still feels like preserving or participating in a sum of male power, while

---

⁶ Excerpts from *Le Ménagier de Paris* (c. 1392) have been translated in *Women's Lives in Medieval Europe*, ed. Emilie Amt (New York: Routledge, 1993), 322. The OF text is available in *Le Ménagier de Paris*, ed. Georgine E. Brereton and Janet M. Ferrier (Oxford: Clarendon, 1981).

⁷ Shahar, *Fourth Estate*, 89.

⁸ *Ibid.*

⁹ Chaucer's own *Tale of Melibee* may offer somewhat of a challenge, but Dame Prudence never challenges her 'lord's' power. She is not in a struggle for equality with her husband or for mastery over him; instead she embodies the humble, self-effacing wife who attempts to influence her husband in the privacy of their own home. She does not assume her husband's place and, in fact, goes out of her way to preserve his public image of mastery over her. See my discussion below.

for a man to undergo any change in the course of a relationship with a woman feels like a radical degeneration of substance.'[10]

When Chaucer's male characters lose a competition for power with women, the women are blamed: the male narrators label them shrewish or unnatural. The Man of Law, for example, lauds female obedience in the character of Custance and damns the two powerful widows who actively shape events in the world of the tale: the Sultaness and Donegild. The Sultaness, Custance's first mother-in-law, obtains a leadership position and designs a plan of action to protect her country from Christianity. To carry out her design, she feigns Christian conversion and a motherly cheerfulness toward Custance; then she slays her own son at his marriage banquet 'for she hireself wolde al the contree lede.' Outraged, the Man of Law-narrator calls her a 'cursed crone':

> O Sowdanesse, roote of iniquitee!
> Virago, thou Semyrame the secounde!
> O serpent under femynynytee,
> Lik to the serpent depe in helle ybounde!
> O feyned womman, al that may confounde
> Vertu and innocence, thurgh thy malice,
> Is bred in thee, as nest of every vice! (II,358–64)

Donegild, Custance's second mother-in-law, is 'ful of tirannye,' a traitor, a 'mannysh' ally of the fiend whose 'spirit is in helle.' She uses deception to work her evil plan, tampering with the letters carried between the court and her son, Alla, in order to drive Custance out of Britain. The Man of Law represents both Donegild and the Sultaness as angry, head-strong, somewhat independent older women who are beyond the control of men, women who seek and abuse power to maintain their own private interests. Both of these evil, designing old women are considered unfeminine (labelled 'mannysh' and 'virago'), and that, in a woman, is clearly no virtue in this tale.[11] When their worlds change, Donegild and the Sultaness attempt to exert some control; they act, and this is condemned. For the Man of Law, ideal and virtuous women (embodied in the character of Custance) submit; when Custance's world changes, she yields, for 'there reigneth in hir no tirannye.' As V. A. Kolve argues, 'Custance . . . lives . . . by submitting to time and [by] refusing to become 'shaper' of her own life.'[12]

Chaucerians commonly assume the praise of obedient women in the *Tales* exists, at least in part, as didactic teachings spoken to benefit women listeners (at least the Wife of Bath and all women like her). Surely that is part of the story. Tales praising obedient women and condemning rebellious ones are part of the

---

[10] E. K. Sedgwick, *Between Men: English Literature and Male Homosocial Desire* (New York: Columbia University Press, 1985), 45.

[11] Creon, in the *Knight's Tale*, is a good comparison since he is a vicious tyrant. Although he, too, is outrageous and cruel, his masculinity is never questioned, nor is gender used as a way of criticizing him.

[12] V. A. Kolve, *Chaucer and the Imagery of Narrative: The First Five Canterbury Tales* (Stanford: Stanford University Press, 1984), 332–33. He cites lines 822–26, 866–68, and 950–52 as evidence.

cultural instruction communicated to the audience.[13] But that is not the whole story. Elaine T. Hansen, for example, has suggested that even though the *Clerk's Tale* contains an epitome of womanly obedience in the character of Griselde, it 'is not a poem about women at all, and [that] it certainly offers no solutions to the problems faced by human beings bound to debilitating definitions of femaleness.' She says, 'It is, rather a poem about men and, like so many of Chaucer's poems, about the men who tell and listen to stories about women.'[14] Historical evidence supports her contention. Even though scholars, influenced by the Corpus Christi illumination, might like to imagine Chaucer reading his work before an audience which included many women, the facts suggest otherwise. Richard Firth Green has established that the court for which Chaucer wrote his early poetry and before which he would have performed it contained few women. Examining Edward IV's *Liber Niger*, 'the fullest account of a late medieval royal household to survive in England,' Green notes that 'we find not one female servant.'[15] Instead, he discovers:

> Men looked after the king's clothes, dressed and undressed him, made his bed, and cleaned his chamber; men served his meat, poured his wine, washed his hands, and cooked his food; not only did men look after his horses and his hawks, they did his laundry and washed his dishes. Many of his more important servants were allowed to keep (male) servants of their own at court at the king's expense, but the *Liber Niger* says nothing of their wives.[16]

Even when Chaucer was attached to the queen's household rather than King Richard's, the late medieval queen's household (commonly segregated from the king's) also contained far more men than women. Margaret of Anjou's household, for example, included one-hundred male servants and only sixteen females.[17] Although Richard II's Court certainly included women, and although women gradually became more a part of the court in the late fourteenth century, Green concludes that the royal household was generally segregated; the king and queen, he notes, rarely even ate meals together:

> . . . in the normal run of things the king would have gone about his business surrounded by his own (male) servants, and only exceptionally would his entourage have included his consort and her ladies. If, then, in calling Chaucer a court poet, we mean that he would have read his poems aloud after supper in the king's [or queen's] chamber or hall . . ., we must think of him reading to an audience which was primarily, if not exclusively, male.[18]

---

[13] In his manual for his wife, the anonymous Ménagier de Paris writes: 'you should be humble and obedient to [your husband] after the example of Griselda. . . . you should dwell in continence and chastity, after the example of Susanna, of Lucretia, and others,' *Le Ménagier de Paris* translated and cited in *Women's Lives in Medieval Europe*, ed. E. Amt, 319.

[14] E. T. Hansen, 'The Powers of Silence,' 237.

[15] Richard Firth Green, 'Women in Chaucer's Audience,' *ChauR* 18 (1983): 147.

[16] *Ibid.*, 147–48.

[17] *Ibid.*, 148.

[18] *Ibid.*, 149.

If the court contained few women, the audience for the *Canterbury Tales* would have consisted of a different demography, since the *Tales* were written and compiled at a time when Chaucer had apparently moved to Kent and was somewhat removed from the court. Donald Howard argues that the intended audience for the *Tales* was 'a "middle," literate group, a mercantile group.'[19] He writes:

> . . . as the majority of pilgrims are male, the audience is conceived as a male audience. We see things through men's eyes; even when we see into a woman's world, as in the Wife's prologue, we see from a male viewpoint . . . [I]n *The Canterbury Tales*, when Chaucer implied an audience of men, he probably had in mind friends and acquaintances like Gower or Hoccleve, an audience of chamber knights and well-to-do merchants . . . men of affairs who, however, had literary interests, who wrote, who read, who liked to play critic . . .'[20]

Should we choose to disregard the historical audience, the fictional audience within the *Tales* is itself predominantly male: there are roughly thirty men on the pilgrimage and three women. In her article, 'Taking the Gold Out of Egypt: The Art of Reading as a Woman,' Susan Schibanoff asserts that it is a 'well-established topos of manuscript literature that women readers [and listeners] alone are offended by antifeminist texts. When men were the fictional audience of antifeminist material, the author assumed that misogyny neither troubled nor offended them.'[21] Schibanoff finds apologies for antifeminist material occurring only when women are a major part of the intended audience. This is what happens in Chaucer's *Troilus and Criseyde*, but it happens much less in the *Tales*. Although the Clerk questions Walter's behavior toward Griselde, his Envoy is anything but sensitive to women; the Reeve never apologizes for his despicable treatment of women in his tale, nor do the Physician or the Merchant. Schibanoff also notes that antifeminist statements were sometimes purposefully encoded in Latin for the male audience because it was more readily known by men than women. In this light, she calls attention to Chaunticleer's '*mulier est hominis confusio.*'[22] The tales men tell on the pilgrimage to Canterbury are not literally or directly aimed at the Wife, the Prioress, or the Second Nun in the same way the *Reeve's Tale* is very much and very literally aimed at the Miller and the way the *Friar's Tale* is very literally aimed at the Summoner. The male pilgrims' narratives include no tales about nuns, and widows are rarely allowed to stay widows – their autonomy is either terminated in death (if they are aggressive) or subsumed in marriage (if they are virtuous) as is the case in the

---

[19] Donald Howard, *Chaucer: His Life, His Works, His World* (New York: Dutton, 1987), 407.

[20] Howard, *Chaucer*, 408. See also Patricia J. Eberle, 'Commercial Language and the Commercial Outlook of the General Prologue,' *ChauR* 18 (1983): 161–74.

[21] Susan Schibanoff, 'Taking the Gold Out of Egypt: The Art of Reading as a Woman,' in *Gender and Reading: Essays on Readers, Texts, and Contexts*, ed. Elizabeth A. Flynn and Patrocinio Schweickart (Baltimore: Johns Hopkins University Press, 1986), 84.

[22] Schibanoff, 'Taking the Gold,' 101–02, n. 5. She also calls attention to Walter J. Ong's study, *Orality and Literacy: The Technologizing of the Word* (New York: Methuen, 1982), 112–115 for further support.

Man of Law's Tale. Wives and daughters, rather than widows and nuns, people the male narrator's fictions. Even though the three female narrators on the pilgrimage – the Prioress, the Second Nun, and the Wife of Bath – live lives free of direct male control, when the male pilgrims tell stories about women, they usually situate women directly under the control of a man. By way of contrast, the Second Nun, the Wife of Bath, and the Prioress create women in their narratives who assume some authority and who are not always subject to direct male control. The Second Nun's St Cecilia may not be able to avoid marriage, but she maintains a species of autonomy within marriage and refuses to give her husband access to her body (albeit through her alliance with the male divinity). In the *Prioress's Tale*, the little clergeoun's mother (a widow) is featured as mother, not wife. And the Wife of Bath, of course, imagines two female characters with power to influence the outside world: Guenevere, who, though married, assumes the role of judge over the young rapist-knight, and the old unmarried crone who uses her power to preserve life and to snag herself a handsome young husband. The male narrators generally avoid tales about autonomous women, preferring to situate women in their tales as piously obedient to men or as abhorrently rebellious to men. This disparity, regardless of any speculations about authorial intent, suggests that the male pilgrims may not see or may not choose to see women as autonomous (or even potentially autonomous) beings. So, if the tales of ideal, obedient women are told by men primarily to men, what perceptions are men really sharing or reinforcing about gender roles here? And what is it men are expressing in these representations of saintly women?

First, men's tales of obedient women – specifically the *Man of Law's Tale*, the *Physician's Tale*, and the *Clerk's Tale* – may reveal ways their male narrators respond to the suffering women experience because of their gender oppression. Despite the men's apparent blindness to the more independent women on the pilgrimage, these three narrators could be said to acknowledge the disenfranchised status of women in late medieval society. Custance may represent such disenfranchisement through exile, Griselde through repeated and prolonged losses (her children, upperclass status, and her marriage), and Virginia may figure an extreme disenfranchisement when she obeys her father and loses her life at his hands. On the other hand, these same male narrators praise women for their obedience. The more extreme the suffering and the more absolute the obedience, the better the woman. The Clerk, the Man of Law, and the Physician each construct women characters who acquiesce and who do not overtly challenge or sustain a challenge to men's power. Female passivity may spawn an eventual reward, but this phenomenon also supports the culture's dominant discourse surrounding masculinity: it confirms for men that women are to be governed and that women who would wish otherwise are not virtuous. Commenting on Virginia's obedience in the *Physician's Tale*, Thomas Hanson says, 'the Physician has told the . . . story in such a way as to suggest not that virtue will be rewarded in Heaven but that virtue leads inexorably to death.'[23] Whatever their religious convictions, whatever their belief in a Christian model, the Physician, the Clerk, and the Man of Law do not represent Christ's non-

---

[23] Thomas Hanson, 'Chaucer's Physician as Storyteller and Moralizer,' *ChauR* 7 (1972): 138.

violence, his obedience and acceptance, his suffering using male characters; instead the Christian model is dramatized or realized by female characters.[24]

Even though the model of acceptance or obedience may be applicable to any Christian regardless of gender, no male character within the male pilgrim's fictional narratives exemplifies acceptance (though a few male characters do achieve an understanding of it). Penelope Curtis writes:

> If one asks the obvious question, why a principle of accepting authority *or* enduring oppression should be commended to everyone *via* the obedience peculiarly expected of wives, the obvious answer is that these things are acceptable when they take a female form and not when they don't. The 'circumstances imposed on' Custance are of a kind typically imposed on women rather than men, and/or on Christians in a heathen world, and/or on exiles. Indeed, in the patterns of associations shared by these . . . [tales], women are made correlative to early Christians and both are seen as exiles. . . . [Both Custance and Griselde] are . . . disinherited beings, wanderers on the face of the earth and sea. To a large extent the impulse towards radical Christianity in the *Tales* is narrowed to that of the alienate and disenfranchised soul, whose emblem is the pious woman . . .[25]

On the one hand, Curtis's analysis suggests that the narratives about obedient women demonstrate a sensitivity toward women since the tales perceive their major female characters as 'alienate' 'exiles' or 'wanderers' in a world where power is denied them, but as she also notes, the narrators perceive this condition as 'acceptable.' Praising women for their 'stillnesse,' these tales uphold the Aristotelian gender binaries of male and female virtues: 'the courage of a man is shown in commanding, of a woman in obeying. . . . Silence is a woman's glory, but this is not equally the glory of man.'[26]

Second, the praise for women's silence suggests that the feminine heroism described by the Clerk, the Man of Law, and the Physician occurs in the inward realm of the will where the will controls itself more than it imposes itself on the

---

[24] This idea is developed fully by Edward I. Condren in his article, 'The *Clerk's Tale* of Man Tempting God,' *Criticism* 26 (1984): 99–114. Condren argues for parallels between Griselde and Christ. He cites James 1: 13–14: 'Let no man say when he is tempted, that he is tempted by God; for God is no tempter to evil, and he himself tempts no one. But everyone is tempted by being drawn away and enticed by his own passion.' Condren concludes that 'though Walter had attempted to govern his world with standards of temporal worth-finery, beauty, passion, cruelty-Griselde's virtues of patience, constancy, and fortitude ultimately govern him.' Walter is the human, Griselde, the divine. Condren argues against a host of critics who have interpreted the *Clerk's Tale* as if Walter were the divinity and Griselde, the human. Cf. Bernard Huppe, *A Reading of the Canterbury Tales* (Albany: State of New York Press, 1964), 164; George Kittredge, *Chaucer and His Poetry* (Cambridge, Mass.: Harvard University Press, 1915), 196; D. W. Robertson, Jr, *A Preface to Chaucer* (Princeton: Princeton University Press, 1962), 82–83, 269, 288, 366. The Second Nun's St Cecile fits this category too, but I will discuss her more extensively later since she is featured in a narrative told by a female narrator.

[25] Penelope Curtis, 'Some Discarnational Impulses in the *Canterbury Tales*,' in *Medieval English Religious and Ethical Literature: Essays in Honour of G. H. Russell*, ed. Gregory Kratzmann and James Simpson (Cambridge: D. S. Brewer, 1986), 136.

[26] Aristotle, from *The Works of Aristotle*, ed. W. David Ross, trans. J. F. Beare et al, vol. 10 (Oxford: Oxford University Press, 1921).

external environment; it can be even self-immolating. Although major male characters in the *Physican's Tale*, the *Clerk's Tale* and the *Man of Law's Tale* express their wills in the form of action and control over the external environment, the female characters express their wills – not in shaping events – but in conforming to events, making a 'virtue of necessity.' Women, here, are heroic because they control themselves, and control is defined as body purity and a nearly silent acceptance of suffering, qualities which imitate the Virgin Mary and thereby reinscribe the common cultural discourse surrounding femininity. Such a valuation of women again reaffirms men's (and God's) position as shapers of worldly events, for if these ideal women can be said to influence the public world significantly, they do so, like the Virgin Mary, as instruments of someone else's design.[27] In the *Man of Law's Tale*, for example, Custance does not establish order, law, or social relations. Instead, she is an object in the design of God, Satan, men, and evil women. In fact, if we define 'hero' rather traditionally, as one who actively participates in and shapes the story, God is the rightful hero of the *Man of Law's Tale*. God is the one who acts; Custance's role is to reveal God's heroic nature. He governs events and passes judgment; she is his instrument, a mediating sign of divine control. He preserves Custance from the satanic designs of two pagan stepmothers and from the hazards of the open seas. By the 'wyl of Crist,' she lands at Northumbria where, through her, God converts pagan Britons. He is the one whose hand smites the false knight dead and his is the voice that declares to Alla and his court: 'Thou has desclaundred, giltelees, / The doghter of hooly chirche in heigh presence' (II, 674–75). When Custance marries Alla, the narrator comments: 'And thus hath Crist ymaad Custance a queene' (693). Christ provides her with food and water to survive in the boat where she drifts 'as liked Cristes sonde' (902), and Christ and Mary intervene to save Custance from the would-be rapist (950–52).[28] As John Yunck describes it, 'The real protagonist is God himself.' Chaucer's purpose, he claims, is to write 'a drama of Providence, of the greatness of divine power and the helplessness of man in the face of worldly vicissitudes.'[29] But, I would add, the 'helplessness' of 'man' is projected on a female body.

Although Custance is an object in God's design and an object, consequently, of Satan's attack, she is also an object in the designs of mortal men and women. Her marriages are determined by men. She does not fall in love, men fall in love with her. When Syrian merchants describe her to the Sultan, he falls in love with her and determines to marry her or die. She is the remedy to his love-sickness. The Church and the nobility of Rome view her as an avenue for the 'destruccioun of mawmettrie, / And [the] encrees of Cristes lawe deere' (236–37). Her feelings, her perspective are of no concern: 'But forth she moot, wher-so she wepe or synge' (294). King Alla chooses to marry her, two lecherous men attempt to rape her, and the most evil designs of Satan assault her through the agency of evil mother-in-laws. Her challenge is to accept her fate. The

---

[27] For an argument that assumes Griselde has power, though not a masculine form of power, see Hansen's article, 'The Powers of Silence: The Case of the Clerk's Griselda,' 230–49.

[28] The extensive actions of God are well-documented and discussed in John A. Yunck's article, 'Religious Elements in Chaucer's *Man of Law's Tale*,' *ELH* 27 (1960): 249–61.

[29] *Ibid.*, 252, 256–57.

Physician's Tale is similar: Virginius and Apius act, whereas Virginia submits; and in the *Clerk's Tale*, Walter completely controls and shapes Griselde's external world; (she acquiesces with no hesitation). Griselde's freedom is internal; only in the realm of the heart and mind can she choose her own response to external circumstances.

Since the drama of the major female character takes place in the inner realm of the soul and the will, one might expect the male narrators to focus on that inner life. Instead, they downplay it, ignore it, or hint at its elusiveness. Like an object, Custance, Griselde, and Virginia are perceived by their narrators predominantly from the outside. They are unquestionably obedient; there is little or no struggle for these female 'heroines.' Obedience *is*; it is an essence of these female characters; it does not *become*. John Yunck has even gone so far as to say that Custance, 'as [a] character . . . is nothing,' and Edward Block sees her as 'too perfect to be a credible human being.'[30] Stephen Manning, arguing that the flatness of Custance's character comes from the flatness of characterization typical of hagiographic romance, says:

> Chaucer has difficulty harmonizing the elements of the cosmic and the human in Constance. . . . by her very name . . . she drifts into waters allegorical as well as hagiographical. . . . Chaucer explores neither the theological nor the psychological dimensions of Constance, and his treatment of his theme seems ultimately superficial.[31]

Whether we interpret this superficiality of character as a function of Chaucer's perspective or the Man of Law's (or as a function of genre) is a question I will raise and simply leave for the time being, but the point is that Custance's obedience simply exists; we do not see her actively create it within herself.[32]

The *Consolation of Philosophy*, widely known in the Middle Ages and translated by Chaucer, describes a male character, Boece, caught in the downward turn of Fortune's Wheel much like a Custance or a Griselde, but his inner experience, his struggle with his will, and his intellectual, emotional, and spiritual journey receives all the attention of the text. He reaches acceptance only

---

[30] Yunck, 'Religious Elements,' 257; Edward Block, 'Originality, Controlling Purpose, and Craftsmanship in Chaucer's *Man of Law's Tale*,' *PMLA* 68 (1953): 572–616. Similarly Charles Muscatine comments that Griselde is 'a model of "vertuous suffrance," and of nothing more specific. She will wither at the touch of practical realism,' *Chaucer and the French Tradition* (Berkeley: University of California Press, 1957), 193. See also Eugene Clasby, 'Chaucer's Constance: Womanly Virtue and the Heroic Life,' *ChauR* 13 (1979): 221–33, and V. A. Kolve, *Chaucer and the Imagery of Narrative*, chapter VII (esp. 303–04) where Kolve admits that the poem is centered around moral simplicities of either/or and good/bad characters.

[31] Stephen Manning, 'Chaucer's Constance, Pale and Passive,' in *Chaucerian Problems and Perspectives: Essays Presented to Paul E. Beichner, C.S.C.*, ed. Edward Vasta and Zacharias Thundy (Notre Dame: University of Notre Dame Press, 1979), 13–14.

[32] Many readers account for Custance's flatness of character by claiming that Chaucer's purpose here is to use the character as an emblem or as an archetype representing Virtue, the True Wife, the Church, the human soul, or the 'ideal and suffering Christian.' They argue that Chaucer's purpose is to illustrate morality, to praise virtue and blame vice more than it is to develop characters or plot. See Robertson, *A Preface to Chaucer*, Huppe, *A Reading of the Canterbury Tales*, 91–107; John Speirs, *Chaucer the Maker* (London: Faber and Faber, 1951), 135; Michael Paull, 'The Influence of the Saint's Legend Genre in the *Man of Law's Tale*,' *ChauR* 5 (1971): 179–94.

after a long internal struggle and debate. Chaucer's considerable attention to the inner drama of the male will is exhibited by his dream vision narratives and is particularly evident in the conversation between Geoffrey and the Man in Black in the *Book of the Duchess*. The Boethian struggle also informs the articulation of Troilus's inner struggle within *Troilus and Criseyde*. The *Man of Law's Tale*, however, so heavily indebted to the *Consolation* for its philosophic content, provides us only glimpses into Custance's internal experience. She does not dialogue or debate with another character, not even herself; no songs or soliloquies express her thoughts. Stephen Manning, acknowledging pervasive Boethian influences on the *Man of Law's Tale*, believes Chaucer's narrative places so much emphasis on divine Providence that the active decision-making crucial to Boethian epistemology becomes obscured. He claims it 'tends to cancel out some of [Custance's] awareness of the emotional cost of yielding to divine will,' and he continues: 'Finally it also raises questions about the analysis of the entire problem of Providence: the treatment is warmed-over Boethius, the point is naively reiterated over and over and over, and no aspect of it seems pursued very far.'[33] Even when Custance converts the Constable, we are not given her dialogue, no direct evidence of her intellectual capabilities.[34] Instead, the male-narrator steps back from the scene and reduces her ability to convert a man into a three-line summary:

> And so ferforth she gan oure lay declare
> That she the constable, er that it was eve
> Converted, and on Crist made hym bileve. (II, 572–74)

The same slant occurs in the narrative when King Alla and his court are converted. God's action, smiting the knight-murderer and speaking to the court, receives at least fifteen lines:

> An hand hym smoot upon the nekke-boon,
> That doun he fil atones as a stoon,
> And bothe his eyen broste out of his face
> In sighte of every body in that place.
>
> A voys was herd in general audience,
> And seyde, 'Thou has desclaundred, giltelees,
> The doghter of hooly chirche in heigh presence;
> Thus hastou doon, and yet holde I my pees!'
> Of this mervaille agast was al the prees;
> As mazed folk they stonden everichone,
> For drede of wreche, save Custance allone.
>
> Greet was the drede and eek the repentance
> Of hem that hadden wrong suspecioun
> Upon this sely innocent, Custance . . . (II, 669–82)

[33] Manning, 'Chaucer's Constance,' 20.
[34] This receives commentary or response, perhaps, in the *Second Nun's Tale* where a female narrator imagines her female saintly character with an extremely active intellect, debating and challenging Almachius.

Custance's 'mediation' is given one-and-a-half lines: 'And by Custances mediacioun, / The kyng – and many another in that place – / Converted was, thanked be Cristes grace!' (684–86). If the tale lacks the drama of intellectual and emotional struggle found in the *Consolation of Philosophy*, it also eliminates references to many of the intellectual achievements ascribed to Constance in Chaucer's source – Nicholas Trivet. Unlike his source, Chaucer's Man of Law de-emphasizes his female character's assertive actions, her educational interests, and her independent decisions.[35] Trivet's Custance is an only child of an emperor who educates her as if she were male. She gets training:

> en lez sept sciences, que sount logicience, naturel, morale, astronomie, geometric, musique, perspective, que sount philosophies seculares apelez, e . . . en diverse languages . . . et theologie.[36]

As John Yunck comments, Chaucer's Custance is 'quite unburdened by an academic curriculum.'[37] Furthermore, Trivet's Custance actively converts the Syrian merchants who are dazzled not only by her beauty but also by her mental acuity. Not so in the *Man of Law's Tale*; Custance never even speaks to the merchants. Trivet's Custance also exhibits a will and a direction of her own, a self-motivated desire to convert the pagans in Briton, for example. But this active quality of mind is suppressed in the Chaucerian version. The *Clerk's Tale* is shaped similarly, as Charles Muscatine has noted: Chaucer's revisions of Petrarch 'heighten Griselda's submissiveness and deepen the pathos of her situation.'[38]

Now it has been common to see these tales as a defense of women, to see them as answering the antifeminist charge made against women in the late Middle Ages that they were inconstant, like bodies. And yet, by making the female characters unchangeable, the narrators make them into transcendent ideas, into signs which restrict them to such a degree that modern readers can scarcely recognize their portraits as a defense of women. For the modern reader, the extreme form of obedience evidenced in Custance, Griselde, and Virginia carries with it a sense of fusion, a threat of disintegration. By conforming so absolutely to the will of another, ego boundaries seem to melt. To imagine someone in this extreme condition of self-erasure is to imagine them in a kind of death-in-life, a form of fusion evident in the *Clerk's Tale* where Griselde says:

> 'Ye been oure lord, dooth with youre owene thyng
> Right as yow list; axeth no reed at me.
> For as I lefte at hoom al my clothyng,
> Whan I first cam to yow, right so,' quod she,

---

[35] For Trivet's account see W. F. Bryan and G. Dempster, *Sources and Analogues of Chaucer's Canterbury Tales* (Chicago: University of Chicago Press, 1941), 155–206. See also Block's article, 'Originality, Controlling Purpose, and Craftsmanship in Chaucer's *Man of Law's Tale*,' and Robert Pratt's study: 'Chaucer and *Les Cronicles* of Nicholas Trivet,' in *Studies in Language, Literature and Culture of the Middle Ages*, ed. Atwood and Hill (Austin: University of Texas Press, 1969), 303–311.

[36] Cited in Bryan and Dempster, *Sources and Analogues of Chaucer's Canterbury Tales*, 165.

[37] Yunck, 'Religious Elements,' 251.

[38] Muscatine, *French Tradition*, 193.

'Lefte I my wyl and al my libertee,
And took youre clothyng; wherfore I yow preye,
Dooth youre plesaunce, I wol youre lust obeye.'   (IV, 652–58)

She agrees to die should Walter desire it: 'For wiste I that my deeth wolde do
yow ese, / Right gladly wolde I dyen, yow to plese' (664–65). In lines 716–17
the Clerk-narrator comments that 'Ther nas but o wyl; for, as Walter leste, / The
same lust was hire plesance also.'[39] Even when Griselde's children are taken
away from her, even when she believes they will be murdered, her tone,
manner, and stance do not waver; she remains obedient: 'She neither weep ne
syked, / Conformynge hire to that the markys lyked' (545–46).

Custance, Virginia, and Griselde are fascinating for their male narrators
because they represent that 'other' quality, the quality of submission these men
see as particularly 'feminine.' That also becomes our fascination or abhorrence.
We watch them as they react to other people's designs. Whereas we watch
Theseus, Nicholas, Absolon, Old John, Palamon and Arcite, Symkyn and the
young clerks create plans and designs and attempt to carry them out, in the *Man
of Law's Tale*, the *Clerk's Tale*, and the *Physician's Tale*, we watch women's
reactions to those male powers that design. We judge the male characters, to
some degree, on how good their plans are and how successfully they carry out
those plans; but not so with Custance or Griselde or Virginia. Instead, we
wonder, will they ever revolt? Will they ever assert themselves in active
opposition to the forces around them? If there is suspense around these female
characters, it revolves around that question. But neither Custance, nor Griselde,
nor Virginia ever revolt. The closest they come even to questioning authority is a
far cry from the classically male heroic struggle. Virginia's struggle to accept
death is contained in only nineteen lines. Although she begs for mercy and
questions her father's decision to sacrifice her life rather than her virginity, she
readily submits. Even when she asks for some time to prepare herself for death,
we are not privy to her thoughts. She is dispatched summarily:

'O mercy, deere fader!' quod this mayde,
And with that word she bothe hir armes layde
Aboute his nekke, as she was wont to do.
The teeris bruste out of hir eyen two,
And seyde, 'Goode fader, shal I dye?
Is ther no grace, is ther no remedye?'
     'No, certes, deere doghter myn,' quod he.
'Thanne yif me leyser, fader myn,' quod she,
'My deeth for to compleyne a litel space;
For, pardee, Jepte yaf his doghter grace
For to compleyne, er he hir slow, allas!
And, God it woot, no thyng was hir trespas,

---

[39] The fusion of the female will with the male is also evident in the way the Physician describes
Nature. At first, (feminine) Nature takes credit for having created the beautiful Virginia, but then
she acknowledges that she is but the 'vicaire general' for the divine god in control. She adds, 'My
lord and I been ful of oon accord. / I made hire to the worshipe of my lord; / So do I alle myne
othere creatures . . .' (25–27).

But for she ran hir fader first to see,
To welcome hym with greet solempnitee.'
And with that word she fil aswowne anon,
And after, whan hir swownyng is agon,
She riseth up, and to hir fader sayde,
'Blissed be God, that I shal dye a mayde!
. . .

And with that word she preyed hym ful ofte
That with his swerd he sholde smyte softe;
And with that word aswowne doun she fil.
Hir fader, with ful sorweful herte and wil,
Hir heed of smoot, and by the top it hente,
And to the juge he gan it to presente . . .   (VI, 231-48; 251-56)

As Anne Middleton comments, Virginia hardly has a self; she is 'simply an extension of Virginius, himself. There is no question of her *choosing* death over dishonor . . . her wishes are weightless in the moral balance struck between Apius and her father.'[40]

Custance, too, may display a momentary reluctance to marry the Sultan, she may weep 'Alas, alas!' but she concludes by saying, 'Wommen are born to thraldom and penance, / And to been under mannes governance' (II, 286-87). Each of these three women justifies her own oppression and accepts her position as 'thral.' Custance, in her prayer, gives one rationale:

'Mooder . . . and mayde bright, Marie,
Sooth is that thurgh wommanes eggement
Mankynde was lorn, and damned ay to dye,
For which thy child was on a croys yrent . . .'   (841-44)

These lines echo, of course, the severe antifeminist statements common in Church writings. They are couched in a woman's voice, but they are the teachings of male theologians and express the dominant patristic view of women. Of course, in the context of the narrative, the lines also rationalize women's suffering. Custance, as particularly female, is suffering because of her sex. Just as it was 'thurgh wommanes eggement / Mankynde was lorn,' she says (or the Man of Law says), so it is that through her sex she is nearly lost herself, and this takes us to a third key idea about gender being communicated by these tales.

Obviously Custance's femininity has something to do with the ideas being communicated here. J. A. Burrow has stated that 'Constance is reduced by her character *and sex* to a state of passivity so complete that she seems more like a saint than a heroine of romance' (my emphasis).[41] Her sex, according to the narrative, reinforces the idea of human helplessness, passivity, obedience and acquiescence being represented in the tale. And yet, feminine sexuality is also

---

[40] Anne Middleton, 'The *Physician's Tale* and Love's Martyrs: "Ensamples mo than ten" as a method in the *Canterbury Tales*,' ChauR 8 (1973): 13.

[41] J. A. Burrow, *Medieval Writers and Their Work: Middle English Literature and its Backgrounds, 1100-1500* (Oxford: Oxford University Press, 1982), 82.

portrayed as an awesome power in this tale. It causes Custance incredible misery. The tragedy of her temporal experience is not caused by pride or by greed or by an action, as is common with male heroes; instead, it is a product of her sexuality. From the security of Rome, she travels to marry a prince who has fallen hopelessly in love with her picture. When he is murdered by his own mother at the wedding banquet, Custance is put out to sea. As soon as she finds peace in the quiet stability of the Constable's home, she is accosted by a lecherous knight who murders Hermengild as a way to get revenge on Custance. Custance is put on trial for the murder, and at the trial King Alla falls in love with her. From a seemingly secure second marriage to Alla, she winds up exiled on the sea with her new-born child. She is almost raped but finally lands in Rome again where she is eventually restored to her position as wife of Alla until his death and ultimately, her own. In each of these incidents, the Man of Law attributes her misfortune to her sex; the narrative is shaped so as to demonstrate that her sexuality attracts destructive forces into her life. The Sultan would never have married her had she not been so physically attractive to him. Her beauty and his subsequent attraction to her causes her suffering. If she had not been the bride to the Sultan, she would never have been put out to sea by the evil Sultaness. Her role as wife – a sexual category – causes the jealous mother-in-law to act. Once Custance is peacefully established in Northumbria, it is a lecherous knight who, lustful of Custance's body, enraged by her rebuffs, murders Hermengild. This act brings Custance to Alla's attention. If she had never been bride to Alla, her mother-in-law would never have found a way to exile her on the open sea. And if she were not an attractive and vulnerable female, the Steward would never have attempted to rape her. The Man of Law cannot resist commenting on her sexuality and sexual bondage. He enjoys, for example, reporting on Custance's nuptial night with Alla, and the language is telling:

> They goon to bedde, as it was skile and right;
> For thogh that wyves be ful hooly thynges,
> They moste take in pacience at nyght
> Swiche manere necessaries as been plesynges
> To folk that han ywedded hem with rynges,
> And leye a lite hir hoolynesse aside,
> As for the tyme, – it may no bet bitide.   (II, 708–14)

For the Man of Law, Custance's holiness diminishes slightly when she actively participates in sexual behavior. If she simply *exists* as a female being, fine; if she *acts* as a sexual being, she is slightly corrupted. This same point is made later in the tale in reference to her chastity. The Senator of Rome comments to Alla:

> 'But God woot,' quod this senatour also,
> 'So vertuous a lyvere in my lyf
> Ne saugh I nevere as she, ne herde of mo,
> Of worldly wommen, mayde, ne of wyf.
> I dar wel seyn hir hadde levere a knyf

Thurghout hir brest, than ben a womman wikke;
There is no man koude brynge hire to that prikke.'   (1023-29)

Similar assumptions about women's bodies surface in the *Physician's Tale* where Virginia, made so exquisitely beautiful by Nature, suffers because Apius wants her as his concubine. To preserve her physical 'purity,' and to keep her from being sexually violated, her own father kills her. As Harry Bailly sees it, 'hire beautee was hire deth.' And, in the *Clerk's Tale*, Griselde suffers because Walter chooses her to be his wife. The kinds of suffering Griselde endures are closely related to her gender role as mother and wife. She is forced to give up her two children to a man she believes is their executioner. She is sent back to her father because her husband would marry a younger woman. And she is forced to decorate the palace for Walter's new bride because, Walter says, 'I have no wommen suffisaunt' to decorate 'after my lust' (960, 962). Walter has, in fact, a specifically sexual perception of Griselde, for he states that his purpose is 't'assaye' Griselde's 'wommanheede' (1075).

If we compare the reasons the narrators give for these ideal women's suffering to the reasons given for King Alla's suffering, we can see the difference. King Alla suffers because he does not see the truth clearly and because he is betrayed and deceived. He makes a mistaken decision. But why do Custance and Griselde and Virginia suffer? According to the Man of Law, the Clerk, and the Physician, they suffer because of Providence and because of their bodies. They suffer at the hands of forces well beyond their control.

The three male narrators shape their narratives to suggest that a woman's external circumstances are determined by her body. As such, they also suggest that these three female characters are not simply universal or allegorical abstractions representing all human suffering. The attention each narrator gives to the sexuality of all three women belies their universality, and it is a way of perceiving women which reinscribes the dominant medieval discourse on femininity. Since this discourse on the bodily nature of women is codified in legal, scientific, and theological/philosophical writings, it is not surprising that the Man of Law, the Physician, and the Clerk (representatives of the law, science, and the Church, respectively), say little or nothing to challenge the culture's definitions of femininity. These tales admire and pity female characters who arc chaste, obedient, silent, self-effacing, self-sacrificing and beautiful; they do not suggest that women should be otherwise. By locating suffering in the female body, the male narrators distance themselves, in fantasy, from their own bodily suffering. Projecting the vulnerability of the body onto women is a powerfully consoling (if fictional) move for the male narrator.[42]

If these tales uphold the debilitating images of obedient women, they do not, however, simply affirm the culture's gender discourses surrounding masculinity. The gender dynamics here are more complex than that. These tales offer up a challenge to men's governance by describing the suffering of women under cruel male domination and by eliciting empathy from the reader/listener. The

---

[42] Cf. the discussion of eroticism, physicality, and idealism in R. Howard Bloch's *Medieval Misogyny and the Invention of Western Romantic Love* (Chicago: University of Chicago Press, 1991), 143-64.

Man of Law, for example, ponders the wisdom of the Roman men who decide to dispatch Custance to a non-Christian Syria. Although he never castigates Custance for her acceptance of marriage, and although he does not imagine her actively asserting herself on the plot events, his emotional reaction to the men who govern Custance's life is evident:

> Impudent Emperour of Rome, allas!
> Was ther no philosophre in al thy toun?
> Is no tyme bet than oother in swich cas?
> Of viage is ther noon eleccioun,
> Nemely to folk of heigh condicioun?
> Noght whan a roote is of a burthe yknowe?
> Allas, we been to lewed or to slowe! (II, 309–15)

The Clerk, too, is outraged at times by men.[43] He cannot stand Walter's pointless and willful determination to test Griselde. Registering his reservations at the beginning of his tale, he says that he admired Walter 'save in somme thynges that he was to blame' (IV, 76). The Clerk-narrator finds Walter's design 'subtil,' 'nedeless,' 'cruel,' and 'wikke[d].' He says: 'But as for me, I seye that yvele it sit / To assaye a wyf whan that it is no nede, / And putten hire in angwyssh and in drede' (460–62). And this criticism is echoed throughout the tale. After the first test, the Clerk-narrator remarks that Walter doggedly holds to his plan despite Griselde's obedience, 'As lordes doon, whan they wol han hir wille,' because, he says, 'wedded men ne knowe no mesure, / Whan that they fynde a pacient creature' (581, 622–23). And after the second test, the Clerk comments critically on Walter's 'lustful will,' charging him with rigidity and mercilessness:

> . . . ther been folk of swich condicion
> That whan they have a certein purpos take,
> They kan nat stynte of hire entencion,
> But, right as they were bounden to a stake,
> They wol nat of that firste purpos slake. (701–05)

Elizabeth Salter has found Walter to be so vividly and adversely portrayed that, she says, 'we are inclined – indeed encouraged – to believe in his heartlessness rather than in his inscrutability.'[44] Additionally, the Clerk-narrator is outraged

---

[43] The Clerk's outrage is an element Chaucer has, most likely, added to his source. See W. A. Cate, 'The Problem of the Origin of the Griselda Story,' *SP* 29 (1932): 405.

[44] Elizabeth Salter, 'Chaucer: The *Knight's Tale* and the *Clerk's Tale*,' *Studies in English Literature* No. 5 (London: Edward Arnold, 1963), 58. Although Walter has produced a wide variety of scholarly interpretations, many critics agree with Salter that Walter is somewhat of a tyrant. See Donald Reiman, 'The Real *Clerk's Tale*; or Patient Griselda Exposed,' *TSLL* 5 (1963): 356–73; Donald Baker, 'Chaucer's Clerk and the Wife of Bath on the subject of *Gentilesse*,' *SP* 59 (1962): 631–40. Joseph Grennan, 'Science and Sensibility in Chaucer's Clerk,' *ChauR* 6 (1971): 90 sees Walter as 'a parody of divine lordship.' Charles Muscatine, *Chaucer and the French Tradition* (195) argues that the tale intensifies the 'political aura' and makes the Petrarchan tale into an image 'of lordship and domination.' John McNamara even goes so far as to see Walter's character approaching the role of the devil, 'Chaucer's Use of the Epistle of St James in the *Clerk's Tale*,'

at Walter's faithful Sergeant, criticizing him for obeying Walter without question:

> A maner sergeant was this privee man,
> The which that feithful ofte he founden hadde
> In thynges grete, and eek swich folk wel kan
> Doon execucioun in thynges badde. (519–22)

Even though the Sergeant obeys his ruler explicitly, just like Griselde, he is depicted as horrible. The Clerk describes him:

> Suspecious was the diffame of this man,
> Suspect his face, suspect his word also;
> Suspect the tyme in which he this bigan. (540–42)

Here again, we can perceive the Clerk's gender bias. Whereas Griselde is praised for her extreme obedience, the male sergeant is not. The Clerk-narrator never wonders at the wisdom of Griselde's complete obedience to a tyrannical Walter, although some contemporary critics do. Donald Reiman, for example, has commented that Walter's actions become progressively 'odious' until he succeeds at so enslaving Griselde's mind that 'she acquiesces to the unnatural murders [of her own children] without a murmur of protest.' He continues:

> Griselda completely surrenders her moral freedom and disobeys God's law to follow the whims of a fellow creature. . . . Griselda, who possesses more of the theological virtues of faith, hope, and charity, than does the high-born marquis, misdirects them by submitting patiently and obediently, not to God's law, but to the arbitrary and evil desires of a 'mortal man'; she is, therefore, guilty of idolatry. . . . [Her] great 'patience' was as much a source of evil as was Walter's arbitrary wilfullness.[45]

But this is not the perspective taken by the pilgrim-narrators; instead, they admire their fictional, obedient women. Harriet Hawkins has even suggested that their admiration borders on wish-fulfillment, that the *Clerk's Tale*, for example, 'enacts what may be a common masculine fantasy: to have the beautiful, faithful, and perfectly obedient wife, yet remain free to get rid of her without worrying about any claims or recriminations on her part.'[46] However true this may be, it is also true that these three narrators, by telling a tale which focuses on women, find an avenue for levelling criticism at men. When a male narrator takes on a female persona or tells a tale surrounding a female persona, that persona may become a disguise allowing the male narrator to articulate ideas

---

ChauR 7 (1973): 192. See also Carol Heffernan, 'Tyranny and *Commune Profite* in the *Clerk's Tale*,' *ChauR* 17 (1983): 332–40, and Robert Stepsis, 'Potentia Absoluta and the *Clerk's Tale*,' *ChauR* 10 (1975): 129–46.

[45] Reiman, 'The Real *Clerk's Tale*,' 363.

[46] Harriet Hawkins, 'The Victim's Side: Chaucer's *Clerk's Tale* and Webster's *Duchess of Malfi*,' *Signs* 1 (1975): 341.

culturally taboo or restricted if voiced by a male persona; and, indeed, these three tales level severe criticism at rulers, the upper class, and at men. The *Man of Law's Tale* passes judgment on ambitious queens, lecherous knights, and rapist stewards. The tale sides with women who, like Custance, become unwilling targets of men's sexual desires and who, like Custance, become targets of powerful women's jealousy. The *Physician's Tale* openly criticizes judges who misuse the law for personal gain and more indirectly, through the plot, criticizes tyrannical fathers who demand absolute control over their children's lives. The tale may well be directed even against what Donald Howard has called the 'misguided moralism' of the Physician-narrator himself.[47] The Physician condemns Apius harshly but empathizes with a murderer. In his article 'Jephthah's Daughter and Chaucer's Virginia,' Richard Hoffman argues that the tale indicates the Physician-narrator does not really understand what chastity is, 'or that a woman whose chastity is forcibly violated may remain chaste. To his anatomical mind, virginity is nothing more than Fielding thought it was to Richardson – physical intactness merely.'[48] Whatever the tale may be saying about the Physician's moral absolutism, the plot elicits our outrage at the death of an innocent woman. The narrative condemns Virginius's detached absolutism as well as Apius's lust. That the tale attacks the misuse of legal power is obvious.[49]

The *Clerk's Tale* contains potential criticisms of the aristocracy. The privileged and rather narcissistic, upperclass marquis – who would lie to, and 'pley' with, his people, his wife, and his children – is a man who unabashedly draws the Pope into his own 'cruel' game simply to satiate his own curiosity and willfulness. Walter contrasts with the low-born, naturally virtuous woman who is able to govern openly and honestly, whose words and deeds are in accord: 'Ther nas discord, rancour, ne hevynesse / In al that land, that she ne koude apese, / And wisely brynge hem alle in reste and ese' (432–34). The contrast has prompted Elaine T. Hansen to suggest that 'if a peasant woman can in fact be as good a ruler as a noble man – or even a better one – then Walter's birthright and the whole feudal system on which it depends are seriously threatened.'[50] The resilience Griselde ascribes to her own oppressed class and gender is evident, too, in her remark to Walter concerning his prospective new bride, a woman of much greater privilege:

---

[47] Howard, *Idea*, 334.

[48] Richard Hoffman, 'Jephthah's Daughter and Chaucer's Virginia,' *ChauR* 2 (1967): 30.

[49] See Beryl Rowland, 'The Physician's "Historical Thynge Notable" and the Man of Law,' *ELH* 40 (1973): 165–78. Sheila Delany finds the political content of the *Physician's Tale* considerably watered down in Chaucer's version of the tale. She argues that Chaucer's sources made such criticism far more explicit. She regards Chaucer's version as verging 'on a kind of pornographic or free-floating sadistic sensationalism, with the murder as its only real centre,' 'Politics and the Paralysis of Poetic Imagination in the *Physician's Tale*,' *SAC* 3 (1981): 57.

[50] Hansen, 'The Power of Silence: the Case of Griselda,' in *Women and Power in the Middle Ages*, 234. Of course, such a reading assumes a more literal political and social reading of the poem. In discussion, Russell Peck has suggested that Walter may be demonstrating Griselde's superior nature to his people, including Janicula, who still assume that aristocratic birth miraculously confers superior nature upon individuals. Cf. Chaucer's short poem, 'Gentilesse,' where human virtue originates from 'the firste stok,' [presumably God] rather than from social status.

'O thyng biseke I yow, and warne also,
That ye ne prikke with no tormentynge
This tendre mayden, as ye han doon mo;
For she is fostred in hire norissynge,
Moore tendrely, and, to my supposynge,
She koude nat adversitee endure
As koude a povre fostred creature.'   (1037–43)

The *Clerk's Tale*, in its plot, moves us to sympathize with the victim, Griselde, and it challenges the tyranny of any husband or ruler who would dominate and manipulate, rather than love, his wife or people.

As critiques of male misgovernance and abuse against women, these three tales challenge an uncritical allegiance to the dominant cultural discourses on masculine control, but they remain aligned with the culture's assumptions about the nature of ideal women: women are to be obedient, chaste, and silent. Terry Eagleton, commenting on literary depictions of ideal women, writes, 'The "exaltation" of women, while undoubtedly a partial advance in itself, also serves to shore up the very system which oppresses them. For the eighteenth-century woman, as indeed for women of any epoch, the pedestal is never very far from the pit.'[51]

The Man of Law, the Clerk, and the Physician do not go unchallenged, for the *Canterbury Tales* include narratives which counter these three narrators' assumptions about women's obedience. The *Franklin's Tale*, for example, posits a marriage which requires both partners to submit and both to rule. Although Arveragus wants to preserve the outward appearance of 'soveraynetee' (V, 751–52), the Franklin-narrator seems to extol a reciprocity in male-female relationships in a move that challenges the dominance of men like Walter and Virginias as well as the unquestioning obedience of women like Griselde and Virginia. He writes:

That freendes everych oother moot obeye,
If they wol longe holden compaignye.
Love wol nat been constreyned by maistrye.
Whan maistrie comth, the God of Love anon
Beteth his wynges, and farwel, he is gon!
Love is a thyng as any spirit free.
Wommen, of kynde, desiren libertee,
And nat to been constreyned as a thral;
And so doon men, if I sooth seyen shal.   (V, 762–770)

The Franklin also questions the absolutism characteristic of the *Man of Law's Tale*, the *Physician's Tale*, and the *Clerk's Tale*. He never attempts to posit an absolutely ideal man or woman; instead, he believes that 'in this world, certein, ther no wight is / That he ne dooth or seith somtyme amys' (779–80).

---

[51] Terry Eagleton, *The Rape of Clarissa: Writing, Sexuality, and Class Struggle in Samuel Richardson* (Oxford: Blackwell, 1982), 15.

Furthermore, he suggests that any absolute adherence to masculine domination or feminine submission may be rigid, backward, and ultimately uninformed by mercy. So whereas the Physician-narrator never questions the appropriateness of a woman dying to preserve her chastity, the Franklin-narrator does. Although Dorigen contemplates suicide in rather overblown fashion when she learns she must commit adultery to preserve her word, she chooses to live instead. The humorous tone in the passage may well even further the point: namely, that considering suicide as way of preserving integrity is hardly viable. Like Virginius, Dorigen initially thinks an unchaste woman can only choose between two extremes: death or dishonor; but she finally chooses life. In this tale, harsh judgments revert to mercy; so, the Franklin's young bachelor, Aurelius, awe-struck by the 'gentilesse' of husband and wife, finally releases Dorigen from her promise, and subsequently, the philosopher-clerk also releases Aurelius from his contract. The *Franklin's Tale* is comedy, and as such it advocates life and mercy, offering an alternative to the moral rigidity of the Man of Law's representation of Custance, the Clerk's Griselde, and the Physician's Virginia. The Franklin-narrator assumes, apparently, that women consist of more than merely maidenheads or wombs, that their value – like men's – lies in living. As the Franklin sees it, 'Trouthe [or, more accurately, the appearance of trouthe] is the hyeste thynge that man [or woman] may kepe' (1479), though not at the expense of life itself.

The comedy of the *Franklin's Tale* also reinforces objections to male domination which surface throughout the *Canterbury Tales*, suggesting that men are more virtuous, or, at least, more civilized, when they forgive others than when they willfully assert themselves over others as Virginius and Walter do. Whereas Walter cunningly deceives Griselde to the point of sadistic psychological torture, Aurelius, even though he initially sets up a test for Dorigen, backs away from his manipulation of her, and unlike Walter, who tests and retests Griselde's pledge, Aurelius releases Dorigen from her promise:

> 'I have wel levere evere to suffre wo
> Than I departe the love bitwix yow two.
> I yow relesse, madame, into youre hond
> Quyt every serement and every bond
> That ye han maad to me as heerbiforn,
> Sith thilke tyme which that ye were born.
> My trouthe I plighte, I shal yow never repreve
> Of no biheste, and heere I take my leve,
> As of the treweste and the beste wyf
> That evere yet I knew in al my lyf.' (1531–40)

Despite these 'answers' to the Man of Law, the Clerk, and the Physician, the *Franklin's Tale* persists in presenting us with a major female character who conforms to men's desires, except, here, conformity is made to appear ridiculous. Dorigen jokingly and flippantly promises Aurelius that he can have her sexually if he removes the rocks from the coastline. When, through magic, he claims they have disappeared, Dorigen does not challenge him nor does she defend herself. Instead of reasoning with Aurelius about the true intent of her words, she submits. And when Arveragus tells her she must keep her word to Aurelius, she conforms to his wishes, too – she never challenges her husband.

Dorigen cannot be said to be ideal, by any stretch of the imagination, but in the *Tale of Melibee*, Chaucer creates an admirable woman whose virtue comes, not from silence but from speaking, not from accepting, but from successfully and gently challenging her husband. Like two other assertive women in the *Canterbury Tales* – the Wife of Bath and St Cecile – Dame Prudence's challenge to Melibeus takes the form of speaking. In fact, the tale consists of dialogue nearly to the exclusion of anything else. Commenting on this, Charles A. Owen writes that Prudence's 'appeal for Chaucer was in what she says rather than in what she does: she preaches virtue instead of suffering for it as Chaucer's other heroines do; her reality, as befits a figure in allegory, is primarily in the realm of the intellect, [of] disembodied ideals and qualities. . . .'[52] The conflict presented in the tale involves the issue of what to do in the face of violent assault. Melibeus, consistent with cultural definitions of competitive masculine behavior, opts initially for retaliation. Prudence patiently argues with him and finally persuades him to practice mercy instead.[53] Her influence comes from her ability to serve as a mediator between a host of male authorities and Melibeus's conscience. We are still a ways away from the Wife of Bath's experientially-based challenge. Prudence's arguments and her words are men's. She is the vessel carrying the 'honey' of male authorities to her husband. Ultimately, Melibeus is persuaded by the wisdom of men filtered through a female voice, as Prudence cites Cicero, Peter Alfonce, Cassiodorus, Cato, Ovid, St Augustine, St Jerome, and many others, but even though Prudence uses men's words, she does so to persuade her husband to her own way of thinking. Melibeus may think 'that alle wommen been wikke,' he may consider any man a fool to go against the counsel of many men (VII, 1075), and he may find it unnatural or 'contrarious' for his wife to 'have maistrie,' but she patiently and reasonably convinces him to forgive his enemies rather than to make war on them: 'His herte gan enclyne to the wil of his wif, considerynge hir trewe entente, / and conformed hym anon, and assented fully to werken after hir conseil' (1871–72). So, unlike Custance, Griselde, or Virginia, Prudence does not conform to someone else's will; instead, she shapes her husband's actions.

Some scholars, like Dorothy Palomo, have found Chaucer's Prudence to be 'domineering' and have accused her of 'conspicuous verbal overkill.'[54] Others have thought her lengthy speeches, so heavily laden with proverbial lore, to be humorous commentary on women's supposed loquaciousness.[55] But to suspect that Chaucer is poking fun at Prudence, 'you have to ignore [the tale's] content,' argues Donald Howard.[56] The tale, as we know, had great success and

---

[52] Charles A. Owen, Jr 'The *Tale of Melibee*,' *ChauR* 7 (1973): 270. On the tale as allegory see also Paul Strohm, 'The Allegory of the Tale of Melibee,' *ChauR* 2 (1967): 32–42.

[53] The story of Prudence and Melibeus occurs as an exemplum in *Le Ménagier de Paris*: 'forbid [members of your household] to quarrel with each other or with your neighbors; forbid them to speak ill of others. . . . Forbid revenge to them and teach them in all patience by the example of Melibeus, of whom I have told you,' cited in Amt, *Women's Lives*, 326.

[54] Dorothy Palomo, 'What Chaucer Really Did to *Le Livre de Melibee*,' *PQ* 53 (1974): 316.

[55] W. W. Lawrence, 'The *Tale of Melibeus*,' in *Essays and Studies in honor of Carleton Brown* (New York: New York University Press, 1940), 100–110.

[56] Howard, *Idea*, 310.

popularity from the mid-thirteenth to the fifteenth centuries, and its popularity resulted from the wisdom of its contents, not from any subtle, ironic look at women. Assuming the content of the tale is intended to be serious, there must be other explanations for the length of Dame Prudence's speeches. The most obvious one is that the tale belongs to the genre of philosophical debate. However, the length of the tale may also reflect what Elizabeth Lunz identifies as 'male obtuseness rather than female prolixity.'[57] Charles Owen accounts for the length of Dame Prudence's speeches and the ponderous frequency of quotations in yet another way. He writes: 'The patient and painstaking way in which the arguments develop suggests the difficulty of stopping the violence decided on in the beginning' by Melibeus.[58] However we read her lengthy speeches, it is clear that her words are her actions. Prudence shapes her challenge to Melibeus gently and carefully. She avoids being silenced or disregarded by strategically citing male authorities and maintains a consistently deferential manner. She never challenges her husband in public but always waits to discuss her views with him in the privacy of their home; and she must do this, for within the fictional world of the narrative, she is dealing with a rather volatile man who would consider himself shamed if his friends knew he was following his wife's counsel.[59] Prudence challenges Melibeus only 'as ferforth as she doste,' and she calls him 'sire' and 'lord' innumerable times throughout the dialogue. She also takes care to listen to him 'ful debonairly and with greet pacience.' Only 'in ful humble wise whan she saugh hir tyme' does she approach her husband to ask 'of hym licence for to speke' (1051, 1064). Even when she devises a plan to get Melibeus's enemies to repent and ask forgiveness, she pretends she speaks to them without Melibeus's knowledge in order to save face for her husband. So, although she is unafraid to challenge her husband's authority, she is careful about how she challenges him. There is no 'quiting' here, no competition surfaces between husband and wife, and Prudence has, always, her husband's best interest at heart. She even promises him that he need never publically acknowledge her role in his decision-making, and he never does. Prudence is not interested in winning power 'over' her husband or even gaining recognition; her concern is to protect Melibeus and assist peace. Never directly censoring her husband, she works only to change his mind.[60] As a nurturing female, even as a vessel through whom we hear male words, she actively shapes the world of the tale, but, it must be granted that Dame Prudence conforms to many of the

---

[57] Elizabeth Lunz, 'Chaucer's Prudence as the Ideal of the Virtuous woman,' *Essays in Literature* 4 (1977): 7.

[58] Owen, 'The *Tale of Melibee*,' 272.

[59] See *The Book of the Knight of the Tower*, trans. William Caxton, EETS, SS, no. 2 (London: Oxford University Press, 1971), 129: 'I shalle telle yow another ensample of the quene Hester/ whiche was wyf to the grete kynge of Surye/ She was a good lady and a wyse/ and loued and drad her lord/ . . . The kyng her lord was a felon man & dyuers[/] And said to her many outragyous wordes/ but for ony thynge that he sayd/ she ansuerd hym nothynge before the folke/ wherby he myght be wrothe/ but after whanne she had hym alone/ and sawe the tyme and the place be conuenyente/ she blamed hym/ and curtoysly shewed hym his fawte/ And therfore the kynge loued her moche/ and sayd att his secrete/ that he myght not be wrothe with his wyf/ by cause she repreued hym by soo fayre and swete wordes[.]'

[60] Lunz notes, 'she is careful not to fall into the unpardonable error of prideful conflict with Melibeus for power,' 'Chaucer's Prudence,' 5.

medieval culture's concepts of ideal femininity, even as she presents a challenge to male authority. Significantly, her rebellion against one form of male power stems from her allegiance to another form of male power, one considered more authoritative: the patriarchal tradition in philosophy and theology. Furthermore, as a 'disembodied' allegorical figure, she can easily be understood to represent one part of Melibeus's mind – the prudent element within him. Such an interpretation fragments the female and makes her significant only as part of a male whole, just as Eve (the rib) was made from, or split off from, Adam (the whole) in the Genesis narrative. Of course, the flatness of Prudence's character, her one-dimensional nature, is typical of allegorical figures, but in the long tradition of personified concepts, virtues and vices, abstract representations of virtue remained predominantly female. Real human, biblical figures associated with virtues were almost always male.[61] In this way, Dame Prudence echoes the objectification of women found in the absolutist category of 'the virtuous woman' in the *Man of Law's Tale*, the *Clerk's Tale*, and the *Physician's Tale*.

Despite her allegorical function, Prudence also represents one form of femininity (particularly as wife) in the pantheon of women found within the *Canterbury Tales*. Germaine Dempster raises an objection to such a reading, charging that the portrait of wisdom as feminine and folly as masculine 'is only the frame of the allegory; otherwise, that is, as possible illustration of feminine wisdom versus masculine impulsiveness, it is of no . . . interest to Chaucer.'[62] While I might assent to Dempster's interpretation if the tale existed in isolation, it does not; it is woven into the complex fabric of tales presented in the *Canterbury Tales*. As such, it comments on other tales and is commented upon by other tales and by other voices in the storytelling game. Since issues of sovereignty exerted by both men and women form the central foci of other tales, Dame Prudence and Melibeus function not only as allegorical figures, but also as representations of male and female.[63] What Geoffrey's *Tale of Melibee* depicts in Prudence is a strong female intellectual capability, though no aspiration to 'maistrie.' As Elizabeth Lunz maintains, Dame Prudence's speeches 'serve to demonstrate scholarly wisdom coming from a brilliant, phenomenally retentive mind, and so to suggest the possibility and the power of such learning in a medieval woman.'[64] But it must be acknowledged that Dame Prudence exists in this tale only to nurture her husband. The action, if we can call it that, involves the movement and transformation of Melibeus's will. Will he decide to forgive his enemies or won't he? That is the suspense. Prudence, like Custance or Griselde, remains the same from start to finish. Melibeus is the one who changes; he is the one who enacts the public peace-making; and he is the one who enters the political realm and asserts himself.[65] He is the governor.

[61] See Michael Evans, 'Allegorical Women and Practical Men: The Iconography of the *Artes* reconsidered,' in *Medieval Women*, ed. Derek Baker (Oxford: Oxford University Press, 1978), 305–330.

[62] Germaine Dempster, 'A Period in the Development of the *Canterbury Tales* Marriage Group of Blocks B2 and C,' *PMLA* 68 (1953): 1143.

[63] Harry Bailly surely interprets the allegorical character as potentially real, when he wishes his wife could become a bit more like Dame Prudence.

[64] Lunz, 'Chaucer's Prudence,' 6.

[65] As a representation of masculinity, Melibeus offers a challenge to the dominant cultural discourse because he submits to the will of his wife; furthermore, the narrative advocates precisely that.

Prudence is an advisor. She can influence, but the final decision and action rests with Melibeus. Yet, however much Prudence shares with the other objectified and idealized women in the *Tales*, her influence does assert itself over a man's mind. Here is no silent woman. Dame Prudence is the intelligence with which we are allied as we hear or read the tale, and her interpretation of the world is offered up as far more sagacious than her husband's.

Melibeus opens himself to the mind and experience of another person by accepting her advice. Judith Ferster comments: 'The person who requests and receives advice must decide what to do with the piece of the outside world he has let in: accept or reject it. A good deal of the *Melibee* is taken up with when to ask, how to ask, and what to do with what one gets when one asks. Thus, it is also about the boundaries of the self,' *Chaucer on Interpretation* (Cambridge: Cambridge University Press, 1985), 19. Melibeus allows a woman to cross over the boundaries of his selfhood. But what is particularly unique is that within this tale, the lowering of defenses is depicted as appropriate and good, and it does not harm him.

CHAPTER NINE

'Female' Narrators and Chaucer's Masquerade: the Second Nun, the Prioress, and the Wife of Bath

The representations of women included in the male pilgrims' tales are filtered through several layers of male perception: first, Chaucer has a man (the pilgrim-narrator) create a representation of a woman; then he has that man represent her to yet another man (Geoffrey) who represents the representation and who is, of course, yet another man's persona, Chaucer's. As Elaine Hansen has noted, we do not hear 'a swelling chorus of female voices entering the text and speaking for and about themselves, but something of a monotone making known both feminine absence and masculine anxiety,' and 'what often sounds like a woman's voice, what is spoken in the name of women . . . always enters and leaves Chaucerian story not as the enunciation of an autonomous speaker, but as an urgent problem for the gendered identity of male characters, male narrators, and (?male) readers.'[1] There are several tales, however, in which Chaucer attempts to move closer to a female perspective. In the *Tale of Melibee*, Chaucer's persona, Geoffrey, begins this exploration of 'female' perspective, oscillating back and forth between the feminine voice and the masculine. Even though his tale does represent the feminine voice far more extensively than any of the other male pilgrims' narratives, Chaucer's most imaginative experimentation with the feminine voice obviously occurs in the *Second Nun's Tale*, the *Wife of Bath's Tale*, and the *Prioress's Tale*. Unlike the male pilgrims, who usually simplify women's inner worlds, unlike their tendencies to avoid or to mute the feminine voice, separating themselves from that 'other' by using the third-person narrative, Chaucer tries to embrace the fusion and experiments with a feminine first-person; he takes on the masquerade of the female voice.[2] In these

---

[1] Hansen, *Chaucer and the Fictions of Gender* (Berkeley: University of California Press, 1992), 12.

[2] Notice, however, that Chaucer distances himself at times from the female narrator by including the phrase 'quod she.' See, for example, the *Prioress's Tale* (VII, 454 and 581) and the *Wife of Bath's Prologue and Tale* (III: 169, 188, and 854). The fusion of Chaucer/Geoffrey's narrative voice with the Wife's is also disrupted by two interruptions: one from the Pardoner (163–87), the other from the Friar and the Summoner (829–56). See Hansen, *Chaucer and the Fictions of Gender*, 14: she argues that Chaucer's representations of women and women's voices always reinscribe patriarchal

three tales, women are represented through fewer filters of male perception: Chaucer represents Geoffrey's representation of a female voice.

Chaucer's three 'female' narrators are free to speak and to assert themselves unlike any female character found within the narratives of the *Tales*. Their participation in the competitive storytelling game is welcomed; within that context, at least, they have the potential to win, to defeat each other, and to defeat the men on the pilgrimage as well. Nowhere does the text record an objection to the female narrators' participation in the competitive world of the game, although a Sedgwickian reading of their presence might demonstrate ways both they and their tales are territories across which homosocial desire flows. They are not silent, not always self-effacing and, through language, through interpretation, they participate in shaping the game and in shaping their own texts. These 'female' voices, though far outnumbered by male voices, carry considerable power within the text; indeed, no thorough discussion of the *Canterbury Tales* can disregard them. Consequently, it would appear that Chaucer's text is challenging the discourse surrounding femininity, arguing that women are not simply rebellious or obedient but that they are also creating the game (and, by implication, the world). Furthermore, within their tales the 'female' narrators create main characters who, through words, rather than silence, assert considerable influence on the world, and that influence is positive. Their tales also challenge or critique the dynamic of male domination and female subordination. Although the extent of their challenge is hardly equivalent to a modern feminist challenge, it is, however, far greater than any challenge to the culture's assumptions about femininity raised by the male pilgrims' narratives.

The Second Nun's St Cecile, for example, represents a form of womanhood consistent with that posited by the Man of Law, the Clerk, and the Physician, yet we find in her some striking differences, too. Although the Second Nun calls attention to her character's body and sexuality, although St Cecile is awesomely beautiful, and although her virginity takes a center stage in the early part of the narrative, the saintly woman's body – her virginity – is a power, not a liability. It allows a kind of autonomy and separateness not found in characters like Griselde, Virginia, or Custance. Where female characters like Custance or Emelye rather conventionally wish they could stay maidens, St Cecile, through the force of her faith and will, carries that wish into action. She may not be able to avoid the marriage her parents have arranged for her, but she can maintain her virginity within it. She need not die for her virginity, nor does she need a father to 'protect' it for her; instead, she maintains her bodily autonomy herself. In fact, her virginity/autonomy is guarded so strongly by her own will and her own faith that any man who would attempt to violate her risks death.[3] The Second Nun, describing Cecile's wedding night, says:

privilege. She writes, 'the female character is always redefined as other than the male characters and speakers in the texts in a variety of predictable ways: she is generically fixed and fully engendered; in every instance she is dead, or mutilated, victimized, violated, anesthetized, abandoned, mystified; or she lacks art, or she lacks desire.'

[3] The assumption, here, is that 'clene' love is non-sexual. F. N. Robinson, in his notes to the text, assumes St Cecile and her husband maintain virginity. The crown of lilies and roses which the two receive are, he notes, 'symbols of martyrdom and purity.' St Jerome, 'in an epistle to Furia (*PL*,

> The nyght cam, and to bedde moste she gon
> With hire housbonde, as ofte is the manere,
> And pryvely to hym she seyde anon,
> 'O sweete and wel biloved spouse deere,
> Ther is a conseil, and ye wolde it heere,
> Which that right fayn I wolde unto yow seye,
> So that ye swere ye shul it nat biwreye.'
>
> Valerian gan faste unto hire swere
> That for no cas, ne thyng that myghte be,
> He sholde nevere mo biwreyen here;
> And thanne at erst to hym thus seyde she:
> 'I have an aungel which that loveth me,
> That with greet love, wher so I wake or sleepe,
> Is redy ay my body for to kepe.
>
> 'And if that he may feelen, out of drede,
> That ye me touche, or love in vileynye,
> He right anon wol sle yow with the dede,
> And in youre yowthe thus ye shullen dye;
> And if that ye in clene love me gye,
> He wol yow loven as me, for youre clennesse . . .'
>
> (VIII, 141–60)

In this passage, the female narrator 'reads' virginity as equivalent to autonomy
and power, a reading quite different from the male narrators' interpretations of
virginity found sprinkled throughout the *Canterbury Tales*, and this stems partly
from the Second Nun's narrative location within the genre of the Saint's Life, a
genre not embraced fully by any other narrators. Undeniably, Cecile's virginity
is protected by God just as Custance's chastity is, but the Second Nun focuses
her attention on St Cecile's words rather than God's action. In the *Man of Law's
Tale*, by contrast, we do not hear Custance say anything to protect herself from
the rapist-steward. The Man of Law downplays an active role for Custance by
narrating rather than dramatizing:

> A theef, that hadde reneyed oure creance,
> Cam into ship allone, and seyde he sholde
> Hir lemman be, wher-so she wolde or nolde.
>
> Wo was this wrecched womman tho bigon;
> Hir child cride, and she cride pitously.
> But blisful Marie heelp hire right anon;
> For with hir struglyng wel and myghtily
> The theef fil over bord al sodeynly,

22, col. 557), . . . ascribes lilies to virgins and roses to martyrs, as does also St Ambrose in his
commentary on the Song of Songs (*PL*, 15, col. 1871). . . . The crowns are brought to [Cecile]
and her husband, not at the moment of martyrdom, but as soon as they determine to live a life of
virginity in marriage.' Robinson cites numerous sources, both modern and medieval, which
assume that St Cecile maintains virginity, not just chastity, within her marriage. See Robinson,
Chaucer, 758, notes to lines 220ff.

And in the see he dreynte for vengeance;
And thus hath Crist unwemmed kept Custance.   (II, 915–24)

But in the *Second Nun's Tale*, St Cecile's words become the very focus for the narrative; both her words and her body are powerfully autonomous. Where the male pilgrim narrators generally assume their heroines are vulnerable because of their bodies, Chaucer's Second Nun makes no such assumption. Like Custance, St Cecile winds up in an arranged marriage to a pagan husband, but unlike Custance, she registers her resistance by wearing a hair shirt beneath her wedding gown. This sign proclaims to us, to herself, and to Valerian the boundaries she has established around her body. She warns Valerian that if he violates her, he will be struck down by an angel; and when Almachius attempts to silence her words by assaulting her body, her words become even more powerfully subversive of his authority. Any invasive force directed against her body is nullified by greater force.

St Cecile's fate is not determined by her sex; it is determined by her religious faith. Her destiny is shaped, not by men's attraction to her, but by her own choices – her faith, her Christian belief. Except for her husband, people in the tale are not attracted to her sexually, even though she is beautiful; they are drawn to her because of her faith, her ideas, her words. In the male pilgrims' narratives, men are frequently attracted to women out of lust. And this lust, when it is spurned, leads to anger and violence. In the *Man of Law's Tale*, the lecherous knight kills Hermengild because Custance refuses his advances. Custance's separateness, her assertion of her own integrity, provokes him to murderous revenge. In the *Second Nun's Tale*, this pattern takes a very different turn. We still have a young man, Valerian, who very much desires his wife, and when he is rebuffed, he, too, is angered. He says:

'Lat me that aungel se, and hym biholde;
And if that it a verray angel bee,
Thanne wol I doon as thou hast prayed me;
And if thou love another man, for sothe
Right with this swerd thanne wol I sle yow bothe.'
(VIII, 164–68)

But his ire is transformed by the power of her faith. Where he was initially 'ful lyk a fiers leoun,' he becomes 'meke as evere was any lomb . . .' (198, 199). (Of course, Almachius is provoked to a murderous rage because St Cecile will not submit to his authority nor to his gods, but he is not trying to seduce her.)

Unlike the obedient and malleable women in the men's narratives, Cecile becomes a designer in the plot of the tale; her words shape events. She sends Valerian off to St Urban where he is baptized, and through her, Tiberius converts. Because she guides these men to Christianity, they are taken captive, executed by Almachius, and thereby obtain the Christian salvation awaiting martyrs. Cecile's efforts to convert large numbers of people result in her summons before Almachius for questioning, and because of her faith, her words, she is ultimately martyred. Where the Clerk represents Griselde as a virtuous woman controlled by Walter's designs, the Second Nun provides us with a St Cecile defiantly marching into Almachius's prison, converting people and defiantly refusing to acknowledge men's earthly authority. She defends herself eloquently and attacks her enemy forcefully with words. She calls Almachius 'a lewed officer and a veyn justise,' a 'blynde,' man, a 'ministre of deeth.' When he says, 'Ne takestow noon heede / Of my power?' She replies:

> 'Youre myght . . . ful litel is to dreede,
> For every mortal mannes power nys
> But lyk a bladdre ful of wynd, ywys.
> For with a nedles poynt, whan it is blowe,
> May al the boost of it be leyd ful lowe.'   (437–441)

Nor does she stop there; she claims that he, 'with a wood sentence,' frames innocent Christians and thereby perverts justice. When he insists she sacrifice to his gods, 'the hooly blisful faire mayde / Gan for to laughe.' Almachius wonders how Cecile can treat his authority with such disrespect, and he says:

> . . . 'Unsely wrecche,
> Ne woostow nat how fer my myght may strecche?
> Han noght oure myghty princes to me yiven,
> Ye, bothe power and auctoritee
> To maken folk to dyen or to lyven?
> Why spekestow so proudly thanne to me?'   (468–73)

She responds by accusing him of the sin of pride and by refusing to be awed by his power over her life and death: 'Thy power is ful naked,' she says. Where the Physician never questioned the power of men over (especially woman's) life and death, the Second Nun laughs at such pretenses. From her Christian perspective, life is so transitory that men's secular power is hardly worth much anyway; she believes that the most potent power over eternal life or eternal death lies with a divine power. Indeed, when Almachius tries to have Cecile's body burned, he fails, and when he tries to have her decapitated, he fails. Although the 'tormentour' can pierce her neck, he cannot sever it from her body completely.[4] His action has been constrained by a woman's words. Cecile remarks, 'I axed this of hevene kyng / To han respit thre dayes and namo / . . . er that I go' (542–44). No man will ultimately determine her death. Her body is still under her own command (although also in service to God). The definition of the ideal woman in the Second Nun's narrative challenges the definitions given in the male pilgrims' narratives. Here is a dedicated, strong-willed and vocal woman who sees through the pretenses of male power, both her husband's and her governor's. Hardly silent and accepting, she suffers violence at the end of the tale because she chooses to do so. Chaucer, moving into greater fusion with a feminine perspective, taking on the voice of a 'female' narrator, grants far more

---

[4] Note the contrast with Virginia's beheading scene in the *Physician's Tale*:
> Hir fader, with ful sorweful herte and wil,
> Hir heed of smoot, and by the top it hente
> And to the juge he gan it to presente . . .   (VI, 254–56)

autonomy to St Cecile than the other male narrators grant to their female characters.[5]

Like her character, the Second Nun-narrator also challenges the male pilgrims. The tale she tells, late in the journey, responds and takes exception to the representations of ideal women given earlier by the male narrators. Where the men have fashioned ideal women as supremely obedient or cautiously influential (like Geoffrey's Dame Prudence), the Second Nun paints her ideal woman as openly defiant and autonomous. St Cecile's faith constitutes her only authority. But the Second Nun's challenge is, perhaps, even more immediate than that. In the Prologue to her tale, she, like the Parson-narrator who will follow her, questions the morality of Harry's storytelling game, arguing that idle words and works are sinful:

> And for to putte us fro swich ydelnesse,
> That cause is of so greet confusioun,
> I have heer doon my feithful bisynesse
> After the legende, in translacioun
> Right of thy glorious lif and passioun,
> Thou with thy gerland wroght with rose and lilie –
> Thee meene I, mayde and martyr, Seint Cecile.   (22–28)

Where so many other tales have caused 'greet confusioun,' the Second Nun's does not, at least not from the Christian vantage point which informs the tale. The prologue, plot, action, dialogue, and narrative are never in conflict. Although ambivalence is a common feature of the other tales, it is not a feature of the *Second Nun's Tale*. Recall for a moment the confusion in the *Physician's Tale* when the Physician-narrator condemns Apius but not Virginius, when he refrains from criticizing a man who insists on murdering his own innocent child but lauds the same man for begging the people to spare the life of Claudius, a man who had conspired to abduct and violate his daughter. Or recall the *Clerk's Tale* with its ambivalence toward Walter and its contradictory and confusing multiple endings. Where we have to work hard to account for discrepancies in other narratives, we have no such task before us in this tale. The tale and its purpose are free of the entanglements and pronounced ambiguities that mark so many of the other tales.

But if the tale avoids entanglements from a traditional Christian perspective, it certainly encompasses entanglements for the modern reader. First of all, a Christian perspective must be assumed to make this reading work; without it, Cecile's sacrifice appears to be a tragic death-wish. Secondly, the overt and assertive female resistance to male power praised in the tale becomes problematic when we see that the consequence of laudable resistance is death. As such, the *Second Nun's Tale*, like the *Man of Law's Tale* and the *Clerk's Tale*, represents the ideal woman as self-sacrificing and long-suffering. Where the Knight-narrator can consider Theseus admirable, not because he suffers, but because he learns to rule with mercy; where Geoffrey admires the Parson and

---

[5] Russell Peck notes the strong possibility that the *Second Nun's Tale* was originally narrated by Chaucer himself. See his article, 'The Ideas of "Entente" and Translation in Chaucer's *Second Nun's Tale*,' *AnM* 8 (1967): 17–37.

the Plowman because they actively lead their communities to greater peace, Griselde, Custance, Virginia, and St Cecile are admired because they obey God and/or men without hesitation and pay a high price. The sacrifice required of these women is self-effacement, either physical (Virginia and St Cecile) or psychological (Griselde and Custance). In this way, St Cecile, ever obedient to God, joins the ranks of the other sacrificed and suffering women represented in the *Canterbury Tales*.

The *Second Nun's Tale*, as part of the Christian content of the poem, assumes that the shape of life, at least St Cecile's life, is a procession from, and a return to, God the Father – a problematic assumption for most modern feminist readers. Cecile is a woman who, like so many female saints, receives great praise from the culture for denying her sexuality, her female body. And we may well ask, 'For whom is this representation of heroic femininity actually a step forward?' The answer, from a skeptical and secular feminist viewpoint, certainly isn't 'women,' for St Cecile may assert herself, but the price she pays for doing so is death. Her martyrdom which, from a Christian perspective, is the most noble narrative a person can live out, appears to be a denial of life from a secular perspective. She embraces death to obtain union with God the Father, placing herself in the category of saintly women whom feminist theologians may view as 'serv[ing] the masters' purposes.'[6] From the vantage point of modern feminist skepticism, St Cecile is praised by a Christian medieval world and by a male text because she sacrifices herself to further belief in God the Father. Her words gain great authority, and she receives the highest accolade because she dies. Through the negation of the body, she is affirmed in spiritual union with God.

This same dynamic exists in Chaucer's depiction of the Second Nun, herself. Within the context of the *Tales* where so many pilgrim narrators are described, the Second Nun receives no description, and this lack of description, this effacement, allows her more authority than either of the other two women narrators and more than most of the male narrators. Once captured in language (more or less), a narrator becomes subject to various interpretations (depending on how one hears or reads the tone of Chaucer's remarks), but by leaving the Second Nun un-named, invisible, Chaucer prevents us from erring in our interpretation of her. She is the ideal woman created by absence: she exists as an authority because she is a disembodied voice. We cannot locate any potential irony or hypocrisy because we cannot locate her; in modern feminist terms, 'she is where she is not.'[7]

Chaucer's representation of the Prioress, on the other hand, is extensive, and it thereby opens the door to ambiguity and interpretation. The Prioress, like the other disobedient women who appear in the male pilgrims' narratives, gets classified as 'disobedient' because Geoffrey, in the *General Prologue*, stresses her disregard for her vows. Although Geoffrey seems quite oblivious to the implications of his observations, we as readers, whether modern or medieval, can recognize the satire aimed at the Prioress.[8] She fastidiously tends to her

[6] Mary Daly, *Gynecology: The Metaethics of Radical Feminism* (Boston: Beacon, 1978), 8.

[7] Cf. Hélène Cixous, *Sorties*, in Catherine Clément and Hélène Cixous, *The Newly Born Woman*, trans. Betsy Wing (Minneapolis: University of Minnesota Press, 1986), 67.

[8] For a discussion of the satire levelled at the Prioress, see E. Talbot Donaldson, 'The Masculine

clothing, her food, and her pets rather than to her soul. Her wimple, 'ful semly' and 'pynched,' reveals her very worldly, very material aesthetic concerns. As Chauncey Wood points out, Chaucer carefully crafts his portrait of the Prioress so that 'where one would expect . . . a sign of unworldliness we find stylishness as a sign of worldliness.'[9] The entire portrait is constructed so that what, at first, seems appropriate, turns out to be inappropriate. Rather than a 'Sister Mary Francis,' we have a 'Madame Eglentyne,' a nun whose name comes from the fictional world of medieval romance rather than from the spiritual world of Christianity. And Madame Eglentyne feigns a courtly manner in nearly everything she does, from smiling, to singing, to dressing, to eating:

> Ther was also a Nonne, a Prioresse,
> That of hir smylyng was ful symple and coy;
> Hire gretteste ooth was but by Seinte Loy;
> And she was cleped madame Eglentyne.
> Ful weel she soong the service dyvyne,
> Entuned in hir nose ful semely,
> And Frenssh she spak ful faire and fetisly,
> After the scole of Stratford atte Bowe,
> For Frenssh of Parys was to hire unknowe.
> At mete wel ytaught was she with alle:
> She leet no morsel from hir lippes falle,
> Ne wette hir fyngres in hir sauce depe;
> . . .
> Hir over-lippe wyped she so clene
> That in hir coppe ther was no ferthyng sene
> Of grece, whan she dronken hadde hir draughte.
> . . .
> She was so charitable and so pitous
> She wolde wepe, if that she saugh a mous
> Kaught in a trappe, if it were deed or bleede.
> Of smale houndes hadde she that she feede
> With rosted flessh, or milk and wastel-breed.
>
> (I, 118–29; 133–35; 143–47)

The essence of the Prioress is masquerade: she 'peyned hire to countrefete cheere / Of court' (139–40). Both as an imitation of a nun and as an imitation of a lady, she is 'counterfeit,' and the irony of the *General Prologue* condemns her for attempting to confound territories or cross the boundaries of 'Lady' and 'Nun.'[10] The irony accomplishes several things. From one perspective, it

Narrator and Four Women of Style,' in *Speaking of Chaucer*, 46–64. Jill Mann, in her *Chaucer and Medieval Estates Satire*, catalogues Chaucer's use of traditional satirical material and also shows how Chaucer refuses the biting cynicism and severe judgment usually found in Estates Satire.

9 Chauncey Wood, 'Chaucer's Use of Signs in His Portrait of the Prioress,' in *Signs and Symbols in Chaucer's Poetry*, ed. John P. Hermann and John J. Burke, Jr (University, AL: University of Alabama Press, 1981), 86.

10 Of course, these rigid boundaries surrounding identity and activity show up in Chaucer's representations of the male clergymen as well.

criticizes the Prioress for her inadequate obedience to spiritual values, thereby reinscribing cultural assumptions about women by defining her in terms of obedience and disobedience. At the same time, the portrait challenges the simplistic discourse on women by refusing to simplify the Prioress. Her identity is a conglomerate of 'nun' and 'lady,' thereby demonstrating the inadequacy of either/or categories. Between the Second Nun's renunciation of the world and the Wife of Bath's earthy embrace comes the would-be esthete, a woman more concerned with appearances, style, and manners than with the real-life plight of starving people or tortured Jews. The Prioress lies mid-way between the disembodied voice of the Second Nun and the very embodied voice of the Wife of Bath in the same way her little clergeoun lies for a time half-way between life and death. Unlike the *Second Nun's Tale* which carries authority because its narrator is disembodied, the *Prioress's Tale* is qualified by the very real hypocrisy of a very present narrator who is both lady and nun, Christian and bigot.

Given her 'counterfeit,' or 'confounding' nature, it becomes quite ironic that she tells a tale about a child whose faith is so absolutely pure and simple, so unmediated by social sophistication or pretense. But if we assume the Canterbury narratives function as signs for the inner worlds of narrators just like bodies, clothing, gestures, and physiognomy, then the *Prioress's Tale* about a child who memorizes rather than understands Latin, may possibly reveal her own inadequate knowledge, her own mimetic and masquerading life in which she speaks a language inadequately understood. The child in her tale *understands* the religious meaning which lies behind the prayer he sings, although he does not understand its literal meaning, and so he contrasts ironically with his narrator who can rather eloquently construct poetic forms to contain a tale and yet *can not*, apparently, understand its spiritual meaning.

Whatever the spiritual concerns of her tale, she fashions adult men as murderers, hasty judges, and dubiously pious monks; the little clergeoun, the widowed mother, and the Virgin Mary are the most admirable characters within her tale. Furthermore, the Prioress quite obviously sees herself figured in the little child. The prayer to the Virgin which opens the tale invites the comparison:

> 'My konnyng is so wayk, o blisful Queene,
> For to declare thy grete worthynesse
> That I ne may the weighte nat susteene;
> But as a child of twelf month oold, or lesse,
> That kan unnethes any word expresse,
> Right so fare I, and therfore I yow preye,
> Gydeth my song that I shal of yow seye.'   (VII, 481–87)

The Prioress's self-representation echoes the end of Dante's *Paradiso*, the moment when Dante imagines himself to be a helpless infant. Piero Boitani, who has also noted the correspondence, writes: 'She, the teller, is indeed like a baby, smaller even than her protagonist, and incapable of words, whereas he, the little child of her tale, will sing, and in Latin, to the greater glory of Mary and God.'[11]

---

[11] Piero Boitani, 'His desir wol fle withouten wynge: Mary and Love in Fourteenth-Century

The feminist reader may think of a number of questions to raise about this 'female' narrator's self-representation. Why is the Prioress characterizing herself as a twelve-month old baby? Is she, by placing herself beneath the Latin-singing clergeoun, saying, 'men don't know much, but I know even less than a male child'? Is she signing herself in the image of the protagonist who is speaking and speaking the same thing over and over with a cut throat, singing and singing in a state of living death? Is she signing herself in the image of the child trying to live in a hostile world? Is she suggesting that on some level she lives a life which corresponds to that of a child who is murdered and thrown away?[12] Robert Hanning offers a 'speculative interpretation,' suggesting that the Prioress's 'treatment of her lapdogs, her sympathy for trapped mice, dead or bleeding, suggests an identification with small, helpless things, trapped and punished in a world ruled by men. . . . Within the shell of extraversion and schooled, courtly competence that this large and (in an institutional sense) successful woman has carefully constructed, there exists a frighteningly different self-image: an imprisoned, helpless creature, vulnerable to men who would menace or tyrannize her.'[13]

However we may interpret the correspondence or contrast between the Prioress and her little clerk, Chaucer quite obviously diminishes her authority in the same way he undercuts so many of the male representatives of professional spirituality, by giving her a markedly material presence and an extensive concrete description. Consequently, the Prioress commands little authority from a Christian perspective, and yet, despite this, her tale shares some features with the Second Nun's. Both female narrators tell tales about women and children attaining heavenly bliss through love. Unlike the Parson whose expository prescription for salvation is a heavy dose of penitence, the Second Nun and the Prioress tell tales which Boitani notes 'represent the only examples of religious narrative [or story] and the only two celebrations of human love for God in a fully Christian sense in the *Canterbury Tales*.'[14] The *Parson's Tale*, which emphasizes human sinfulness, the need for purification, and the necessity of obeying the law – of God the Father – is balanced by these two female narrators who give greatest emphasis to the power of love. The way to heaven emphasized by the Parson's sermon is the way of penance and atonement, of 'thou shalt not sin'; the way to heaven emphasized in the *Prioress's Tale* and the *Second Nun's Tale* is the way of revelation, the way of 'thou shalt see, believe, and love.'

Among the major characters featured *within* the Canterbury narratives, only the Prioress's child and the Second Nun's St Cecile obtain sainthood. Only they live the perfect pilgrimage of the Christian to the divine. Within the context of the spiritual pilgrimage which gives rise to the storytelling game, the Second Nun may even be the winner of the game. If we adopt a Christian perspective from which to evaluate the *Tales*, we can see that her tale is the only one which

Poetry,' in *Chaucer's Frame Tales: The Physical and the Metaphysical*, ed. Joerg O. Fichte (Tubingen: Gunter Narr Verlag/ Cambridge: D. S. Brewer, 1987), 119.

[12] The Prioress's anti-semitism here is obvious in that she characterizes Jews as the agents of a hostile world.

[13] Robert W. Hanning, 'From *Eva* and *Ave* to Eglentyne and Alison: Chaucer's Insight into the Roles Women Play,' *Signs* 2 (1977): 588–89.

[14] Boitani, 'His desir wol fle,' 119.

explicitly dramatizes the Christian's perfect search for, obedience to, and vision of, God. And unlike the Prioress, and so many other pilgrim-narrators who possess an inadequate understanding of faith and mercy, the Second Nun quite obviously understands the meanings and implications of her own religious tale. But even if we entertain the notion that the Second Nun 'wins' the storytelling contest, thereby completely upsetting the stereotypical gender hierarchy, or even if we see her tale posit a viable 'wey' to reach salvation that is equal to the Parson's, her tale does not do as much to upset or challenge the pilgrims' perceptions of gender roles as does the Wife of Bath and her tale. In the guise of Dame Prudence, St Cecile, or the Second Nun, Chaucer still creates a representation of 'woman' which is closely allied with powerful patriarchal ideals. These women are largely disembodied mediators between men and wisdom, men and God. As vessels of wisdom, as nurturers of men, they are still closely related to a Custance or a Griselde. But Chaucer takes a greater risk when he takes on the masquerade of the Wife of Bath, for in her, he imagines a woman very much 'in the body' whose own life experience is the grounding for her perceptions and judgments.

Where Dame Prudence's perceptions of the world are shaped by an extensive knowledge of male writings, where the Prioress, the Second Nun, and her character, St Cecile, are women whose words and judgments stem from their religious beliefs, the Wife of Bath takes experience to be her authority: 'Experience, though noon auctoritee / Were in this world, is right ynogh for me . . .' (III, 1-2). And where Dame Prudence never challenges Melibeus's ultimate authority, where she patiently endures his stubbornness, Dame Alysoun physically fights with her husband, Jankyn, and refuses to endure oppressive marriages calmly and quietly. St Cecile, Chaucer's Antigone, is a Christian woman who upbraids non-Christian men of a former time, but the Wife of Bath, in her Prologue, takes on men of the here and now: Christian men, not pagans. She steps beyond the rather subtle challenges to patriarchal structures found in the *Prioress's Tale* and the *Second Nun's Tale* where religious purpose obscures the critique of male dominance.

The Wife's refusal to be silent or accepting is the most brazen refusal of the three 'female' narrators. The Second Nun tells us nothing about herself; the Prioress says little and tells the briefest narrative of the three female pilgrims; but the Wife of Bath spends twice as much time revealing herself in her lengthy Prologue as she does telling her tale. Her flagrant enjoyment of a feminine identity considered abhorrent by patristic writers has led several modern Chaucerians to interpret her as a grotesque symbol of carnality, cupidity, and proud ignorance.[15] She damns herself before her clerical listeners when she claims for herself all the attributes of women the antifeminist tradition identifies: she relishes her sexuality; she enjoys acquiring wealth and power; she boasts that no man can 'swere and lyen' half as well 'as a womman kan'; and she absolutely tingles at the prospect of deceiving men. David S. Reid, for example,

---

[15] See Robertson, *A Preface to Chaucer*, 321; Hope Phyllis Weissman, 'Antifeminism and Chaucer's Characterization of Women,' in *Geoffrey Chaucer: A Collection of Original Articles*, ed. George Economou (New York: McGraw-Hill, 1975), 93-110; James Boren, 'Alysoun of Bath and the Vulgate "Perfect Wife",' *NM* 76 (1975): 247-56; William Matthew, 'The Wife of Bath and all Her Sect,' *Viator* 5 (1974): 435.

believes such textual material demonstrates that the Wife 'belongs to a vulgar and perennial fund of antifeminist jocularity.'[16] E. Talbot Donaldson, acknowledging the antifeminist caricature in the Wife, also maintains, however, that if Alysoun and women like her are the butt of Chaucer's humor, so are 'the creators of the [antifeminist] tradition and contemporary men who profess to believe it.'[17] Along the same lines, Dorothy Colmer writes, 'If it is presumptuous to suggest that Chaucer may have had some sympathy with the Wife of Bath's point of view, it is equally presumptuous to suppose that he was always and necessarily in accord with the establishment's way of thinking.'[18] Drawing attention to the historical research of May McKisack, Colmer suggests that Dame Alysoun's attack on misogyny and her sermon on 'gentilesse' serve as Chaucer's way to express 'the political disaffections of the age,' particularly women's disaffection and the desire of lower classes to break down the artificial privileges of the aristocracy.[19] In Colmer's view, the Wife's voice both protects and permits Chaucer to level criticism at his culture's misogyny and its social inequities. Viewing the tale from yet another perspective, Judith Tibbetts Schulenberg sees Chaucer, through the Wife of Bath, raise most profound objections to the misogyny of late medieval gender discourse: 'Her delightfully blunt responses to the underlying tensions created by patriarchal assumptions are unequaled in the literature of this period.'[20]

The disagreements over interpretation stem from disagreements about Chaucer's alignment with, or alienation from, Church doctrine and misogynist discourse, a tension which no doubt surfaces when we read other tales within the *Canterbury Tales*, as well as when we read the *Book of the Duchess, Troilus and Criseyde*, and the *Legend of Good Women*. And the modern critical disagreements suggest a number of things. First, since the modern reader usually finds medieval patristic writings on women unenlightened, to say the least, those who find Chaucer so likeable in other respects may have difficulty entertaining the idea that he reinscribes severe antifeminism in the Wife of Bath's portrait. But as David S. Reid suggests, by 'fearing for Chaucer's good name, we [run the risk of] misunderstand[ing] her elaborately.'[21] Antifeminism is so readily

---

[16] David S. Reid, 'Crocodilian Humor: A Discussion of Chaucer's Wife of Bath,' *ChauR* 4 (1970): 73.

[17] E. Talbot Donaldson, *Chaucer's Poetry: An Anthology for the Modern Reader* (New York: Ronald Press, 1958), 914.

[18] Dorothy Colmer, 'Character and Class in the *Wife of Bath's Tale*,' *JEGP* 72 (1973): 329–339. See also Hansen, *Chaucer and the Fictions*, 26–57.

[19] McKisack discusses the role of townspeople and weavers in the Peasants' Revolt in her text, *Oxford History of England: The Fourteenth Century* (Oxford: Oxford University Press, 1959), 413–17. She also notes that during the protests of this period, at Cambridge 'an old woman named Margery Starre cr[ied], "Away with the learning of clerks, away with it!" as she flung the parchments on the fire' (417). Among Wat Tyler's demands at Smithfield was the elimination of all lordship save the position of King; all other men were to be equal.

[20] Judith Tibbets Schulenberg, 'Clio's European Daughters: Myopic Modes of Perception,' in *The Prism of Sex: Essays in the Sociology of Knowledge*, ed. Julia A. Sherman and Evelyn T. Beck (Madison: University of Wisconsin Press, 1979), 34. Walter C. Long goes even further and argues that the Wife provides Chaucer with an avenue by which to undermine the other pilgrims' notions of order and to critique the 'natural' order: 'The Wife as Moral Revolutionary,' *ChauR* 20 (1986): 273–84.

[21] Reid, 'Crocodilian Humor,' 76.

apparent in Chaucer's depiction of Dame Alysoun, we cannot deny her iconographic embodiment of patristic misogyny; hence, D. W. Robertson, Jr, following the patristic lead, interprets her as a representation of 'rampant "femininity." '[22] According to Robertson, the Wife is 'firmly among the evil who are in the Church but not of it.'[23]

On the other hand, Chaucer obviously found this female character's voice so compelling that he gave it tremendous artistic power. It is so strong a statement about the adverse affects of oppression on women's lives that its objections to the culture's definitions of gender must be considered seriously. Perhaps the tension which exists between her disruptive statements and her iconographic conformity stems from the fact that she is a man's depiction of a female's challenge to cultural gender prescriptions. Perhaps the tension reflects (albeit within fiction) actual complexities for medieval women voicing objections and inevitable reinscriptions of the culture's misogyny, complexities well documented in scholarship on Margery Kempe, Christine de Pisan, and Hildegard of Bingen, among others.[24] Undoubtedly, her ambiguous portrait stems from tensions Chaucer can articulate between the complexity of real life and the inadequacies of cultural discourse.[25]

Dame Alysoun's first speech act in her powerful and extensive Prologue dramatizes her struggle with the dominant discourse on gender found in male-authored texts and in male glossings of those texts. She criticizes St Paul, St Jerome, Ovid, Jean de Meun, Walter Map, and others because they categorize women in ways she finds objectionable. More than individual men, whom she would thoroughly enjoy, these texts are her enemies.[26] Men, she says, love to 'devyne and glosen, up and doun' (26); they love to interpret, distort, and imagine they know the truth. The Wife knows the representations of women popular in Church writings are inadequate and biased. As Judith Ferster notes, she 'knows that these descriptions represent choices,' and she knows that the patristic representations of women draw on select passages within scripture, particularly those passages demeaning women.[27] So, for example, she objects to clerics who privilege virginity to such a degree that they sometimes condemn marriage, and she takes them on using their own weapon, the Bible, against

---

[22] Robertson, *Preface*, 321.

[23] *Ibid.*, 327.

[24] See Karma Lochrie, *Margery Kempe and Translations of Flesh* (Philadelphia: University of Pennsylvania Press, 1991); Sheila DeLany, ' "Mothers to Think Back Through": Who Are They? The Ambiguous Example of Christine de Pizan,' in *Medieval Texts and Contemporary Readers*, ed. Finke and Schichtman (Ithaca: Cornell University Press, 1987), 177–97; Elizabeth A. Petroff, *Body and Soul: Essays on Medieval Women and Mysticism* (Oxford: Oxford University Press, 1994); Barbara Newman, *Sister of Wisdom: St Hildegard's Theology of the Feminine* (Berkeley: University of California Press, 1987).

[25] Cf. Louise O. Fradenberg, 'The Wife of Bath's Passing Fancy,' *Studies in the Age of Chaucer* 8 (1986): 31–58.

[26] See Robert A. Pratt, 'Jankyn's "Book of Wikked Wyves": Medieval Antimatrimonial Propaganda in the Universities,' *AnM* 3 (1962): 5–27. William Matthews, 'The Wife of Bath and All Her Sect,' *Viator* 5 (1974): 413–43. For a comprehensive list of antifeminist literature from the Middle Ages see Francis L. Utley, *The Crooked Rib* (Columbus: Ohio State University Press, 1944), and Alcuin Blamires, ed., *Woman Defamed, Woman Defended* (Oxford: Oxford University Press, 1992).

[27] Judith Ferster, *Chaucer on Interpretation* (Cambridge: Cambridge University Press, 1985), 126.

them. By privileging virginity so exclusively, she argues, patristic writers contradict the Biblical injunction in Genesis: 'Be fruitful and multiply.' Responding to a powerful cultural discourse that valued virginal women above all others, the Wife says defiantly, 'that am nat I' (112). Although her vulnerability to ideology can be seen in her willingness to regard virginity as closer to perfection, she insists that for most humans it is not the way to live: 'And certes, if ther were no seed ysowe, / Virginitee, thannne wereof sholde it growe?' (71–72). Sexual desire and the body, she argues, are God's creation:

> Telle me also, to what conclusion
> Were membres maad of generacion,
> And of so parfit wys a wight ywroght?
> Trusteth right wel, they were nat maad for noght.
> Glose whoso wole, and seye bothe up and doun,
> That they were maked for purgacioun
> Of uryne, and oure bothe thynges smale
> Were eek to knowe a femele from a male,
> And for noon oother cause, – say ye no?
> The experience woot wel it is noght so.
> So that the clerkes be nat with me wrothe,
> I sey this, that they maked ben for bothe,
> This is to seye, for office, and for ese
> Of engendrure, ther we nat God displese.[28]   (115–28)

To those clerks who write against remarriage based upon an incident in the Gospels (John 2:1), who arrive at their condemnation based on an allegorical reading of Christ's visit to only one wedding feast, she asks, where in the Bible is remarriage explicitly forbidden? From her perspective, clerks have over-active imaginations which run wild creating misreadings of Biblical texts.[29] But to argue, as Robertson has, that Alysoun 'disregard[s] the obvious implications' of a writer like St Paul, is hardly credible. She does not 'disregard' him; she 'disagrees' with him.[30] From her 'pre-feminist' position, she seems to be quite aware of the 'obvious implications' of Pauline doctrine – if not always its spiritual meaning, surely its social meaning.

To what degree her 'ignorance' is self-willed or in play and to what degree it may reflect women's exclusion from education raises yet more interpretive possibilities. From a sympathetic perspective, her interpretations of doctrine surely reveal her tremendously capable imagination. And although her revisions

---

[28] Donald Howard comments that 'Fallen man, everyone knew, could not be expected to follow the highest counsels of perfections, and those not specially called should not envy those in higher states of perfection than themselves.' He adds, 'The enthusiasm with which [the Wife of Bath] accepts it . . . doubtless violate[s] the spirit of medieval morality,' *Idea*, 250.

[29] On the Wife's own misuse of sources see Robertson, *Preface*, 317–51. See also Lee Patterson, ' "For the Wyve's Love of Bath"': Feminine Rhetoric and Poetic Resolution in the *Roman de la Rose* and the *Canterbury Tales*,' *Speculum* 58 (1983): 656–95.

[30] Of course, her text shares some similar themes and concerns with the Pauline text. Both are concerned with the body: how to be made young again, how to become the chosen vessel, how to be made full; but the Wife's perspective also clearly differs from Paul's.

of patristic material are iconoclastic and disruptive, we should also note that Chaucer enjoys playing with biblical material and patristic references himself, as the raucous *Miller's Tale* so ably demonstrates.[31] At the least, Dame Alysoun's 'mis'readings affirm that we all do select, interpret, and distort the world as we represent it and form meaning; at the least, her argument with Church doctrine attests to the distortions of women found in patristic discourse. The Wife's Prologue depicts human perceptions, particularly men's perceptions of the world, as often contradictory or 'confusing.' This occurs, she claims, because human interpretation arises out of self-interest and social context. As Peggy A. Knapp suggests, 'The Wife sees textual production and interpretation as deeply aligned with institutional interests[:] . . . the Church and more distantly the court, and with personal intentions. Words and fictions are presented not primarily as statements of the truth about God, people, and Nature, but as instantiations of power. . . .'[32] Quite frequently, Dame Alysoun acknowledges and details her own personal biases and experiences so that we know from what positioning in the world she speaks; as she says, 'I speke after my fantasye'(190).

Of all the characters in the *Canterbury Tales*, we know more about the way Dame Alysoun's perceptions have been shaped than anyone else's. She understands the particularity of voice and word, although this does not always lead her to an awareness of her own blind self-interest.[33] What she knows is that men have seen the world and named it from their own personal, professional, and gender-inflected biases; she knows men's power to 'name' women distorts and inhibits men's perceptions of women, as well as women's perceptions of themselves.[34] Arguing that men's definitions of women reflect men's own fears, desires, fantasies and frustrations, Alysoun knows that the isolated cleric reacts to women and defines women according to his own material relationship with them so that projections and distortions are inevitable:

> The clerk, whan he is oold, and may noght do
> Of Venus werkes worth his olde sho,
> Thanne sit he doun, and writ in his dotage
> That wommen kan nat kepe hir mariage!   (707–10)

Dame Alysoun has intimately experienced the severe repercussions of such inequity. As Robert Hanning comments, 'When we 'gloss' people, we make them mean for us what we want them to and can thus use them either to satisfy our needs, if they accept our self-aggrandizing interpretation of them, or to

---

[31] Laura Kendrick, for example, discusses the potential ambiguities surrounding the notion of 'Goddes Priveytee' in her book, *Chaucerian Game: Comedy and Control in the Canterbury Tales*, 5–19.

[32] Peggy A. Knapp, 'Wandrynge by the Weye,' in *Medieval Texts and Contemporary Readers*, ed. Finke and Schichtman (Ithaca: Cornell University Press, 1987), 145.

[33] On the nature of the knower and his/her relationship to knowledge, see Boethius, *Consolation of Philosophy*, trans. Richard Green (Indianapolis: Bobbs-Merrill, 1962), 111.

[34] For a modern feminist discussion of men's power of naming, see Dale Spender, *Man Made Language* (New York and London: Routledge & Kegan Paul, 1980) and Marilyn Frye, *The Politics of Reality* (Trumansburg, N.Y.: The Crossing Press, 1983).

justify our fears and hatreds, if they do not.'[35] The Wife's recognition of the power men have in a culture which preserves and perpetuates men's interpretations far more than women's reaches its most poignant note as her words encourage us to put aside self-interest (our own versions of deafness) and listen to the voice of the Other to avoid objectifying and harmfully misrepresenting that Other. In this way, regardless of her own generalizations which so obviously (and inevitably) violate her own pleas for adequate representations, she speaks to the modern world as much as she speaks to her own, because she would remind us that words and discourse inevitably misrepresent life.

What the Wife's Prologue reveals is her struggle against the artificial constraints of culturally inscribed definitions of gender, the insufficiency of absolute categories, the insufficient relationship of Word and Experience. Whatever way we read the Wife's Prologue, in it Chaucer revels in the conflicts between the experience of individual lives and the institutional discourses on gender. In one marriage, Alysoun is in complete control:

> An housbonde I wol have, I wol nat lette,
> Which shal be bothe my dettour and my thral
>
> . . .
>
> I have the power durynge al my lyf
> Upon his propre body, and noght he. (154–55, 158–59)

But in another marriage, a different context, a different power arrangement holds: Alysoun must struggle for control. She recalls Jankyn's violence:

> . . . he to me [was] the mooste shrewe;
> That feele I on my ribbes al by rewe,
> And evere shal unto myn endyng day. (505–07)

For the Wife, an accurate representation of marriage includes an account of the inequities of power and the struggles for power she knows exist within marriage, rather than some sort of formulaic gender hierarchy.

In a struggle for power with Jankyn, violence erupts when he hits her in the head and makes her deaf, an event Alysoun mentions not once, but twice (lines 636, 668). Commonly, scholars have interpreted the Wife's deafness as a defect, believing her inability to listen to others marks her self-absorption. Chaucerians have read her deafness as an icon of her wrong-headedness or her misunderstandings. Certainly she is wrong-headed if we assume a traditional Christian perspective on the tale, but such a reading ignores or downplays Jankyn's role, for the Wife did not, alone, make herself deaf. Hit in the head, Alysoun is made deaf. It is her 'war-wound,' so to speak, material evidence of the competitive nature of marriage. Ironically, of all the pilgrims, our deaf Dame Alysoun has heard the gender discourse most clearly and can articulate its artifice most persuasively. But what if we imagine this 'war wound,' her

---

[35] Robert W. Hanning, ' "I Shal Finde It in a Maner Glose": Versions of Textual Harassment in Medieval Literature,' in *Medieval Texts and Contemporary Readers*, ed. Finke and Schichtman, 49.

deafness, as a weapon or as a shield? If she is struggling against the discourse of a patriarchal culture, what better defense than an inability to hear? If Alysoun cannot hear the awesome and oft-repeated voice of anti-feminism in her culture, she cannot be as easily persuaded of its 'truth' either. If she no longer hears it over and over, she may avoid absorbing the discourse as thoroughly as other 'hearing' men and women. Deafness becomes, potentially, a sign of her resistance, then, to anti-feminist discourse in the culture. Not constrained by, not hearing, the verbal definitions of men and women, she can examine her own experience and give it her own interpretation, to some degree. Her experience is not *as* predigested nor *as* precooked as it would be if she 'listened to,' or was limited by, pre-existing linguistic interpretations of it.

Speaking out against men's distorted representations of women, the Wife of Bath finds the double binds most disturbing. There is no way, in the dominant cultural discourse surrounding femininity, for her to be 'named' good. If a woman is beautiful, she is perceived by men as a liability because other men will always be after her. But, she knows, too, that men think 'it is an hard thyng for to welde / A thyng that no man wole, his thankes, helde' (271-72). Being ugly offers no haven, either, for if a woman is ugly, men think she will lust after anyone at any time. Similarly, she notes:

> 'Thou seist to me it is a greet meschief
> To wedde a povre womman, for costage;
> And if that she be riche, of heigh parage,
> Thanne seistow that it is a tormentrie
> to soffre hire pride and hire malencolie.'   (248-52)

Given this cultural straight jacket, it is remarkable that in the Wife of Bath, we hear a 'female' narrator venture to imagine an alternative. She imagines a world upside down, a world in which women can gain 'maistrye.' In the *Tale of Melibee*, Dame Prudence's challenge to her husband's power only goes so far as to prefer Christian mercy to retaliatory violence, and in the *Second Nun's Tale*, St Cecile only imagines another world, after death, in which she can attain union with the divine Father. Although Cecile interprets Almachius's power much differently than he does himself, she does not imagine an alternative world where men do not hold power. But the Wife does. She imagines how different cultural discourse would be if women had control of it:

> Who peyntede the leon, tel me who?
> By God! if wommen hadde writen stories,
> As clerkes han withinne hire oratories,
> They wolde han writen of men moore wikkednesse
> Than al the mark of Adam may redresse.   (692-96)

Her strategy is to expose men's biases by promoting her own. Turning the tables, she hopes that men will understand the influence patriarchy and its dominant anti-feminist discourse has on women.

Like the Second Nun, she complains against men's 'confusing' texts, but unlike the Second Nun, the Wife does not always achieve clarity in her

Prologue. Her own text is wonderfully 'confusing' in places. She disparages the misogynist idea that women are duplicitous, calling it a 'proverbe of a shrewe' (284). And, without acknowledging the contradiction, she boasts, 'for half so boldely kan ther no man / Swere and lyen, as a womman kan' (227–28). If we assume consistency is the mark of a more ordered and self-possessed mind, the Second Nun's St Cecile appears to be a woman far more autonomous and much further along the road to an articulated self than the Wife of Bath. The Wife has been so hurt by antifeminist ideology that she cannot accurately see her own access to power nor perceive ways she imitates and simply reverses the oppression she has experienced. Here, then, we encounter a challenge to the idea, entertained earlier, that Alysoun's deafness may indicate an evasion of ideology, for quite obviously she does not evade it. When she claims that her 'constellation' has determined her personality (615–32), and when she claims that her physiognamy is to blame (608–10), and when she claims that male 'auctorities' and definitions have created her, she demonstrates an awareness that individuals are never fully free to shape themselves. Although she uses these ideas to excuse herself, they also bespeak an awareness of the complexities and complicities of ideology and individual, 'auctoritie' and 'experience.' With this in mind, Lee Patterson observes:

> Try as she (and Chaucer) might, she remains confined within the prison house of masculine language; she brilliantly rearranges and deforms her authorities to enable them to disclose new areas of experience, but she remains dependent on them for her voice. Her performance is a kind of transvestism, and she speaks 'habille en homme.'[36]

(Perhaps, we should also note that Chaucer remains dependent on Alysoun, his 'habille en femme,' for the voice which will permit him to question his culture's gender ideology most blatantly). Noting the intersection of self and external influence in the Wife, Robert W. Hanning argues that Chaucer's representation reveals his sensitivity to the stultifying effects of oppressive circumstances on women: 'Rather than praising or condemning them [women], Chaucer's art shapes our understanding of the interplay of character and social environment.'[37] Surely, what the Wife's Prologue demonstrates is that both culture and individual create the self. The Wife of Bath knows that culture precludes a self beyond ideology, that there are no rigid or absolute boundaries between self and other; that self is a conglomeration of individual desire and social enculturation. It is a perception which, if considered, disallows us from *always* reading the *Tales* from the traditional Christian perspective. It encourages us to embrace the various viewpoints voiced by all the pilgrims and to acknowledge their differences. As such, the Wife of Bath's presence within the text constitutes quite a challenge to any scholarly interpretation which refuses to acknowledge unresolved conflicts and tensions in the *Tales*. Because of this, Alysoun is situated in a competitive relationship with those tales and tellers (both fictional and scholarly) who think they know truth.

---

[36] Patterson, ' "For the Wyves Love of Bath," ' 682.
[37] Hanning, 'From *Eva* and *Ave* to Eglentyne and Alison,' 599.

If the Wife of Bath's Prologue is a challenge to the authority of human perception, particularly men's perceptions, it also reveals the power of patriarchal ideology to impede perception. On several different levels the tale challenges the culture's gender prescriptions, and yet, it also reinscribes them. Literally, of course, the narrative exposes and upbraids a rapacious and duplicitous male character (the figure of the rapist-knight) and makes him dependent upon women for his survival: if he cannot discover what it is that women desire most, he will lose his head. The Wife enjoys making him squirm as the hag plays with him a bit and tests his pledge, but his is only a momentary testing: the Wife-narrator lets him off the hook quite easily. In the *Clerk's Tale*, where Walter tested and tortured a completely innocent Griselde, and in the *Physician's Tale*, where no remedy could save the pure Virginia, women who were completely innocent were subjected to horrendous 'testing.' But in the *Wife of Bath's Tale*, the knight being tested deserves to be tested; he is a rapist. The Wife-narrator's 'testing' of the knight is, however, quite mild. Even though the knight is guilty of a crime, the hag nurtures him, assists him, and forgives him. The Wife's story ultimately embraces and restores the sinner (the knight) to the community (figured in the marriage). If the Wife's 'testing' story is read this way, it advocates forgiveness and mercy, the Christian imperative, and thereby challenges the competitiveness and vengefulness which characterizes humanity in so many of the other pilgrims' narratives.

One wonders, however, if any 'real-life' Alysoun, married off at age twelve, would interpret the narrative this way. Does the Wife's leniency toward the rapist-knight indicate a controlling ideology or a controlling male viewpoint behind the 'female' voice? The image of the old woman who rescues and marries a rapist, who transforms herself into a beautiful young maiden, who ultimately surrenders herself to him is surely problematic. At the end of the tale, we learn that the hag 'obeyed' the rapist-knight 'in every thyng / That myghte doon hym pleasaunce or likyng' (1255-56). Lee Patterson claims:

> The Tale tells us, first, that the husband who abandons *maistrye* will receive in return a wife who will fulfill his every wish. . . ., and second, that what women most desire is to be just this sort of obedient wife. The feminine desire that is anatomized throughout the Tale is here revealed to be, in its authentic form, determined by a desire that is not only masculine but is beyond scrutiny. The Wife's 'queynte fantasye,' in short, is a masculine wish-fulfillment, and one in which she appears to be fully complicit.[38]

Such a narrative promotes the cultural stereotype of women as nurturers of men, even when men violate women, and the hag's transformation into the beautiful woman reinforces the absolute, 'either/or' categories which men tend to assign to women and which women tend to assign to themselves (all bad, threatening crones and witches, or all good, submissive maidens).

Notably, the tale the Wife tells is set in a distant time, in a 'land fulfild of fayerye,' in an irrecoverable world 'of manye hundred yeres ago.' And the Wife

38 Patterson, ' "For the Wyves," ' 682-83.

tells a tale of an elf-queen who danced 'with hir joly compaignye . . . in many a grene mede.' But this old world, the magic be-witched world of women's fantasy, has been colonized, she claims, by more modern and male institutions. Is this another 'pre-feminist' perception? Is the Wife perhaps lamenting the enculturation of the pre-institutionalized individual or society into an institutionalized and 'limited' patriarchal, Christian mode of perception that both she and her husbands have struggled with?

> But now kan no man se none elves mo,
> For now the grete charitee and prayeres
> Of lymytours and othere hooly freres,
> That serchen every lond and every streem,
> As thikke as motes in the sonne-beem,
> Blessynge halles, chambres, kichenes, boures,
> Citees, burghes, castels, hye toures,
> Thropes, bernes, shipnes, dayeryes –
> This maketh that ther ben no fayeryes.
> For ther walketh now the lymytour hymself
> In undermeles and in morwenynges,
> And seyeth his matyns and his hooly thynges
> As he gooth in his lymytacioun.   (864–77)

These lines would seem to offer confirmation. The feminine magical world (possibly an image of Alysoun's imagination) has been 'limited' and strongly influenced by the Church and by institutionalized knowledge and perceptions. So the modern world and its discourses and categories have codified and limited the fictional world, the world of the imagination (in this case, particularly the feminine imagination). This aspect of the Wife's tale must be acknowledged along side her aberrant readings of doctrine. The Wife may struggle not to hear the codified and powerful cultural discourse, but she cannot really escape it. If escape is possible, it is escape through fiction, possibility, and imagination, and it resides in a 'fayerye' world, a remembered world, a dream world. But the Wife knows, 'now kan no man se none elves mo.' She tells a fantasy, a fairy tale. What the Wife perceives when she looks at gender is echoed in contemporary feminism. She knows what the dominant culture's patriarchal dream of ideal marriage is, and she knows her own dream is different. It is a perception which weaves in and out of women's history from ancient myth to contemporary theorists like Hélène Cixous, who writes/imagines:

> Man's dream: I love her – absent, hence desirable, a dependent nonentity, hence adorable. Because she isn't there where she is. As long as she isn't where she is. How he looks at her then! When her eyes are closed, when he completely understands her, when he catches on and she is no more than this shape made for him: a body caught in his gaze.
>   Or woman's dream? It's only a dream. I am sleeping. If I weren't asleep, he wouldn't look for me, he wouldn't cross his good lands and my badlands to get to me. Above all, don't wake me up! What anguish! If I have to be entombed to attract him. And suppose he kissed me? How can I

will this kiss? Am I willing? What does she want? To sleep, perchance to dream, to be loved in a dream, to be approached, touched, almost, to almost come (jourir). But not to come: or else she would wake up. But she came in a dream, once upon a time.[39]

And yet, by telling a tale, a fiction, the Wife can imagine a different world, and during the time we listen to the story, past and present, fiction and reality blur. The past, reiterated in the present, is born again in the present. We may not see fairies or elves dancing on the green, we may not perceive crones turning into young maidens, yet we can imagine such celebrations and transformations, and by speaking them, create them anew. The utopian fairy world exists in the imagination; and, in the mind that can imagine the folktale, the old crone can also be the young maid.[40]

If the Wife of Bath's words allow Chaucer to entertain a challenge to the misogyny of his culture to some degree, this gat-toothed, sensual woman's body is also a challenge, for the old woman narrator, whose very body depicts flux and change, tells a tale in which flux and change are redemptive.[41] Where male narrators generally resist change, mourn the loss it brings, or struggle to transcend its awesome power, the Wife embraces it. By way of contrast consider the Pardoner who thinks on change and flux and associates it with death, associates it with the old man longing for an end, a finality. Or consider the Knight-narrator who, for all his Boethian concepts, laments change or loss. He does not spend time in his narrative describing the promise of rejuvenation, the marriage of Palamon and Emelye; instead, he details the violence of emotional transformation (love) and physical transformation (death). He offers a detailed representation of Arcite's dying body, the male body in change, but almost nothing which documents the changes in Palamon's body or Emelye's, the characters who marry, who are transformed from the virginal state to the married, whose changes promise new life. The *Miller's Tale* and the *Reeve's Tale* effect no positive change in their characters either; change is rape, ravishment, illicit sexuality, or broken bones. And, of course, the Man of Law and the Physician, as we have seen, chastise change, praising constancy and 'sameness.' For most of the male narrators, ideal women are women who transcend change and cycle.

Harry Bailly, too, belongs with the large group of men who privilege finality and security. Although he will ultimately change from leader to follower by turning his authority over to the Parson, as long as he leads the storytelling game, he carefully watches the time, always urging the narrators to make a good end. His discomfort with time or change is registered when he characterizes it as a murder, burglary, and sexual conquest:

> '. . . the tyme wasteth nught and day,
> And steleth from us, what pryvely slepynge,

---

[39] Hélène Cixous, *Sorties*, 67.

[40] Perhaps the Wife's utopian or nostalgic desire for another world is also, ironically, a recognition of the impossibility of reforming rapists or of remaining young. Perhaps, then, it contains a bitter statement: 'The day no one grows old, rapists will be reformed.'

[41] Cf. Robertson, *Preface*, 317–33.

And what thurgh necligence in oure wakynge,
As dooth the streem that turneth nevere agayn,
Descendynge fro the montaigne into playn.
Wel kan Senec and many a philosophre
Biwaillen tyme . . .
    . . .
"But los of tyme shendeth us," quod he.
It wol nat come agayn, withouten drede,
Namoore than wole Malkynes maydenhede,
Whan she hath lost it in hir wantownesse.'   (II, 21-24; 28-31)

In this particular passage, Harry Bailly 'reads' time through the image of the female body. In this brief passage, the Wife of Bath may well hear (if she's listening) the gender-talk she would like to escape. Harry has made a 'confusing' text. Change is horrible; it 'steals' from men when they're not looking and when they're not attentively protecting their own best interests. Time is an adversary; time is, in a sense, a rapist. On the other hand, since time is like a woman's body, it can be possessed, penetrated, and controlled, if a man isn't negligent. Harry's prevailing response to time (change) and to Woman (as sexual body) involves a sense of loss. Time's conquest over humanity, in other words, death, and men's conquest over women's bodies, in other words, sex, are interwoven in the language of this passage.

The Wife of Bath, obviously, 'reads' change and time quite differently; and she 'reads' the female body quite differently. Instead of privileging the hymen and mourning its rupture, the Wife privileges the erotic and the cycles of a woman's body. For the Wife of Bath, the old hag can recapture her maidenhood and her time. If time is, in any sense, a rapist, the Wife imagines herself disarming and manipulating him for her own pleasure. She can live in a cycle of regeneration. Desiring to begin again and again, she would embrace change. She welcomes another marriage: 'Welcom the sixte, whan that evere he shal. / For soothe, I wol nat kepe me chaast in al' (45-46). Rather than connecting the female body with loss and death, as Harry Bailly does, the Wife equates the female body with new beginnings. And in her imagination, at least, there are no distinct borders between death and rebirth, old age and youth.

In the Wife of Bath's prologue, tale, voice, and body, boundaries become amorphous.[42] Here, individual speech and cultural discourse, word and experience, self and others blur together. Crone and maid, past and present, beginnings and endings, the corrupt and the beautiful, fiction and truth all unite to pull together and against one another in a single character. Chaucer/Alysoun, she/he is a product of both 'experience' and 'auctoritie' – experience perceived in a context of authority or ideology and authority perceived from within a context of experience. Here is Chaucer's greatest challenge to the culture's discourse surrounding femininity. Unlike his male pilgrim narrators, Chaucer embraces and enjoys the multiplicities of character, whether male or female. What attracts him to Dame Alysoun is the complexity of the human, not the simplicity of artificial social or cultural definitions.

[42] Cf. Caroline W. Bynum, *Fragmentation and Redemption: Essays on Gender and the Human Body in Medieval Religion* (New York: Zone, 1991).

CHAPTER TEN

Conclusion
and Notes Toward Further Inquiry

Chaucer's *Canterbury Tales*, with its collection of people who, for the most part, don't know one another, typifies the human dynamics of an emerging, early modern and urban world. The relationships between men which are foregrounded in the text reflect a competitive, fourteenth-century London society experiencing the rise of capitalism. The tribe, the village, the somewhat isolated community, was gradually giving way to a more impersonal and bureaucratic world. Recent research examining the formation of the state, makes clear that 'the mature state is one in which bureaucracy dominates kinship; the early state is one in which kinship still dominates bureaucracy,' and that, furthermore, bureaucracy heralds a loss of status and rights for women and a loss of close, interdependent relationships among men.[1] Chaucer's world was not, of course, simply (or yet) a bureaucracy, but late fourteenth-century courts, cities, and states were moving gradually in that direction. Wariness toward other people in the Middle Ages existed, however, as a commonplace before the rise of a monied economy and a more consolidated state. Not unique to men nor unique to the late medieval urban scene, wariness was an everyday phenomenon for people living without security of person or property. Where people have little or no recourse to an effective police force and where they have infrequent or unequal access to a legal system, they defend their lives and livelihoods as best they can, and this need for survival on a very basic level promotes vigilance. Quite some time ago, Norbert Elias imagined that 'life on the main roads' of medieval society would 'demand[] a constant readiness to fight,' as well as a constant readiness to unleash all of one's 'emotions in defense of one's life or possessions.'[2] Corroborating his views, a number of recent studies have persuasively demonstrated that the late Middle Ages had a relatively high

---

[1] Richard Lee and Richard Daly, 'Man's Dominance and Woman's Oppression: The Question of Origins,' in *Beyond Patriarchy*, 36–37. See also Rosalind Coward, *Patriarchal Precedents: Sexuality and Social Relations* (London: Routledge, Kegan Paul, 1983).

[2] Norbert Elias, *Power and Civility: The Civilizing Process: Volume II*, trans. Edmund Jephcott (Oxford: Basil Blackwell, 1982), 233; originally published as *Uber den Prozess der Zivilisation*, vol. 2 (Basel, 1939).

tolerance threshold for violence.[3] But besides its location at a crossroads in the development of the modern bureaucratic state, a crossroads where relationships between men were increasingly distant and competitive, fourteenth-century London elite culture preserved, incorporated, and cultivated chivalric discourses which also promoted competition and control.

Germanic, Norman, French, and Anglo-Saxon chivalric discourses surrounding masculinity emphasized 'the warrior' and produced a formidable legacy which, in its literature, idealized the comitatus, the war band, filial and feudal devotion, and devoted friendship.[4] But if we might naively imagine men's lives in earlier heroic and feudal periods to have been at least emotionally more homosocial, Peggy Reeves Sanday, in her book, *Female Power and Male Dominance* (Cambridge, 1981), has found that men's lives in preindustrial cultures are still marked by emotional isolation. She says men in such societies often are, for example, distanced from their children and expect complete obedience from them.[5] In societies where competitiveness and control are valued masculine attributes, men tend to view women as inferior and unworthy of trust, she claims, but other men are not trustworthy either, since the culture promotes competition. She notes that such a culture is perceived as hostile by its people, that it is experienced as a series of power struggles, viewed with suspicion, and marked by competition and sexual antagonism, features quite prominent in the world of Chaucer's *Canterbury Tales*.[6] Hostility, she says, is a common feature of preindustrial society, even if its members cannot describe it as such. But what of the male bonding that we assume common in patriarchal cultures? Joseph Pleck explains in his book, *The Myth of Masculinity*, that at least in the Western world, male-to-male bonding is unreal, a facade. It is, he says, 'not a vehicle for male-male emotional relationships, but rather a substitute for them.'[7] Thus, the cultural expressions of competition can be understood to function (to some degree) as mirrors of, or compulsions for, the emotional isolation of men from one another. Men in the *Tales* are, in many ways, strangers to one another, and this dynamic reflects not only tensions between discourses of masculinity in the culture, but more complex institutional alignments and dissonances as well.

Indeed, when the male pilgrims in Chaucer's text look out into the world, they typically find adversaries more often than friends, and, because they expect to find adversaries, they also participate in creating the presence of adversarial relationships on the pilgrimage. The expectation of conflict quite obviously

---

[3] See Richard Kaeuper, *War, Justice and Public Order: England and France in the Later Middle Ages* (Oxford: Clarendon, 1988) and James B. Given, *Society and Homicide in Thirteenth-Century England.* (Stanford: Stanford University Press, 1977).

[4] Cf. *The Song of Roland, The Battle of Maldon, Amis and Amiloun, Beowulf.* See also Cicero's *De Amicitia*, and Aquinas on friendship in the *Summa* (Prima Secundae; Secunda Secundae, ques. 114 art. 1.), and his commentary on Book 8 of Aristotle's *Ethics*.

[5] For a careful evaluation of medieval family life, see David Nichols, *The Domestic Life of a Medieval City: Women, Children, and the Family in Fourteenth-Century Ghent* (Lincoln: University of Nebraska Press, 1985). Part II, entitled 'Honor Thy Fathers: The Children of Ghent' (109–72), offers historical evidence of parent-child relationships.

[6] Peggy Reeves Sanday, *Female Power and Male Dominance* (Cambridge: Cambridge University Press, 1981), 63.

[7] Joseph H. Pleck, *The Myth of Masculinity* (Cambridge, Mass.: Harvard University Press, 1981), 150. Cf. Sedgwick, *Between Men* and Middleton, *The Inward Gaze*, for alternative analyses of competition within the formation of masculinity.

shapes the interpersonal dynamics dramatized in the *Tales*. In the frame narrative, the Friar and the Summoner, the Miller and the Reeve create conflict where none previously existed. And Chaucer weaves this dynamic into his portraits and dramatic interchanges; in fact, the competitive game relationship is foundational for his narrative. If we look in the *Canterbury Tales* to find men whose relationships to each other exhibit openness, honesty, or intimacy, we are disappointed; close friendships between men are hardly represented. Granted, there is the friendship, ever so briefly mentioned in the *Knight's Tale*, between Theseus and Perotheus; and the Parson and the Plowman have a nurturing sibling relationship, according to the *General Prologue*, but it is never explored or dramatized in the course of the pilgrimage; and in the *Second Nun's Tale*, Valerian demonstrates a love for his brother, Tibertius, but these kinds of male-to-male relationships are rare; rather more typical are rivalry and competitiveness. The more loving relationships between men are woven into the background – as 'details' easily overlooked.

In the frame narrative, when male pilgrims do speak gently and more personably, they are separated to preserve the game, the competition. At the end of the *Squire's Tale*, for example, the Franklin praises the Squire and says he wishes his own son were like the Squire. He wishes his son were a man of 'discrecioun,' eloquence, and virtue. The Franklin complains that his son gambles away his money and that 'he hath levere talken with a page / Than to comune with any gentil wight / Where he myghte lerne gentillesse aright' (V, 692–94). The host, irritated by this personal exchange between the Franklin and the Squire, intrudes:

> 'Straw for youre gentillesse!' quod oure Hoost.
> 'What, Frankeleyn! pardee, sire, wel thou woost
> That ech of yow moot tellen atte leste
> A tale or two, or breken his biheste.'   (695–98)

Apparently, it goes against the rules of the game to speak so. The Franklin responds:

> 'That knowe I wel, sire,' quod the Frankeleyn.
> 'I prey yow, haveth me nat in desdeyn,
> Though to this man I speke a word or two.'   (699–701)

And Harry Bailly commands: 'Telle on thy tale withouten wordes mo' (702). 'Gentillesse' may be a trait Chaucer admires, but the Host prefers gamesmanship.

Historical research has also established that although men had enjoyed a fuller range of relationships with each other (including homosexual ones) in the early and high Middle Ages, early modern Europe began systematically persecuting men for having too intimate a relationship with other men. From the 1300s onward, greater strictures and blatant aggression against homosexuality inhibited men's relationships with men, whether homosexual or not, and men feared being labelled a 'sodomite.'[8] Although the twelfth century witnessed a revival of gay culture, by the fourteenth century, Philip IV could destroy the Templars using the charge of rampant homosexuality as a way to justify his greed and his violence against them. In the twelfth century, a king could easily and without opposition advance his male lover within the court or within the episcopate; in the fourteenth century, England's Edward II, whom John Boswell calls 'the last overtly homosexual monarch of the Middle Ages,' could be executed primarily because of his intimate relationships with men.[9] Boswell offers the evidence and concludes that many of the complaints made against Edward 'seem to camouflage the real conflict over his attachments to Gaveston and Hugh le Despenser.'[10] Noting this growing intolerance in the fourteenth century, Boswell writes:

> Only a century before, . . . a cleric convicted of habitual sodomy would have suffered at worst demotion and religious penance. Now 'sodomy' could be used as a charge carrying the death penalty and justifying – in the minds of some – the dissolution of an entire order of Christian knights [the Templars]. Mere suspicion of the act was considered sufficient to warrant such torture that many of the Knights died under it.[11]

Obviously, this cultural climate of hostility toward men loving men affected all men's relationships with other men, regardless of sexual orientation, making them especially wary of getting too close. Although Chaucer seems to cast doubt on his own virile masculinity – writing his body as small, elfish, childish, like a 'popet' – he distances himself (and his audience) from the Pardoner, the pilgrim who most trespasses the embodied definitions of masculinity. His body – unreadable because it fails to conform adequately to the category of maleness – lies somewhere between 'a geldyng or a mare' (I, 691).[12] Whatever critical gymnastics we perform with this figure, whatever the rhetorical brilliance of his prologue, Geoffrey's observations in the *General Prologue* coupled with Chaucer's choice of a despairing and macabre tale for the character distance him from us. This 'freend' and 'compeer' of the Summoner (670), this opportunistic Pardoner speaks with a voice 'as smal as . . . a goot' and 'feyn[s] flaterye and japes' to defraud 'povre' people (688, 705, 702). If his body moves into the sexually subversive or 'dangerous' realm, his tale counters any homosocial or homosexual affection by reinscribing mythic and violent betrayals men perpetrate on one another. The three rioters, who each betray the others to gain

---

[8] John Boswell's recent historical investigation into this topic is an excellent place to find supporting evidence for this change in social regulation. The information included at this point in my text is indebted to his extensive research: *Christianity, Social Tolerance and Homosexuality: Gay People in Western Europe from the Beginning of the Christian Era to the Fourteenth Century* (Chicago: University of Chicago Press, 1980).

[9] See Boswell, *Christianity*, 297-98.

[10] *Ibid.*, 298; 298, n. 86.

[11] *Ibid.*, 297.

[12] For insightful discussions of the Pardoner see Carolyn Dinshaw, *Chaucer's Sexual Poetics* (Madison: University of Wisconsin Press, 1989) and Lee Patterson, *Chaucer and the Subject of History* (Madison: University of Wisconsin Press, 1991). Although the two discussions have different aims, both examine the Pardoner and the construction of his body and voice thoroughly.

wealth, begin as carousing friends: 'Togidres han thise thre hir trouthes plight / To lyve and dyen ech of hem for oother,/ As though he were his owene ybore brother' (VI, 702–04), and each lies dead at the end of the tale, simultaneously victim and perpetrator of homicide. In the sermonizing sections of the *Pardoner's Tale*, intertextual resonances of mythic and biblical narratives reaffirm a dynamic of betrayal and violence among men. We hear of Adam, the 'gloton' cast out of paradise, whose sin dooms all men to suffering; of Christ's betrayal and crucifixion; of Herod who 'yaf his heeste / To sleen the Baptist John, ful gilteless' (490–91); and of Death, the 'adversarie,' the 'privee theef' who 'with his spere . . . hath a thousand slayn' (675–82). The Old Man in the tale (as a figural Cain) wanders the earth searching either for mercy from a young man willing to take his place or for Death to grant him release, and neither will. He says:

> '. . . For I ne kan nat fynde
> A man, though that I walked into Ynde,
> Neither in citee ne in no village,
> That wolde chaunge his youthe for myn age;
> And therfore moot I han myn age stille,
> As longe tyme as it is Goddes wille.
> Ne Deeth, allas, ne wol nat han my lyf.
> Thus walke I, lyk a restelees kaityf . . .'

Besides telling one of the bleakest and despairing of tales (thereby repressing or destroying any notion of homosocial affection), the Pardoner, by his very presence, becomes an 'other' Chaucer uses to reaffirm the male pilgrims' masculinity and his own culture's gender definitions. As Lee Patterson notes, 'in both his mutilation [as a eunuch] and in his willingness to imagine sufficiency in Oedipal terms, the Pardoner at once enacts masculinism's deepest fears and challenges a theological orthodoxy that is itself sustained by profoundly masculinist assumptions.'[13] The pilgrims distance themselves (at the expense of the Pardoner and the effeminate Absolon in the *Miller's Tale*) from any male bodies or voices that wander too far from normative gender categories. When the Pardoner invites Harry Bailly to kiss the relics hanging in a pouch right in front of his genitals, his language moves into the sexual: 'Com forth, sire Hoost, and offre first anon, / And thou shalt kisse the relikes everychon, / Ye, for a grote! Unbokele anon thy purs' (943–45). Harry, outraged, cries:

> '. . . it shal nat be . . .
> Thou woldes make me kisse thyn olde breech,
> And swere it were a relyk of a seint,
> Though it were with thy fundement depeint!
> But, by the croys which that Seint Eleyne fond,
> I wolde I hadde thy coillons in myn hond
> In stide of relikes or of seintuarie.
> Lat kutte hem of, I wol thee helpe hem carie;
> They shul be shryned in an hogges toord!'   (947–55)

---

[13] Patterson, *Chaucer and the Subject of History*, 397.

And 'al the peple lough' (961). The threat Harry Bailly perceives coming from the Pardoner is answered with a violent verbal attack, apparently enjoyed by the other pilgrims. The Knight's intervention reconciles the host with the Pardoner, his action a distant echo of Theseus's intervention in the duel between Palamon and Arcite.

The male pilgrims' desire to declare, in some way, their masculinity and power over the others, suggests connections between the storytelling contest, medieval codes of masculinity, and analyses of contemporary Euro-American masculinity. For example, when men speak in *The Canterbury Tales*, they most often are involved in what Clyde Franklin terms 'impression management'; that is, they are speaking so as to manipulate or control the perceptions other people have of them. Of course, women can do the same thing, but Franklin identifies 'impression management' as one key element in the modern male gender role. He writes:

> . . . it is likely that males try their hardest to control and manage impressions when they interact with other males. This is due to the possibility that while men seek validation of their masculinity from women, the ultimate validation of a male's masculinity comes from more 'powerful' others – other males. Why? Because generally other males validate a crucial requirement for a particular male's masculinity – whether he has established sufficient distance from femininity.
>
> As a result of males' concerns about other males validating this important aspect of their masculinity, males tend to give their most dramatic masculine 'performances' in social situations where other males are present. Such 'performances' can be seen in much male-male social interaction where men frequently exhibit competitively their mental and physical skills. The motivation behind these frequent exhibitions, in addition to male desires to compete and win male games, includes attempts by males to gain validation of their masculinity from other males.[14]

Even though Clyde Franklin's concept and analysis of 'impression management' arises out of a twentieth-century context, it may speak to a fourteenth-century world as well. Franklin's concept of male 'performance' may help explain why we don't see more 'gentillesse' among the pilgrims in the frame narrative or in the stories the male narrators tell. If by giving these performances, the male narrators are seeking validation for their masculinity from 'powerful' male others, it not surprising that emotional intimacy is inhibited: each pilgrim thinks he is controlling and managing the information he allows the others to have about him. Direct self-disclosure is risky, for a man may accidentally disclose 'weaknesses' or what he considers to be 'feminine' parts of himself.[15] Of course, it is also difficult to self-disclose or to empathize with someone else if one's subtext involves anxious questions like 'Am I masculine enough? ' 'Is he masculine enough?' Those men set up as authorities over male gender identities are not likely to be embraced as close friends. And obviously, men who are

---

[14] Clyde W. Franklin, *The Changing Definition of Masculinity*, Perspectives in Sexuality (New York and London: Plenum, 1984), 98.
[15] See Elaine T. Hansen, *Chaucer and the Fictions of Gender*.

making gender role assessments are distanced from those they are judging as well. So the desire to (or the compulsion to) conform to the culture's prescribed codes of masculinity creates emotional distance. On the surface, men must conform, draw together, be men. Under the surface? Competition, wariness, judgment.

Although I disagree with Peter Schwenger's comment that 'there seems to be little explicit questioning of the male role, in literature or outside of it, until our own century,' his work illuminates yet some other features of masculinity represented in the *Canterbury Tales*.[16] Schwenger (focusing on modern literature) has been moving toward an understanding 'the masculine mode,' and he suggests that the mode is exemplified by texts which 'attempt to render a certain *maleness of experience*' and which take male sexuality 'as their explicit subject.'[17] Chaucer does not demonstrate the mode to the degree (or in the same way) that Yukio Mishima, Ernest Hemingway, Lincoln Kirstein, and Philip Roth do, but, in so far as masculinity and male sexuality form a central issue for *The Canterbury Tales*, he participates in 'the masculine mode.' Here, as in modern texts, the 'explorations of maleness . . . are not straightforward but riddled with contradictions and paradoxes,' and here we have several narrators who perform what Schwenger calls 'a deliberate distancing from the sense of self-awareness.' The 'confessional element[s],' the 'mistrust of words,' 'the [linguistic and literary] styles that to various degrees annihilate themselves,' and the 'deliberate distancing' which help identify Schwenger's 'masculine' texts also characterize the *Tales* but are especially features found in Chaucer's persona, Geoffrey, the super-narrator. Exposing himself with gentle mockery, illustrating a mistrust of linguistic signs, creating a kind of self-consuming art, and performing always at ironic distance, Chaucer's persona shares key features with Schwenger's 'masculine mode.' Geoffrey displays himself naively before us, calling attention to his small, plump, rather emasculated body; at the same time, this naive and highly observant persona provides the 'deliberate distancing' so crucial for Chaucer's pervasive irony. Lee Patterson has noticed the 'unrecognizability' of Chaucer's narrator, and has investigated the significance of the question Harry Bailly asks Geoffrey: 'What man artow?' Patterson understands the answer to the question to rest in the tensions Chaucer registers as he attempts 'to establish a modernist (i.e., classicizing) poetic in opposition to fashionable courtly "makyng."'[18] Patterson also argues that Chaucer locates himself in the negation, the irony, and the satire of his texts . . ., as well as in the ironic persona, Geoffrey, who narrates so many of his earlier works: 'It is the positive that is missing from this picture, a social identity commensurate with Chaucer's literary practice: he is the originator of a national literature in a culture that lacks both the concept of literature and a social identity for those who produce it.' Patterson continues: 'Lacking a recognizable role within the social whole, Chaucer is obliged to locate himself outside it'; finally, he argues, Chaucer locates himself in the image of the child or in the hopeful

---

[16] Peter Schwenger, 'The Masculine Mode,' in *Speaking of Gender*, ed. Elaine Showalter (New York: Routledge, 1989), 102.

[17] *Ibid.*

[18] Lee Patterson, ' "What Man Artow?": Authorial Self-Definition in *The Tale of Sir Thopas* and *The Tale of Melibee*,' *SAC* 11 (1989): 117–75. My citations here occur on p. 117 and p. 123.

longing represented in the image of the child with 'its paradoxical mixture of anticipation and nostalgia,' 'birth and death,' 'origin and termination.'[19] Patterson's analysis, which (among other things) highlights Chaucer's emphasis on his persona's body, is echoed in Schwenger's discussion of 'masculine' writing: 'In the masculine mode, . . ., the [male] body's paradoxes operate with unusual force.'[20] Although writers frequently avoid or erase the body, focusing instead on dialogue or on the internal worlds of characters, Schwenger notes that a 'masculine mode' of literature explores 'the paradoxes and complexities of being-in-the-world' which 'center on the body.'[21]

Patterson's analysis of Chaucer's yearning identification with the child is also provocative when set next to Roland Barthes's description of Oedipal narrative. In his essay, 'Introduction to the Structural Analysis of Narratives,' Barthes writes, 'It may be significant that it is at the same moment (around the age of three) that the little human "invents" at once sentence, narrative, and the Oedipus.'[22] Barthes argues elsewhere that the imprint of the Oedipal/masculine dynamic is integral to both the narrative structure and the aesthetic experience of any text:

> The pleasure of the text is . . . an Oedipal pleasure (to denude, to know, to learn the origin and the end), if it is true that every narrative (every unveiling of the truth) is a staging of the (absent, hidden or hypostatized) father – which could explain the solidarity of narrative forms, of family structures, and of prohibitions of nudity.[23]

We can see the *Tales* produce exactly this kind of pleasure as each tale 'denudes' its teller, as each tale 'unveils' its ethical or moral dilemma, and as each tale offers up its own meaning (often focusing on family relationships, as Patterson has noted). If exposure is a feature of Oedipal/masculine narrative, one can readily identify many of Chaucer's *Tales* as participating in that type of narrative. In the *Miller's Tale*, for example, all that is 'deerne' and 'privete' is known and exposed in the end. Furthermore, the impetus toward exposure (here also a feature of the dynamic of competition) provides the motivation for a number of storytelling duels in the frame narrative. The Reeve tells a tale designed to expose the Miller; the Miller tells a tale designed to expose the pretenses of the Knight or his genre; the Friar reveals the Summoner; the Summoner likewise denudes the Friar; and the Canon's Yeoman parades the Canon's secrets, and so forth.

The Oedipal, or masculine, informs the *Tales* in yet another way. If we examine Chaucer's work to find where pleasure originates and where meaning originates, we find it 'tracking . . . from the point of view of Oedipus,' to

---

[19] *Ibid.*, 135; 160–75.

[20] Schwenger, 'Masculine Mode,' 103.

[21] *Ibid.*

[22] Roland Barthes, 'Introduction to the Structural Analysis of Narratives,' in *Image-Music-Text*, trans. Stephen Heath (New York: Hill and Wang, 1977), 124.

[23] Barthes, *The Pleasure of the Text*, trans. Richard Miller (New York: Hill and Wang, 1975), 10. For a feminist critique of these assumptions about reading and pleasure, see Teresa de Lauretis, *Alice Doesn't: Feminism, Semiotics, Cinema* (Bloomington: Indiana University Press, 1984), especially chapter five.

borrow a key phrase from Teresa de Lauretis; 'its movement is that of a masculine desire.'[24] If we ask what happened to May after her encounter with Damian, or what happened to Alisoun after her affair with Nicholas, we do not know. These female perspectives are not represented in the *Tales*. How did Custance feel about indirectly causing her dear friend Hermengild's death? What is Judith's perspective on Holofernes or Delilah's on Samson in the *Monk's Tale*? What happened to Sophia who lies so badly wounded in the *Tale of Melibee*? How did Malyne feel after being seduced, used, and thrown away? What happened to the girl the knight raped in the *Wife of Bath's Tale*? How did the unnamed mother of Virginia feel when her husband killed her only child? When we pose these kinds of questions, the gender perspective which pervades the tales (regardless of the gender of the narrator) becomes apparent. For the most part, the narratives exist to express man's desires, to express his perspective and to ask his questions. The stories are told *for* men and to provide answers *to* men. The male figure is most frequently the one who is transformed, the 'hero' the one who has a problem to solve or a difficulty to be overcome. Emelye, Alisoun, and Virginia function as goals to be achieved, and a character like Griselde functions as both an object for Walter's testing and as a mystery for the Clerk to explain. Most, if not all, of the women characters in the *Tales* are 'inscribed in hero narratives, in someone else's story, not their own; so they are figures or markers of positions – places and topoi – through which the hero and his story move to their destination and . . . meaning.'[25] Women form the boundaries or the obstacles for men to overcome, explain, or out-maneuver. Whether representing knowledge, power, or sexuality, women in the *Tales* become the problem to be solved or the thing to be possessed. When they do pose a threat for men, they resemble the Medusa, the Gorgon, and the Sphinx, figures de Lauretis discusses because they function within narratives as a threat to men's vision. Damian, January, Palamon, Arcite, Nicholas, Absolon, and the Sultan from the *Man of Law's Tale* are all striken in the eye by the visual image of a woman. Woman's power in Oedipal/masculine narrative, according to de Lauretis, stems from her ' "to-be-looked-at-ness," ' and from her 'luring of man's gaze into the "dark continent," ' . . . the enigma of femininity.'[26] The fear of seeing the feminine, of gazing upon the mother's 'lack' and the masculine fear of castration attendant to that gaze, are cornerstones of the Oedipal and cornerstones of Western masculinity, albeit as it is theorized in the twentieth century.

But even if we disregard the terms of contemporary, twentieth-century discussions of masculinity, Chaucer's concerns with masculinity and gender are still clearly central to the *Canterbury Tales*. From the opening lines of the *General Prologue* to the last lines of the retraction, the *Canterbury Tales* establishes its concern with male characters, male subjectivity, masculinity, and male sexuality. Indeed, the very beginning of the work emphasizes male sexuality as a regenerative force. Although nature is most often associated with the feminine in medieval literature, Chaucer equates Spring with male energy:

---

[24] de Lauretis, *Alice Doesn't*, 108.
[25] *Ibid.*, 109.
[26] *Ibid.*, 110.

> Whan that Aprill with his shoures soote
> The droghte of March hath perced to the roote,
> And bathed every vegne in swich licour
> Of which vertu engendred is the flour;
> When Zephirus eek with his sweete breeth
> Inspired hath in every holt and heeth
> The tendre croppes, and the younge sonne
> Hath in the Ram his halve cours yronne,
> And smale foweles maken melodye,
> That slepen al the nyght with open ye
> (So priketh hem nature in hir corages);
> Thanne longen folk to goon on pilgrimages.   (I, 1–12)

April, Zephirus, the sun, and the Ram are all constituted as male images and personifications which have regenerative influence on the natural world and on the humans within that natural world. Nouns, verbs, adjectives all resonate through this passage connoting male creative and sexual energy. April's 'shoures soote,' his 'licour,' 'perced' the arid March soil, engendering the flower with potency (or 'vertu'), and he 'priketh' nature in the hearts of birds. Echoing the creation story where God, the male omnipotence, breaths life into Adam, Zephiris inspires life in the fallow landscape.[27] Both the masculine-sexual rebirthing of nature and the male saint's power to renew the pilgrims spiritually establish a male sexual/spiritual background for the pilgrimage which, in turn, features some thirty male travellers and three women who participate in a male-adjudicated storytelling competition.

Chaucer's concerns with masculinity are, obviously, complex, and he turns the phenomenon around and around, now one way, now another. His concerns are also noticeable in the persona Chaucer creates for himself – the pilgrim Geoffrey, this strange little narrator.[28] If Geoffrey expresses the frustrations Chaucer faced – the poet caught between making courtly amusements and writing didacticism, the poet yearning for 'poesy' – this persona also surely registers discomfort with the masculine codes and categories of a late medieval, chivalric society. In the *Canterbury Tales*, Geoffrey tries to avoid being drawn into the limelight. He feels vulnerable to the judgments of others, and so he frequently turns to us either to excuse himself or to justify himself. He is the observer – judging (often incorrectly), perceiving (often incorrectly) the others in the *Tales*. His isolation is apparent in his profession as well, for he is the artist in the midst of tradesmen, clerics, warriors, and landowners. His 'elfishness' suggests that he originates in some other world. This is a stance Chaucer uses in all depictions of himself. He is poignantly solitary in the dream visions where he reads alone late at night, sleeps alone, and, of course, experiences the world of

---

[27] The passage from Genesis 2:7 reads: 'the Lord God had not caused it to rain upon the earth, and there was not a man to till the ground. / But there went up a mist from the earth, and watered the whole face of the ground. And the Lord God formed man of the dust of the ground, and breathed into his nostrils the breath of life; and man became a living soul.' For a more detailed discussion of the parallels, see J. C. Nitzsche, 'Creation in Genesis and Nature in Chaucer's *General Prologue, 1–18,*' *Publications in Language and Literature* 14 (1978): 459–64.

[28] Cf. Hansen, *Fictions*, 14–15.

his dreams alone. Geoffrey is the sole earthly body in the *House of Fame*; he is the human in a world of birds in the *Parlement of Foules*; he is the artist on trial in the *Legend of Good Women*. Only in the *Book of the Duchess*, written early in Chaucer's career, does Geoffrey carry on a truly intimate conversation with another man, the Man in Black. After Chaucer travels abroad in Italy, after he is exposed to the Italian Renaissance, his persona, Geoffrey, is always an outsider. One can only suspect that once Chaucer had ventured beyond medieval Anglo-Norman culture, once he had stepped into the early modern world of Renaissance Italy, he wrote from the outside, though he also obviously gained such a perspective from his philosophical bent and from the influence of writers like Jean de Meun and Boethius as well. His social and political positioning, as I suggested in chapter two, most likely contributed to this sense of being outside, for Chaucer was always living both within and without the court world and within and without the London middle class. Given this historical and biographical context, it is not surprising to find Chaucer's male characters are frequently isolated from one another. Their isolation may stem from gender role definitions, cultural and historical contexts, but it may also reflect Chaucer's particular positioning within his own socio-political world.

Whatever the source, the foreignness of one man to another carries with it the implied separation of men from themselves. Because men are looking outward so much in the world of the *Canterbury Tales*, it is difficult for them to perceive themselves accurately. This creates, of course, some of our enjoyment of the poem, for we like to scrutinize tale and teller, body and voice to see discrepancies and unintended revelations. Through irony of this kind, Chaucer demonstrates the insufficiency of his characters' projected image. Over and over the characters reveal themselves without knowing they do so. Our own desires are implicated and/or tantalized by the way the narrative fiction pretends to situate us outside the maze of self-contradictions and chaos located in the pilgrim narrators. Although Chaucer's cultivated ambiguity disallows our interpretive tyranny over the text and thus mirrors the impossibility of full or correct knowledge within the temporal world, considering the gendered narrative dynamics which pervade the *Tales*, their 'tracking from the point of view of Oedipus,' a masculine perception and locus situates both affirmations and negations of gender (of both masculinity and femininity).

Chaucer, ever observant of human behavior, sees, to some extent, the price men themselves pay for an uncritical adherence to the culture's gender ideology. Nowhere here do we get an *unambiguous* image of the epic warrior who typically silences the reflective inner world and risks his body for the purposes of fame and glory.[29] Nowhere in the *Canterbury Tales* do we see the tough guy unreservedly praised; and where Chaucer represents a character's allegiance to logic and philosophy, he encourages us to examine his motivations. Nowhere does Chaucer value empirical reasoning without also valuing intuition and the inner knowing of the dream; as Chaunticleer asserts, 'dremes been significaciouns'(2979). In the General Prologue, Chaucer writes:

---

[29] Although Theseus embodies many virtues we associate with epic heroes, Chaucer's text contains ambiguity around this character. See my discussion above in chapter four.

For many a man so hard is of his herte,
He may nat wepe, althogh hym soore smerte.
Therfore in stede of wepynge and preyeres
men moote yeve silver to the povre freres.   (I, 229–32)

These lines, delivered by Geoffrey in typically naive fashion, suggest that 'many a man' in Geoffrey's world is detached, 'hard-hearted,' or cold – emotionally distant both from himself and from others. Chaucer's irony suggests he does not approve. In the Parson's prescription for 'perfit Penitence,' heart-felt grief is very much at the center and foundational: 'Thanne shal man looke and considere that if he wole maken a trewe and profitable confessioun, there moste be foure condiciouns. / First, it 'moot been in sorweful bitternesse of herte' (X, 982–83). Second, penance requires humility, 'and this humylitee shal been in herte' (989). Third, 'thy shrift sholde be ful of teeris, if man may, and if man may nat wepe with his bodily eyen, lat hym wepe in herte' (993). Since a perfect penitential pilgrimage involves intense self-examination and genuine grief over one's sins, and since Chaucer's text endorses Christian spirituality, it criticizes men who prefer to buy their penance with 'pieces of silver.' The *Parson's Tale* is critical of a culture which promotes a split for men between the intellect and the heart, at least as long as the heart is longing for union with God the Father.[30] A twentieth-century reader might well wonder whether or not the pursuit of 'God the Father' and the desire for union with 'Him' – represented by the pilgrimage to the shrine of St Thomas à Becket – might here, as in innumerable other Judeo-Christian texts, express male longings for genuine male-to-male friendship and nurturing within a competitive and patriarchal society.[31]

Theorizing the development of civilization, we, in the late twentieth century, have come to understand ways civilization establishes its domination over individual desires by subjugating and damning up the flood of human desire.[32] Chaucer's text, as cultural phenomenon, records ways patriarchal civilization keeps men apart and ways it regulates male homosocial/ homoerotic desire through religion and competition. The *Canterbury Tales* both reinscribes and challenges the category of 'manliness,' and Chaucer's critique always also marks the loss or lack of the ideal heroic warrior, the pure cleric, the devoted lover, and the correct scholarly interpreter.[33]

---

[30] His opposition to men indulging in 'excessive' love of women is discussed above in chapter five.

[31] Cf. Rene Girard, *Deceit, Desire and the Novel*, trans. Yvonne Freccaro (Baltimore: Johns Hopkins University Press, 1972) and Eve Kosofsky Sedgwick, *Between Men: English Literature and Male Homosocial Desire* (New York: Columbia University Press, 1985), esp. 1–48. See also Jonathan Rutherford, *Men's Silences: Predicaments in Masculinity* (London and New York: Routledge, 1992), esp. 123–198.

[32] See Foucault's prolific writings on the power of the cultural construction and institutional regulation of human subjects.

[33] For a modern look at the gender reinscriptions and challenges that can and cannot be made in language, see Judith Butler, *Bodies that Matter: On the Discursive Limits of 'Sex'* (London and New York: Routledge, 1993). Discussing the term and category 'woman,' in a way that is usefully applied to any generalizing term, Butler writes (221–22), 'The claim to have achieved

Jonathan Rutherford, writing on nostalgia and its role in the construction of masculinity, observes, in his book, *Predicaments of Masculinity* (1992):

> Nostalgic myth mediates between the past and individual consciousness. It can function by erasing a memory or an object from the past and displacing the anxiety induced by it into a more pleasurable and less threatening object or scene. The significance of the psychological element in nostalgia is not in the image that is evoked but in the object or scene displaced from the narrative. . . . Nostalgic myth maintains the power relations between hegemonic identities and others. It doesn't actually represent men's sense of loss so much as evade it. . . . nostalgia . . . is voluble, chattering memories that skirt around the central and unspoken dilemma of the predicament. The function of nostalgia is to evade anxiety and the effect of predicaments within male subjectivity.[34]

Chaucer's *Canterbury Tales* expresses, simultaneously, nostalgia and critique. What is repudiated continues, of course, to structure the discourse of/on gender within the *Tales*. Likewise, if competition and aggression are foregrounded in the definition of masculinity, love between men remains foreclosed and outside but also necessary to that same definition. Channelling homosocial desire into the competitive arena, into an exchange of words, and into religious discourse, the *Tales* seem to long for a unity of male with male beyond competition: Father with Son, God with pilgrim. The Parson defines hell as a place of separation where there 'is no solas ne no freendshipe' (206) and as a place of separation from God, imagined as a kind of violence: 'for certes, right as a swerd departeth a thyng in two peces, right so consentynge departeth God fro man' (356). Heaven is, on the other hand, a place of unity where 'joye hath no contrariousee,' where 'the blisful compaignye' resides 'that rejoysen hem everemo, everich of otheres joye,' and where 'the body of man' is 'so strong and so hool that ther may no thyng apeyren it' (1077, 1078); in heaven, the soul is 'replenysshed with the sighte of the parfit knowynge of God' (1079).

The storytelling game of the *Canterbury Tales* allows competition to surface between individuals and yet sets boundaries around it.[35] It allows the

such an impartial concept or description shores itself up by foreclosing the very political field that it claims to have exhausted. This violence is at once performed and erased by a description that claims finality and all-inclusiveness. To ameliorate and rework this violence, it is necessary to learn a double movement: to invoke the category and, hence, provisionally to institute an identity and at the same time to open the category as a site of permanent political contest. That the term is questionable does not mean that we ought not to use it, but neither does the necessity to use it mean that we ought not perpetually to interrogate the exclusions by which it proceeds. . . .'

34 Jonathan Rutherford, *Predicaments of Masculinity* (London: Routledge, 1992), 127.
35 See Carol Gilligan, *In a Different Voice: Psychological Theory and Women's Development* (Cambridge, Mass.: Harvard University Press, 1982), 9–11, who cites Janet Lever's 1976 study of children's playground games and writes, 'Boys . . . by participating in controlled and socially approved competitive situations, [. . .] learn to deal with competition in a relatively forthright manner–to play with their enemies and to compete with their friends – all in

homosocial but orchestrates and contains it. On the one hand, the game is a civilizing agent, channelling aggression into play; on the other hand, the *Parson's Tale*, placed in an authoritative final position in the *Tales*, chastises men for their rivalries and expresses a desire for the oneness of man and man, thereby voicing criticisms of a culture which increasingly encouraged competition.

accordance with the rules of the game. In contrast, girls' play tends to occur in smaller, more intimate groups, often the best-friend dyad, and in private places. This play replicates the social pattern of primary human relationships in that its organization is more cooperative. . . . It fosters the development of the empathy and sensitivity necessary for taking the role of "the particular other" and points more toward knowing the other as different from the self.'

SELECT BIBLIOGRAPHY

Adams, Marilyn McCord. *William Ockham*. 2 Vols. Notre Dame: Notre Dame University Press, 1987.

Aers, David. *Chaucer*. Brighton: Harvester Press, 1986.

——. *Chaucer, Langland, and the Creative Imagination*. London: Routledge & Kegan Paul, 1980.

——. *Community, Gender, and Individual Identity: English Writing, 1360-1430*. London and New York: Routledge, 1988.

——. 'Criseyde: Woman in Medieval Society.' *ChauR* 13 (1979): 177-200.

Alighieri, Dante. *Dante in Hell: The De Vulgari Eloquentia: Introduction, Text, Translation, Commentary*. Ed. Warman Welliver. Ravenna: Longo Editore, 1981.

Allen, Judson B. 'The Old Way and the Parson's Way: An Ironic Reading of the *Parson's Tale*.' *Journal of Medieval and Renaissance Studies* 3 (1973): 255-71.

Allen, Judson B. and Theresa A. Moritz. *A Distinction of Stories: The Medieval Unity of Chaucer's Fair Chain of Narratives for Canterbury*. Columbus: Ohio State University Press, 1981.

Allmand, Christopher. *The Hundred Years War: England and France at War c. 1300-c. 1450*. Cambridge: Cambridge University Press, 1988.

——., ed. *Society at War: the Experience of England and France During the Hundred Years War*. Edinburgh, 1973; New York: Barnes and Noble, 1973.

Amt, Emilie., ed. *Medieval Women's Lives: A Sourcebook*. New York: Routledge, 1993.

Ancrene Riwle. The English Text of the Ancrene Riwle (MS. Pepys 2498). Ed. A. Zettersten. EETS OS 274. London: Oxford University Press, 1976.

Aquinas, Thomas. *The Basic Writings of Saint Thomas Aquinas*. 2 vols. Trans. and ed. Anton C. Pegis. New York: Random House, 1945.

——. *Summa Theologica*. Ed. and trans. The Fathers of the English Dominican Province. New York: Benzinger, 1947.

Aristotle. *De Generatione Animalium*. Ed. J. A. Smith and W. D. Ross. in *The Works of Aristotle*. Vol. 5. Oxford: Clarendon, 1912.

——. *The Works of Aristotle*. Trans. J. F. Beare, et al. Ed. W. D. Ross. Oxford: Oxford University Press, 1927.

Aston, Margaret. *Lollards and Reformers: Images and Literacy in Late Medieval Religion*. London: Hambledon Press, 1984.

Atkinson, Clarissa W. *The Oldest Vocation: Christian Motherhood in the Middle Ages*. Ithaca: Cornell University Press, 1991.

Auerbach, Erich. *Mimesis: The Representation of Reality in Western Literature*. Trans. Willard Trask. Garden City: Doubleday, 1957.

Augustine. 'Of the Work of Monks.' Trans. H. Browne. In *A Select Library of the Nicene and Post-Nicene Fathers of the Christian Church*. Ed. Philip Schaff, et al. Vol. 3. Buffalo: The Christian Literature Co., 1887.

——. *On Christian Doctrine*. Trans. D. W. Robertson, Jr. New York: Bobbs-Merrill, 1958.

Baker, Derek., ed. *Medieval Women*. Oxford: Blackwell, 1978.

Baker, Donald C. 'Chaucer's Clerk and the Wife of Bath on the Subject of Gentilesse.' *SP* 59 (1962): 631–40.

Bakhtin, Mikhail M. *Rabelais and His World*. Trans. Hélène Iswolsky. 1968; Bloomington: Indiana University Press (Midland): 1984.

——. *Speech Genres and Other Late Essays*. University of Texas Press Slavic Series, No. 8. Trans. Vern W. McGee. Ed. Caryl Emerson and Michael Holquist. Austin: University of Texas Press, 1986.

Barber, Richard. *The Knight and Chivalry*. 2nd ed. Woodbridge: The Boydell Press, 1974.

Barker, Judith R. V. *The Tournament in England, 1100–1400*. Woodbridge: The Boydell Press, 1986.

Barnie, John. *War in Medieval English Society: Social Values in The Hundred Years War, 1337–99*. Ithaca: Cornell University Press, 1974.

Barthes, Roland. *Image-Music-Text*. Trans. Stephen Heath. New York: Hill and Wang, 1977.

——. *The Pleasure of the Text*. Trans. Richard Miller. New York: Hill and Wang, 1975.

Baum, Gregory. *Man Becoming*. New York: Herder and Herder, 1970.

Baum, Paul F. 'Chaucer's Puns.' *PMLA* 71 (1956): 242–46.

Beichner, Paul E., C. S. C. 'Absolom's Hair.' *MS* 12 (1950): 222–33.

——. 'Baiting the Summoner.' *MLQ* 22 (1961): 367–76.

——. 'Characterization in the *Miller's Tale*.' In *Chaucer Criticism*. 117–29. See Schoeck 1960.

——. 'Chaucer's Pardoner as Entertainer.' *MS* 25 (1963): 160–72.

——. 'Daun Piers, Monk and Business Administrator.' In *Chaucer Criticism*. 152–62. See Schoeck 1960.

Bennett, J. A. W. *Chaucer at Oxford and at Cambridge*. Toronto and Oxford: Toronto: University of Toronto Press, 1974.

Bennett, Judith M. *Women in the Medieval English Countryside*. Oxford: Oxford University Press, 1987.

Benson, C. David. *Chaucer's Drama of Style: Poetic Variety and Contrast in the Canterbury Tales*. Chapel Hill: University of North Carolina Press, 1986.

Benson, Larry D. 'The Order of *The Canterbury Tales*.' *SAC* 3 (1981): 77–120.

Benton, John F. 'Clio and Venus: An Historical View of Medieval Love.' In *The Meaning of Courtly Love*. 19–42. See Newman 1968.

——. 'The Court of Champagne as a Literary Center.' *Speculum* 36 (1961): 551–91.

Berndt, David E. 'Monastic *Acedia* and Chaucer's Characterization of Daun Piers.' *SP* 68 (1971): 435–50.

Birney, Earle. *Essays on Chaucerian Irony*. Ed. Beryl Rowland. Toronto: University of Toronto Press, 1985.

Blake, Kathleen A. 'Order and the Noble Life in Chaucer's *Knight's Tale*.' *MLQ* 34 (1973): 3–19.

Blamires, Alcuin., ed. *Woman Defamed and Woman Defended: An Anthology of Medieval Texts*. Oxford: Clarendon, 1992.

Bloch, R. Howard. *Medieval Misogyny and the Invention of Western Romantic Love*. Chicago: University of Chicago Press, 1991.

——. *The Scandal of the Fabliaux*. Chicago: University of Chicago Press, 1986.

Block, Edward A. 'Originality, Controlling Purpose, and Craftsmanship in Chaucer's *Man of Law's Tale*.' *PMLA* 68 (1953): 572–616.

Bloomfield, Morton W. 'Authenticating Realism and the Realism of Chaucer.' *Thought* 39 (1964): 335–58.

——. 'The *Man of Law's Tale*: a Tragedy of Victimization and a Christian Comedy.' *PMLA* 87 (1972): 384–90.

Boccaccio, Giovanni. *Boccaccio on Poetry*. Trans. and ed. Charles G. Osgood. Princeton: Princeton University Press, 1930.

——. *The Book of Theseus*. Trans. Bernadette M. McCoy. New York: Medieval Text Association, 1974.

Boethius. *The Consolation of Philosophy*. Trans. Richard Green. Indianapolis: Bobbs-Merrill, 1962.

Boitani, Piero. *Chaucer and Boccaccio*. Medium Aevum Monographs. Oxford: Society for the Study of Mediaeval Languages and Literature, 1977.

——. 'His desir wol fle withouten wynge: Mary and Love in Fourteenth-Century Poetry.' In *Chaucer's Frame Tales*. 83–128. See Fichte 1987.

——., and Anna Torti., eds. *Intellectuals and Writers in Fourteenth-Century Europe*. The J. A. W. Bennett Memorial Lectures, Perugia, 1984. Cambridge: D. S. Brewer, 1986.

Boone, Joseph A., and Michael Cadden., eds. *Engendering Men: The Question of Male Feminist Criticism*. New York: Routledge, 1990.

Boren, James. 'Alysoun of Bath and the Vulgate "Perfect Wife." ' *NM* 76 (1975): 247–56.

Born, L. K. 'The Perfect Prince: A Study in 13th and 14th Century Ideals.' *Speculum* 3 (1928): 470–504.

Boswell, John. *Christianity, Social Tolerance, and Homosexuality*. Chicago: University of Chicago Press, 1980.

——. *Same-Sex Unions in Premodern Europe*. New York: Villard, 1994.

Brewer, Derek S. 'The Arming of the Warrior in European Literature and Chaucer.' In *Chaucerian Problems*. 221–43. See Vasta 1979.

——., ed. *Chaucer and Chaucerians: Critical Studies in Middle English Literature*. London: Nelson, 1966.

——., ed. *Chaucer: The Critical Heritage*. 2 vols. London: Routledge and Kegan Paul, 1978.

——. *Geoffrey Chaucer*. Writers and Their Background series. Athens, Ohio: University of Ohio Press, 1975.

Bridenthal, Renate, Claudia Koonz, and Susan M. Stuard., eds. *Becoming Visible: Women in European History*. 2nd ed. Boston: Houghton-Mifflin, 1987.

Brooke-Rose, Christine. 'Woman as a Semiotic Object.' In *The Female Body in Western Culture*. Ed. Susan R. Suleiman. 305–16. Cambridge, Mass.: Harvard University Press, 1986.

Brooks, Douglas, and Alaistair Fowler. 'The Meaning of Chaucer's *Knight's Tale*.' *MAE* 39 (1970): 123–46.

Brownlee, Marina S., Kevin Brownlee, and Stephen G. Nichols., eds. *The New Medievalism*. Baltimore: Johns Hopkins University Press, 1991.

Brundage, James A. *Law, Sex, and Christian Society in Medieval Europe*. Chicago: University of Chicago Press, 1987.

Bryan, W. F., and G. Dempster., eds. *Sources and Analogues of Chaucer's Canterbury Tales*. Chicago, 1941; New York: The Humanities Press, 1958.

Burlin, Robert B. *Chaucerian Fiction*. Princeton: Princeton University Press, 1977.

Burnley, J. D. *Chaucer's Language and the Philosophers' Tradition*. Woodbridge: D. S. Brewer, 1979.

——. 'Chaucer's Termes.' *Yearbook in English Studies* 7 (1977): 53–67.

Burrow, John A. *Medieval Writers and Their Work: Middle English Literature and its Background, 1100–1500*. Oxford: Oxford University Press, 1982.

Butler, Judith. *Bodies that Matter: On the Discursive Limits of 'Sex'*. New York: Routledge, 1993.

——. *Gender Trouble: Feminism and the Subversion of Identity*. New York: Routledge, 1990.

Bynum, Caroline W. *Fragmentation and Redemption: Essays on Gender and the Human Body in Medieval Religion*. New York: Zone, 1991.

Cambrensis, Giraldus. *Chronicles and Memorials of Great Britain and Ireland During the Middle Ages. Cambrensis Opera*. Vol. 8. Ed. George F. Warner. London: Eyre and Spottiswoode, 1891.

Campbell, Joseph. *The Masks of God: Occidental Mythology*. New York: Viking Press, Compass Edition, 1970.

Carlson, David. 'Religious Writers and Church Councils on Chivalry,' in *The Study of Chivalry*. Ed. Howell Chickering and Thomas H. Seiler. 141–71. Kalamazoo: Western Michigan University Press, 1988.

Carruthers, Mary. 'The Wife of Bath and the Painting of Lions.' *PMLA* 94 (1979): 209–22.

Casey, Kathleen. 'The Cheshire Cat: Reconstructing the Experience of Medieval Women.' In *Liberating Women's History: Theoretical and Critical Essays*. Ed. Berenice A. Carroll. 224–49. Urbana: University of Illinois Press, 1976.

Cate, W. A. 'The Problem of the Origin of the Griselda Story.' *SP* 29 (1932): 389–405.

Certaldo, Paolo da. *Libro di buoni costumi*. Ed. Alfredo Schiaffini. Firenze: F. Le Monnier, 1945.

Chaucer, Geoffrey. *The Complete Poetry and Prose of Geoffrey Chaucer*. Ed. John H. Fisher. New York: Holt, Rinehart and Winston, 1977.

——. *The Riverside Chaucer*. 3rd. ed. Ed. Larry D. Benson. Boston: Houghton Mifflin, 1987.

——. *The Works of Geoffrey Chaucer*. 2nd ed. Ed. F. N. Robinson. Boston: Houghton Mifflin, 1961.

Cherubino da Siena. *Regole della vita matrimoniale*. ed. Francesco Zambrini and Carlo Negroni. Bologna: Commissione per i testi di lingua, 1969.

Christine de Pisan. *The Book of the City of Ladies*. Trans. Earl Jeffrey Richards. New York: Persea Books, 1982.

——. *The Book of Fayttes of Armes and of Chyualrye*. Trans. William Caxton. Ed. A. T. P. Byles. EETS OS 189. London: Oxford University Press, 1932.

Cixous, Hélène. 'Castration or Decapitation.' Trans. Annette Kuhn. *Signs* 7 (1981): 41–55.

——. 'The Laugh of the Medusa.' Trans. Keith and Paula Cohen. *Signs* 1 (1976): 875–93.

——, and Catherine Clément. *The Newly Born Woman*. Trans. Betsy Wing. Theory and History of Literature, Vol. 24. Minneapolis: University of Minnesota Press, 1986.

Clanvowe, Sir John. *The Works of Sir John Clanvowe*. Ed. V. John Scattergood. Cambridge: D. S. Brewer, 1975.

Clasby, Eugene. 'Chaucer's Constance: Womanly Virtue and the Heroic Life.' *ChauR* 13 (1979): 221–33.

Code, Lorraine., Sheila Mullett, and Christine Overall., eds. *Feminist Perspectives: Philosophical Essays on Method and Morals*. Toronto: University of Toronto Press, 1988.

Coleman, Janet. *Medieval Readers and Writers, 1350–1400*. New York: Columbia University Press, 1981.

Colish, Marcia L. *The Mirror of Language: A Study in the Medieval Theory of Knowledge*. rev. ed. Lincoln: University of Nebraska Press, 1983.

Colmer, Dorothy. 'Character and Class in The *Wife of Bath's Tale*.' *JEGP* 72 (1973): 329–39.

Condren, Edward I. 'The *Clerk's Tale* of Man Tempting God.' *Criticism* 26 (1984): 99–114.

Contamine, Philippe. *War in the Middle Ages*. Trans. Michael Jones. Oxford: Basil Blackwell, 1984.

Coward, Rosalind. *Patriarchal Precedents: Sexuality and Social Relations*. London: Routledge, Kegan Paul, 1983.

Crane, Susan. *Gender and Romance in Chaucer's Canterbury Tales*. Princeton: Princeton University Press, 1994.

Crump, C. G. *Life in the Middle Ages*. New York: MacMillan, 1910.

——, and E. F. Jacob., eds. *The Legacy of the Middle Ages*. Oxford: Clarendon, 1926.

Currie, Felicity. 'Chaucer's Pardoner Again.' *Leeds Studies in English*. 4 (1970): 11–22.

Curry, Walter Clyde. *Chaucer and the Mediaeval Sciences*. Rev. ed. New York: Barnes and Noble, 1960.

Curtis, Penelope. 'Some Discarnational Impulses in the *Canterbury Tales*.' In *Medieval English Religious and Ethical Literature*. 128–45. See Kratzmann 1986.

Daly, Mary. *Beyond God the Father: Toward a Philosophy of Women's Liberation*. Boston: Beacon, 1973; rpt 1974.

——. *Gynecology: The Metaethics of Radical Feminism*. Boston: Beacon, 1978.

David, Alfred. 'Criticism and the Old Man in Chaucer's *Pardoner's Tale*.' *College English* 27 (1965): 39–44.

——. *The Strumpet Muse: Art and Morals in Chaucer's Poetry*. Bloomington: Indiana University Press, 1976.

Dean, Christopher. 'Salvation, Damnation, and the Role of the Old Man in the *Pardoner's Tale*.' *ChauR* 3 (1968–69): 44–49.

Debax, Jean-Paul. 'Et voilà pourquoi votre femme est muètte.' *Caliban* 17, (1980): 23–37.

de Beauvoir, Simone. *The Second Sex*. Trans. H. M. Parshley. New York: Vintage, 1974.

Delany, Sheila. 'Politics and the Paralysis of Poetic Imagination in The *Physician's Tale*.' *SAC* 3 (1981): 47–60.

——. *Writing Woman: Women Writers and Women in Literature, Medieval to Modern*. New York: Schocken, 1983.

Delasanta, Rodney. 'Chaucer and the Problem of the Universal.' *Mediaevalia* 9 (1983): 145–63.

——. 'Penance and Poetry in the *Canterbury Tales*.' *PMLA* 93 (1978): 240–47.

——. 'Sacrament and Sacrifice in the *Pardoner's Tale*.' *AnM* 14 (1973): 43–72.

de Lauretis, Teresa. *Alice Doesn't: Feminism, Semiotics, Cinema*. Bloomington: Indiana University Press, 1984.

——. *The Practice of Love: Lesbian Sexuality and Perverse Desire*. Bloomington: Indiana University Press, 1994.

——. *Technologies of Gender: Essays on Theory, Film, and Fiction*. Bloomington: Indiana University Press, 1987.

——. 'Upping the Anti(sic) in Feminist Theory.' In *Conflicts in Feminism*. 255–70. See Hirsch 1990.

D'Emilio, John. *Sexual Politics, Sexual Communities*. Chicago: University of Chicago Press, 1983.

Dempster, Germaine. 'A Period in the Development of the *Canterbury Tales*' Marriage Group of Blocks B2 and C.' *PMLA* 68 (1953): 1142–59.

de Rougemont, Denis. *Love in the Western World*. Rev. ed., trans. Montgomery Belgion. Princeton: Princeton University Press, 1940; rpt 1983.

Diamond, Arlyn. 'Chaucer's Women and Women's Chaucer.' In *The Authority of Experience: Essays in Feminist Criticism*. See Diamond 1977.

——. '*Troilus and Criseyde*: The Politics of Love.' In *Chaucer in the Eighties*. 93–104. See Wasserman 1986.

Dinshaw, Carolyn. *Chaucer's Sexual Poetics*. Madison: University of Wisconsin Press, 1989.

Dionysius the Areopagite. *Dionysius the Areopagite: On the Divine Names and The Mystical Theology*. Trans. C. E. Rolt. London, 1966; New York: MacMillan, 1970.

Doiron, M. 'Margaret Porete: *The Mirror of Simple Souls*: A Middle English Translation.' *Archivio italiano per la storia della pieta* 5 (1968): 241–355.

Dollimore, Jonathan. *Sexual Dissidence: Augustine to Wilde, Freud to Foucault*. Oxford: Clarendon, 1991.

Donaldson, E. Talbot. *Chaucer's Poetry: An Anthology for the Modern Reader*. 2nd ed. New York: Ronald, 1975.

——. *Speaking of Chaucer*. New York, 1970; Durham, N. C.: Labyrinth Press, 1983.

Doresse, Jean., ed. and trans. *The Secret Books of the Egyptian Gnostics*. Paris, 1958; New York: Viking, 1960.

Doyle, James A. *The Male Experience*. Dubuque: William C. Brown, 1983.

Dronke, Peter. *Women Writers of the Middle Ages: A Critical Study of Texts from Perpetua (d. 203) to Marguerite Porète (d. 1310)*. Cambridge: Cambridge University Press, 1984.

Duby, Georges. *The Three Orders: Feudal Society Imagined*. Trans. Arthur Goldhammer. Chicago: University of Chicago Press, 1980.

Dyer, Christopher. 'The Social and Economic Background to the Rural Revolt of 1381.' In *The English Rising of 1381*. 9–42. See Hilton 1984.

——. *Standards of Living in the Later Middle Ages*. Cambridge: Cambridge University Press, 1989.

Eadmer. *The Life of St Anselm Archbishop of Canterbury by Eadmer*. Trans. and ed. R. W. Southern. London: Nelson, 1962.

Eagleton, Terry. *Literary Theory: An Introduction*. Minneapolis: University of Minnesota Press, 1983.

——. *The Rape of Clarissa: Writing, Sexuality, and Class Struggle in Samuel Richardson*. Oxford: Blackwell, 1982.

Eberle, Patricia J. 'Commercial Language and the Commercial Outlook of the *General Prologue*.' *ChauR* 18 (1983): 161–74.

Economou, George., ed. *Geoffrey Chaucer: A Collection of Original Articles*. New York: McGraw-Hill, 1975.

Eisenstein, Hester., and Alice Jardine., eds. *The Future of Difference*. Boston: 1980; rpt Rutgers University Press, 1985.

Elbow, Peter. 'How Chaucer Transcends Oppositions in the *Knight's Tale*.' *ChauR* 7 (1972): 97–112.

——. *Oppositions in Chaucer*. Middleton, Conn.: Wesleyan University Press, 1975.

Eliade, Mircea. *Myth and Reality*. Trans. Willard R. Trask. New York: Harper and Row, 1963. Rpt Harper Colophon, 1975.

Elias, Norbert. *The History of Manners: The Civilizing Process, Volume I*. Trans. Edmund Jephcott. New York: Urizen, 1978.

——. *Power and Civility: The Civilizing Process, Volume II*. Trans. Edmund Jephcott. Oxford: Blackwell, 1982.

Elliot, R. W. V. 'Chaucer's Reading.' In *Chaucer's Mind and Art*. 46–68. See Cawley 1969.

Ellmann, Mary. *Thinking About Women*. New York: Harcourt, 1968.

Erler, Mary., and Maryanne Kowaleski., eds. *Women and Power in the Middle Ages*. Athens: University of Georgia Press, 1988.

Erzgaber, Willi. ' "Auctorite" and "Experience" in Chaucer.' In *Intellectuals and Writers in Fourteenth-Century Europe*. 67–87. See Boitani 1986.

Evans, G. R. 'Wyclif on Literal and Metaphorical.' In *From Ockham to Wyclif*. 259-66. See Hudson 1987.

Evans, Michael. 'Allegorical Women and Practical Men: The Iconography of the Artes Reconsidered.' In *Medieval Women*. 305-330. See Baker 1978.

Ferguson, Margaret W., Maureen Quilligan, and Nancy J. Vickers., eds. *Rewriting the Renaissance: The Discourses of Sexual Difference in Early Modern Europe*. Chicago: University of Chicago Press, 1986.

Ferrante, Joan M. 'The Conflict of Lyric Convention and Romance Form.' In *In Pursuit of Perfection: Courtly Love in Medieval Literature*. 136-78. See Ferrante 1975.

——. and George Economou, et al., eds. *In Pursuit of Perfection: Courtly Love in Medieval Literature*. Port Washington, N.Y.: Kennikat Press, 1975.

——. 'Public Postures and Private Maneuvers: Roles Medieval Women Play.' In *Women and Power in the Middle Ages*. 213-29. See Erler 1988.

——. *Woman as Image in Medieval Literature*. New York: Columbia University Press, 1975.

Ferster, Judith. *Chaucer on Interpretation*. Cambridge: Cambridge University Press, 1985.

Fetterley, Judith. *The Resisting Reader: A Feminist Approach to American Fiction*. Bloomington: Indiana University Press, 1978.

Fichte, Joerg O., ed. *Chaucer's Frame Tales: The Physical and the Metaphysical*. Tubingen: Gunter Narr; Cambridge: D. S. Brewer, 1987.

——. 'Man's Free Will and the Poet's Choice: The Creation of Artistic Order in Chaucer's *Knight's Tale*.' *Anglia* 93 (1975): 335-60.

Fiedler, Leslie. 'Literature as an Institution: The View from 1980.' In *English Literature: Opening Up the Canon, Selected Papers from the English Institute, 1979*. 73-91. Ed. Leslie Fiedler and Houston A. Baker, Jr. Baltimore: Johns Hopkins University Press, 1981.

Finke, Laurie A., and Martin B. Schichtman., eds. *Medieval Texts and Contemporary Readers*. Ithaca: Cornell University Press, 1987.

Finlayson, John. 'The Satiric Mode and the *Parson's Tale*.' *ChauR* 6 (1971): 94-116.

Fisher, John H. *John Gower: Moral Philosopher and Friend of Chaucer*. New York: New York University Press, 1964.

Fleming, John V. 'The Antifraternalism of the *Summoner's Tale*.' *JEGP* 65 (1966): 688-700.

Flynn, Elizabeth A., and Patrocinio P. Schweickart., eds. *Gender and Reading: Essays on Readers, Texts, and Contexts*. Baltimore: Johns Hopkins University Press, 1986.

Foucault, Michael. *The History of Sexuality, Volume I*. Trans. Robert Hurley. New York: Vintage, 1980.

Fradenberg, Louise O. 'The Wife of Bath's Passing Fancy.' *SAC* 8 (1986): 31-58.

Franklin, Clyde W., II. *The Changing Definition of Masculinity*. Perspectives in Sexuality. New York and London: Plenum, 1984.

French, Marilyn. *Beyond Power, On Women, Men, and Morals*. New York: Simon & Schuster, Summit, 1985.

Frye, Marilyn. *The Politics of Reality: Essays in Feminist Theory*. Trumansburg, New York: The Crossing Press, 1983.

Fuss, Diana. *Essentially Speaking: Feminism, Nature & Difference*. New York: Routledge, 1989.

Ganim, John. 'Bakhtin, Chaucer, Carnival, and Lent.' *SAC* 8 (1986): 56-71.

Gaylord, Alan T. 'Sentence and Solaas in Fragment VII of the *Canterbury Tales*: Harry Bailly as Horseback Editor.' *PMLA* 82 (1967): 226-35.

Geoffrey of Vinsauf. *The Poetria Nova of Geoffrey of Vinsauf*. Trans. Margaret F. Nims. Toronto: Pontifical Institute of Mediaeval Studies, 1967.

Gilligan, Carol. *In a Different Voice: Psychological Theory and Women's Development.* Cambridge, Mass.: Harvard University Press, 1982.

Girard, Rene. *Deceit, Desire, and the Novel.* Trans. Yvonne Freccero. Baltimore: Johns Hopkins University Press, 1965.

Gist, Margaret A. *Love and War in the Middle English Romances.* Philadelphia: University of Pennsylvania Press, 1947.

Given, James B. *Society and Homicide in Thirteenth-Century England.* Stanford: Stanford University Press, 1977.

Gold, Penny S. *The Lady and the Virgin: Image, Attitude, and Experience in Twelfth-Century France.* Chicago: Chicago University Press, 1985.

Gottfreid, Barbara. 'Conflict and Relationship, Sovereignty and Survival: Parables of Power in the *Wife of Bath's Prologue.*' *ChauR* 19 (1985): 202–24.

Gower, John. *The Major Latin Works of John Gower.* Trans. and ed. Eric W. Stockton. Seattle: University of Washington Press, 1962.

Green, Richard Firth. 'Chaucer's Victimized Women.' *SAC* 10 (1988): 3–21.

——. 'The *Familia Regis* and the *Familia Cupidinis.*' In *English Court Culture and the Late Middle Ages.* 87–108. See Scattergood 1983.

——. *Poets and Princepleasers: Literature and the English Court in the Late Middle Ages.* Toronto and Buffalo: University of Toronto Press, 1980.

——. 'Women in Chaucer's Audience.' *ChauR* 18 (1983): 146–54.

Grennan, Joseph E. 'Chaucer's Man of Law and the Constancy of Justice.' *JEGP* 84 (1985): 498–514.

——. 'Science and Poetry in Chaucer's *House of Fame.*' *AnM* 8 (1967): 38–45.

Gross, C. 'Great Reasoner in Scripture: The Activities of Women Lollards, 1380–1530.' In *Medieval Women.* 359–80. See Baker 1978.

Hahn, Thomas. 'Money, Sexuality, Wordplay, and Context in the *Shipman's Tale.*' In *Chaucer in the Eighties.* 235–49. See Wasserman 1986.

——., and Richard W. Kaueper. 'Text and Context: Chaucer's *Friar's Tale.*' *SAC* 5 (1983): 67–101.

Halley, Janet., and Sheila Fisher., eds. *Seeking the Woman in Late Medieval and Renaissance Writings.* Knoxville: University of Tennessee Press, 1989.

Hanawalt, Barbara., ed., *Chaucer's England: Literature in Historical Context.* Medieval Studies at Minnesota, Vol. 4. Minneapolis: University of Minnesota Press, 1992.

——. 'Peasant Resistance to Royal and Seigniorial Impositions.' In *Social Unrest in the Late Middle Ages.* 23–47. See Newman 1986.

Hanning, Robert. ' "I shal Finde it in a Maner Glose": Versions of Textual Harassment in Medieval Literature.' In *Medieval Texts and Contemporary Readers.* 27–50. See Finke 1987.

——. 'From *Eva* and *Ave* to Eglentyne and Alisoun: Chaucer's Insight into the Roles Women Play.' *Signs* 2 (1977): 580–99.

Hansen, Elaine Tuttle. *Chaucer and the Fictions of Gender.* Berkeley: University of California Press, 1992.

——. 'The Feminization of Men in Chaucer's *Legend of Good Women.*' In *Seeking the Woman.* See Halley 1989.

——. 'The Powers of Silence: The Case of the Clerk's Griselde.' In *Women and Power in the Middle Ages.* 230–49. See Kowalkeski 1988.

Hanson, Thomas B. 'Chaucer's Physician as Storyteller and Moralizer.' *ChauR* 7 (1972): 132–39.

——. 'Physiognomy and Characterization in the *Miller's Tale.*' *NM* 72 (1971): 477–82.

Hawkins, Harriett. 'The Victim's Side: Chaucer's *Clerk's Tale* and Webster's *Duchess of Malfi.*' *Signs* 1 (1975): 339–61.

Hazelton, Richard. 'The *Manciple's Tale*: Parody and Critique.' *JEGP* 62 (1963): 1–31.

Heffernan, Carol. 'Tyranny and Commune Profit in the *Clerk's Tale.' ChauR* 17 (1983): 332–40.

Henriques, Julian., et al., eds. *Changing the Subject: Psychology, Social Regulation and Subjectivity.* London and New York: Methuen, 1984.

Herlihy, David. *Medieval Households.* Cambridge, Mass.: Harvard University Press, 1985.

Hermann, John P., and John J. Burke, Jr, eds. *Signs and Symbols in Chaucer's Poetry* (University, AL: University of Alabama Press, 1981).

Hewitt, Herbert J. *The Black Prince's Expedition of 1355–57.* Manchester: University of Manchester Press, 1958.

——. *The Organization of War Under Edward III, 1333–62.* Manchester, 1966; New York: Barnes and Noble, 1966.

Hilton, Rodney H. *English Peasantry in the Later Middle Ages.* Oxford: Clarendon, 1975.

——. *Peasants, Knights, and Heretics.* Cambridge: Cambridge University Press, 1976.

Hoccleve, Thomas. *Regement of Princes.* Ed. F. J. Furnivall. EETS ES 72. London: K. Paul, Trench, Trubner. 1897.

Hoffman, Richard. 'Jephthah's Daughter and Chaucer's Virginia.' *ChauR* 2 (1967): 20–31.

Holley, Linda T. 'The Function of Language in Three Canterbury Churchmen.' *Parergon* 2 (1980): 36–44.

The Holy Bible, in the Earliest Version made from the Latin Vulgate by John Wycliffe and his Followers. Ed. Josiah Forshall and F. Madden. Oxford: University Press, 1850.

Horrell, Joe. 'Chaucer's Symbolic Plowman.' *Speculum* 14 (1939); rpt in *Chaucer Criticism.* 84–97. See Schoeck 1960.

Horowitz, Maryanne Cline. 'Aristotle and Woman.' *Journal of the History of Biology* 9 (1976): 183–213.

Howard, Donald R. *Chaucer: His Life, His Works, His World.* New York: Dutton, 1987.

——. *The Idea of the Canterbury Tales.* Berkeley: University of California Press, 1976.

Hudson, Anne., ed. *Selections from English Wycliffite Writings.* Cambridge: Cambridge University Press, 1978.

——., and Michael Wilks, eds. *From Ockham to Wyclif.* Studies in Church History: Subsidia 5. Oxford: Basil Blackwell, 1987.

Huizinga, Johan. *Homo Ludens: A Study of the Play-Element in Culture.* London: Routledge & Kegan Paul, 1949.

——. 'The Political and Military Significance of Chivalric Ideas in the Late Middle Ages.' In his *Men and Ideas: History, the Middle Ages, the Renaissance: Essays.* 196–206. Trans. James S. Holmes and Hans van Marle. Princeton: Princeton University Press, 1984.

——. *The Waning of the Middle Ages.* Trans. F. Hopman. London: E. Arnold, 1924.

Humbert of Romans, *De Eruditione Predicatorum, Treatise of Preaching,* ed. W. M. Conlon, O.P. (Westminster, Md.: Newman Press, 1951).

Huppe, Bernard. *A Reading of the Canterbury Tales.* Albany: State of New York Press, 1964.

Irigaray, Luce. 'And the One Doesn't Stir Without the Other.' Trans. Helene V. Wenzel. *Signs* 7 (1981): 60–67.

——. 'When Our Lips Speak Together.' Trans. Carolyn Burke. *Signs* 6 (1980): 69–79.

Jack Upland; Friar Daw's Reply; and Upland's Rejoinder. Ed. P. L. Heyworth. London: Oxford University Press, 1968.

Jameson, Fredric. *The Political Unconscious: Narrative as a Socially Symbolic Act.* Ithaca: Cornell University Press, 1981.

Jardine, Alice. *Gynesis: Configurations of Woman and Modernity*. Ithaca: Cornell University Press, 1985.

Jarrett, Bede. *Social Theories of the Middle Ages, 1200–1500*. Boston: Little Brown, 1926; rpt, New York: F. Ungar, 1966.

John of Garland. *Parisiana Poetria*. Yale Studies in English, 182. Trans. and ed. Traugott Lawler. New Haven: Yale University Press, 1974.

John of Salisbury. *Metalogicon*. Ed. C. C. J. Webb. London: 1932.

———. *The Metalogicon*. Trans. Daniel D. McGarry. Berkeley: University of California Press, 1955.

Jordan, Robert M. *Chaucer and the Shape of Creation: The Aesthetic Possibilities of Inorganic Structure*. Cambridge, Mass.: Harvard University Press, 1967.

Joseph, Gerard. 'Chaucerian "Game"–"Ernest" and the "Argument of Herbergage,"' in the *Canterbury Tales*.' *ChauR* 5 (1970): 88–89.

Jusserand, J. J. *English Wayfaring Life in the Middle Ages*. Trans. Lucy Toulmin Smith. 1888; London: Benn, 1950.

Kaeuper, Richard. 'An Historian's Reading of the *Tale of Gamelyn*.' *MEA* 52 (1983): 51–62.

———. *War, Justice and Public Order: England and France in the Later Middle Ages*. Oxford: Clarendon, 1988.

Kail, J., ed. *Twenty-Six Political and Other Poems (Digby 102)*. EETS OS 124. London: K. Paul, Trench, Trubner, 1904.

Kampf, Louis., and Paul Lauter., eds. *The Politics of Literature: Dissenting Essays on the Teaching of English*. New York: Pantheon, 1972.

Kane, George. 'Some Fourteenth-Century "Political" Poems.' In *Medieval English Religious and Ethical Literature*. 82–91. See Kratzmann 1986.

Kaufman, Michael., ed. *Beyond Patriarchy: Essays by Men on Pleasure, Power, and Change*. Toronto and New York: Oxford University Press, 1987.

Kelly, Douglas R. *Medieval Imagination: Rhetoric and the Poetry of Courtly Love*. Madison: University of Wisconsin Press, 1978.

Kelly, Henry. A. *Love and Marriage in the Age of Chaucer*. Ithaca: Cornell University Press, 1975.

Kendrick, Laura. *Chaucerian Play: Comedy and Control in the Canterbury Tales*. Berkeley: University of California Press, 1988.

Keohane, Nannerl O., Michelle Z. Rosaldo, and Barbara C. Gelpi., eds. *Feminist Theory: A Critique of Ideology*. Chicago: University of Chicago Press, 1982.

Keuls, Eva C. *The Reign of the Phallus: Sexual Politics in Ancient Athens*. New York: Harper, 1985.

Kiernan, Kevin S. 'The Art of the Descending Catalogue, and a Fresh Look at Alisoun.' *ChauR* 10 (1975): 1–16.

Kinsman, Gary W. 'Men Loving Men.' In *Beyond Patriarchy*. 103–19. See Kaufman 1987.

———. *The Regulation of Desire*. Montreal: Black Rose, 1986.

Kirshner, Julius, and Suzanne F. Wemple., eds. *Women of the Medieval World*. Oxford: Oxford University Press, 1985.

Kittredge, George L. *Chaucer and His Poetry*. Cambridge: Mass.: Harvard University Press, 1915.

Klapisch-Zuber, Christiane., ed. *A History of Women in the West, Volume II: Silences of the Middle Ages*. Cambridge, Mass.: Belknap Press of Harvard University Press, 1992.

Kleinbaum, Abby W. *The War Against the Amazons*. New York: McGraw Hill, 1983.

Knapp, Peggy A. *Chaucer and the Social Contest*. New York: Routledge, 1990.

———. 'Wandrynge by the Weye.' In *Medieval Texts and Contemporary Readers*. 142–57. See Finke 1987.

Knight, Stephen. *Geoffrey Chaucer.* Oxford: Oxford University Press, 1986.
——. 'Chaucer's Religious *Canterbury Tales.*' In *Medieval Religious and Ethical Literature.* 156–66. See Kratzmann 1986.
Knowles, David. *The English Mystical Tradition.* London: Burns & Oates, 1961.
Koff, Leonard M. *Chaucer and the Art of Storytelling.* Berkeley: University of California Press, 1988.
Kolodny, Annette. 'Dancing Through the Minefield: Some Observations on the Theory Practice, and Politics of a Feminist Literary Criticism.' *Feminist Studies* 6 (1980): 1–25.
Kolve, V. A. *Chaucer and the Imagery of Narrative: The First Five Canterbury Tales.* Stanford: Stanford University Press, 1984.
Kratzmann, Gregory., and James Simpson., eds. *Medieval English Religious and Ethical Literature: Essays in Honour of G. H. Russell.* Cambridge: D. S. Brewer, 1986.
Kretzmann, Norman., et al., eds. *The Cambridge History of Later Medieval Philosophy.* Cambridge: Cambridge University Press, 1982.
Kristeva, Julia. 'How Does One Speak to Literature?' In her *Desire in Language: A Semiotic Approach to Literature and Art.* Trans. Thomas Gora, Alice Jardine, and Leon S. Roudiez. Ed. Leon S. Roudiez. 92–123. New York: Columbia University Press, 1980.
Langland, William. *Piers Plowman.* Ed. Rev. Walter W. Skeat. London and New York: Oxford University Press, 1964.
Lawler, Traugott. *The One and the Many in the Canterbury Tales.* Hamden, Conn.: Archon, 1980.
——., ed. *Patterns of Love and Courtesy: Essays in Memory of C. S. Lewis.* Evanston: Northwestern University Press, 1966.
Lawrence, W. W. 'The *Tale of Melibeus.*' In *Essays and Studies in Honor of Carleton Brown.* 100–110. New York: New York University Press, 1940.
Lee, Richard., and Richard Daly. 'Man's Dominance and Woman's Oppression: The Question of Origins.' In *Beyond Patriarchy: Essays by Men on Pleasure, Power and Change.* 30–44. See Kaufman 1987.
Leff, Gordon. *The Dissolution of the Medieval Outlook.* New York: New York University Press, 1976.
——. *Heresy in the Later Middle Ages: The Relation of Heterodoxy to Dissent, c. 1250–c. 1450.* 2 Vols. Manchester: Manchester University Press, 1967.
——. *Medieval Thought: St Augustine to Ockham.* Baltimore: Penguin, 1958; 1965.
——. *Paris and Oxford Universities in the Thirteenth and Fourteenth Centuries: An Institutional and Intellectual History.* New York and London: John Wiley & Sons, 1968.
——. *William of Ockham: The Metamorphosis of Scholastic Discourse.* Manchester: Manchester University Press, 1965.
Leicester, H. Marshall, Jr. *The Disenchanted Self: Representing the Subject in the Canterbury Tales.* Berkeley: University of California Press, 1990.
Lerer, Seth. *Chaucer and His Readers: Imagining the Author in Late-Medieval England.* Princeton: Princeton University Press, 1993.
Lester, G. A. 'Chaucer's Knight and the Medieval Tournament.' *Neophilologus* 66 (1982): 460–68.
Lévi-Strauss, Claude. *The Raw and the Cooked.* Trans. John and Doreen Weightman. 1969; rpt New York: Harper and Row, 1970.
Levy, Bernard S., and George R. Adams. 'Chaunticleer's Paradise Lost and Regained.' *MS* 29 (1967): 178–92.
Lindahl, Carl. *Earnest Games: Folkloric Patterns in the Canterbury Tales.* Bloomington: Indiana University Press, 1987.

Little, Lester K. 'Pride Goes before Avarice: Social Change in Latin Christendom.' *American Historical Review* 76 (1971): 16–49.

Lorde, Audre. *Sister Outsider: Essays and Speeches*. Trumansburg, New York: Crossing Press, 1984.

Lucas, Angela. *Women in the Middle Ages: Religion, Marriage, and Letters*. New York: St Martins, 1983.

Luke, Carmen., and Jennifer Gore., eds. *Feminisms and Critical Pedagogy*. New York: Routledge, 1992.

Lumiansky, Robert. 'Chaucer's Philosophical Knight.' *Tulane Studies in English* 3 (1952): 47–68.

Lunz, Elizabeth. 'Chaucer's Prudence as the Ideal of the Virtuous Woman.' *Essays in Literature* 4 (1977):

Mackay, Louis H. '*Inter Nocturnas Vigilias*: A Proof Postponed.' In *Medieval Texts and Contemporary Readers*. 69–99. See Finke 1987.

The Malleus Maleficarum of Heinrich Kramer and James Sprenger. Trans. and ed. Rev. Montague Summers. 1928; New York: Dover, 1971.

Mann, Jill. *Chaucer and Medieval Estates Satire*. Cambridge: Cambridge University Press, 1973.

———. *Geoffrey Chaucer*. Atlantic Highlands: Humanities Press, 1991.

Manning, Stephen. 'Chaucer's Constance, Pale and Passive.' In *Chaucerian Problems*. 13–23. See Vasta 1979.

Matthew, William. 'The Wife of Bath and all Her Sect.' *Viator* 5 (1974): 413–43.

McFarlane, K. B. *Wycliffe and the Beginnings of English Nonconformity*. London: English Universities Press, 1952.

McKisack, May. *The Fourteenth Century, 1307–99*. Oxford: Clarendon, 1959; 1971.

McNamara, Jo Ann., and Suzanne Wemple. 'The Power of Women through the Family in Medieval Europe 500–1100.' *Feminist Studies* 1 (1973): 126–41.

McNamara, John. 'Chaucer's Use of the Epistle of St James in the *Clerk's Tale*.' *ChauR* 7 (1973): 184–93.

Meese, Elizabeth A. *Crossing the Double-Cross: The Practice of Feminist Criticism*. Chapel Hill: University of North Carolina Press, 1986.

Middleton, Anne. 'The *Physician's Tale* and Love's Martyrs: "Ensamples mo than ten" as a method in the *Canterbury Tales*.' *ChauR* 8 (1973): 9–32.

Middleton, Peter. *The Inward Gaze: Masculinity and Subjectivity in Modern Culture*. New York: Routledge, 1992.

Migne, J.-P., ed. *Patrologia Latina*. Paris. 1844–91.

Miller, Robert P., ed. *Chaucer: Sources and Backgrounds*. New York: Oxford University Press, 1977.

———. 'Chaucer's Pardoner: the Scriptural Eunuch and the *Pardoner's Tale*.' *Speculum* 30 (1955): 180–99.

———. 'The *Miller's Tale* as Complaint.' *ChauR* 5 (1970): 147–60.

Minnis, A. J., ed. *Gower's Confessio Amantis: Responses and Reassessments*. Cambridge: Brewer, 1983.

———. *Chaucer and Pagan Antiquity*. Cambridge: Brewer, 1982.

Mitchell, Jerome., and William Provost., eds. *Chaucer the Love Poet*. Athens, GA: University of Georgia Press, 1973.

Mohl, Ruth. *The Three Estates in Medieval and Renaissance Literature*. New York: F. Ungar, 1962.

Moller, Herbert. 'The Social Causation of Courtly Love Complex.' *Comparative Studies in Society and History* 1 (1958/59): 137–63.

Mum and the Sothsegger. Ed. Mabel Day and R. Steele. EETS OS 199. London: Oxford University Press, 1936.

Muscatine, Charles. *Chaucer and the French Tradition*. Berkeley: University of California Press, 1957.

Myers, Alec R. *The Household of Edward IV*. Manchester: University of Manchester Press, 1959.

Neuse, Richard. 'The Knight: The First Mover in Chaucer's Human Comedy.' *UTQ* 31 (1962): 299-315.

Newman, Francis X., ed. *The Meaning of Courtly Love*. Albany: State University of New York Press, 1968.

——., ed. *Social Unrest in the Late Middle Ages*. Papers of the Fifteenth Annual Conference of the Center for Medieval and Early Renaissance Studies. Binghamton, New York: Center for Medieval and Early Renaissance Studies, 1986.

Nicholas, David. *The Domestic Life of a Medieval City: Women, Children, and the Family in Fourteenth-Century Ghent*. Lincoln, Nebraska: University of Nebraska Press, 1985.

Oberman, Heiko. 'Fourteenth-Century Religious Thought: A Premature Profile.' *Speculum* 53 (1978): 80-93.

Olson, Paul. 'Poetic Justice in the *Miller's Tale*.' *MLQ* 24 (1963): 227-36.

Ong, Walter J. *Orality and Literacy: The Technologizing of the Word*. London and New York: Methuen, 1982.

Ortner, Sherry B., and Harriet Whitehead., eds. *Sexual Meanings: The Cultural Construction of Gender and Sexuality*. Cambridge: Cambridge University Press, 1981.

Owen, Charles. 'Chaucer's *Canterbury Tales*: Aesthetic Design in Stories of the First Day.' *ES* 35 (1954): 49-56.

——. 'The *Tale of Melibee*.' *ChauR* 7 (1973): 267-80.

Owens, Craig. 'The Discourse of Others: Feminists and Postmodernism.' In *The Anti-Aesthetic: Essays on Postmodern Culture*. Ed. Hal Forster. 57-82. San Francisco: Bay Press, 1983.

Owst, Gerald R. *Literature and Pulpit in Medieval England*. Cambridge, 1933; New York: Barnes and Noble, 1966.

Ozment, Steven. *The Age of Reform, 1250-1550: An Intellectual and Religious History of Late Medieval and Reformation Europe*. New Haven: Yale University Press, 1980.

Pagles, Elaine. 'What became of God the Mother?: Conflicting Images of God in Early Christianity.' *Signs* 2 (1976): 293-303.

Palomo, Dorothy. 'What Chaucer Really Did to *Le Livre de Mellibee*.' *PQ* 53 (1974): 304-20.

Partner, Nancy F., ed. *Studying Medieval Women: Sex, Gender, Feminism*. Cambridge, Mass.: Medieval Academy of America, 1993.

Patterson, Lee. *Chaucer and the Subject of History*. Madison: University of Wisconsin Press, 1991.

——. ' "For the Wyve's Love of Bath" ': Feminine Rhetoric and Poetic Resolution in the *Roman de la Rose* and the *Canterbury Tales*.' *Speculum* 58 (1983): 656-95.

——. *Negotiating the Past: The Historical Understanding of Medieval Literature*. Madison: University of Wisconsin Press, 1987.

——. 'The *Parsons' Tale* and the Quitting of the *Canterbury Tales*.' *Traditio* 34 (1978): 331-80.

Paull, Michael R. 'The Influence of the Saint's Legend Genre in the *Man of Law's Tale*.' *ChauR* 5 (1971): 179-94.

Peck, Russell A. 'Chaucer and the Nominalist Questions.' *Speculum* 53 (1978): 745-60.

——. 'The Idea of "Entente" and Translation in Chaucer's *Second Nun's Tale*.' *AnM* 8 (1967): 17-37.

——. 'St Paul and the *Canterbury Tales*.' *Mediaevalia* 7 (1981): 91-131.

Penninger, Elaine. 'Chaucer's *Knight's Tale* and the Theme of Appearance and Reality in the *Canterbury Tales.*' *South Atlantic Quarterly* 63 (1964): 398–405.

Peters, Edward., ed. *The First Crusade: The Chronicle of Fulcher of Chartres and Other Source Materials.* Philadelphia: University of Pennsylvania Press, 1971.

Philippe de Navarre. *Les Quatres Ages de L'Homme.* Ed. Marcel de Freville. Paris: Librairie de firmin didot, 1888.

Pickering, Frederick P. 'Historical Thought and Moral Codes in Medieval Epic.' In *The Epic in Medieval Society.* 1–7. See Scholler 1977.

Pleck, Joseph H. *The Myth of Masculinity.* Cambridge, Mass.: MIT Press, 1981.

Plimpton, George A. *The Education of Chaucer: Illustrated from the School Books in Use in his Time.* London & New York: Oxford University Press, 1935.

Pollock, Frederick., and F. W. Maitland. *The History of English Law.* 2 Vols. London: Cambridge University Press, 1898; rpt 1968.

Post, R. R. *The Modern Devotion: Confrontation with Reformation and Humanism.* Leiden: E. J. Brill, 1968.

Power, Eileen. *Medieval Women.* Ed. M. M. Postan. Cambridge: Cambridge University Press, 1975.

——. 'The Position of Women.' In *The Legacy of the Middle Ages.* 405–34. See Crump 1926.

Pratt, Robert A. 'Chaucer and *Les Cronicles* of Nicholas Trivet.' In *Studies in Language, Literature, and Culture of the Middle Ages.* 303–11. Ed. Atwood and Hill. Austin: University of Texas Press, 1969.

——. 'The Importance of Manuscripts for the Study of Medieval Education, as Revealed by the Learning of Chaucer.' In *Progress of Medieval and Renaissance Studies in the United States and Canada.* 43–51. Ed. S. Harrison Thomson. Boulder, Colo., 1949.

——. 'Jankyn's "Book of Wikked Wyves": Medieval Antimatrimonial Propaganda in the Universities.' *AnM* 3 (1962): 5–27.

Rabine, Leslie Wahl. 'A Feminist Politics of Non-identity.' *Feminist Studies* 14 (1988): 11–31.

Rashdall, Hastings. *The Universities of Europe in the Middle Ages.* 3 Vols. Ed. F. M. Powicke and A. B. Emden. 1895; Oxford: Clarendon, 1936.

Reid, David S. 'Crocodilian Humor: A Discussion of Chaucer's Wife of Bath.' *ChauR* 4 (1970): 73–89.

Reidy, John. 'The Education of Chaucer's Duke Theseus.' In *The Epic in Medieval Society: Aesthetic and Moral Values.* 381–408. See Scholler 1977.

Reiman, Donald. 'The Real *Clerk's Tale*: or Patient Griselde Exposed.' *TSLL* 5 (1963): 356–73.

Reiss, Edmund. 'Chaucer's deerne love and the Medieval View of Secrecy in Love.' In *Chaucerian Problems and Perspectives.* 164–79. See Vasta 1979.

——. 'Chaucer's Parodies of Love.' In *Chaucer the Love Poet.* See Mitchell 1973.

——. 'The Symbolic Surface of the *Canterbury Tales.*' *ChauR* 2 (1967–68): 254–72.

——. 'The Symbolic Surface of the *Canterbury Tales*, Part II.' *ChauR* 3 (1969): 12–28.

Renna, Thomas. 'Wyclif's Attack on the Monks.' In *From Ockham to Wyclif.* 267–80. See Hudson 1978.

Rich, Adrienne. *Blood, Bread, and Poetry: Selected Prose 1979–1985.* New York: Norton, 1986.

——. *On Lies, Secrets, and Silence: Selected Prose 1966–1978.* New York: Norton, 1979.

Rickert, Edith. 'Chaucer at School.' *MP* 29 (1931–32): 257–74.

——. 'Was Chaucer a Student at the Inner Temple.' *The Manly Anniversary Studies in Language and Literature.* 20–31. Chicago, 1923.

Ridley, Florence. 'The State of Chaucer Studies: A Brief Survey.' *SAC* 1 (1979): 3–16.

Riehle, Wolfgang. *The Middle English Mystics*. Trans. Bernard Standring. London: Routledge & Kegan Paul, 1981.

Richardson, Janette. *Blameth Nat Me: A Study of Imagery in Chaucer's Fabliaux*. The Hague: Mouton, 1970.

——. 'Friar and Summoner: The Art of Balance.' *ChauR* 9 (1974-75): 227-36.

Robert of Brunne. *Handlyng Synne*. Ed. F. J. Furnivall. EETS OS 119. London, 1901.

Robertson, D. W., Jr. *A Preface to Chaucer: Studies in Medieval Perspectives*. Princeton: Princeton University Press, 1962.

Robinson, Ian. *Chaucer and the English Tradition*. Cambridge: Cambridge University Press, 1972.

Robson, James. A. *Wyclif and the Oxford Schools*. Cambridge: Cambridge University Press, 1961.

Rogers, Katharine. *The Troublesome Helpmate: A History of Misogyny in Literature*. Seattle: University of Washington Press, 1966.

Rowland, Beryl. 'The Physician's "Historical Thynge Notable" and the Man of Law.' *ELH* 40 (1973): 165-78.

Rose, Mary Beth., ed. *Women in the Middle Ages and the Renaissance: Literary and Historical Perspectives*. Syracuse: Syracuse University Press, 1986.

Rouse, Richard H., and Mary A. Rouse. 'The Franciscans and Books: Lollard Accusations and the Franciscan Response.' In *From Ockham to Wyclif*. 364-84. See Hudson 1987.

Rudat, Wolfgang. 'Chaucer's Mercury and Arcite: *The Aeneid* and the World of the *Knight's Tale*.' *Neophilologus* 64 (1980): 307-19.

Russell, Frederick. H. *The Just War in the Middle Ages*. Cambridge: Cambridge University Press, 1975.

Rutherford, Jonathan. *Men's Silences: Predicaments in Masculinity*. London: Routledge, 1992.

Salter, Elizabeth. 'Chaucer: The *Knight's Tale* and the *Clerk's Tale*.' *Studies in English Literature* 5. London: Edward Arnold, 1963.

——. *English and International: Studies in the Literature, Art, and Patronage of Medieval England*. Ed. Derek Pearsall and Nicolette Zeeman. Cambridge: Cambridge University Press, 1988.

Sanday, Peggy Reeves. *Female Power and Male Dominance: On the Origins of Sexual Inequality*. Cambridge and New York: Cambridge University Press, 1981.

Saul, Nigel. 'Chaucer and Gentility.' In *Chaucer's England*. 41-55. See Hanawalt 1992.

Scattergood, V. John. 'Chaucer and the French War in *Sir Thopas* and *Melibee*.' In *Court and Poet: Selected Proceedings of the Third Congress of the International Courtly Literature Society*. Ed. Glyn Burgess. Liverpool: Francis Cairns, 1981.

——. 'Literary Culture at the Court of Richard II.' In *English Court Culture*. 29-43. See Scattergood 1983.

——. *Politics and Poetry in the Fifteenth Century*. Blandford History Series. London: Blandford Press, 1971.

Schibanoff, Susan. 'Taking the Gold Out of Egypt: The Art of Reading as a Woman.' In *Gender and Reading: Essays on Readers, Texts, and Contexts*. 83-106. See Flynn 1986.

Schollar, Harald., ed. *The Epic in Medieval Society: Aesthetic and Moral Values*. Tubingen: Max Niemeyer Verlag, 1977.

Schulenberg, Jane Tibbets. 'Clio's European Daughters: Myopic Modes of Perception.' In *The Prism of Sex*. Ed. Julia A. Sherman and Evelyn Torton Beck. 33-53. Madison: University of Wisconsin Press, 1977.

——. 'The Heroics of Virginity: Brides of Christ and Sacrificial Mutilation.' In *Women in the Middle Ages and the Renaissance: Literary and Historical Perspectives*. 29–72. See Rose 1986.

Schweitzer, Edward. 'Fate and Freedom in the *Knight's Tale*.' *SAC* 3 (1981): 13–46.

——. 'The Misdirected Kiss and the Lover's Malady in Chaucer's *Miller's Tale*.' In *Chaucer in the Eighties*. 223–33. See Wasserman 1986.

Schwenger, Peter. 'The Masculine Mode.' In *Speaking of Gender*. 101–110. Ed. Elaine Showalter. New York: Routledge, 1989.

Sedgwick, Eve Kosofsky. *Between Men: English Literature and Male Homosocial Desire*. New York: Columbia University Press, 1985.

——. *The Epistemology of the Closet*. Berkeley: University of California Press, 1990.

Severs, J. Burke. 'Chaucer's Clerks.' In *Chaucer and Middle English Studies in Honour of Rossell Hope Robbins*. Ed. Beryl Rowland. 140–52. London: Allen & Unwin, 1974; Kent, Ohio: Kent State University Press, 1974.

Shahar, Shulamith. *The Fourth Estate: A History of Women in the Middle Ages*. Trans. Chaya Galai. New York and London: Methuen, 1983.

Shepherd, Geoffrey. 'Religion and Philosophy in Chaucer.' In *Geoffrey Chaucer*. Writers and Their Background. 262–89. See Brewer 1975.

Sherwin, Susan. 'Philosophical Methodology and Feminist Methodology: Are They Compatible?' In *Feminist Perspectives: Philosophical Essays on Method and Morals*. 13–28. See Code 1988.

Silverman, Kaja. *Male Subjectivity at the Margins*. New York: Routledge, 1992.

Shoaf, R. A. *Dante, Chaucer, and the Currency of the Word: Money, Images, and Reference in Late Medieval Poetry*. Norman, Oklahoma: Pilgrim, 1983.

Showalter, Elaine. 'Feminist Criticism in the Wilderness.' *Critical Inquiry* 8 (1981): 179–205.

——., ed. *The New Feminist Criticism: Essays on Women, Literature, Theory*. New York: Pantheon, 1985.

Smith, Paul. *Discerning the Subject*. Minneapolis: University of Minnesota Press, 1988.

Smith-Rosenberg, Carroll. 'Writing History.' In *Feminist Studies/Critical Studies*. Ed. Teresa de Lauretis. 31–54. Bloomington: Indiana University Press, 1986.

Speirs, John. *Chaucer the Maker*. London: Faber and Faber, 1951.

Spender, Dale. *Man Made Language*. New York and London: Routledge & Kegan Paul, 1980.

Spivak, Gayatri Chakravorty. *In Other Worlds: Essays in Cultural Politics*. New York: Methuen, 1987.

——. 'The Politics of Interpretation.' *Critical Inquiry* 8 (1981): 259–78.

——. 'Translator's Forward to "Draupadi" by Mahasveta Devi.' *Critical Inquiry* 8 (1981): 381–92.

Spurgeon, Caroline F. E., ed. *Five Hundred Years of Chaucer Criticism and Allusion*. 3 Vols. Cambridge: The University Press, 1925.

Stenton, Doris Mary. *The English Woman in History*. London: Allen & Unwin, 1957; New York: Shocken, 1977.

Stepsis, Robert. 'Potentia Absoluta and the *Clerk's Tale*.' *ChauR* 10 (1975): 129–46.

Stillwell, Gardiner. 'The Political Meaning of Chaucer's *Tale of Melibee*.' *Speculum* 19 (1944): 433–44.

Strohm, Paul. 'The Allegory of the *Tale of Melibee*.' *ChauR* 2 (1967): 32–42.

——. *Social Chaucer*. Cambridge, Mass.: Harvard University Press, 1989.

——. 'Some Generic Distinctions in the *Canterbury Tales*.' *MP* 68 (1971): 321–28.

Suleiman, Susan R., ed. *The Female Body in Western Culture*. Cambridge, Mass.: Harvard University Press, 1986.

Szittya, Penn R. *The Antifraternal Tradition in Medieval Literature*. Princeton: Princeton University Press, 1986.

Tatlock, John S. P., and Arthur G. Kennedy. *A Concordance to the Complete Works of Geoffrey Chaucer and to the Romaunt of the Rose*. Concord: Carnegie Institute, 1927.

Taylor, P. B. 'Chaucer's Cosyn to the Dede.' *Speculum* 57 (1982): 315-27.

Tellenbach, Gerd. *Church, State and Christian Society*. Trans. R. F. Bennett. Oxford: Basil Blackwell, 1940; 1948.

Theweleit, Klaus. *Male Fantasies, Volume One: Women, Floods, Bodies, History*. Trans. Stephen Conway. Minneapolis: University of Minnesota Press, 1987.

Turner, Victor., and Edith Turner. *Image and Pilgrimage in Christian Culture: Anthropological Perspectives*. New York: Columbia University Press, 1978.

Underwood, Dale. 'The First of the *Canterbury Tales*.' *ELH* 26 (1959): 455-69.

Utley, Francis Lee. *The Crooked Rib*. Columbus: Ohio State University Press, 1944.

Van, Thomas A. 'Imprisoning and Ensnarement in *Troilus* and the *Knight's Tale*.' *Papers on Language and Literature* 7 (1971): 3-12.

Vance, Eugene. *Mervelous Signals: Poetics and Sign Theory in the Middle Ages*. Lincoln: University of Nebraska Press, 1986.

——. 'Semiotics and Power: Relics, Icons, and the Voyage de Charlemagne à Jérusalem et à Constantinople.' In *The New Medievalism*. See Brownlee 1991.

Vasta, Edward., and Zacharias P. Thundy., eds. *Chaucerian Problems and Perspectives: Essays Presented to Paul E. Beichner, C.S.C.* Notre Dame: University of Notre Dame Press, 1979.

Wall, John. 'Penance and Poetry in the Late Fourteenth-Century.' In *Medieval Religious and Ethical Literature*. 179-91. See Kratzmann 1986.

Wasserman, Julian N., and Robert J. Blanch., eds. *Chaucer in the Eighties*. Syracuse: Syracuse University Press, 1986.

Waugh, Patricia. *Feminine Fictions: Revisiting the Postmodern*. New York: Routledge, 1989.

Webb, H. J. 'A Reinterpretation of Chaucer's Theseus.' *Review of English Studies* 23 (1947): 289-96.

Weeks, Jeffrey. *Sex, Politics, and Society*. London: Hutchinson, 1981.

Weil, Kari. *Androgony and the Denial of Difference*. Charlottesville: University of Virginia Press, 1992.

Weissman, Hope Phyllis. 'Antifeminism and Chaucer's Characterization of Women.' In *Geoffrey Chaucer: A Collection of Original Articles*. 93-110. See Economou 1975.

Weltner, Peter N. *Myth and Masculinity*. Harper Studies in Language and Literature. New York: Harper & Row, 1975.

Wetherbee, Winthrop. 'Some Intellectual Themes in Chaucer's Poetry.' In *Geoffrey Chaucer: A Collection of Original Articles*. 75-91. See Economou 1975.

White, Robert B. 'Chaucer's Daun Piers and the Rule of St Benedict: The Failure of an Ideal.' *JEGP* 70 (1971): 13-30.

Wilks, Michael. 'Royal Patronage and Anti-Papalism.' In *From Ockham to Wyclif*. 150-63. See Hudson 1987.

Wood, Chauncey. 'Chaucer's Use of Signs in His Portrait of the Prioress.' In *Signs and Symbols in Chaucer's Poetry*. 81-101. See Hermann 1981.

Woolf, Virginia. *A Room of One's Own*. London and New York: Harcourt Brace Jovanovich, 1929; rpt 1957.

Wright, Thomas., ed. *Political Poems and Songs relating to English History, Composed during the Period from the Accession of Edw. III. to that of Ric. III.* 2 Vols. London: Longman, 1859-61.

Wyclif, John. *De Universalibus*. Trans. Anthony Kenny. Oxford: Clarendon: 1985.

——. *The English Works of John Wyclif Hitherto Unprinted*. Ed. F. Matthew. EETS OS 74. London: Trubner, 1880.

——. *Select English Works of Wyclif*. Ed. T. Arnold. 3 Vols. Oxford: Clarendon, 1869–71.

Yunck, John. 'Religious Elements in Chaucer's *Man of Law's Tale*.' *ELH* 27 (1960): 249–61.

Zacher, Christian. *Curiosity and Pilgrimage: The Literature of Discovery in Fourteenth-Century England*. Baltimore: Johns Hopkins University Press, 1976.

Zumthor, Paul. *Speaking of the Middle Ages*. Trans. Sarah White. Ed. Eugene Vance. Regents Studies in Medieval Culture. Lincoln: University of Nebraska Press, 1986.

INDEX

Printed in the United Kingdom
by Lightning Source UK Ltd.
127676UK00001B/96/P

9 780859 914819